Praise for *Yiddish Scholarship Comes to America*

"The YIVO Institute for Jewish Research is a unique institution in the American landscape of Jewish scholarship. Conceived in Weimar Berlin, built in Vilna (then in Poland, now the Lithuanian capital Vilnius), and transplanted to New York after the outbreak of World War II, it has served as a second home and a source of knowledge for hundreds—if not thousands—of authors of books, dissertations, and articles. Its role in the preservation and development of Yiddish can hardly be overestimated. Kalman Weiser's excellent research on the institute's American period is an important contribution to our understanding of the history of Jewish studies outside of 'regular' academia at research universities."

—Gennady Estraikh, professor emeritus, New York University

"Weiser illuminates not only the fate of Yiddish in the wake of the Holocaust but also how survivors reacted to their immense losses, adjusted to their new American home, and carried on the legacy of eastern European culture. This is an important contribution to the history of Jewish scholarship, American Jewish history, and Yiddish studies."

—Cecile E. Kuznitz, Patricia Ross Weis '52 Chair in Jewish History and Culture, Bard College

"Anyone with an interest in the history of modern Yiddish culture should read Kalman Weiser's study of YIVO in America. This book is well written and based on a wealth of fascinating archival material."

—Samuel Kassow, Charles H. Northam Professor of History, Emeritus, Trinity College

YIDDISH SCHOLARSHIP COMES TO AMERICA

YIDDISH SCHOLARSHIP COMES TO AMERICA

THE YIVO INSTITUTE AT 100

KALMAN WEISER

WAYNE STATE UNIVERSITY PRESS
DETROIT

ISBN 9780814353394 (paperback)
ISBN 9780814353387 (hardcover)
ISBN 9780814353400 (ebook)

Library of Congress Control Number: 2026936223

On cover: Chana Mlotek née Gordon and Zosa Szajkowski on stairs in front of the YIVO building, 535 West 123rd Street, 1945. (Courtesy of YIVO Institute for Jewish Research.) Cover design by Will Brown.

Grateful acknowledgment is made to the YIVO Institute for Jewish Research and Ruth Levine for the generous support of the publication of this volume.

Wayne State University Press rests on Waawiyaataanong, also referred to as Detroit, the ancestral and contemporary homeland of the Three Fires Confederacy. These sovereign lands were granted by the Ojibwe, Odawa, Potawatomi, and Wyandot Nations, in 1807, through the Treaty of Detroit. Wayne State University Press affirms Indigenous sovereignty and honors all tribes with a connection to Detroit. With our Native neighbors, the press works to advance educational equity and promote a better future for the earth and all people.

Wayne State University Press
Leonard N. Simons Building
4809 Woodward Avenue
Detroit, Michigan 48201-1309

Visit us online at wsupress.wayne.edu.

CONTENTS

Acknowledgments vii

Introduction 1

1. Coming to America? 29

2. From Yiddish Scientific Institute to the YIVO Institute for Jewish Research 64

3. YIVO and the Holocaust 112

4. YIVO Yiddish 157

5. A Generation Goes, a Generation Comes 200

Conclusion 242

Notes 261

Additional Sources Consulted 331

Index 333

ACKNOWLEDGMENTS

Like so many scholars of Yiddish and Jewish, especially eastern European Jewish, history, I owe YIVO a debt of gratitude. The institute has been central to my education and career for some three decades. Needless to say, this book could not have been written without its assistance through the years.

I first encountered YIVO by chance as a Stuyvesant High School student who stumbled past the Vanderbilt mansion (now the Neue Galerie), its longtime home at the corner of Fifth Avenue and Eighty-Sixth Street, in early 1990. I was drawn in by the words צוריק אַהיים on a poster announcing a bilingual exhibit curated by Jack Kugelmass and Jeffrey Shandler: "Going Home: How American Jews Invent the Old World." A few years later, I returned as a Yale College undergraduate to make use of YIVO's Yiddish press collection to write a thesis about Displaced Persons in post–World War II Germany. Soon afterward, as a Yiddish studies graduate student, I attended the Uriel Weinreich Yiddish Summer Program, became acquainted with YIVO's staff, learned about the history of the institute, and conducted research in its archives.

Mine was likely the last cohort of students to be trained by Rakhmiel Peltz and colleagues in a Yiddish immersion graduate program at Columbia University with close ties to YIVO. We—Beatrice (Brukhe) Lang, Vera Szabó, Naomi Kadar z"l, Eddy Portnoy, Rebecca Margolis, Marc Miller, and I—benefited immeasurably from our language, culture, and history tutorials at YIVO's Max Weinreich Center for Advanced Jewish Studies in the mid-1990s. Above all, I was inspired by weekly meetings with my teacher Beatrice (Bina) Silverman Weinreich. She not only read Max Weinreich's challenging *Geshikhte fun der yidisher shprakh* (*History of the Yiddish Language*) with me but inspired me with tales of YIVO's founding generation in America. This included her beloved husband and intellectual partner Uriel (about whom she gleefully told how he practiced a

Yiddish "r" with her on their honeymoon) and her esteemed father-in-law, Max Weinreich. In one way or another, I have been trying to comprehend the Weinreichs' vast legacy and the fortunes of Yiddishism ever since then.

As with almost any book, there are too many people to thank, and I will almost certainly overlook some inadvertently. I apologize in advance. First of all, I would like to thank the entirety of YIVO's staff and leadership—past and present—for all their help and support in the decades that I have visited the institute and made use of its collections. This includes, but is not limited to, my teachers Lucian Dobroszycki z"l and Beatrice (Bina) Weinreich z"l; archivists Gunnar Berg, Ettie Goldwasser, Leo Greenberg, Stefanie Halpern (present Director of Collections), Solomon (Shloyme) Krystal z"l, Fruma Mohrer, Eleanor (Chana) Mlotek z"l, Yakov Sklar, Marek Web z"l, and Vital Zajka; reading room staff Herbert Lazarus and Yeshaye Metal; librarians Dina Abramowicz z"l, Aviva Astrinsky, Zachary Baker, and Lyudmila Sholokhova; sound archivists Lorin Sklamberg and Eléonore Biezunski; former Max Weinreich Dean Paul (Hershl) Glasser; Senior Academic Adviser and Director of Exhibitions Eddy Portnoy; Academic Adviser in Yiddish Language, Pedagogy, and Linguistics Dovid Braun; Director of Public Programs Alex Weiser; Director of Education Ben Kaplan; and Executive Director and CEO Jonathan Brent.

In gathering material for this book, I am particularly indebted to Clair Padgett and Corbin Alliardice. They did much of the heavy lifting of expertly sorting through and scanning hundreds of pages of documents for me in YIVO's archives, including unprocessed collections, during the tail end of the COVID pandemic, when access to the archives was limited and travel to the United States difficult. My current and former students Ricki (Birnbaum) Prince in Jerusalem and Sam Bick in Montreal also helped me gather archival and periodical materials. Along the way, many friends, teachers, and colleagues—among them Isaac Bleaman, Leyzer Burko, Kenneth Moss, Rakhmiel Peltz, William Pimlott, and Eddy Portnoy—also helped by sharing relevant documents, feedback on my work, and/or their own scholarship.

This project would not have been possible without the generous financial support of many parties, above all YIVO itself. York University's Koschitzky Centre for Jewish Studies and the Frankel Center at the

University of Michigan, the latter being where I spent a semester as a fellow in 2010, also provided funding that made research for this book possible. My colleagues and students at the Koschitzky Centre have been extremely supportive of all my academic efforts, both serving as intellectual interlocutors and helping provide me with the time and resources necessary to write this book. It has been an honor to work closely with Julie Feinberg, the Centre's coordinator, and David Koffman, the Centre's associate director, while serving as Koschitzky Centre director. At the University of Toronto, my colleague Sol Goldberg patiently talked through many issues related to this book and my other research projects through the years. Naomi Seidman, who teaches too at that university, has also been a source of encouragement and insights into Max Weinreich and Yiddish culture.

I would also like to express my gratitude to the staffs of the University of Michigan–Ann Arbor Special Collections Library; the Central Archive for the History of the Jewish People, Jerusalem; and the Archive of the Hebrew University, Jerusalem. Special thanks go to my friend Mr. David Birnbaum, who curates the Nathan and Solomon Birnbaum Family Archives in Toronto, for giving me years of open access to his father's and grandfather's collections and for sharing information and insights about his remarkable family that would be available nowhere else.

I am particularly indebted to Alex Weiser and Stefanie Halpern, who shared invaluable comments and corrections on early drafts of the book manuscript, as did my York colleague historian David Koffman and the two anonymous readers on behalf of Wayne State University Press. Cecile Kuznitz, author of the most important study of YIVO's European era and herself a former YIVO archivist, has been unfailingly generous with her time and private collection to assist me with my research, to answer questions, and to provide guidance. Similarly, Zachary Baker, YIVO's former chief librarian, has not only shared with me rare documents from his personal collection; he has always made himself available to discuss various topics and figures in the institution's history—whether in person, via Zoom, or via email. Of course, all errors of fact and interpretation remain my own.

My understanding of YIVO has been shaped not only by examining printed and archival sources but also by conversations with teachers and colleagues through the years. These include David Fishman,

Miriam Hoffman, Rakhmiel Peltz, David Roskies, Bilha Shilo, Nancy Sinkoff, Mordkhe Schaechter z"l, and Jeffrey Shandler. Fortunately, I began interviewing figures in the history of YIVO and Yiddish studies for class assignments in the 1990s and have continued with this effort as a private project to this day. Among those who graciously permitted me to interview them about subjects with direct relevance to this book are Zachary Baker, Nikolai (Kolya) Borodulin, Deborah Dash Moore, Sandy Feiner, Joshua Fishman z"l, Itzik Gottesman, Benjamin Harshav z"l, Bella Hass Weinberg, Miriam Hoffman, Barbara Kirshenblatt-Gimblett, William Labov z"l, Chava Lapin z"l, Jeffrey Shandler, Lorin Sklamberg, James Matisoff, Dan Miron, Chana Mlotek z"l, Anita Norich, Samuel Norich, Rakhmiel Peltz, Mordkhe Schaechter z"l, Gabriel Weinreich z"l, Ruth Wisse, and Renate Zeitlin z"l.

I also wish to thank acquisitions editor Sandra Korn and the team at Wayne State University Press and Saryta Brent of YIVO for their assistance in preparing this manuscript and ensuring its publication in a timely fashion.

Finally, I wish to express my profound appreciation for the love and support of my wife, Sharon, and my daughters, Orly and Talia. I hope my Yiddish-speaking daughters will grow up to appreciate YIVO's legacy as more than the Max Weinreich action figure on my bookshelf.

INTRODUCTION

In 2025, the YIVO Institute for Jewish Research celebrated its one hundredth anniversary. Having begun its storied history in Europe in 1925, YIVO (an acronym for *Yidisher visnshaftlekher institut* or Yiddish/Jewish [social] Scientific Institute) transferred its world headquarters from Vilna (Wilno), Poland (today's Vilnius, Lithuania), to New York City during World War II. It is today a well-established American Jewish institution and preeminent center for the study of eastern European Jewry best known for its unparalleled library and archival collections. Its numerous and pioneering publications, conferences, public programming, and educational endeavors have also helped establish the place in American scholarship of such fields as eastern European and American Jewish history, Yiddish studies, and Holocaust studies. Its Uriel Weinreich Yiddish Summer Program alone has immersed thousands of students in Yiddish language and culture since it began in 1968 and has inspired similar programs over the decades in cities such as Oxford, Paris, Berlin, Warsaw, and even Vilnius.

Located since 1999 in the Center for Jewish History on West Sixteenth Street in Manhattan, YIVO maintains an independent identity and finances while sharing library infrastructure as well as exhibition and programming facilities with partners encompassing a cross section of the contemporary and historical experience of America's Jewish community: the Yeshiva University Museum, the American Jewish Historical Society, the Leo Baeck Institute, and the American Sephardi Federation. The stately building, YIVO's fifth home in America, reflects the figurative distance the institute has traveled from its humble origins as the three-room American branch of a global organization headquartered in Poland until the present.

In the early years after World War II, YIVO in New York was an impoverished institution staffed almost exclusively by immigrant and refugee intellectuals from eastern Europe, all of them Yiddish speakers and many of them Holocaust survivors. Their painful losses and traumatic personal experiences only strengthened their resolve to salvage all that they could of eastern European Jewry's heritage and to continue

YIVO's mission of producing knowledge, as Yiddish-language scholar and educator Yudel Mark expressed it in 1926, "from the folk, for the folk, with the folk" in America and the larger world.[1] But how could this mission be pursued when the largest part of that folk—the Yiddish-speaking masses of eastern Europe—was no longer alive?

Yiddish speakers were the primary victims of Hitler's "war against the Jews," to borrow from the title of the 1975 history of the Holocaust written by Lucy Dawidowicz, another scholar with close ties to YIVO.[2] There still remained millions of Yiddish speakers around the world after World War II, but Yiddish-speaking civilization was destroyed in its eastern European heartland. Relatively few Jews outside the Soviet Union, which repressed Jewish culture in the postwar era, still lived in compact masses in the lands where the language and its culture had taken shape over the course of centuries. Prior to the war, eastern European Jews and their descendants had established sizable communities across the continents, particularly in the Americas, South Africa, and what is today Israel. In all these places, however, language shift from Yiddish to the dominant language of the land was advancing rapidly outside of some *haredi* ("Ultra-Orthodox") communities, particularly among youth, despite the best efforts of Yiddishists to transmit the language.

Moreover, the ideal of national cultural autonomy within multiethnic states—part of the platform of those Jewish political parties in interwar eastern Europe that supported YIVO, even if it was almost nowhere fully implemented—was impracticable in lands of immigrant settlement.[3] In almost all lands that Yiddish speakers called their new homes, Jews constituted a tiny minority and were officially treated (and frequently understood themselves) as a religious community rather than as a national group deserving state support to preserve their languages and culture.[4] Israel was, of course, the exception, as it was conceived as a national homeland for the Jewish people. But Zionist ideology was then dedicated to the creation of a Hebrew-speaking society that would unify—and, in the process, erode cultural differences between—diasporic Jewish communities. It discouraged the perpetuation of "foreign" (including other Jewish) languages—above all, Yiddish—as languages of home, community, and society in a Jewish state, even if practical use was made of them (such as in the form of newspapers sponsored by political parties) in the state's early years. Yiddish was not only the most widely spoken Jewish language and the focus of its own nationalist movement—and hence a rival to Hebrew—but long considered emblematic of the allegedly deforming qualities of Diaspora life that were to be shed as part of the construction of a "new Jew" in the ancient Jewish homeland.[5]

It was thus hardly clear to YIVO's staff and supporters in the 1940s that an organization dedicated to serving the intellectual and cultural needs of a global, Yiddish-speaking Jewish nation could take root in the radically different circumstances of postwar America and prove relevant in the long run to generations not born and raised in eastern Europe. Even the very decision early in the war to transfer the institute's headquarters from Vilna, whose future was deeply uncertain, to the safety of New York City was greeted with more than a little trepidation on both sides of the Atlantic. These anxieties only intensified as the extent of the devastation unfolding in Nazi-controlled Europe became apparent and as the likelihood that Jewish communal life in Europe would be revived after the cessation of hostilities became increasingly remote. Nonetheless, YIVO soldiered on in New York, seeking to remain true to its prewar mission while articulating a vision for American Jewry's leadership role in the postwar era.

World War II and the Holocaust were, of course, the major catastrophes affecting YIVO in the 1940s and beyond. But the postwar peace immediately brought its own share of challenges. The wartime alliance between the capitalist United States and the communist Soviet Union yielded to a growing rivalry for political and economic hegemony between them that had profound effects on efforts to reclaim what had survived of YIVO's prewar collections. Further, the emergence of Israel as a modern Jewish nation-state raised the question of the relationship of an institute animated by its commitment to the flourishing of the Jewish Diaspora to a new country that understood itself as the center of Jewish life and inheritor of Europe's destroyed Jewish communities. Simultaneously, questions arose as to how YIVO in New York, now itself elevated from the status of periphery to center of a world organization, would relate to its affiliates outside the United States as well as to the study of American Jewish history and culture and to the experience of non-Yiddish-speaking Jews around the world.

Most profound, however, was the challenge of cultivating a relationship with the largest segment of American Jewry that, even if it spoke or understood Yiddish, did not share YIVO's valorization of Yiddish and of social science scholarship about the recent past and present as a means to better Jewish life and was consequently little inclined to support it morally or financially. The institute struggled over the course of decades not only to survive financially but to ensure that it would find an audience beyond the generation of its founders and their immigrant supporters. Questions concerning its direction, activities, and leadership and even the language of its daily operations were the subject of often bitter disputes within the institute and the circles of its supporters.

The process of YIVO's transplantation from Vilna and its transformation from the aspiring academy of a Yiddish-speaking nation transcending political boundaries into an American Jewish research institute firmly rooted in New York is the subject of this book. Its focus is the crucial years from 1940 to 1970, which encompass the final years of YIVO's European era and the foundational years of its still-unfolding American one. These years mark a transitional period in the institute's history during which YIVO struggled to establish itself on a new continent, to reclaim what had survived of its European collections and commemorate a lost world, and to chart a course for scholarship and public engagement that would remain true to its founding ethos. At the same time, it strived to acclimate itself to a society in which many of its founding commitments were deemed foreign or found little resonance within the mainstream Jewish community seeking integration into American society. Significantly, these years also represent the time when Yiddish scholar Max Weinreich assumed the reins of YIVO's preexisting American division and guided its evolution toward an American YIVO. It is Weinreich, the chief architect of the American YIVO, who provided the main rationale for YIVO's continued activity even after the destruction of eastern European Jewry, and it is his vision and imposing personality that provided much of its direction and impetus in the years that would follow. Weinreich's role as a scholar, administrator, and teacher whose influence extended to virtually all spheres of YIVO's activity places him at the center of this study.

More than adapt YIVO to America, Weinreich sought to adapt American Jewish life to YIVO's mission of Jewish nation-building through scholarship. In his words, he sought to "Vilnaize" it—to activate its intellectually motivated youth and culturally creative forces in and on behalf of Yiddish and YIVO's approach to Jewish scholarship on the model of eastern European, especially prewar Vilna Jewry.[6] Naturally, the institute underwent a large degree of Americanization—both welcome and contested—in its new home. But while YIVO under Weinreich's leadership could not remake American Jewry in the image of eastern European Jewry, it could furnish it with a treasure house of knowledge about the Jewish past and present as well as the social scientific tools to interpret them. As Weinreich was fond of saying, YIVO would provide not only *visnshaft* ([social] science) but *visn vos shaft*, knowledge that creates. Only an unbiased record of the Jewish past and sober understanding of the problems of the Jewish present, YIVO scholars maintained, would offer American Jewry the means to sustain a secular Jewish identity. This book explores those ways by which Weinreich and his colleagues pursued their goals and to what extent they were successful.

YIVO's formative European period (1925–39) has been reconstructed and analyzed by historian Cecile Kuznitz in her magisterial work *YIVO and the Making of Modern Jewish Culture*. Her "biography" of YIVO represents an important contribution not only to the institute's history but to the already very substantial and rapidly growing body of scholarship about Jewish culture, society, and politics in interwar Poland that has developed especially since the opening of eastern European archives following the dissolution of the Soviet Union.[7] It is particularly valuable for its insights into the development of Diaspora Nationalism and Yiddishism—the movement to make Yiddish language and culture the focal point of a modern, secularized Jewish identity—as often closely linked and mutually shaping political and cultural ideologies. Kuznitz's work is complemented by a number of studies about personalities active in the Vilna YIVO and aspects of its scholarly production in that period, as well as by studies of Jewish academic institutions established in pre–World War II eastern Europe.[8]

In contrast, the still-unfolding American chapter in the institute's history has so far escaped comprehensive scholarly treatment despite the fact that YIVO has called New York City its home for eighty-five years—more than five times longer than it was active in Vilna. Several monographs have appeared in recent years about the fate of YIVO's Vilna library and archival collections in the early postwar era. Because of their focus, however, these works tend to situate the dramatic reclamation and transfer of materials to New York City more as the conclusion of or a coda to the European era in YIVO's history than as an early chapter in its expanding American one.[9] Beyond them, the early decades of YIVO's activity in America typically receive at most passing mention in scholarship about American Jewish history in this period, usually as a reflection of the vibrancy of New York's Jewish intellectual scene in the 1940s or in discussions of the decline of Yiddish language and culture by the 1960s.[10] Similarly, the field of Yiddish studies, which is intimately linked to the history of YIVO, has so far given little systematic attention to the institute's postwar contributions.[11]

Recent scholarship has definitively cast aside the notion of Yiddish-speaking intellectuals' silence during the Holocaust and debunked the myth of the post-Holocaust "death of Yiddish" by revealing the existence of a still vibrant world of Yiddish letters, scholarship, and culture from the 1940s through the 1970s in the Americas and even in an Israel long known for its opposition to Yiddish.[12] Indeed, Yiddish speakers continued to play an important role as public intellectuals in the post–World War II era and made tremendous contributions to the development of a variety of fields of scholarly inquiry, including Holocaust studies. And likely no one locus brought together more Yiddish-speaking intellectuals in its daily operations, publications, and annual conferences than YIVO.

Nonetheless, we know surprisingly little about so important an institution as YIVO for shaping Jewish scholarship and public life in America. Apart from in its administrative records (most of which awaits processing by archivists), YIVO's history as an institution in America from 1940 to 1970 is chiefly reflected in addresses delivered at annual conferences, scattered references in memoir literature, evaluations by boosters and critics appearing in Jewish (mainly Yiddish) newspapers and periodicals, and in speeches delivered by staff members at its events. Beyond works already mentioned above, a small number of recent articles and monographs, mainly by historians, also help us to trace YIVO's encounter with America through the examination of specific projects and the careers and achievements of individual YIVO-affiliated scholars such as linguist Max Weinreich and historian Lucy Dawidowicz.[13]

Surviving members of the founding generation active in YIVO were themselves more inclined to commemorate and reflect publicly on the institute's milieu and its achievements during its European than its

American era.[14] Even the content of the fiftieth anniversary issue of *Yivo bleter* (*YIVO Pages*), the institute's main journal, is overwhelmingly dedicated to the "Vilna years."[15] The European chapter was decisively closed and hence lent itself more readily to summary and analysis than the conflictual and open-ended present during which many despaired about the future of the language and culture that animated the institute, if not the very future of American Jewry. Moreover, they often felt morally compelled to memorialize the world in which they had come to maturity as well as those whom they had tragically lost. Evocations of YIVO's European period in the institute's publications as well as in the Yiddish press and memoirs are consonant with a trend found in what former YIVO librarian Zachary Baker describes as the "Silver Age" of Yiddish publishing. The quarter century after World War II saw an outpouring of commemorative writing as well as literary production by Yiddish writers and memoirists now dispersed around the world that focused on the prewar and wartime eras in eastern Europe.[16]

Literary scholar Jan Schwarz's *Survivors and Exiles: Yiddish Culture After the Holocaust* vividly depicts how Silver Age writers not only endeavored to capture a lost world and transmit its values but struggled with the question of their own relevance as artists and intellectuals working in a language accessible to a dwindling readership. They employed a variety of strategies, including translating and reshaping their works to appeal to the sensibilities of an English-reading audience.[17] Focusing on historians of the same generation, Mark L. Smith analyzes the foundational contributions that a global cohort of survivor scholars originating in Poland and writing largely in Yiddish made to the development of Holocaust historiography in his *The Yiddish Historians and the Struggle for a Yiddish History of the Holocaust*. Like Schwarz's book, his study examines the contributions of a number of prominent YIVO associates but does not seek to paint a larger picture of YIVO's postwar activities as an institution or its relationship to America and its Jews.[18] Nonetheless, both works reflect the centrality of YIVO and New York, home to a still sizable Yiddish writing community after the Holocaust, to postwar Yiddish scholarly and cultural production around the world.

Seldom does scholarship recognize YIVO as an institute that strove to remain relevant as more than an archive and library to generations beyond Yiddish-speaking immigrants. A notable exception is Markus

Krah's *American Jewry and the Re-Invention of the East European Jewish Past*. Krah demonstrates how YIVO initiated a conversation about harnessing selective elements of eastern European Jewry's cultural legacy to shape post–World War II Jewish identity in the United States that was later taken up by intellectuals, artists, and community leaders spanning the Jewish political, cultural, and religious spectrum in their construction of a "usable past" for American Jewry.[19] In particular, Krah highlights Weinreich's Freudian analysis of what he identified as American Jewish youth's discomfort with its Jewishness and his ambitions for YIVO to assume a leading role in the intellectual life of English- as well as Yiddish-speaking Jewry. Krah's insightful study rightly recognizes the limits of YIVO's appeal to a chiefly English-speaking American Jewry imposed by its foundational commitment to Yiddishism. But given the book's limited survey of YIVO's activities between 1940 and 1965, it also misses ways in which YIVO activities—including those focused on Yiddish—ultimately proved successful in bringing generations of American Jews closer to their eastern European Jewish heritage.[20]

Jeffrey Shandler offers a more sanguine evaluation of YIVO's efforts to engage American Jewry in his meditation on Jewish museums, *Homes of the Past: A Lost Jewish Museum*. For Shandler, YIVO's project, launched during World War II, to solicit personal items from immigrant and American-born Jews to create a museum about the vanishing world of eastern European Jewry marks an inflection point "between studying this population as a living culture and examining it as a bygone phenomenon." In his evaluation, the project, which was ultimately aborted for reasons not wholly clear, arrived "too early" for an American Jewish audience preoccupied with pressing postwar concerns, such as caring for Holocaust survivors and combating antisemitism, and not yet intellectually and emotionally ready to appreciate the vibrant culture that had been lost. Nonetheless, the project anticipated more successful efforts by later generations of YIVO associates to represent the world of eastern European Jewry, albeit from the perspective of American Jews who had not experienced that civilization firsthand.[21] Arguably, Shandler's characterization of the project as precocious is apt for much of YIVO's enterprise during its early decades in America. During these, the "Weinreich years," YIVO attempted or planted the seeds for many farsighted endeavors that yielded fruit only decades later, when changes in American Jewry made it more receptive to its heritage and to YIVO's goals.

For YIVO to succeed in its mission in America, however, not only did American Jewry need to change in its relationship to the eastern European Jewish historical and cultural legacy; YIVO too necessarily changed, including in its attitudes toward Yiddish, Yiddishism, and Diaspora Nationalism.

In the last two decades alone, researchers have produced a slew of monographs about the movement in noncommunist eastern Europe to acquire national cultural autonomy for Jews, including state support for Yiddish cultural institutions, prior to World War II.[22] They have also examined the contrasting case of the Soviet Union, where the regime supported Yiddish-language schools as well as academic and cultural institutions conforming to Bolshevik ideology until changes in the nationalities policy in the mid-1930s led to their decline and frequent closure. While Yiddish cultural forces were reinvigorated during the war years through their recruitment in the struggle against Nazi Germany, remaining Jewish cultural organizations were shuttered by 1949, and the last few Soviet Yiddish schools closed by 1951 following an antisemitic campaign launched by Stalin's regime.[23]

In postwar Poland, Jewish cultural organizations, including schools, ultimately did not fare much better despite initial efforts to rebuild an infrastructure for Jewish communal life. A state-sponsored Yiddish theater, Jewish Historical Institute, and Yiddish newspaper, however, continued to exist in communist Poland. In fact, the Polish Yiddish newspaper *Folks-sztyme* (Voice of the People) published writers not only from Poland but offered almost the only platform for Soviet Yiddish writers until the journal *Sovetish heymland* (Soviet Homeland), a highbrow literary and political journal, was launched in 1961 to placate foreign sympathizers (particularly Western communists pressing for a revival of Yiddish culture) as well as to serve as a mouthpiece for Soviet ideology in the post-Stalinist era. It served as the single forum for established Yiddish writers to publish their work in the USSR as well as an opportunity to train new ones.[24]

In contrast, no legal obstacles existed to the promotion of secular Yiddish culture in the United States. How did proponents of Jewish cultural autonomy and Yiddishists of various stripes who survived the

Holocaust come to terms with the decline of their ideologies in postwar conditions and try to imbue their organizations and institutions with revised or expanded meaning once settled in America?[25] In addition to providing an account of the Weinreich years in YIVO's American history, this book is chiefly occupied with the intertwined questions of how the institute responded to the catastrophe that engulfed European Jewry and endeavored to invest ideologies—above all, Yiddishism—with new meaning after they had lost much of their practical, although not personal, significance for surviving eastern European Jews.

Scholars studying the afterlife of movements promoting Yiddish-centric cultural autonomy for Jews in the Diaspora have demonstrated, for example, that both the anti-Zionist Bund, one of the most popular Jewish parties in Poland in the period between the two world wars, and the much smaller Freeland League did not abruptly quit their activities or cease having influence in shaping Jewish political discourse in the postwar period. But the Bund, the Marxist political party in which many YIVO associates were active, was unsuccessful in finding a mass audience for its commitments to socialism and secular Yiddish culture among English-speaking, increasingly middle-class Jews in Cold War America or among young Jews in most other countries. While continuing its political activities globally in attenuated form, it became increasingly relevant more as a source of community, a center of Yiddish cultural activity, and a locus for collective commemoration of the Holocaust for its aging members. Tellingly, YIVO absorbed its massive archives in 1992.[26]

Similarly, the ambition of the Freeland League, a small intellectual movement that also found adherents within YIVO, to create an autonomous Jewish settlement in an underpopulated territory outside of Palestine lost much of its appeal in a world where a Jewish nation-state now existed and that saw movements calling for the decolonization of European-controlled territories. It ultimately survived in the form of the League for Yiddish, an organization that maintained its support for Yiddish as Jews' vernacular and a language of higher culture but relinquished its territorialist and anti-Zionist political commitments.[27] The collection of Freeland League (and YIVO) cofounder Isaac N. Steinberg, which contains much of the organization's files, is also to be found in YIVO's archives.

Secular Yiddish supplementary schools and summer camps provide an alternative model for adjustment to the decline of vernacular

Yiddish culture and politics. They grappled since their inception in the pre–World War II era with how to adapt curricula grounded in eastern European political-cultural ideologies to the realities of American life. Their audience consisted of children immersed in English-language culture and educated in American public schools rather than European transplants. As studies such as Fradle Pomerantz Freidenreich's *Passionate Pioneers*, Naomi Prawer Kadar's *Raising Secular Jews*, and Sandy Fox's *The Jews of Summer* reveal, it became increasingly difficult even before the war to preserve Yiddish as the language of activities, as fewer and fewer children arrived from Yiddish-speaking homes. Further, the ideological convictions championed by working-class city dwellers in the early decades of the twentieth century were decreasingly appealing to an American Jewry that was becoming not only overwhelmingly English-speaking but also increasingly middle class, suburban, and drawn into general American cultural and political concerns. Ultimately, anxiety about communist and socialist affiliations in general American society, particularly during the McCarthy era, and the widespread discrediting of the Soviet Union in Jewish circles following the revelation of Stalinist purges (including the murders of prominent Yiddish cultural figures) left virtually all "radical" ideologies suspect among American-born Jews. Together with language and demographic shift, this contributed to the decline of Yiddish camps and schools. Left-leaning Yiddish schools and camps increasingly emphasized Jewish peoplehood and Holocaust commemoration—sometimes alongside support for the State of Israel and secularized elements of Jewish religious tradition, depending on where they lay on the political-ideological spectrum—in combination with core values such as labor and social justice.[28]

In the process, Yiddishism itself was transformed from a form of eastern European cultural nationalism into a tool for building a distinctive, left-leaning American Jewish identity. As Fox demonstrates, even in those camps most committed to Yiddish (such as the nonpartisan Sholem Aleichem Folk Institute's Camp Boiberik and the Bundist Camp Hemshekh until their closing by the late 1970s), the language became more a symbol of secular Jewish identity and eastern European Jewish heritage (however interpreted) to be celebrated and performed through announcements, declarations, rituals, and song than employed as a vehicle for everyday functions and spontaneous expression.[29] In this way, camps were a harbinger of a phenomenon known today as "postvernacular" culture, which emphasizes the emotive and symbolic functions of language over purely communicative ones that presume linguistic competence.[30]

YIVO, by contrast, grew rather than withered with the transition from prewar to postwar politics and the decline of secular Yiddish culture for reasons that will be explored in this study. Unlike other Jewish archives and research institutes that came into existence in America both prior to World War II (such as the American Jewish Historical Society, founded in 1892) and after it (such as the Leo Baeck Institute, founded in 1955 to preserve the history and culture of German-speaking Jewry), YIVO distinguished itself not only through its holdings and publications but also through its training and educational programs as well as its cultural programming directed at a broad audience.[31] It never aimed to serve solely as a resource for scholars or as an "ivory tower" institute, despite its commitment to high academic standards. Rather, it has always been motivated by a desire for a symbiotic relationship with a living *folk*, even if maintaining such a relationship has at times proven difficult. YIVO has been animated since its inception by a unique fusion of popular and elite (and at times elitist) academic impulses. This dynamic tension has both strained and invigorated the institute across a century of tumultuous change but ultimately enabled it to preserve much of the core of its prewar values forged in Vilna while remaining relevant, in different ways, to both eastern European and American-born generations in the postwar era.

The YIVO in Vilna

YIVO came into existence in order to serve as a national university, language academy, and library for a diasporic, Yiddish-speaking Jewry at a time before Jewish studies, let alone Yiddish itself, was widely recognized in academia. It was the brainchild of Yiddish scholar Nokhem Shtif, a Ukrainian-born linguist and literary historian residing in Berlin, then home to a large cohort of Jewish refugee scholars fleeing the violence, poverty, and political instability of post–World War I eastern Europe. Shtif authored a memorandum in 1924 envisioning the creation of a Yiddish academic institute for researchers that would ideally be located in a western European capital with an established Jewish scholarly tradition such as Berlin or Vienna. But his plan, which he circulated among Yiddish scholars in New York and Vilna, found its greatest resonance in eastern Europe, the heartland of Yiddish culture. Its chief executors were Max Weinreich and journalist and literary scholar Zalmen Reyzen, who convened a meeting of Yiddish educational organizations in Vilna to discuss it in the spring of 1925. They endorsed Shtif's memorandum with modifications (summarized as the "Vilna Theses"), giving greater emphasis to teaching and stressing a connection to the Yiddish-speaking masses, especially via the Yiddish secular schools that had emerged in eastern Europe during World War I. Delegates from western and eastern Europe met that summer in Berlin, where they determined the contours of the institute's research and publication activities as well as established its organizational structure.[32]

YIVO was not alone in seeking to professionalize and raise the standards of Jewish scholarship. That same decade also saw the birth of the Polish-language Instytut Nauk Judaistycznych (Institute for Jewish Studies) in Warsaw as well as Jewish academic institutions in Palestine (the Hebrew University in Jerusalem) and in the USSR (the Institute of Jewish Proletarian Culture in Kiev [Kyiv, in Ukrainian] and a Jewish department of the Institute for Belorussian Culture in Minsk). YIVO was, however, from its outset meant not only to support Yiddishist ideology but to be a global institute, with academic sections projected in Vilna, Warsaw, and Berlin. An American branch was founded that same year in New York and an Argentine one in Buenos Aires in 1928. Throughout the 1920s and '30s, local supporters also created "Friends of YIVO" societies to assist with the collection of materials, fundraising, and other tasks not only in Poland and neighboring countries but throughout the far-flung diaspora of Yiddish-speaking Jews originating in eastern Europe, including cities in the Americas, Australia, Belgium, England, France, Palestine, and South Africa. On the eve of World War II, these societies existed in more than thirty countries the world over.[33]

But YIVO's primary headquarters were in Vilna, Poland, the famed "Jerusalem of Lithuania"—a city of some two hundred thousand that was about 28 percent Jewish on the eve of World War II. So strong was the commitment of the city's secular Jewish intelligentsia to the ideal of building a modern, Yiddish-speaking future for eastern European Jewry that the city was crowned with the unofficial title of "the capital of Yiddishland."[34] While YIVO-affiliated scholars elsewhere, particularly in Warsaw, contested Vilna's "hegemony" in the organization and the tendency to promote Vilna-based linguistic norms, it was hard for anyone to deny the centrality of that city in Jewish history or the high degree of enthusiasm for YIVO shown by its Jewish inhabitants. The very location of YIVO's building outside the older Jewish section of Vilna emphasized its modern character while asserting its continuity with the city's history as a center of traditional religious study (of which the revered Vilna Gaon was only the most illustrious example), *Haskalah* (the secularizing nineteenth-century Jewish Enlightenment), and modern Jewish movements such as Zionism and Bundism, not to mention Hebrew and Yiddish publishing. YIVO's technologically up-to-date appointments and physical attractiveness were a source of pride and made it a tourist destination for Jews from throughout Poland and beyond.

The institute found its primary constituency among the impoverished Jewish masses of non-Soviet eastern Europe, especially in eastern Poland and the Baltic states. There, support for Yiddish and YIVO's ideals was greater than in more linguistically assimilated regions of Poland, such as the former Galicia (today's southeastern Poland and western Ukraine, where Kraków and Lwów/Lviv are located) and Congress Poland (today's central Poland, where Warsaw and Łódź are found). With little budget for the acquisition of publications and data for its collections and research, YIVO relied largely on the submissions of thousands of *zamlers*—amateur, volunteer collectors from all walks of life, who sent books and information—as well as participants in its essay contests. Many *zamlers* were uneducated or semieducated workers and merchants who felt elevated by their participation in a sacred mission to gather artifacts and data, such as folklore and vocabulary, for what would normally be considered recondite research by a tiny elite. Collecting materials, always central to YIVO's mission, not only served as a means to assemble the necessary repository of information to document and analyze Jewish life, including folkways and elements of culture believed likely to disappear with the advance of secularization, industrialization, and migration; it was also a means to engage the broad Jewish public in a project to build consciousness of belonging to a Jewish nation rooted in eastern Europe but with "colonies" throughout the world and to inspire pride in its language and culture. YIVO branches and "Friends of YIVO" societies on virtually every continent also collected money and materials to be sent to Vilna. As early as 1926, YIVO cofounder Max Weinreich wrote to his colleague Jacob Shatzky in New York, "When we reveal how much we were able to amass in YIVO, the world will be astounded what can be done with sheer devotion and without as much as a penny."[35]

This relationship between YIVO and its supporters was mutual. YIVO not only relied on the Jewish masses for material; it cultivated the ideals of empiricism and objective scholarship as a means for Jews to acquire the self-knowledge necessary to improve their present-day conditions and to help them build secular Yiddish culture.[36] Its four "sections"—Philological (for the study of language, literature, and folklore), Historical, Social-Economic (later, Economic-Statistical), and Pedagogical (later, Psychological-Pedagogical)—applied the latest techniques in the social sciences to gather information about Jews' past and present lives. Its commitment to scientific objectivity as an ideal meant striving to retain political neutrality as much as possible in the bitterly divided atmosphere of interwar Jewish society rather than conducting scholarship through the lens of a given ideology or in the service of a specific political orientation beyond its general commitment to Yiddish and the Diaspora. Thus, it did not draft policy or lobby the Polish government to effect legal change, even when Yiddish secular schools—especially those of the *TSYSHO* (*Tsentrale yidishe shul organizatsye*, Central Yiddish School Organization) network, closely affiliated with YIVO—were harassed by state officials who opposed them as expressions of Jewish nationalism and leftist ideologies. It sought instead to furnish the data and understanding that would help Jewish communal and political leaders improve Jews' material conditions, bolster Jews' psychological health and educational levels, and defend Jews against discrimination and harassment. Hence, for example, historian Jacob Shatzky noted with great pride that data YIVO had gathered about Jews' economic and social conditions were used by Jewish politicians in the Polish parliament to refute baseless claims made by parties hostile to Jews. Similarly, Max Weinreich analyzed hundreds of autobiographies submitted to its essay contests to understand the social and psychological factors shaping individual and collective identity among Polish Jewish youth and to gain insight into their strategies for facing a hostile world.[37]

At the same time, YIVO endeavored to disseminate its research findings through exhibitions, courses, and publications aimed at popular as well as expert audiences. To this end, the institute made use of Yiddish, the language of the Jewish masses of eastern Europe and its global diaspora, as the language of its daily operations and regular publications. It also made major contributions to the modernization of the language itself, collecting terminology for various professions and working in particular with Yiddish secular schools in Poland to elaborate and spread a standardized system of spelling. In 1938, YIVO's Vilna headquarters proudly possessed a collection of some forty thousand books, ten thousand volumes of periodicals, seventy-five thousand manuscripts, and more than one hundred thousand objects of folk art.[38]

YIVO's relationship to Yiddish was, however, more than pragmatic. The language was widely derided by Jews and non-Jews alike as a corruption of German, with which it shared medieval roots. It was seen as a grammarless folk language (*folkshprakh*) and accorded a status within Jewish society inferior to that of Hebrew, a classical language associated with religion and an established intellectual and literary tradition, and to languages of European high culture such as Russian and Polish. Building on the agenda for language reform of the 1908 First Yiddish Language Conference in Czernowitz (today's Chernivtsi, Ukraine, then a city in the Habsburg monarchy), which famously pronounced Yiddish "a national language" of the Jewish people, YIVO sought to raise the status of the much-maligned traditional vernacular of Ashkenazic Jewry in the eyes of both Jews and the wider world. It also contributed to the cultivation of emerging secular, European-style elite and popular cultures in the language. In doing so, YIVO and its scholars hoped to further the project, underway since the late nineteenth century, to construct a modern identity grounded in the traditional folk language and its culture on behalf of a (Ashkenazic) Jewish people that was increasingly scattered and linguistically, politically, and religiously divided. This emphasis on Yiddish and support for Jewish national cultural autonomy in the Diaspora distinguished it in particular from the Hebrew University. The latter represented the instantiation of Zionist aspirations for the creation of a modern, secular Hebrew culture focused on Jews' ancient homeland. While championing different languages as emblematic of Jewish identity, Yiddishism and Hebraism agreed on the desirability of attaining national monolingualism, thereby undoing centuries of Hebrew-Yiddish diglossia (the use of related "high" and "low" languages for distinct but complementary functions) within Jewish society.[39]

YIVO was intended to serve as the pinnacle of an entire Yiddish-language educational network that had emerged around the time of World War I—from kindergarten to a hoped-for university—in Poland and beyond. This network would cultivate a generation of producers and consumers of highbrow Yiddish culture, thereby assuring the existence of an economic base for that culture and its intelligentsia. Its founders and staff had by necessity received whatever higher education they possessed in languages other than Yiddish (usually German, Russian, or Polish) and were sometimes—as was the case of philologists Nokhem Shtif, who studied in both polytechnical and law schools, and Noah Prylucki, a lawyer and journalist by profession—autodidacts in the fields they sought to develop. Of its leadership, in fact, only Max Weinreich possessed a doctorate in the area in which he was chiefly active (German philology, from the University of Marburg). By elaborating an academic register for the language and demonstrating its suitability as a vehicle of European high culture, they aimed to stay the growing "defection" of Jews to more prestigious state languages such as Polish in the pursuit of intellectual and cultural opportunities, material gain, and prestige. YIVO accordingly set for itself the goals of standardizing terminology for use by educators (for example, in teaching the natural sciences and mathematics), health-care workers, writers, and cultural, social, and political organizations as well as providing guidance in what it considered proper use of the language. At the same time, the collection and standardization work of its Terminological Commission was not limited to white-collar professions. It thus collected vocabulary from practitioners of a variety of crafts and trades, traditional and modern, from tailors to auto mechanics.[40]

After Poland reemerged as a state from the wreckage of the Russian, Austro-Hungarian, and German Empires following more than a century of partition in November 1918, it was obliged by the victorious Western Allies to guarantee a measure of cultural autonomy for its national minorities (above all, Ukrainians, Jews, Belarusians, and Germans), which made up almost a third of its population, as a condition for international recognition. YIVO did not, however, receive the vital support to which it felt entitled under provisions in the Polish constitution: support for educational work in the languages of national minorities, including Yiddish. It therefore appealed to Polish municipalities, arguing that they were obliged to uphold the state's responsibility by sharing a portion of taxes paid by Jewish citizens in the form of subsidies for YIVO. Similarly, in the absence of a sovereign Jewish state that could tax its citizens, YIVO maintained that it was the duty of Jewish organizations in Poland and beyond to support it as a national institution serving the needs of Yiddish-speaking Jews everywhere.[41]

In this way, YIVO managed to cobble together financial support from a combination of meager sources: grants from Polish municipalities and subsidies from *kehilot* (state-recognized Jewish communities), private donations and contributions from individuals and Jewish organizations in Poland and, above all, abroad, especially in the United States. It survived with a budget often on the verge of bankruptcy, unable to pay its staff their full wages for months at a time. At the beginning of

YIVO instructors (including Max Weinreich, second row on the right, and Zalmen Reyzen, last row, second from the right) and *aspirantn* (including Lucy Shildkret, front row in the middle) stand in front of its building in Vilna in 1939. Credit: YIVO Institute for Jewish Research

the academic year 1938–39, it included fourteen professional and clerical workers on its staff. Sixteen students were enrolled in its *aspirantur*, the graduate-level program for training scholars under the guidance of senior staff. It also maintained a *proaspirantur* program to prepare students without university experience to enter the *aspirantur*. Such achievements, however, could not undo the harsh economic reality and bleak professional horizon: Paradoxically, some scholars in training (called *aspirantn*) prolonged their stay in the program precisely because it was virtually impossible to find jobs in the fields in which YIVO was training them and because they lacked other sources of income.[42]

Despite—or perhaps because of—widespread poverty, eastern European Jewish society in the period between the two world wars was riven by ideological divides. A small minority of "Assimilationists," to use the language of the day, viewed Jews chiefly or exclusively as a religious community and preached their integration into the dominant national group among whom they lived—for example, Poles. Most Jews (and Gentiles), however, understood Jews as a unique people distinguished not merely by religion but by such characteristics as language, culture, and economic profile. While both religious Jews and secularists accepted this understanding, they differed in that the former saw devotion to God and observance of Jewish law (halakha) as the sine qua non of Jewish identity, whereas the latter saw Jewish nationhood as not dependent on religious criteria. Specifically Jewish political parties offered competing visions for a better future, clashing over such issues as the role of religion in Jewish society, where Jews should live (in diasporic lands or a Jewish autonomous territory or state), what language(s) they should use (Hebrew, Yiddish, or the language of the land), and what economic system (capitalism or socialism) was most just and conducive to generating prosperity for the largest number of people.

YIVO sought to be a nonpartisan institute, studying Jews of all walks of life and accepting contributions from across the ideological spectrum to its mission to collect and expand knowledge. It pursued a "big tent" approach, welcoming anyone—including Zionists and Orthodox Jews—who embraced its scholarly mission and commitment to Yiddish. Practically speaking, however, its assumption of a secular definition of Jewish nationhood made it difficult to include Orthodox Jews, many of whom were already suspicious of Yiddishism as a form of idolatry that fetishized language and sought to uproot religion from Jewish life. YIVO's supporters were mainly to be found among liberal and leftist elements, who pressed it to adopt an overtly ideological stance beyond devotion to the Diaspora and Yiddish. Socialists such as Bundists and pro-Yiddish Labor Zionists (Left Poale Zion), not to mention Communists, rejected its nonpartisan stance, accusing its leadership of bourgeois, ivory tower aloofness from the urgent needs of the working masses in a time of growing poverty and discrimination. They pressed for an explicitly class-based position to dictate the research agenda as well as for greater involvement in politically left-leaning Yiddish secular schools. Speaking to pressing contemporary problems while retaining intellectual independence and integrity in the face of political pressures was thus a perennial source of tension within the institute.

While YIVO's administration and Philological Section, headed by Max Weinreich, were located in Vilna, the heads of YIVO's other sections were to be found elsewhere. The Psychological-Pedagogical Section was directed by Leibush Lehrer from New York, but its meetings, attended mainly by educational activists, were held in Vilna. Meanwhile, the Historical and Economic-Statistical Sections, headed by Elias Tcherikower and Jacob Lestschinsky, respectively, were located until 1933 in Berlin and then in Paris (Tcherikower) and Warsaw (Lestschinsky). Warsaw was also home to a number of young YIVO-affiliated historians, such as Emanuel Ringelblum and Raphael Mahler, as well as Philological Section member Noah Pryłucki.

The Amopteyl

The most important of YIVO's branches outside its center in Vilna was to be found not in Warsaw, the Polish capital and a major center of Jewish life since the nineteenth century, or some other European Jewish metropolis but in New York City. On the eve of World War II, more than two million Jews lived in New York City, making up more than 25 percent of its population. In comparison, Warsaw, home to Europe's largest Jewish community, had some 375,000 Jews in 1939—about 30 percent of the city's population.[43] Some fifty years after the beginning of the wave of mass emigration of Jews from eastern Europe to the United States in the 1880s, the country's nearly five million Jews—many of them Yiddish-speaking immigrants or their progeny—were comparatively affluent and supported a vibrant literary scene and an eclectic array of labor organizations, mutual aid societies, newspapers, theaters, supplementary schools for children, and other cultural institutions functioning in Yiddish.[44]

YIVO's American division, the Amopteyl (short for *Amerikaner opteyl*), was founded in late 1925 by a group of eastern European Jewish intellectuals who had settled in New York City. The main organizers were folklorist Yehuda Leib Cahan, influential literature critic Samuel Charney (better known by his pen name Shmuel Niger),[45] educator Leibush Lehrer, and historian Jacob Shatzky, who served as the group's secretary

Group photo of the founders of American YIVO Section with Max Weinreich, then visiting America. Including Jacob Shatzky (seated, first on right), Max Weinreich (seated, second from right), Samuel Charney (seated, middle), Y. L. Cahan (seated, second from left), David Berezer, Morris (Moyshe) Odoner, Sh. Weiner, Gustav Eisner, Sh. Faks, 1929. Credit: YIVO Institute for Jewish Research and hosted its meetings in his apartment. Under their combined leadership, the Amopteyl enjoyed a positive reputation thanks to its annual conference and the publication of a number of important scholarly works. These included collections of documents about the history of the Yiddish theater and press that Shatzky edited as well as the journals *Der pinkes* (*The Record Book*; 1927–29) and *Yorbukh fun amopteyl* (*Yearbook of the Amopteyl*; two volumes published in 1938 and 1939). Moreover, as Cecile Kuznitz notes, through its fundraising campaigns and solicitation of donations from organizations such as the American Joint Distribution Committee, "the section became crucial to YIVO's fundraising efforts, with American sources contributing as much as two-thirds of the institute's total budget."[46]

By the outbreak of World War II in September 1939, not only was Lehrer, the secretary of YIVO's Psychological-Pedagogical Section, a resident of New York; so was a majority of the members of YIVO's Philological Section—language scholars Yudel Mark and Judah A. Joffe, along with literary critic Charney—as well one of the institute's European cofounders, Jacob Lestschinsky, a pioneering economic demographer of Jewish life. Expelled from Germany in 1933 for denouncing the Nazi regime on the pages of the New York Yiddish *Forverts* (known also by its English name, *The Jewish Daily Forward*), Lestschinsky left Berlin—where he headed YIVO's Economic-Statistical Section—for Prague and then Riga. He settled in Warsaw in 1934 but was barred by the government of Poland from returning after a vacation abroad for writing articles critical of that country.[47] When he arrived in the United States in 1938, he brought with him the section's library, further expanding the Amopteyl's collections.[48]

Yet despite the presence of so many prominent YIVO associates in New York and the Amopteyl's significant contributions, the Vilna YIVO and much of the Amopteyl's own staff themselves saw the Amopteyl as playing an auxiliary role in the broader YIVO organization. In this way, it mirrored the image common among eastern European intellectuals of Jewish America as a culturally dependent (and culturally inferior) "colony" of eastern Europe, despite its impressive demographic, political, and financial weight.[49] Moreover, differences in fundraising strategies and scholarly methodology proved a frequent source of tension between Vilna and New York.[50] It remained subordinate to Vilna, the unofficial capital of secular Yiddish culture and the universally acknowledged center and home of YIVO.

In Vilna, YIVO possessed a modern building of its own that housed the bulk of its staff and a rich library and archival holdings. It received the loyal support of a public whose lives it aimed to study and enrich. Jews from throughout the region took pride in the institution, coming to visit and marvel at its building and exhibits. In contrast, the Amopteyl was housed in comparatively small, drab quarters—three rented rooms at 425 Lafayette Street in downtown Manhattan in a building formerly housing the Astor Library that it shared with the Hebrew Immigrant Aid Society (HIAS) and other Jewish organizations.[51] Neither YIVO nor the Amopteyl was a household name among American Jews outside of circles of immigrants and their children, especially those associated with Yiddishism or left-leaning, especially labor, movements.

Even the work of the Amopteyl focused primarily on researching Jewish life in eastern Europe, not the United States, and on helping support and maintain the center in Vilna. Symbolic of Vilna's centrality to YIVO's mission as a Yiddishist academic institution was the publication of *Yivo bleter*, the institute's flagship journal, exclusively in Vilna. Moreover, materials collected around the world about local Jewish life were routinely sent to Vilna, fulfilling the ideal of creating a collective archive for eastern European and Yiddish-speaking Jewry regardless of the geographic provenance of items.[52] In addition to a steady flow of money and occasional emergency remittances, the Amopteyl sent to Vilna both published and archival materials, rare periodicals, theater posters, photographs, and more that represented the distinct experience of American Jewry. Only a minority of those active in the Amopteyl objected that doing so deprived American Jewry of the documents necessary to study its own past or promote a distinctly American Jewish identity. Typical of such attitudes was Jacob Shatzky's hyperbolic comment: "There isn't anything to write about America historically. There is no history at all; it is a Sodom."[53]

Nor was cooperation between Amopteyl and anglophone American Jewish scholars to produce a body of scholarship about American Jewry seen as an attractive or practical option. Speaking at the Amopteyl's 1935 conference, literary critic Alexander Mukdoyni (pen name of Aleksander Kapel) complained of the absence in the auditorium of Jewish studies scholars who work in English. He pointed to it as evidence of what he considered an unbridgeable gap between two worlds. English-language Jewish scholarship had, with few exceptions, thus far given little serious attention to the Yiddish language or its culture. On the contrary, English-language scholars frequently considered them primitive and inferior—at best a transient phenomenon of the "ghetto" to meet the needs of the immigrant generation and at worst an obstacle to Jews' integration into American society. Eastern European Jewish scholars, conversely, viewed American Jewry as lacking in historical consciousness and poor in cultural achievements. Indeed, little of the bounty of modern scholarship about Jewish history and culture produced in eastern Europe since the turn of the twentieth century had been translated into English.[54] Mukdoyni maintained, "[American Jewish scholars] do not understand our enthusiasm, they cannot have our sense of purpose and therefore they cannot unite with us."[55]

Still, American Jewish history and culture was not wholly overlooked as a subject of study by the Amopteyl, even by its detractors. In fact, an issue of the Amopteyl's annual edited by Shatzky was devoted to studies of aspects of Jewish history and literature in America in 1938. Meanwhile, European-based YIVO scholars such as Noah Pryłucki and Max Weinreich saw fit to write about Yiddish language and folklore in the United States and Canada following visits to North America.[56] American Jewry, however, was understood not as an independent entity but as part of a larger world organism whose beating heart was found in eastern Europe.

The combined German and Soviet invasion of Poland in September 1939 necessitated a fundamental reassessment of this transatlantic relationship. Wherever YIVO was active, its associates sensed that, regardless of the length or outcome of the war, an inflection point had been reached in Jewish life. Would the conditions of war now impel YIVO to relocate its center from the heartland of Yiddish culture to its American periphery? What would become of its eastern European center? Could the Yiddish cultural movement, as well as the Yiddish language itself, sustain itself indefinitely in the conditions of a comparatively integrationist America, especially without reinforcements in the form of immigrants from *di alte heym* (the Old Country)? Would American Jewry, long dependent on Europe for cultural guidance, embrace not only scholarship but a leadership role for world Jewry in a time of crisis? Such questions troubled YIVO's staff in Vilna and New York even before it became clear that the war and the ensuing devastation would spell an end in Europe to what Max Weinreich later called the "Yiddish era" in Jewish history.[57] They lie at the heart of the current investigation of YIVO's adaptation to and evolution in America.

Chapter Outline

Chapter 1, "Coming to America?," focuses on the crucial period from September 1939 until the summer of 1941 during which YIVO remained active in Vilna while a new center was also emerging in New York City. It begins with Max Weinreich stranded in Copenhagen at the outbreak of World War II and examines his agonized decision to continue on to America. The question of where YIVO's center lay—and, implicitly, its periphery as well as those of Yiddish culture and world Jewry—aroused passions in Vilna, New York, and elsewhere as long as the Vilna headquarters continued to operate independently. Debates among YIVO's staff members on both sides of the Atlantic reveal anxiety over the future of the institute both as an organization to be administered in its own right and as a symbol of the continued relevance and even survival of eastern European Jewry, as they sensed a seismic shift was underway in Jewish life.

The second chapter, "From Yiddish Scientific Institute to the YIVO Institute for Jewish Research," picks up in 1943, when emotions among YIVO's staff in New York had reached their nadir with awareness of the unfolding genocide. It examines YIVO's responses to the catastrophe engulfing European Jewry and efforts to prepare American Jewry, widely deemed materially secure but intellectually and psychologically immature, to assume the anticipated burden of intellectual and cultural leadership of world Jewry in the postwar era. YIVO struggled in the 1940s and '50s to strike an elusive balance between its long-standing focus on eastern European Jewry—and its commitment to the survivors of that civilization and the legacy of the Vilna YIVO—and the necessity of "Americanization"—cultivating scholarship and programming, in Yiddish and English, about Jewish life in America both for its inherent value and to appeal to American-born generations.

The third chapter, "YIVO and the Holocaust," focuses on the late 1940s until the early 1960s to examine YIVO's development as a center for documentation, research, and education about the Holocaust both during and after the war. The chapter emphasizes the ways in which YIVO's commitments to a "vanished world" not only reinforced its attachment to eastern Europe but simultaneously contributed to its identity as a world and, above all, American institution. At its heart is a discussion of the fate of the personnel and collections of the Vilna YIVO under German occupation, YIVO's efforts in New York to bring the Holocaust and German crimes to the world's attention, and the challenges it faced in recovering surviving parts of its Vilna library and archival collections against the backdrop of the emerging Cold War. YIVO's efforts to recover Jewish cultural treasures brought to the fore the question of who the legitimate inheritor of a murdered eastern European Jewry was—the Jewish community of the United States, the young State of Israel, or the eastern European countries in which Jews had lived prior to the war.

Next, "YIVO Yiddish," chapter 4, examines the changing meaning of Yiddish for YIVO as the language increasingly became a heritage language among American Jews and how this evolving relationship to the language was reflected in its operations and activities. The chapter takes its name from the fact that YIVO was not only engaged in the promotion of Yiddish but also associated with controversial spelling, pronunciation, and lexical norms that were rejected by many native speakers but embraced in the classroom. The chapter focuses on YIVO's projects to record dialects and standardize the language in the 1950s and '60s before the final generation of eastern European Yiddish speakers had disappeared as well as its work to introduce the language into universities.

The book's fifth chapter, "A Generation Goes, a Generation Comes," looks at the close of the immigrant period in YIVO's history and at the emergence of a new one in which individuals who came to maturity after World War II became prominent in the staffing and administration of the institute. This new period—which symbolically begins following the deaths in the late 1960s of both Max and his son Uriel Weinreich, an important scholar and YIVO associate in his own right—saw simultaneously a crisis in leadership and the fruition of a long-standing ambition within YIVO to cultivate a modest regrowth of scholarly and culturally creative forces. It is reflected above all in the creation of an academically innovative graduate center and a pioneering immersive Yiddish-language and culture summer program that mark the start of a process of change and revitalization in the institute. They were followed by several other innovative projects in the 1970s that brought YIVO into increasing contact with American-born generations eager to "reclaim" their eastern European cultural heritage on their own terms. In retrospect, these years appear as a golden era for YIVO as an American Jewish institute despite its financial instability and a perceived crisis in leadership and direction. The chapter ends by briefly surveying major developments into the 1990s that paradoxically both increased YIVO's stature as an American institution and undermined its utility as a training center for future generations of scholars in Yiddish culture and eastern European Jewish studies.

The book's conclusion begins with the revelation in 1989 of the survival of additional YIVO materials in Vilnius and the twenty-first-century digitalization of surviving collections, a remarkable achievement that both revived unresolved questions and serves in some ways as a metaphor for the larger history of the institute since 1940. This final chapter evaluates the period in YIVO's history bookmarked by the arrival and death of Max Weinreich in New York in order to appreciate not only the institute's achievements—both successes and failures—since its transplantation to "new soil" but also the extent to which it has remained loyal to Yiddishism and the mission first articulated and pursued in Vilna as well as transformed and transcended them.

The only secular Jewish institution to survive transition from eastern Europe to America, YIVO—and the history contained in its collections, educational programs, exhibitions, and cultural programming—has become in many ways emblematic of the experience of the largest part of American Jewry, which traces its origins to the massive waves of migration that brought Yiddish-speaking Jews from that region to North America. The institute's longevity and the transmission of knowledge about Yiddish and eastern European Jewry are owed largely to the good fortune of a small number of refugee scholars who transformed YIVO's American division into not merely the institute's world center but an American institution aspiring to a global reach.

A Note About Spelling and Usage

For the sake of consistency, I have generally spelled personal names in the text and notes as they appear in *The YIVO Encyclopedia of Jews in Eastern Europe*. When there seems to be no convention for the spelling of an eastern European Jewish name that appears only in Hebrew-letter sources, I have romanized that name according to YIVO rules found in Uriel Weinreich's *Modern English-Yiddish Yiddish-English Dictionary*.[58] I have followed the same system to romanize names within the titles of Yiddish- and Hebrew-language sources. Hence "Max Weinreich" appears in the body of the text and as an author's name, but "Maks vaynraykh" appears in the title of a Yiddish article about Max Weinreich. For North American–born YIVO associates, I use the name under which they published in English in the body of the text even if they were widely known by their Yiddish names in YIVO circles. Hence "Beatrice" instead of "Bina" Weinreich and "Joshua" instead of "Shikl" Fishman. Eleanor Mlotek is the exception, as she widely published as "Chana" in both Yiddish and English.

In the case of toponyms, I have tried to employ those widely known to English speakers. Hence, for example, I use "Warsaw" and not "Warszawa." I do, however, distinguish between Vilna and Vilnius, using the former to refer to the city in pre–World War II Poland and when referring to Jewish life and death during the war years (e.g., the Vilna Ghetto; Vilna—or more precisely, Vilne—is the Yiddish name for the city). In contrast, I refer to the capital of independent and Soviet Lithuania as Vilnius. Similarly, following contemporary scholarly convention in the writing of Polish Jewish history, I use Łódź to indicate the city in Poland but refer to the Lodz Ghetto, since most Jews imprisoned in that ghetto knew the city by its Yiddish name (Lodzh, usually rendered Lodz in English) rather than its Polish one. These distinctions may seem arbitrary but are meant to convey meaningful political and cultural distinctions, including the Jewish dimension of the history of these cities, without making them overly foreign to the reader.

1
COMING TO AMERICA?

In early October 1939, YIVO's Amopteyl in New York City released a pressing announcement in the *Forverts* regarding the institute's future as a world organization. A month earlier, Nazi Germany and the Soviet Union had divided Poland between them in accordance with a secret protocol of the now-infamous Molotov-Ribbentrop Pact. The historically contested, multiethnic city of Vilna, which had belonged to Poland for most of the interwar period, was now under Soviet authority. The scant information then available to the Amopteyl revealed that YIVO and its collections in Vilna remained intact despite the presence of the Red Army. But with the city's future uncertain, the Amopteyl announced that Vilna could not continue to serve, at least for the duration of the war, as YIVO's world center. Rather, the Amopteyl, YIVO's "main backbone and chief support," would temporarily assume the institute's primary functions, including publications and acquisitions. Jews everywhere were urged to send materials intended for YIVO scholars and archives in Vilna, including letters and other items related to the current war, instead to the Amopteyl's offices in Lower Manhattan.[1]

Soon after this announcement appeared in the American Yiddish press, the Red Army's forty-day occupation of Vilna came to an unanticipated end. The Soviets transferred the city into Lithuanian hands in mid-October as part of an agreement ensuring Lithuanian independence in return for Soviet use of military bases—a deal tiny Lithuania could hardly reject. Vilnius, as Lithuanians call the city they knew as their historic capital, was made the capital of the independent Lithuanian Republic in mid-October 1939.[2] Fears of the Sovietization of the institute and the complete severing of Lithuanian Jewry from the West were allayed, at least for the time being. But the future of YIVO in Vilna, like the fate of eastern European Jewry as a whole, remained a matter of profound anxiety. After having weathered the increasingly antisemitic climate of Poland in the late 1930s and survived a Soviet takeover without damage to its building or collections,[3] YIVO found itself under a new regime whose attitude toward it could not be predicted. Further, the war cut the institute off from its material and cultural base, the more-than-three-million-strong Jewish community of Poland. Meanwhile, much of YIVO's academic and administrative leadership was to be found abroad.

Despite the murkiness of the emerging picture, YIVO's staff on both sides of the Atlantic sensed that a new era in Jewish history was dawning. Since the Nazi and Soviet invasions of Poland in September 1939, they acknowledged, Polish Jewry had experienced a veritable *khurbn*, a destruction of historic, if yet unknown, proportions.[4] The temporary administration of YIVO in Vilna, a mixture of old and newly co-opted members, found itself confronted with an existential dilemma. Should it continue and perhaps even expand its activities despite a paucity of material resources to meet the needs of the influx of Jewish refugees from occupied Poland to Vilna along with those of the native Lithuanian Jewish population? Or should it suspend and perhaps even transfer its operations, collections, and select personnel, as the Amopteyl urged, to the distant safety of New York City? Meanwhile, members of the Amopteyl questioned their own readiness to assume the mantle of YIVO's world leadership, whether temporarily or for the indefinite future.

Symbolically, the public announcement to recognize the Amopteyl as YIVO's world center in October 1940—a full year after YIVO leaders began to debate the best location for the organization's home—marks the end of the "Vilna period" in the institute's history even if YIVO staff in Vilna continued to function in some capacity until the following summer. Practically speaking, however, YIVO's still-unfolding "American period" begins with the arrival of Yiddish scholar Max Weinreich, secretary of its Philological Section, in New York in the spring of 1940. Weinreich's flight from Hitler's Europe not only helped ensure maximum continuity between Vilna and New York and the survival of YIVO as an institution. His program to transform the Amopteyl from the American subsidiary of an eastern European institution into the center of an American and world Jewish organization focused on meeting what he perceived as the needs of the postwar Jewish world shaped YIVO's course for decades to come.

Weinreich's Dilemma

Max Weinreich found himself in Copenhagen in August 1939, enjoying a visit to the city and his colleagues there while on his way to represent YIVO at an international linguistics conference in Brussels scheduled for the following month. He was accompanied on this trip to western Europe by his wife, Regina, a teacher in Vilna's Yiddish school system, and his thirteen-year-old son, Uriel. Their younger son, Gabriel, then eleven years old, was left in the care of Regina's mother, the Vilna notable Stefania Szabad.[5]

Soon after the signing of the Soviet-German nonaggression pact, Regina returned to Vilna at the behest of her mother. Convinced that Germany would now invade Poland with impunity, Stefania Szabad urged her daughter to return home before it was too late. Despite the ferocity of Nazi antisemitic pronouncements and the cruelty of German conduct thus far, it was expected that the German army would not deliberately harm women and children.[6] A more optimistic Max chose to remain, hoping to enjoy the sights of Copenhagen a bit longer before continuing on to the conference, which was postponed and ultimately canceled.[7] Consequently, Max and Uriel found themselves separated from their family when war erupted on 1 September 1939, desperate to return home to Vilna. But with their Polish passports effectively worthless and any travel across Europe difficult and fraught with danger, they had no choice but to wait. Nonetheless, Weinreich struggled with the dilemma of risking life and limb to return home to his family and an uncertain future in Vilna or accepting assistance from YIVO's American division to travel to safety in New York.

Their personal funds severely limited, Weinreich and his son relied largely on support provided by the Amopteyl and the generosity of the local community of eastern European Jews in Copenhagen during a near-six-month, anxiety-ridden stay there. A visit from Lucy (Libe) Shildkret (the future historian Lucy Dawidowicz) provided a few days of diversion and cemented a sense of solidarity. A graduate of New York's Yiddish secular schools, Shildkret had traveled to Vilna with the encouragement of her teacher Jacob Shatzky to spend the academic year 1938–39 studying with Weinreich and other YIVO scholars in the *aspirantur*, the institute's postgraduate training program. With war imminent, she hurried back to New York at the urging of the American embassy and her friends in Vilna YIVO circles.[8]

Above all at this time, Weinreich feared that the Red Army would remain in Vilna. While his political activism on behalf of the socialist Bund had waned by the late 1920s—especially because he wished to keep YIVO above partisan politics beyond a general commitment to Yiddishism—he retained its fervently anti-Bolshevik stance. He understood well that Soviet policy had led to the arrests of Yiddish cultural figures and the closure of most Yiddish schools and cultural institutions by the late 1930s. More recently, the Soviets had arrested one of YIVO's main figures, the philologist and newspaper editor Zalmen Reyzen, along with other important Jewish political and cultural figures, when they occupied Vilna.[9]

Philologist Zelig Kalmanovitch, who was away when the Soviets took hold of the city, shared Weinreich's despair at the possibility of a Soviet Vilna. Writing from Ponevezh (Panevėžys) in Lithuania to Jacob Shatzky in New York in September 1939, Kalmanovitch urged the Amopteyl to take the reins:

> I do not have to search for a proof that now, when the collapse of Polish Jewry is a fact, there remains but one hope for a "Jewish people with secular culture," that is, American Jewry . . . Is it at all possible? I have a dream that all this time, when building a Jewish community in Eastern Europe is out of the question, a spirit of defiance will overtake the American Jews. They cannot expect anymore the word to come out [of] Vilna. They, and they alone, must create the new *yidishkeit.* If they don't, no one else will. So, now, this is the question: are there any such young people amongst you who will have the strength to awake[n] the American Jews to a "Jewish" life?[10]

Once the Soviets had departed from the city in October, however, he dutifully returned to Vilna. As the only member of the prewar executive bureau possessing Lithuanian citizenship, Kalmanovitch begrudgingly accepted approval as the institute's curator by the new Lithuanian regime.

Writing to the Amopteyl after the transfer of Vilna into Lithuanian hands in October 1939, Weinreich in Copenhagen expressed hope that YIVO would survive and even flourish under a regime more favorably inclined to Jewish culture than Poland's. Conditions under independent Lithuanian rule could be far better for YIVO and Yiddish culture than in Poland, since in his words, in Lithuania, "there is no assimilation."[11] There, in contrast with Poland, where most Jewish children had attended tuition-free Polish-language public schools and were increasingly adopting Polish as their preferred language, generous state support for schools in Jewish languages existed throughout the interwar period, even after official support for Jewish cultural autonomy was otherwise rescinded. While an education in Hebrew or a combination of Hebrew and Yiddish was a more popular option for Jewish children than exclusively Yiddish schools in interwar Lithuania, Jews remained overwhelmingly Yiddish speaking.[12] Consequently, Weinreich argued, Yiddish schools would continue to grow there and necessarily turn to YIVO for guidance in questions of language and pedagogy. This would justify the need for the *aspirantur* and *proaspirantur* that prepared researchers, teachers, and social workers.

In independent Lithuania, the dream of a self-sustaining, multigenerational intellectual and academic culture in Yiddish seemed possible. "If Vilna does not become a backroom of Russia, it can again become a major Jewish city—not only for Lithuanian Jews" but for Jews arriving from elsewhere too, wrote Weinreich to Nathan (Naftole) Feinerman, who headed the Amopteyl in New York. As long as there would be no Soviet intervention in Lithuania's domestic affairs, he maintained, "YIVO is saved, then my place is in Vilna." If not, he wrote, "We must think about saving the collections and people by transporting them to America and ending the European period of YIVO's history."[13]

Feinerman was less sanguine about the future of YIVO's Vilna center. He confided in a letter to Elias Tcherikower in Paris, a YIVO cofounder and head of its Historical Section, that he feared that Weinreich and Kalmanovitch would be lured by the siren song of Lithuanian control to return to the city. It would only be a matter of time, Feinerman predicted, before Stalin returned and Sovietized Lithuania, endangering the independent operation and holdings of the institute.[14]

Seeking to take maximum precautions, the Amopteyl endeavored to bring as many YIVO scholars working in neutral lands to the United States as possible. Meetings of the Amopteyl leadership explored the possibility of sending a delegate to help transport archival materials and rare items from Vilna to New York. The Amopteyl also considered obtaining a microfilm machine from the philanthropic Rockefeller Foundation to photograph documents.[15] Tcherikower shared Feinerman's pessimistic evaluation of Vilna's future, and he hoped to make YIVO's branch in Paris, to which he had fled from Berlin in 1933, its European center. He cautioned Feinerman, however, not to underestimate the profound psychological impact that the transfer of materials and key people across the ocean would have on those who had no choice but to remain.[16]

The Amopteyl implored Max Weinreich to come with his wife and sons to stay in America, at least until after the summer of 1940. It promised to take care of his travel expenses and support him in New York City. If he did not intend to head first to Vilna to take stock of the situation and settle matters there, Feinerman urged, Weinreich should come directly to America with Uriel. Tirelessly appealing for aid from American consular authorities and academics, the Amopteyl would arrange for the necessary visas.[17] Still in Vilna, Regina and Gabriel Weinreich would have to travel independently to join them in America.

America was not terra incognita for Weinreich. In 1929 he made a tour of its major Jewish centers, delivering lectures and raising substantial sums for YIVO on the eve of the Depression.[18] During this visit, he made connections with several prominent intellectuals, not the least of whom was Edward Sapir. A pioneer in the field of linguistic anthropology, best known today for his scholarship about Indigenous North American languages, Sapir also published in English about his native Yiddish at a time when American scholars seldom paid it serious attention.[19] Encouraged by Sapir, Weinreich returned in 1932 to spend an academic year as a research fellow at Yale University's Institute of Human Relations with the support of the Rockefeller Foundation in New York. In New Haven, he represented Yiddish-speaking Jewry, a "nationality" lacking its own state, among scholars representing various countries in a Seminar on the Impact of Culture on Personality led by Sapir and the sociologist John Dollard. There Weinreich immersed himself in the literature of the American social sciences with a focus on the experiences of Native Americans, Black Americans, and immigrants.[20]

Weinreich admired American academia for its rigor and intellectual innovation and had formed positive relationships with American colleagues, whose respect he enjoyed. He also knew that he would be received with open arms in New York City, home to several YIVO colleagues and a vibrant Yiddish literary and cultural scene. Still, the thought of leaving behind his friends and colleagues as well as Vilna and, above all, the institute that meant so much to him—even if only temporarily—proved agonizing for Weinreich. He wrote to his YIVO colleague Leibush Lehrer in New York that neither he nor his wife, Regina, could contemplate leaving Vilna behind; nor could he conceive of "starting over" at his advanced age—forty-six.[21]

Riddled with anxiety about the fate of his own family in Vilna as well as the future of the institute, Weinreich attempted from Copenhagen to coordinate YIVO's activities between New York and Vilna, cities between which communication had become unreliable. Privately, he expressed doubts about the continued viability of Vilna as YIVO's center and mulled over coming to America. But he asked that Feinerman keep this possibility a secret.[22] Publicly, in contrast, both he and Kalmanovitch, who shared his doubts, projected confidence in the institute's continued functioning in Vilna.

While Weinreich worried about the sense of abandonment that the transfer of YIVO's center to New York would evoke in Vilna, he was also critical of colleagues in that city. Almost two weeks later, he wrote in January 1940 to remind them that the institute was a global organization belonging to all Jews, not only those in Lithuania or only those in America. From its inception, YIVO associates had contributed from around the world. It was an error for the center in Vilna to treat the Amopteyl as a subordinate body that existed for fundraising purposes rather than as an integral part of the organization. Apart from stressing the need for YIVO's constituent parts to cooperate as much as possible in these difficult circumstances, Weinreich stressed that YIVO must retain its focus on research and training students as part of its core commitment to scholarship—as represented by the two letter *vovs* that made the "v" in YIVO's Yiddish name, standing for *visnshaft* (scholarship). Scholarship is what, he maintained, distinguished YIVO from other Jewish organizations that also possessed collections, some more impressive than its own.[23]

An American Center?

Meanwhile, the Amopteyl in New York continued to make preparations to assume Vilna's responsibilities. Writing to colleagues in Vilna in early

January 1940, Feinerman urged YIVO to keep its activities there to a necessary minimum, to finish only those projects it had undertaken before the war, and to catalog its holdings. Encouraged by Weinreich, Feinerman announced to Vilna colleagues that publication of *Yivo bleter* would continue in New York City until further notice because "the Jewish community in Poland is now destroyed; it is technically impossible to deliver *Yivo bleter* to America. So, for whom will Vilna print them?"[24] Prior to the war, America was the single largest destination for issues of the journal, accounting for as much as 65 percent of its copies in 1934.[25] In the evaluation of Yiddish author Joseph Opatoshu, who was active in the Amopteyl, recent events definitively spelled the end of the Vilna period in YIVO's history and the beginning of a new, American era: "In Jewish history, such cases are already known when one center is destroyed and another arises in a different land."[26]

Not all in America shared Opatoshu's fatalistic conclusion or possessed optimism about the cultural potential resident in American Jewry. Despite making rational arguments for concentrating Vilna's operations in America, Feinerman harbored doubts about the degree of enthusiasm with which American Jews would support YIVO's academic mission, especially in wartime, if it were located outside eastern Europe. Writing to Tcherikower in Paris, Feinerman worried, "The wide public is taken with the justified feeling of sympathy and will certainly give for shrouds for the dead and bread for the living. Will it also want to give for cultural matters, especially for Jewish cultural institutions in America—God knows?"[27]

Expanding the Amopteyl's activity, in addition to providing support to Vilna and YIVO colleagues elsewhere, also meant rising costs. YIVO colleagues in London, Paris, and Buenos Aires, Feinerman explained to Weinreich, all suggested that YIVO's center shift to America given the circumstances in Europe. But whereas they had all previously sent money to support the Vilna center, they now asked instead for America to send them money in light of their own financial straits. Meanwhile, the Amopteyl understood that the task of raising money was rendered all the more difficult by the urgent need to aid Jews in immediate danger: "Our position is extremely difficult. Fund raising is monopolized in the USA by the Joint, the Zionist Organization, and the Jewish Labor Committee."[28] The Joint Distribution Committee (Joint or JDC) was founded during World War I by American Jewish notables to centralize allocations of aid to Jewish war sufferers but had grown to provide a variety of services—medical, sanitary, rehabilitation, educational, and more—or funding for them to stricken and impoverished Jews, particularly in eastern Europe. Prior to the outbreak of World War II, it had been one of the major contributors to YIVO in Vilna. But since the war's outbreak, it was mainly concerned with facilitating emigration from Europe and providing assistance to Jews in German-controlled territories. Similarly, Zionists were also engaged in efforts to help Jews escape imminent danger, especially to bring them to Palestine despite stringent British quotas on Jewish immigration. The youngest of these organizations, the Jewish Labor Committee, was founded in 1934 by Yiddish-speaking labor activists to unite noncommunist Jewish groupings in opposition to Nazism. It worked to rescue Jewish political and cultural figures, as well as both Jewish and Gentile socialists and labor leaders, from capture by the Germans and to transport them to safety.[29]

Beyond concerns about fundraising in such desperate times, however, the question loomed in American YIVO circles: Would broad sections of American Jewry embrace YIVO's academic mission? Even before the war, as Cecile Kuznitz observes, YIVO's founders "complained of the 'inertia' of 'farbiznevet [commercialized]' New York that 'poisoned' the atmosphere for cultural work."[30] "The problem with our America," wrote the *Forverts* in New York in March 1940, was not a lack of Judaica scholars but "what is called here making 'a living,' and in the present time it diverts much time and causes much concern. It is, however, different in Vilna. There, they don't make a living. The means don't exist. . . . Therefore, they have more time and more patience for scholarly work. Our Americans can help them very much now with the work but it won't do for our Americans to try to become the heirs of Vilna."[31] Members of the Amopteyl's Executive Board voiced similar concerns about American Jewry, prompting historian Jacob Shatzky to emphasize the need for the Yiddish press to prepare American Jews psychologically to give money to YIVO not because it represented Vilna—that is, a metonym for the entire population of Jewish eastern Europe and its traditions—but because it represented modern Jewish scholarship no matter where YIVO's center lay.[32]

Yiddish writer H. Leivick adamantly argued for the Amopteyl to expand its functions in the case that Vilna disappeared. Its members, he wrote, must cease seeing themselves "only as helpers in America and not as independent builders." The need for the Amopteyl to rise to the occasion and act independently was hammered home by philologist Judah A. Joffe. He opined, "The same people who complained yesterday of Vilna's hegemony now complain that we can do nothing without it."[33] From Europe, Max Weinreich enjoined the Amopteyl to broaden its activities while seeking to gird its members psychologically for what lay in store: "Now we must at least reckon with the possibility that for years to come, the few dozen of our own people must stand at the fore posts. American Jews are not yet ready. We know that. But you, our people, must be ready to take over the [YIVO] mission."[34]

By bringing key personnel to the United States—including himself from Copenhagen, Zelig Kalmanovitch from Vilna, and the young linguistics *aspirant* Chaim Gininger from Czernowitz (then, Cernăuti, Romania)—Weinreich reckoned that a "jewel of an institute" could be built with ten select people joining forces with the researchers already present in America.[35] As a show of his recognition of the importance of America as a Jewish center, Weinreich supported the publication, in coordination with Vilna, of an American edition of *Yivo bleter* under a name that would indicate the journal's new, hopefully temporary, provenance. He also explained to Feinerman that he was in the midst of preparing a dictionary of literary Yiddish for use by those with competence in English as a second language (users would consult a word known to them in English in order to find its Yiddish equivalent). The choice of English rather than another language, such as Polish or Russian, as the auxiliary language emphasized that "the center of gravity (let us not decree for how long) has moved to you."[36] These publications would thus simultaneously point to the Amopteyl's continuity with the Vilna YIVO while emphasizing its independent identity and asserting its relevance.

Undeterred by the war, from 6 to 8 January 1940, the Amopteyl held its annual conference. It offered the usual opening addresses and academic lectures in addition to expressions of sympathy and solidarity with the suffering Jews of eastern Europe in general and YIVO colleagues in Vilna in particular. It announced that *Yidn in poyln* (Jews in Poland), an anthology of articles by YIVO scholars originally intended to be edited and published in Vilna, was in preparation and was expected to generate wide interest given the circumstances of the day. Beyond this, the conference affirmed the Amopteyl's commitment to execute all duties that could not be performed by the center in Vilna, among them the coordination of activities with YIVO divisions throughout the world.

The Amopteyl also embarked on a program of expansion, including a research agenda that placed a new emphasis on the unique history and culture of American Jewry. This was above all reflected in a plan to found a special commission for trade unions to collect materials and the necessary funds to publish a volume on the history of the Jewish workers' movement in the United States—a subject neglected by scholars of American Jewish history but that had a special resonance for YIVO given its support among labor organizations and the important role Yiddish-speaking Jews had played in them. It also announced having collected $3,000 in contributions from private individuals and organizations for activities in America.[37] Following the conference, the Amopteyl announced, "It is possibly of the greatest importance to emphasize that the time has come for America, which has the largest and most secure Jewish community in the world, also to become the greatest Jewish cultural and academic center in the world."[38]

At the same time, the Amopteyl absorbed the Central Jewish Library and Press Archives, an organization founded by committed Yiddishist intellectuals in 1935 to collect Jewish, particularly Yiddish, books and periodicals in America. While officially independent of the Amopteyl, the relationship was extremely close, as reflected by the presence of several Amopteyl members—among them, Y. L. Cahan, Feinerman, Shatzky, Charney, Joffe, Leibush Lehrer's brother Lipe, and Mordecai Kosover—on the Central Library's administrative board. Indeed, the Central Library saw itself from its inception as fulfilling a function parallel to the YIVO library in Vilna but with a focus on serving the growing intellectual needs of American Jewry. This included not only collecting publications but hosting lectures by Yiddish-speaking intellectuals.

Due to its very limited means, the Central Library relied on donations for its holdings. These included not only contributions from the private collections of writers and intellectuals close to the Amopteyl—such as Cahan, Shatzky, Joffe, and the philosopher and Yiddishist theoretician Dr. Khayim Zhitlovski—but also the library of leading socialist thinker Morris Winchevsky and the papers of prominent

Sign advertising the entrance to YIVO's American Division and the Central Jewish Library and Archives. Credit: YIVO Institute for Jewish Research

Yiddish playwright Jacob Gordon, to name but two examples. School organizations provided copies of educational materials, and commercial publishing houses specializing in Yiddish also made contributions, as did the three major Yiddish dailies—*Der tog* (*The Day*), *Forverts*, and *Morgn-zhurnal* (*Morning Journal*), which provided full volumes and sent daily issues. Organizations across the cultural-political spectrum similarly shared their newspapers and publications, making for an impressive collection of the American Yiddish press all in all. The Central Jewish Library managed to amass some fifteen thousand volumes by 1939, making the five-thousand-square-foot office that it had rented since 1938 in shared premises with the Amopteyl inadequate for its growing collection.[39] The amalgamation not only increased the Amopteyl's holdings. It also expanded its staff to include the Central Jewish Library and Press Archives' librarian and cofounder Mendel Elkin, who assumed the function of the Amopteyl's librarian.

Reflecting the Amopteyl's new importance, volume 15 (January–February 1940) of *Yivo bleter*, a double issue edited by the executive committee of the Amopteyl, appeared in New York City. The journal's name and design remained unchanged to ensure maximum continuity with preceding issues, but its cover announced under the title that the Amopteyl published it. The editors' preface explained that additional issues devoting significant attention to American themes (volume 15 contained only two articles about America) were to follow. Seeking to minimize alarm, however, the journal assured readers that the decision to publish in New York had arisen as a response to the "temporary weakening of publication activity in the Yiddish Scientific Institute" in Vilna. It informed them that this decision had been made "with the agreement of the Vilna leadership."[40] Indeed, Weinreich himself had encouraged the decision.

News of the publication was received, however, with great alarm, dismay, and indignation within YIVO's temporary administration in Vilna. It viewed the publication as an act of usurpation, if not premature burial: "We have heard that a new issue of *Yivo bleter* has appeared in America," Bundist educator Gershon Pludermakher lamented. "This is symptomatic—they probably think that the Vilna YIVO has gone under. The true milieu around the YIVO is in Vilna. The Yiddish movement is not faring well in America."[41] From the perspective of most YIVO members in Vilna, not only was it unthinkable to declare New York YIVO's center, an act that effectively announced an end to the cultural and intellectual preeminence of eastern Europe in the Jewish world; doing so was also wholly unjustified, as Vilna's importance as the symbolic capital of Yiddish-speaking Jewry had only increased with the absorption of a large number of refugees and activists from Poland.

YIVO Under Lithuanian Rule

With Vilna virtually the only escape route from Poland to the free world by late 1939, more than fourteen thousand Polish Jews, including members of political, cultural, and religious elites, gathered there between the outbreak of war and June 1940. The presence of so many refugees coupled with the absorption by Lithuania of some eighty thousand Jews from Vilna province, most of them Yiddish speakers, made Jews now as much as 10 percent of the population of independent Lithuania and contributed to a Jewish cultural efflorescence in Vilna.[42] Lithuanian Jewry had been isolated from its Polish brethren throughout most of the interwar period due to the absence of diplomatic relations between the two countries. Now it received these refugees generously and was eager to benefit from their creative and organizational talents.[43] Preferring that Jews make use of a Jewish language rather than Polish or Russian, the Lithuanian state offered support to schools in Hebrew and Yiddish. Liberal Lithuanian academic circles even evinced enthusiasm for Yiddish culture and YIVO.[44]

During their occupation of Vilna, the Soviets had banned the Hebrew and Yiddish presses apart from a couple of procommunist Yiddish publications and pursued individuals and organizations deemed dangerous to their interests.[45] In contrast, new vistas opened for Jewish culture—as Max Weinreich had hoped—in a more tolerant Lithuania that posed no real impediments to YIVO's activities once the authorities legalized the institute.

Within the temporary administration in Vilna, only Zelig Kalmanovitch openly rejected optimism for the future of the institute in Europe. Since his very return to Vilna, Kalmanovitch expressed grave doubts due to a lack of money and a loss of key personnel. He also had dwindling confidence in Yiddishism, a form of language-based nationalism, as an ideology capable of sustaining Jewish identity in the long run in an age of assimilation.[46] Nonetheless, he was willing to work on YIVO's behalf. His colleagues respected his commitment despite condemning what they saw as his demoralizing negativity.[47] Without granting his accord to its content, Kalmanovitch sent a telegram on behalf of the executive bureau to the Amopteyl to halt the publication of *Yivo bleter* there. In it, he denounced the possibility of dual sites of publication as a sign of disorganization. Personally, however, he argued before his Vilna colleagues that there existed no reason *not* to publish in New York: Two of the journal's editors, Leibush Lehrer (secretary of YIVO's Psychological-Pedagogical Section) and Jacob Lestschinsky (secretary of its Economic-Statistical Section), already lived there, and two others, Weinreich (secretary of the Philological Section) and Tcherikower (secretary of the Historical Section), were also absent from Vilna. New York could also more easily communicate with the rest of the world. Further, Vilna lacked sufficient money to publish.[48]

In response, Feinerman and Charney in New York City wrote to Vilna in February 1940 asking that it not launch any new publications and yield in the matter of *Yivo bleter*. The journal's appearance in New York, they claimed, had deeply impressed the American public and demonstrated that the Amopteyl was not subordinate to the YIVO center in Vilna. Without the publication, a physical symbol of the vitality of the institute, it would be difficult to raise money among Americans.[49] A letter sent the following month to Vilna reiterated these objections concerning *Yivo bleter*. By this time, however, the Amopteyl questioned whether Vilna was even receiving its letters. (Indeed, as reflected by the Vilna YIVO's internal date stamp, the letter, unbeknownst to the Amopteyl, was actually received only in mid-May—some two months after its sending.) YIVO staff in New York consequently concluded that they had better assessed the situation than their overly optimistic colleagues in Vilna and expressed their intention to publish a second double issue of *Yivo bleter*.[50]

At almost exactly the same time, in mid-March 1940, Max Weinreich arrived with his son Uriel aboard a Swedish ship in New York Harbor after a twelve-day voyage from Copenhagen. Only a few weeks later, on 9 April, the German army occupied Denmark. Officially, Weinreich's purpose lay then in launching a fundraising and publicity campaign for

YIVO while visiting America. He intended to return to Vilna after the summer. His presence would also help elucidate the situation in Vilna for the Amopteyl, on whose irregular remissions Vilna depended for survival. YIVO in Vilna would meanwhile take the necessary steps to procure Lithuanian citizenship for him.[51]

Uncharacteristically enthusiastic reports from Kalmanovitch increased the incentive for Weinreich's return. In a departure from his customary pessimism, Kalmanovitch indicated with satisfaction that the situation in Vilna had largely stabilized thanks to the support of the Joint Distribution Committee, YIVO's Argentinian Section (its next largest branch after the Amopteyl), and fundraising and book sales in Lithuania. In his newest evaluation, YIVO there served as an intellectual and cultural center more than ever, despite an alarming desperation for funds. The reading room and exhibitions were drawing record numbers of visitors from the local population, among them representatives of Lithuanian academia. Refugee scholars previously uninvolved in Jewish research now conducted research in their areas of specialization with Jewry as their subject of study. In some cases, they even demonstrated an eagerness to learn Yiddish and Hebrew. A plan was made, although ultimately never realized, for volume 16 of *Yivo bleter* to appear after the summer in Vilna.

Indeed, YIVO in Vilna seemed to have entered a phase of almost unprecedented productivity. At a press conference in June 1940, Kalmanovitch offered an overview of YIVO's impressive activity of the past several months. This included the acquisition of folklore materials from Lithuania, Romania, Palestine, America, England, and elsewhere; the activity of sixty researchers, among them tens of refugees and eleven *aspirantn*; the training of *proaspirantn*; the publication of the sixth volume of a Yiddish translation of Simon Dubnow's *World History of the Jewish People* and the first volume of YIVO folklorist Y. L. Cahan's collected folklore writings; and the preparation of additional publications, including a volume of *Psikhologish-pedagogishe shriftn* (Psychological-Pedagogical Writings) and a monograph about the history of Hasidism. In the preceding four months, YIVO editions had been sold for Lt10,000 (about $1,000). Drawing on the expertise of its enlarged staff, YIVO also organized popular academic lectures about Yiddish grammar, Jewish history, Lithuanian Jewish history, and Jewish literature, folklore, and demography—each lecture

YIVO's building in Vilna, 1933. Credit: YIVO Institute for Jewish Research

drawing an average of eighty listeners. The twenty-fifth anniversary of the death of esteemed writer Y. L. Peretz was marked with ceremonies such as a radio program featuring seminal historian Simon Dubnow, father of Jewish Diaspora Nationalism and a YIVO supporter, and the University of Vilnius's rector, Professor Mykolas Biržiška. An exhibit dedicated to Peretz drew more than five thousand visitors.[52]

All these efforts were crowned by the anticipated opening of a chair for Yiddish language and literature in the humanities faculty of the University of Vilnius in the spring after lengthy negotiations between YIVO representatives and officers of the university. Such a position, even though the local Jewish community rather than the university was expected to raise funds for it, was hardly conceivable when the same institution was still the Stefan Batory University, a Polish state university, less than a year earlier.[53] There Jewish students had been subjected to violent harassment by right-wing Polish nationalist students seeking to confine them to so-called ghetto benches, parts of the classroom ignominiously reserved exclusively for Jewish students. Weinreich had in fact protested the abuse of Jewish students more than once, resulting in his arrest on one occasion and the near complete loss of vision in his right eye on another, when a stone hurled by hooligans shattered his eyeglasses in 1932.[54]

The creation of the position was all the more remarkable not only because of the prestigious place occupied by Vilna in Yiddish culture but because European and world academia had thus far given Yiddish so little serious attention. Orthodox scholar Solomon Birnbaum, who introduced Yiddish courses to the modern European university, taught Yiddish language, linguistics, and literature as a lector at the University of Hamburg until Hitler's ascent to power in 1933 and subsequently at the University of London.[55] But apart from his modest positions, Yiddish scholarship was not to be found in any European institute of higher learning outside of YIVO and Soviet institutions for Jewish culture. The latter were, in any case, headed toward disappearance by the late 1930s as the Bolshevik regime closed many of the academic and cultural institutions it had previously fostered on behalf of minority peoples as expressions of unacceptable "nationalism."

A referendum conducted by telegram among the geographically dispersed members of YIVO's Philological Section nominated Weinreich for the position at the University of Vilnius in expectation of his return by the fall of 1940. The chair, long a dream of the Yiddishist movement, was a fitting honor for a man deemed not only one of Jewish Vilna's leading personalities and a foremost Yiddish expert but also a champion of its Jewish university students.

Parallel to this celebration of the Vilna YIVO's collective accomplishments, literary critic Samuel Charney reflected in New York on what he depicted as a veritable revolution in Jewish scholarship in America since the emergence of YIVO's American center. He argued that Jewish scholarship in America, as exemplified by the American Jewish Historical Society founded in 1892, focused on the "Judaism" of German and Sephardic Jewries that had established themselves prior to the 1880s. Privileging Judaism as a religious system rather than as a civilization with its own unique cultural forms in all aspects of life, it paid little attention to eastern European Jews and *Yidishkeyt*—that is, Judaism as an all-encompassing cultural system shaping all aspects of life. While the Amopteyl deviated from this approach, it had conducted no systematic work on American Jewry and sent materials about it to Vilna. The recent world war had, in Charney's appraisal, brought the "emancipation" of American

Jewish scholarship. The Amopteyl was now forced "to stand on its own feet and to cease being merely an auxiliary agency for YIVO in Vilna."[56] Meanwhile, Elias Tcherikower, secretary of YIVO's Historical Section, managed to make his way to New York in the summer of 1940, adding yet another YIVO founder to the staff of the Amopteyl. Tcherikower also transported with him from Paris a part of the section's library and archives, further expanding the Amopteyl's holdings.[57]

YIVO Under Soviet Rule

For a brief period—from October 1939 until the summer of 1940—YIVO effectively possessed two world centers, each exceptionally productive and convinced of its preeminence (if only for the time being). High hopes for a rejuvenated Vilna YIVO and autonomous Jewish cultural life there came to an end with the return of the Red Army to the city in mid-June 1940 and the annexation of Lithuania as the sixteenth Soviet Socialist Republic in August. Even before changes were made in YIVO, a despondent Kalmanovitch foresaw the worst: "the destruction of not just YIVO but of scholarship, civilization, autonomy." Accordingly, he urged Weinreich to develop the center in New York. Expecting the rapid Sovietization of the institute and its decimation, he was pleasantly surprised that he was able to continue his function there and to communicate with colleagues in New York for weeks to come. Nonetheless, his optimism was very much guarded: "This is a good-bye letter," he wrote Weinreich, "if we cannot continue to correspond."[58] He vowed to Weinreich that he would continue working in Vilna to protect YIVO as long as possible.[59] But by July 1940, Kalmanovitch was ready to leave. The Amopteyl obtained the necessary visa and offered him employment as a "lecturer in linguistics, esp. Arabic and Syriac, for $1,800 per year."[60] But Kalmanovitch, who had a son in Palestine he wished to join, never made the trip to the United States.

In contrast with territories long under Soviet rule, the imposition of Soviet nationalities policy did not spell an immediate end to Jewish culture in Lithuania. On the contrary, it meant that all Jewish schools in Lithuania—including religious and secular Hebrew and Yiddish ones—would now become Soviet Yiddish schools virtually overnight as a means to impart Bolshevik ideology. Further, the plan for a Yiddish chair at the University of Vilnius was to be implemented with full state funding—the fulfillment of Yiddishist dreams impossible elsewhere. It also spelled the eventual purging of YIVO of ideologically unsuitable elements, such as Bundists and others known for their anti-Soviet positions. This resulted in the removal of most of its staff, including Kalmanovitch, who was replaced as curator by the archivist Moyshe Lerer (a committed Marxist) and thereafter eked out a living as a copyeditor.[61] In an article titled "The 'YIVO' Too Is Finally Dragged out of the Swamp," the Vilna Yiddish *Togblat* (*Daily News*) reported that summer that the institute had "returned" under Soviet rule to its rightful owners—the toiling Jewish masses. Previously, it had been in the hands of "pronounced Zionists and Bundists" who, under the protection of reactionary regimes, "exploited the institute as a nest of protectionism and personal careers, on the one hand, and struggle against the Communist Party and its friends, on the other hand."[62]

Converted into an institution devoted exclusively to research, YIVO was integrated in January 1941 into the Academy of Sciences of the Soviet Socialist Republic of Lithuania. Renamed the "Institute for Jewish Culture," it was thus parallel to Lithuanian, Polish, and Byelorussian institutes for the study of linguistics, history, and ethnography housed under the same authority. Soviet officials made the lawyer, journalist, and linguist Noah Pryłucki, a member of YIVO's Philological Section who was himself a refugee from Warsaw, the director and appointed him as docent on a one-year contract to the Yiddish chair. A former parliamentarian representing the Yiddishist and Diaspora Nationalist Folksparty in the Polish parliament, Pryłucki was likely acceptable to the Soviets because he was neither Orthodox nor a Zionist nor Bundist—parties that were considered dangerous ideological opponents of the Bolshevik regime—and had made pro-Soviet statements.[63]

By late 1940, if not sooner, it was clear to Weinreich and colleagues in New York that not only could Vilna no longer serve as YIVO's global center, but the institute as they had known it there had effectively ceased to exist, and the welfare of its collections, not to mention staff, was uncertain at best in Soviet hands. The future of YIVO, at least for the foreseeable future, resided indisputably in America.

The "Father" of YIVO

Of middling height, bespectacled, and graying, the forty-six-year-old Max Weinreich was hardly a physically imposing figure. But Dr. Weinreich, as he was called by almost everyone, commanded universal respect in the Yiddish world for his towering intelligence and polymath scholarship. Raised in a German-speaking family in today's Latvia, then in the Russian Empire, he came to Yiddish as an adolescent through political activity on behalf of the Bund. He subsequently studied history and philology, first at the University of St. Petersburg prior to the Bolshevik Revolution in 1917. After working as a Yiddish newspaper editor and for the organized Jewish community in Vilna for about a year, he moved to Germany, where he completed a doctorate in German philology at the University of Marburg in 1923 with a dissertation concerning the history of scholarship about the Yiddish language.[64] At that time, possessing a doctor title from a German university conveyed enormous prestige, especially among the Jews of eastern Europe.

A well-known public intellectual active in Vilna's various Yiddish educational and cultural organizations, Weinreich was not only a cofounder of YIVO in 1925 and a leading Yiddish scholar; he was, along with fellow scholars-cum-administrators Zalmen Reyzen and Zelig Kalmanovitch, one of its pillars and its guiding spirit. A desk in Weinreich's Vilna apartment served as YIVO's first home, and he treated "the institute," as it was known in his family, as if it were his firstborn child, it having preceded the birth of his flesh-and-blood sons Uriel and Gabriel. He even proposed the institute's acronym, which he modeled on that of the sixteenth-century scholar Rabbi Moses Isserles, known as the Remo among Ashkenazic Jews.[65]

Weinreich was already familiar to readers of the New York daily *Forverts* as a foreign correspondent writing under various pseudonyms about European politics and culture since his student days in Germany. But he was less well known under his own name and for his role in YIVO. On behalf of the Amopteyl, Samuel Charney formally presented Weinreich in October 1940 to members of the American Yiddishist intelligentsia at a gathering in Greenberg's restaurant on the Lower East Side. Prominent figures in the Yiddish press, literature, and theater, along with representatives of the educational and cultural organizations serving

New York's Jewish community, gathered to greet a scholar whom the *Forverts* hailed as YIVO's "leader and father."[66]

Weinreich explained to the assembled that relocating YIVO's nerve center to New York did not simply entail the mechanical transfer of operations and structures from Vilna in order to relocate an eastern European Jewish institution to American shores.[67] On the contrary, in this and other addresses in the early 1940s, Weinreich announced a course to intensify YIVO's research activities in New York, enlarge its library and archival holdings, increase the number of its publications, and expand its audience and financial base. Perhaps most significantly, Weinreich called for what amounted to a radical reorientation in YIVO's attitude toward America and the English language. He spoke of the importance of devoting serious attention not only to Yiddish culture in the United States but to understanding American Jewry and the economic, social, and psychological problems it faced. To achieve these goals, it was essential to draw more scholars into YIVO's orbit, including English-speaking academics, and to begin training a new generation of American-born students in Jewish history and languages, Yiddish philology (linguistics, literature, and folklore), and the broader YIVO tradition of interdisciplinary scholarship in the social sciences—sociology, economics, demography, psychology, and pedagogy.[68]

Speaking to a packed auditorium at Hunter College at YIVO's first conference as the organization's uncontested world center in January 1941, Weinreich asked rhetorically whether coming together to discuss scholarship was justified in such excruciating times. His answer was characteristic of his perspective on the role of YIVO and had not changed since the mid-1930s, when the walls seemed to be closing in on Jewish life in Poland and elsewhere in Europe: "It depends on whether you see research as entertainment for good times or a necessary part of a collective's existence." Research about Jewish life and Jewish problems was, for Weinreich, not a luxury but a necessity for group survival.[69]

YIVO had been called into existence, he reminded his audience, for the benefit of the Yiddish-speaking Jewish masses. In an environment where conditions were so difficult for Jews as in Poland, YIVO contributed to the building of Jewish resilience through self-knowledge. Reflecting a propensity for employing martial metaphors to describe academic pursuits, Weinreich remarked that YIVO was "not a toy that a bunch of bookworms play with for their own pleasure but a great Jewish folk institution to help the collective and the individual with the weapons of scientific research."[70] Yet to understand its significance for Jewish life in Poland, he continued, one could not simply measure the achievements of a few dozen scholars in Vilna working together for uncertain wages to document and study Jewish life. Rather, one needed to appreciate the symbolic, quasi-religious significance the institute possessed as a bastion of modern, secular Jewish learning for a still traditionally rooted eastern European Jewry prior to the war: "A deep faith in YIVO as a new center of Jewish spirituality emanated from all [its] documents; and *Yidishkeyt* is, after all, spirituality." YIVO not only drew the loyalty of large numbers of the Yiddish-speaking folk masses, who took pride in its achievements in their name and in their mother tongue, he maintained; it also drew the increasing respect of both Gentile and linguistically and culturally assimilated Jewish scholars.[71]

Could America emerge as a new center of Jewish intellectual life? Weinreich asked rhetorically. An intellectual disciple of historian Simon Dubnow, Weinreich understood Jews as having possessed multiple demographic and cultural centers rather than a singular center across the millennia. Over the centuries, he explained, Jews had migrated from western Asia to western and then eastern Europe, most recently establishing new centers for their national culture along the way in such places as Frankfurt am Main and Vilna. America possessed a larger Jewish population than Poland and the three Baltic states combined, but it was young and not fully formed. It remained unproven whether it possessed the necessary vitality and resilience to become the next hegemonic center of Jewish civilization.[72] But Weinreich expressed confidence that American Jewry, with YIVO's help, would rise to the task. The institute would be built on American soil with hard work, brick by brick: "Until now there was no Jewish institution in America whose task was to research the entirety of Jewish life, from the present and the past, in America and everywhere with the methods of modern social science. Now there is the Yiddish Scientific Institute. Today it is still small but it will become great."[73]

The Problem of American Jewry

Max Weinreich was certain that American Jewry would assume a—if not *the*—leading intellectual role in world Jewry and contribute to the postwar rehabilitation of European Jewry. But like so many of his YIVO colleagues, he was hardly convinced that it was ready for this historic task. Paradoxically, it could only do so, he judged, under the tutelage of eastern European Jewish immigrants and refugees such as himself. The academic staff of organizations such as the Jewish Labor Committee, the American Jewish Congress, and even the patrician American Jewish Committee, he argued, were drawn largely from eastern European Jews rather than a native-born and educated intelligentsia.[74] Materially and politically secure, American Jewry—particularly its youth—was culturally and psychologically fragile in his evaluation. It also lacked the conscious will for national survival that he attributed to the desperate Jewish youth of prewar eastern Europe.

Throughout the 1940s, especially during the war years, Weinreich expressed his critique of American Jewry from the perspective of a European cultural nationalist who viewed with a jaundiced eye the formation of a specifically American Jewish culture in English and an identity that deviated from eastern European models that emphasized belonging to a national collective. In this respect, he did not differ from a long line of eastern European intellectuals, including YIVO colleagues, who paternalistically regarded American Jewry.[75] Where he differed from other intellectuals was in his application of Freudian analysis and social psychology to American Jewry to diagnose what he saw as its harmful psychological fragmentation, for which he considered Yiddish and YIVO's brand of scholarship a potent remedy.

Speaking at a symposium in New York in 1942 about the postwar future of world Jewry, Weinreich asked rhetorically, "And is our youth happier here? It is happier in its freedom but it is crippled in its personality. Where is the impetus of the fathers, of the first generation of immigrants? Where do so many extinguished eyes come from? They come from the fact that their *Yidishkeyt* is still a burden for them, still a source of dissatisfaction, of oppression."[76]

"Immigrant parents who raised their children without *Yidishkeyt* (sometimes with a bit of Hebrew and bar-mitzvah)," he elaborated in an article written under the name P. Berman, one of his pseudonyms in the *Forverts*, "thought they would raise their children in a Gentile manner as long their children are well . . . [but their children] aren't well. They feel in any case that they are Jews."[77] Weinreich appreciated that

Jews in America benefited from an unparalleled degree of freedom and opportunity as well as low levels of antisemitism, especially of the violent kind, compared with those in Europe. Yet he saw American Jewish youth as struggling with what W. E. B. Du Bois, whose ideas in connection with Black Americans he encountered during his time at Yale, referred to as "double consciousness"—a conflict in the identity of members of a despised minority group engendered by the awareness that their self-image differs from that which the majority society holds of them.[78] Young American Jews internalized the dominant society's prejudices that all that was distinctly Jewish was foreign, old-fashioned, and inherently inferior. It smacked of the "ghetto"—whether represented by eastern Europe or immigrant neighborhoods such as New York's Lower East Side—they sought to leave behind for the sake of integration.

For Weinreich, who had studied the effect of culture on personality at Yale, the desire to downplay or conceal one's Jewishness in order to escape detection by antisemites and to avoid a parochial existence not only amounted to self-effacement and subservience, the true essence of the ghetto mentality. It also presented a real psychological danger: "Belonging to a specific collective, as Jews are, shapes personality characteristics that cannot be erased by denying them on a rationalist basis. Rather, to do so leads toward neuroticism. There is only one cure for the soul: to make conscious this duality, to make it a conscious part of one's personality. It is not enough to pride oneself on having a rich uncle, even if it is Uncle Sam."[79]

In an increasingly secular age, Weinreich maintained, a declining number of Jews could rely on traditional belief in being God's elect or the advent of messianic redemption to shelter them psychologically from the hostility of the external world. Instead, they relied on modern ideologies such as socialism and nationalism as compensation to shore up their self-esteem and hope for a better future. In rejecting their cultural traditions—above all, the Yiddish language—American Jews were merely depriving themselves of a major psychological compensation and defense mechanism against feelings of inferiority, if not self-loathing. Indeed, Weinreich, a native German speaker, had himself "chosen" Yiddish, the language of the poorer and more religiously conservative classes of Jews in eastern Europe. He had devoted himself to Yiddishism since adolescence, despite receiving an elite education in German and

Russian-language institutions where hostility toward Jews was a consistent concern.

Weinreich did not believe that Jews constituted a distinct race in an anthropological sense.[80] He nonetheless expressed alarm when US authorities proposed changing Jews' long-standing racial designation from "Hebrew" to "white" on immigration documents in 1943. YIVO surveyed more than one hundred American intellectuals, Jewish and non-Jewish, to determine their opinions of the proposed reclassification. Weinreich and Jacob Lestschinsky found themselves at odds with most of the survey's respondents, who approved of the reclassification (which was implemented) as a means to protect the individual's right to self-identify in a liberal society. For the YIVO researchers, who were accustomed to obligatory Jewish membership in organized communities in Europe in comparison with the voluntaristic nature of Jewish affiliation in America, the reclassification was undesirable. It rendered identifying Jews more difficult, creating an obstacle to the collection of data necessary for their social scientific study.[81]

Jews in nineteenth-century America had commonly referred to themselves as a *race*—a vaguely defined term suggesting "common descent"—in order to diminish suspicions of foreign nationhood. But such a description posed challenges with the hardening of racial lines along a Black-white divide in American society and the intensification of political antisemitism and opposition to mass immigration in the late nineteenth century. In response, Jews increasingly defined themselves as belonging to a religious community while seeking to mute their other cultural differences. Categorizing Jews as a distinct race was further discouraged due to the association with Nazi-style racial persecution. During World War II, the American government itself encouraged Americans to view Judaism as a religious category parallel to Protestantism and Catholicism to reduce prejudices and facilitate Jews' acculturation and integration—alongside other groups of European descent—into mainstream, white society.[82] For Weinreich, such a definition of Jewish identity, even if intended to shield Jews from discrimination, obscured a fundamental social reality: Jews historically constituted a national group shaped by an ancient drive for cultural distinctiveness, and *Yidishkeyt* was an all-embracing way of life, even in its contemporary secularized forms.[83] Weinreich worried about the effect of the "confessionalization" of Jewish identity, in particular on Jewish youth.

Raised with little formal Jewish education in a highly individualistic society, American Jewish youth, Weinreich argued, experienced a degree of social atomization that only increased with class and secular education in American universities, to which they flocked in numbers impossible in Poland. Educated in public schools to reject ethnic stereotypes and to judge the individual on his own merits alone, they nervously objected to attributing specific cultural qualities and national values to groups as smacking of racism. Yet they were nonetheless painfully aware of the contradiction between theory and reality. While Jewish Community Centers eschewed specifically Jewish topics as embarrassingly parochial, Jews nonetheless congregated together in them. Jewish youth bore non-Jewish first names and received the best grades in English class yet still attended dances at the Jewish Y and felt unwelcome in Gentile social and professional circles. What distinguishes even the most assimilated Jew who maintains no Jewish practices from a Gentile, Weinreich maintained, is precisely his fear of being detected and consequently disapproved of and discriminated against as a Jew.[84]

But whereas others saw in Jews congregating among themselves for secular functions a form of self-imposed segregation, a regrettable but understandable response to exclusion and discomfort among a hostile majority, Weinreich also saw in it something positive—the manifestation of a natural propensity for cohesion no different from that of any people. Jewish youth experienced an affinity with each other and possessed a sense of their difference from non-Jews.[85] But they could not explain this difference, even less so evaluate it positively, because of their lack of Jewish education and hence self-understanding.

Due to the dearth of objective work conducted about Jews in history and the social sciences, such as economics and sociology, Weinreich asserted that American Jewry was ignorant of itself and therefore unable to comprehend its problems. It relied instead on external views that were often misinformed, if not downright hostile to Jews, and feared public discussion of Jewish issues.[86] He worried about the internalization of antisemitic views by American Jewish youth in particular, citing encounters, for example, with individuals who wondered whether "Hitler is right" or whether there does indeed exist a Jewish sect that consumes Christian blood.[87] Those Jewish organizations that did collect data about Jews did so, he maintained, mainly for the purpose of combating antisemitism. They were inclined to suppress information deemed embarrassing in front of Gentiles. At best, American Jews were willing to give money for the study of antisemitism—the primary issue that pained them as Jews—and the production of apologetics to combat it but not to the study of all facets of Jewish life and its strengthening, which was YIVO's raison d'être.[88]

Enviously, Weinreich noted that Poles and other European peoples overrun by foreign occupiers had founded diasporic universities. Meanwhile, Americans had raised half a million dollars to bring the cream of European scholarship to the US, even contemplating the creation of a special institute for them. But no Jewish academic institution, he lamented, had thus far made a concerted effort to bring Jewish scholars to these shores. Only the Jewish Labor Committee, an organization formed by recent immigrants from eastern Europe, had done so, and only YIVO, a small and weak institution, had made efforts to make use of their talents and energies.[89]

Although American Jews made important contributions as individuals to virtually all fields of scientific inquiry, he noted, Jewish scholarship in America was significantly underdeveloped outside of a few fields, such as Semitic philology. Further, it recalled the apologetic tendencies of the *Wissenschaft* school of Jewish scholars in Germany, which had pioneered modern, secular Jewish studies in the nineteenth century—in part as a way to improve Gentiles' as well as Jews' opinions of Jews and Judaism. Since its founding in 1925, YIVO had defined itself against the *Wissenschaft* school, which it reproached—not without exaggeration—with focusing on classic Judaic texts and the distant past at the expense of the contemporary needs of a living Jewish people.[90] His assessment of American Jewish scholarship as inadequate was reinforced by dismissive attitudes about the quality of American Jewish history writing that he encountered not only among YIVO colleagues but among respected historians within American academia, such as professors Oscar Handlin (Harvard University), Salo Baron (Columbia University), and Jacob Rader Marcus (Hebrew Union College). These scholars lamented that most American Jewish history writing was not the work of full-time, university-trained scholars but that of Jewish communal activists and enthusiastic hobbyists who gathered documents and produced filiopietistic studies emphasizing Jews' contributions to American society and its economy to demonstrate their worthiness for inclusion.[91] Even a decade later, Rader Marcus, a founder of the field of American Jewish history, dramatically described the study of American Jewry as being "literally in its swaddling cloth."[92]

American Jewry thus exhibited in Weinreich's view a deplorable lack of more than material interest in itself, the world's most prosperous and influential Jewish community. Its lack of intellectual curiosity, reflected in the dearth of serious research about Jews and Jewish themes in America, was a symptom of a deeper, underlying malaise: a fundamental discomfort with its Jewishness and the resulting desire to avoid anything that drew attention to its difference from other Americans. Hence American Jewry's aversion to Yiddish, the language that united most Jews around the world, and its preference for hiding from rather than confronting directly those specifically Jewish problems—especially antisemitism—that troubled it.[93]

In short, Weinreich likened American Jewry to a patient difficult to treat because it was either unable to recognize its ailment or in denial of it. Only through social science research in the YIVO tradition, Weinreich maintained, could American Jewry come to understand itself, the necessary precondition for addressing its problems. Convincing it to embrace YIVO and its mission was essential for providing a proper diagnosis and then a cure—or at least for helping it develop the necessary resilience to carry on. The vital importance of Jewish scholarship for group survival and the need for self-reliance in this regard had to be impressed upon American Jewry.[94] In order to do so, YIVO would not only need to make itself known to American Jewry, particularly its youth; it would also need to take up American topics that spoke to its specific condition. Embracing YIVO was, as far as Weinreich was concerned, an act of self-preservation for American Jewry. It was the difficult task of YIVO to tailor its mission to meet the needs of American Jewry while remaining true to its eastern European heritage and its primary constituency of Yiddish-speaking Jews.

To be fair, it must be acknowledged that Weinreich's unfavorable depiction of American Jewish scholarship and its response to Jew hatred, while not unique to him at the time, glossed over some significant accomplishments.[95] Weinreich diminished American Jews for what he considered their self-denying tendencies and amateurish, embarrassed efforts at self-defense at a time of rising nativism and antisemitism. American antisemitism drew on the same wellsprings as its European counterpart, similarly decrying Jews as a foreign and dangerous race, economic exploiters, communist revolutionaries, and general threats to the moral fabric of Christian American society. American Jewish anxiety was high, as Weinreich himself observed, even if anti-Jewish violence and legal discrimination were but a pale shadow of what he knew in Europe. Indeed, fundamentally racist motivations lay behind the introduction of a national quota system by Congress in 1924 that effectively reduced immigration from eastern and southern European immigration to a trickle, thereby depriving American Jewry of its primary reservoir for Yiddish linguistic and cultural reinforcement. Further, historian Tony Michels observes, "From the 1920s through the 1940s, discrimination against Jews in hiring, housing, education, social clubs, and elsewhere became pervasive and institutionalized." Meanwhile, organized American Jewry was quite vocal (and sometimes physical) in its opposition—arguably with no lesser success than European Jews—in the 1920s and '30s to such antisemitic elements as Henry Ford, whose *Dearborn Independent* published a version of the notorious *Protocols of the Elders of Zion*, and the pro-Nazi German American Bund.[96]

Moreover, having studied literature in the American tradition of the social sciences at Yale and an omnivorous reader of scholarship, Weinreich was well aware that American Jewry possessed its own historical societies of local and countrywide character as well as a body of literature in fields such as sociology and demographics that grappled with the transformation of American Jewish life since the period of mass immigration from eastern Europe. While his characterization of history writing was largely justified, scholarship about Jewish sociology in particular had made significant strides in American academia by the late 1930s. No doubt he found some of it—such as Louis Wirth's classic study of Chicago Jewish life, *The Ghetto* (1928)—objectionable in its outlook. The study, which he read at Yale, saw the dissolution of Jewish neighborhoods and the distinctive Jewish mentality they conditioned as an inevitable, if not desirable, phenomenon. But questions about contemporary Jewish demography and social problems were also pursued by social workers and researchers for Jewish welfare organizations that were clearly focused on the preservation of Jewish communal life, such as the National Conference of Jewish Social Service.[97] He was also probably familiar with the work of Horace Callen, the "father" of cultural pluralism in the United States, but passed over it too in silence.[98]

Most likely, Weinreich relied on a negative depiction of scholarship, particularly that sponsored by Jewish self-defense organizations long dominated by Americanized German Jewish elites such as the American Jewish Committee, as a foil to highlight the uniqueness of YIVO's path in America in pursuing a holistic, social scientific approach to American Jewry's problems.[99] Weinreich believed that the pursuit of the Jewish social sciences in its fullest sense should be the purview of a nonpartisan academic institution—ideally YIVO—and not the work of in-house researchers employed by Jewish welfare and advocacy agencies chiefly to combat antisemitism. Equally important in shaping his depiction of the research landscape was the ambivalence he, a profound admirer of American academic culture, felt toward the very prospect of a Jewish high culture embracing scholarship in English, since it implicitly threatened the vitality of Yiddish culture and YIVO's very purpose. Weinreich wished for YIVO's approach to be enriched by the methodological insights and innovations of American scholarship, not supplanted by it.

But Weinreich's emphatic rhetoric must also be understood as meant to inspire his audience of mainly Yiddish-speaking Jewish immigrants already sympathetic to YIVO's work and to persuade them of the necessity of generously supporting the institute when other priorities consumed their attention. In doing so, he sought to reassure YIVO supporters—and perhaps himself—of the enduring value of the eastern European Jewish cultural tradition in a time of violent upheaval and to convince them that YIVO in America must play a formative role in shaping the global and American Jewish futures.

The Postwar Jewish Future in Palestine and Europe

As a public intellectual leading a prominent research institute, Weinreich was invited to participate in a symposium in 1942 organized by the Jewish Labor Committee about Jewish life in the postwar era. The event was one of several organized by Jewish institutes and organizations, frequently established by the numerous European intellectuals of varying Jewish political orientations who found refuge in New York during the war years, to make plans for the anticipated return of millions of Jews to their countries of origin after the cessation of hostilities. Like many of his YIVO colleagues at this time, Weinreich believed wholeheartedly in the reconstruction of European Jewish life with American assistance after the anticipated defeat of Nazi Germany and its allies.

He did not expect that the reintegration of surviving European Jews into their prewar homelands to be easy, but he clung to a vision of Jewish national cultural autonomy in the Diaspora adopted in some form by Jewish political parties in non-Soviet eastern Europe across the spectrum, from the Bund to Zionists, in the interwar period.[100] He foresaw its implementation guaranteed, however, through a system of treaties and measures of enforcement superior to the minority treaties signed and then largely disregarded or repudiated by Poland and neighboring countries in the League of Nations.[101] Some of his Yiddishist colleagues had despaired of the ideal of cultural autonomy even before World War II and turned away from politics entirely and inward toward their research or toward other political and cultural ideologies such as communism or political Zionism. Weinreich, in contrast, retained his faith.[102] The dream was still attainable, he maintained, if only stronger legal protections were granted—despite apparent evidence to the contrary.

Not all in YIVO agreed with Weinreich's sanguine appraisal of postwar opportunities for Jews. Among his staunchest opponents in this matter was the demographer and economist Jacob Lestschinsky. Like many active in eastern European Jewish politics and culture, Lestschinsky had undergone a number of ideological shifts since the early decades of the twentieth century. He had once been a supporter of Diaspora Nationalism and then territorialism, the movement to create an autonomous Jewish territory outside of Palestine. He then gravitated toward Labor Zionism in the 1930s out of disillusionment with ideologies focused on the Diaspora. By 1941, he made clear that he saw no future in eastern Europe for whatever would remain of the Jews there. He anticipated that the war would end with massive population transfers in order to make states ethnically homogeneous—a prediction that would later prove largely correct, albeit chiefly due to involuntary expulsions and the rearrangement of borders. Jews, he noted, had long been denounced by non-Jewish ethno-nationalists as a foreign, parasitic body sapping the strength of their "host" countries. He predicted that prewar pressures to extrude them from the economy would only intensify after the war, making their survival as a large, organized community wholly untenable in the lands where they had dwelled for centuries.[103]

Lestschinsky was not much more optimistic about the future of the much younger Jewish community in the United States, at least not as a collective. He expressed a common sentiment when, at YIVO's annual conference in 1942, he observed that American immigrant "ghettos" such as New York's Lower East Side served as a sort of "ingathering of the exiles." They united Jews of various backgrounds who were integrated to varying degrees into non-Jewish society in their native lands. For some time, these "ghettos" had resisted waves of cultural assimilation in America. But in the long run, he argued, they would not prove strong enough to generate a national culture capable of resisting those powerful forces.[104]

Yet on the other hand, he also agreed with Weinreich's assessment that Jews could not wholly shed their Jewishness either, even if they wished to do so. Shortly after his arrival in America, Lestschinsky warned in 1939 of the potentially dire consequences of a group that surrenders its national particularity while preserving its group cohesion: "The danger is therefore here, as in many countries, not assimilation but denationalization, giving up one's own face easily, one's own cultural forms, one's own ways of living and remaining somewhere in the deepest recesses a Jew—a Jew to such an extent that even where tens of peoples are easily swallowed, Jews can get stuck in the throat of the future American nation. And no good can come from getting stuck in the throat. You end up being spit out."[105]

There existed widespread consensus in YIVO circles about the fundamental deficiencies of American Jewry, which was deemed insufficiently committed to Jewish peoplehood and the preservation of cultural distinctiveness. The differences, as reflected in the contrasting views of Weinreich and Lestschinsky, consisted chiefly at this time in the degree of conviction that YIVO could make a difference in America in counteracting the perceived decline of Jewish collective identity, of which Yiddish was deemed a significant part and its main carrier. For Weinreich, the answer had to be yes if the Jewish people worldwide were to have a future. For others, the answer was often negative or at least far more tentative.

Conclusion

Max Weinreich's misplaced optimism—his decision to stay in Copenhagen rather than return immediately to Vilna—almost surely saved him and his family. Following months of anxiety-ridden travel by train and ship through Russia, Siberia, and Japan, his wife and younger son miraculously reached San Francisco and then, finally, New York in January 1941.[106] In contrast, most of his colleagues who remained in, returned to, or took refuge in Vilna were murdered at the hands of the Nazis and their accomplices. In retrospect, he was one of the few great Yiddish scholars to escape the conflagration that swallowed European Jewry and to continue his career on a new continent. Weinreich's refusal to accept American Jewry *as it was* has shaped the subsequent history of Yiddish studies as an academic field and of YIVO as an institution, helping make New York City a world center for Jewish research.

Of course, New York City did not emerge as YIVO's headquarters simply with Weinreich's arrival. Nor was the decision to make it the institute's center universally accepted and embraced, either in Vilna or New York. Too strong was the attachment among YIVO's staff to the former city and all that it represented about the past and future of eastern European Jewry; too weak was confidence in the competence and preparedness of the latter one to assume the onus of leadership of either YIVO or of world Jewry.

As soon as war erupted, the Amopteyl began, with Weinreich's encouragement, readying itself for a leadership role despite doubts and objections. The arrival of Weinreich and other refugee scholars helped make the fulfillment of this role possible; the destruction of the Vilna YIVO, as difficult as it was to accept, would make it a necessity if YIVO and its values were to live on. Fortunately, when the time came for the Amopteyl to assert itself publicly as YIVO's undisputed world headquarters in late 1940, it already possessed a tradition of scholarship, as well as the core of a library and archives, upon which to build. The secretaries of its sections were also present in America, as were a cadre of highly committed intellectuals who had already grown accustomed to America.

What it lacked, for the time being, was adequate funding and—even more essential—a significant connection to the broad American Jewish public, especially a Yiddish-speaking youth.

With Max Weinreich's arrival in New York begins a new, American chapter in the history of YIVO. The transfer of the institute's center was reflected in the very language used to refer to its American offices. Weinreich and other insiders ceased to speak of the Amopteyl and began to speak in Yiddish instead of "the YIVO in America" or simply "the YIVO." Moreover, while the American center officially inherited the Vilna center's prewar organization into academic sections, Weinreich quickly assumed de facto academic leadership as its research director, a position specifically created for him. For almost the next thirty years, Weinreich's name would be virtually synonymous with YIVO—perhaps even more so than in Poland, where he was more likely to be considered primus inter pares among fellow administrators Reyzen and Kalmanovitch.

2
FROM YIDDISH SCIENTIFIC INSTITUTE TO THE YIVO INSTITUTE FOR JEWISH RESEARCH

The 1940s and early 1950s were a time of staggering productivity by YIVO associates in New York City, motivated by an urgent sense of purpose in desperate times. Anxiety over the uncertain future of the institution during the war years and their immediate aftermath was naturally exacerbated by growing awareness of the gruesome fate of friends, family, and colleagues in eastern Europe. Further, while those YIVO associates who had escaped Hitler's Europe and made it to New York were mercifully spared genocide, they were tormented by debilitating feelings of rage, despair, depression, and impotence as the dimensions of what we now know today as the Holocaust became clear and penetrated their consciousness. YIVO staff was obliged to invest tremendous time, energy, and expenses into what Weinreich had called in YIVO's foundational period in Vilna the "organization of *Yidishe visnshaft*"—that is, establishing the administrative infrastructure, staffing, and material basis necessary for the institute to conduct its work, even if they were building upon the foundation of the Amopteyl. "And the emotional damage?" linguist Mordkhe Schaechter asked rhetorically, reflecting back on this period years later. "How many hours and how much psychological energy went to mourning eastern European Jewry?"[1]

For the founding generation of YIVO scholars who survived the destruction of eastern European Jewry, Vilna would forever occupy a hallowed place in memory and nostalgia as the embodiment of the youthful aspirations of the institute and its staff. It would never cease to be the yardstick by which all achievements would be measured in an America to whose "stony shores" it was not clear YIVO's mission could be successfully transplanted. The dynamic encounter with a massive American

Jewish community little attuned to the Yiddishist ideals upon which YIVO was founded obliged the institute's staff to reconsider profoundly the institute's ideology, goals, and methods even before the war's end.

By the late 1940s, many colleagues and observers questioned not only Weinreich's vision of broadening YIVO's mandate to make it a center for the study of American as well as eastern European Jewry but also the very wisdom of pursuing a future for the institute beyond circles of eastern European Jews transplanted to a new continent. Alongside personal rivalries and frictions common to any organization, fundamental questions divided YIVO circles for years to come regarding the institute's relationship to America, the nature of its activities, its audience, and how best to attain financial stability. Primary among these questions was whether YIVO still saw itself after the Holocaust as an institution serving the needs of a global Jewish nation or believed its future lay in serving the needs of an American Jewish community. And what role did Yiddish play in this? Weinreich's eventual "ousting" as research director and the changing of YIVO's English name in the 1950s reflect the struggle over the institute's direction.

Forging a Path in America

In September 1943, YIVO resumed publication of its informational bulletin, *Yedies fun yivo*, which had been published irregularly in Vilna prior to the war. Reflecting its understanding of the institute's role in America, *Yedies* (subtitled in English "News of the Yivo") explained to readers, "The Yivo has become the meeting place for those Jewish intellectuals who have preferred to seek knowledge through research rather than to accept preconceived ideas at their face value. Its work is a means of giving the Jew the opportunity to acquire self-knowledge and of providing him with new implements in the intellectual struggle for survival." *Yedies* succinctly declared the main pillars of YIVO's mission as follows: "1. documentation and recording: to collect and preserve materials pertaining to Jewish life, past and present, all over the world; 2. analysis and research: to study past and present Jewish life with the methods of modern social science; 3. training: to train a new generation of social scientists concerned with Jewish life and adequately equipped to study it."[2]

ידיעות פֿון ייִוואָ

נומער 1 — סעפּטעמבער 1943

ייִדישער וויסנשאַפֿטלעכער אינסטיטוט, 535 וועסט 123סטע גאַס, ניו־יאָרק 27, נ״י

אליהו טשעריקאָווער פּלוצלינג געשטאָרבן

שבת, דעם 28סטן אויגוסט, אין דער פֿרי איז פּלוצלינג
געשטאָרבן פֿון אַ האַרצאַטאַק דער סעקרעטאַר פֿון דער היסטאָ־
רישער סעקציע פֿון ייִוואָ — א ל י ה ו ט ש ע ר י ק אָ ו ו ע ר.
זײַן אומגעריכטער טויט איז אַ שווערער קלאַפּ פֿאַר אַלע זײַנע
פֿילצאָליקע פֿרײַנד און אַ גוואַלדיק גרויסע אֲבֵידה פֿאַרן ייִדישן
וויסנשאַפֿטלעכן אינסטיטוט, וואָס דער פֿאַרשטאָרבענער איז
געווען איינער פֿון זײַנע גרונטזײַלן.

נאָך פֿון די ערשטע טריט אָן וואָס דער ייִוואָ האָט גע־
שטעלט איז אליהו טשעריקאָווער געווען איינער פֿון זײַנע
הויפּט־מיטאַרבעטערס. בײַם אָרגאַניזירן די
סעקציעס פֿון ייִוואָ אין 1929 איז ער באַ־
שטעטיקט געוואָרן פֿאַרן סעקרעטאַר פֿון דער
היסטאָרישער סעקציע און פֿון יעמאָלט אָן
איז זײַן גאַנצע וויסנשאַפֿטלעכע אַרבעט גע־
ווען פֿאַרבונדן מיטן ייִוואָ. אליהו טשערי־
קאָווער איז געווען דער רעדאַקטאָר פֿון דרײַ
גרויסע בענד „היסטאָרישע שריפֿטן“, פֿון
אַלע אַנדערע אויסגאַבעס פֿון דער סעקציע,
פֿון די בענד „ייִדן אין פֿראַנקרײַך“ און פֿון
דער „געשיכטע פֿון דער ייִדישער אַר־
בעטער־באַוועגונג אין די פֿאַראייניקטע
שטאַטן“. פֿריִער אין בערלין און נאָך דעם,
ווען היטלער איז געקומען צו דער מאַכט,
אין פּאַריז — האָט ער אָנגעפֿירט די דאָר־
טיקע אַרבעט פֿאַרן ייִוואָ. ווען נאָכן צוזאַ־
מענבראָך פֿון פֿראַנקרײַך איז ער געקומען
קיין ניו־יאָרק, האָט ער דאָ געהאָלפֿן אײַנ־
שטעלן דעם צענטער פֿון ייִוואָ. זײַן פֿעי־
קייט זיך צוצופּאַסן צו נײַע באַדינגונגען,
זײַן אומאויסשעפּלעכע ענערגיע און אַר־
בעטזאַמקייט, זײַן לעבנסלוסטיקייט און די
אַטמאָספֿער פֿון פֿרײַנדשאַפֿט און משפּחהדי־
קייט וואָס ער האָט שטענדיק פֿאַרשפּרייט אַרום זיך אין איינעם
מיט די מידות־טובֿות פֿון געטרײַסטער חבֿרישקייט און גרויס־
מוטיקער קאָלעגיאַלקייט — האָבן זיך שטענדיק אַרויסגעוויזן
אין דער טאָג־טעגלעכער אַרבעט, ווי אויך אין אָרגאַניזירן און
אין זאָרגעוודיקן, מוסטערדיקן רעדאַגירן די אויסגאַבעס פֿון דער
היסטאָרישער סעקציע.

געבוירן אין פּאָלטאַווע דעם 13טן אויגוסט 1881, אין אַן אַנ־
געזעענער משׂכּילישער משפּחה, האָט אליהו טשעריקאָווער זיך
געלערנט אין אָדעס און אין פּעטערבורג און אונטער דער השפּעה
פֿון זײַן רבין און חבֿר שמעון דובנאָוו זיך אָפּגעגעבן דער היסטאָ־
רישער וויסנשאַפֿט. ער איז געווען איינער פֿון די הויפּט־
מיטאַרבעטערס פֿון דער „יעווריייסקאַיאַ ענציקלאָפּעדיאַ“, ווו
ער האָט געשריבן אַ רײַ אַרטיקלען וועגן מאָדערנע געזעלשאַפֿט־
לעכע באַוועגונגען; ער האָט צונויפֿגעשטעלט די געשיכטע פֿון
דער חבֿרה „מפֿיצי השׂכּלה“, ער האָט אויסגעפֿונען און באַאַר־
בעט אַ סך אַרכיוו־מאַטעריאַלן צו דער געשיכטע פֿון ייִדן אין
רוסלאַנד במשך פֿון 19טן י״ה. בשעתן בירגערקריג און די בלוטי־
טיקע שחיטות אויף ייִדן אין אוקראַינע האָט ער געזאַמלט אַ
גרויסן פּאָגראָם־אַרכיוו, וואָס ער האָט אים אַרויסגעראַטעוועט
קיין בערלין און דאָרטן אָרגאַניזירט דאָס
אַרויסגעבן אַט די מאַטעריאַלן. זײַן הויפּט־
אינטערעס ווי אַ היסטאָריקער איז געווען
די ייִדישע געזעלשאַפֿטלעכקייט זינט דער
פֿראַנצייזישער רעוואָלוציע, דער אָנטייל פֿון
ייִדן אין רעוואָלוציעס און בכלל די פּאָלי־
טישע און סאָציאַלע געשיכטע פֿון ייִדן
במשך פֿון די לעצטע 150 יאָר. זײַן צו־
גאַנג צו אַלע פּראָבלעמען איז שטענדיק
געווען אַ טיף נאַציאָנאַלער. געשיכטע איז
פֿאַר אונדזער טײַערן פֿרײַנד געווען אַן אָנ־
שפּאַר אין דעם איצטיקן קאַמף פֿון ייִדישן
פֿאָלק פֿאַר זײַן קיום.

אַן ענערגישער און אומרויִק זוכנדיקער
ייִדישער אינטעליגענט, איז אליהו טשערי־
קאָווער געווען שטענדיק דאָרטן ווו מען
דאַרף אָרגאַניזירן דאָס ייִדישע לעבן; בײַ
דער קאָנגרעס־באַוועגונג אין אַמעריקע בעת
דער ערשטער וועלט־מלחמה, בײַם העלפֿן
שאַפֿן דעם אַלוועלטלעכן ייִדישן קאָנגרעס,
בײַם אויסבויען פֿאַרשיידענע קולטור־אונ־
טערנעמונגען. ער האָט אומעטום אַרויסגע־
וויזן זײַן אָרגאַניזיר־טאַלענט. ער האָט גע־
האַט אַ פֿײַנעם און אייגנאַרטיקן סטיל ווי אַ פּובליציסט און איר־
מעטום מיטגעבראַכט זײַן נשמהדיקע וואַרעמקייט און אַ קוואַל
לעבנספֿרייד.

אַ גענויערע כאַראַקטעריזירונג פֿון זײַנע פֿאַרשיידענע טע־
טיקייטן און די אָפּשאַצונג פֿון זײַנע אויפֿטוען ווי אַן אָרגאַניזאַ־
טאָר פֿון וויסנשאַפֿטלעכע אַרבעטן און ווי אַ וויסנשאַפֿטלער וועלן
אונדזערע פֿרײַנד געפֿינען אין די „ייִוואָ־בלעטער“. אין דעם
קומענדיקן נומער „ידיעות פֿון ייִוואָ“ וועלן מיר לאָזן וויסן,
אויף וואָסער אופֿן עס איז באַשלאָסן געוואָרן צו פֿאַראייביקן זײַן

(סוף — זײַט 2)

אליהו טשעריקאָווער

Cover page of *Yedies fun yivo*, first issue in America, September 1943, announcing the death of Elias Tcherikower. Credit: YIVO Institute for Jewish Research

Tellingly, *Yedies* conveyed its survey of the institute's recent and future activities, archival and library acquisitions, and significant events affecting the institution and its audience not only in Yiddish but also in English translation. This was a noticeable departure from the practice of YIVO's smaller prewar bulletin, which appeared exclusively in Yiddish. The relative proportion devoted to each language in the first issue of *Yedies*—ten pages of Yiddish alongside six pages of condensed English translation—confirmed that it was still very much a Yiddish-speaking institute. Within a few issues, however, the English-Yiddish ratio became more or less equal, no doubt ruffling the feathers of those who saw such accommodation of English speakers as a betrayal of Yiddishist convictions.[3]

This linguistic adaptation was intended to showcase YIVO's achievements beyond its usual constituency, most of whom were working-class immigrants and Yiddishist intellectuals. In Poland, YIVO had found comparatively little resonance among Gentile scholars, and the growing Polonization of Jewish society constituted an existential menace to Yiddishism and Jewish ambitions for national cultural autonomy. In contrast, YIVO had more positive feelings toward English, if chiefly as a means to an end. Not only was English a powerful international language associated with more welcoming governments and societies than Jews had known in eastern Europe. The shift to the dominant language of Gentile society was also more advanced among Jews in the United States, who had a tradition of attending public schools, than those in eastern Europe. Competence in state languages first became widespread there in the period after World War I, when Jews began attending schools in languages such as Polish and Russian en masse.

YIVO scholars in America expressed anxiety about the decline of Yiddish here and what they considered the degradation of the language under the influence of English vocabulary, syntax, phonetics, and grammar.[4] But they did not typically condemn English-speaking Jews as assimilationists or national traitors, terms of contempt with which Yiddishists frequently marked Jews who opted for Gentile languages—allegedly out of the snobbish desire to belong to the "better classes" of society or to conceal their Jewishness.[5] Although a competitor to Yiddish, English was not perceived by Yiddishists as the ethnonational language of a hostile majority. YIVO scholars' reaction toward American Jews' widespread use of English—especially among those with little or no knowledge of Yiddish—was hence more often an expression of disappointment tinged with resignation than of burning indignation or militant rebuke. As Weinreich himself put it, without Yiddish, American Jews were left with all the handicaps of being Jewish—above all, antisemitism and thwarted social integration—but also denied one of its greatest pleasures and sources of comfort.[6]

Rather than reject English altogether, Weinreich hoped to use it in measured doses to interest non-Jewish scholars and Jewish intellectuals who did not know Yiddish in YIVO's work and, ideally, to pique their interest in Yiddish itself. He had already succeeded in recruiting sociologist John Dollard, one of his instructors at Yale in 1932, to travel to Vilna in 1939 to address the YIVO staff about trends in American scholarship.[7] The planned lecture series was, however, canceled due to the outbreak of war. Now Weinreich hoped to draw additional American scholars into YIVO's orbit in order to provide for their mutual enrichment, methodological and otherwise, and to dispel notions that Jewish studies research was inherently primitive or parochial. The following year, YIVO formed its Academic Council to provide advice and acquaint scholars both inside and outside of Jewish studies with YIVO's work. It included forty-seven prominent Jewish and non-Jewish scholars whose association with YIVO enhanced the institute's prestige. Among them were renowned Jewish figures such as physicist Albert Einstein and historian Salo Baron as well as non-Jewish ones such as the biblical archaeologist William F. Albright and French Catholic philosopher Jacques Maritain, who was then involved in bringing persecuted academics, many of them Jews, to America.[8]

Among *Yedies*'s first announcements in that issue was the death of Elias (Elye) Tcherikower, aged sixty-two, shortly before the bulletin went to print. The secretary of YIVO's Historical Section, Tcherikower was perhaps best known for his work about antisemitism and for documenting pogroms that took the lives of tens of thousands of Jews in Ukraine after World War I.[9] Since 1921 he had lived in Berlin, which he left for Paris in 1933 with Hitler's ascent to power. As the Nazis advanced on the latter city, he fled again, this time to New York City, where he arrived in the summer of 1940. His sudden death by heart attack three years later put in question the completion of the planned multivolume *Geshikhte fun der yidisher arbeter-bavegung in di fareynikte shtatn* (History of the Jewish

Labor Movement in the United States) that a team of nearly a dozen YIVO associates (among them historians Rudolf Glanz and Raphael Mahler, Jacob Lestschinsky, and journalist Mark Vishniak) was producing under his editorship and to which he himself contributed more than a third of the chapters.[10] It was one of several ambitious new projects to which YIVO had committed itself since Weinreich's arrival in New York and a reflection not only of its interest in the social and economic history of immigration and the Jewish working class—a subject virtually untouched by historians of American Jewry—but of its new emphasis on the history of Yiddish-speaking Jews in the United States. Tcherikower was survived by his wife, Rebecca (Rive), herself an intellectual who assumed the de facto role of the American YIVO's chief—and effectively first—archivist. Prior to her engagement, YIVO in America had been receiving archival collections but had not begun processing them.[11] Elias Tcherikower was mourned as "a loyal co-constructor of YIVO, a dear, intimately close member of our family, an unforgettable friend."[12] Jacob Shatzky succeeded him as secretary of the Historical Section.

Along with the death soon afterward of fifty-nine-year-old Nathan Feinerman, the Amopteyl's dedicated and highly capable executive secretary of the previous thirteen years, Tcherikower's demise was an early harbinger of the inevitable: the physical decline of the eastern European–born generation of ideologically committed scholars who formed the largest part of YIVO associates. This phenomenon would become increasingly palpable by the 1950s.[13] In 1943, Weinreich, one of the youngest of YIVO's cofounders, was approaching the age of fifty. He was surrounded by colleagues who were mostly in their fifties or older. The oldest, Judah A. Joffee, an Amopteyl cofounder and member of YIVO's Philological Section, had just celebrated his seventieth birthday.

This growing sense of mortality extended beyond the lives of YIVO associates and, of course, those they had left behind in Europe. It extended to eastern European Jewish civilization as a whole. YIVO's founding mission was inspired by the impulse shared by linguists, folklorists, and historians alike since the turn of the twentieth century to preserve all that could be gathered from Jews' past and traditional way of life, particularly in *shtetls*, before its anticipated disappearance in the face of the juggernaut of modernization—above all, secularization, industrialization, migration, and acculturation. But never before had the possibility been conceived that a centuries-old way of living would disappear without a trace.[14]

Embarking on a program of salvage ethnography, YIVO proposed the creation of a "Museum of Jewish Homes of the Past." The idea was endorsed in March 1944 at a conference to which it invited representatives of *landsmanshaftn*, mutual aid societies organized by Jewish immigrants from a specific hometown or region in eastern Europe.[15] Weinreich hoped to enlist their support in donating materials to commemorate their now destroyed communities. Individual *Yedies* readers were also solicited to contribute materials for the proposed museum, including those of a highly personal nature such as family letters, that reflected Jewish life in eastern Europe. In doing so, YIVO sought to draw on its long-standing practice of what might anachronistically be called crowdsourcing, engaging the Jewish public through appeals in the press to provide data and physical artifacts for its research. Its staff would then study these items and share their analysis with the public in the form of scholarship and exhibitions. *Zamlers* (collectors) throughout eastern Europe, frequently so impoverished that they had requested that YIVO cover the cost of postage stamps, had played an invaluable role in building YIVO's collections. In return, they felt elevated through their involvement in building a Jewish national institution and making possible an enterprise larger than themselves.[16]

Enlisting the aid now of American Jews in documenting a civilization whose cultural artifacts, along with its people, faced an uncertain future was meant to draw them into active engagement *with* and—at the same time—on *behalf* of YIVO's mission. Moreover, the museum was intended to serve an educational purpose—to acquaint American-born generations with the legacy of a world that they did not know directly and to provoke contemplation of their own Jewish identities.[17]

This was not the only project initiated by YIVO during the war years to draw the two worlds—eastern Europe and America—closer. It also launched a contest in 1943 for best immigrant essay addressing the question of "Why I left the old country and what I have accomplished in America" ("Farvos bin ikh avek fun der alter heym un vos hob ikh dergreykht in amerike"). Modeled on contests for best youth autobiography solicited by YIVO in Vilna in the 1930s, it drew 223 submissions—primarily in Yiddish but also in English, German, and Hebrew—from men and women who had immigrated to the United States and Canada. By design, however, the contest appealed to mature individuals—not to youth. Indeed, the majority of participants were aged fifty-one to seventy. YIVO found among the older generation of Jews an appreciation of Yiddish and sympathy for the institute's mission that it seldom encountered among the American-born. A respect for learning for its own sake and a faith in the constructive value of education, knowledge, and culture were in Weinreich's view values rooted in traditional Jewish religious culture that were maintained despite secularization by the Jewish socialist and labor movements in which the immigrant generations—in contrast with their children and grandchildren—were tremendously invested.[18] Such a disparity highlighted, like the campaign for a "Museum of Jewish Homes of the Past," the gap in both knowledge and interest in Yiddish culture and eastern European Jewry dividing immigrant and native-born American Jews—what would prove a perennial struggle for YIVO as it sought to find its footing in America.[19]

To add gravitas to the endeavor and provide public recognition, essay contest participants received a certificate resembling a diploma at a YIVO ceremony acknowledging their contributions. The authors of those essays judged best received prizes in the form of cash awards, ranging from twenty to one hundred dollars, or books. Participants found, however, that the contest was not only financially or intellectually rewarding. As was the case with participants in YIVO's prewar autobiographical contests aimed at youth, adults reported deriving great emotional satisfaction from the opportunity to recount their life stories and from the knowledge that these stories would serve posterity. In comparison with the autobiographies that formed the basis of *Der veg tsu undzer yugnt* (The Path to Our Youth), Weinreich's study of Polish Jewish youth, however, these essays have received relatively little contemporary scholarly attention.[20] Weinreich was himself a leading prewar proponent of applying psychological and sociological methodologies to the study of contemporary Jewish life and aimed to conduct a study about the problems of personality formation among American Jews. But he had precious little time for research projects of his own, and funding was lacking for this and many other projects at the time.[21]

The American autobiographical essays served as the basis for a single study by a YIVO associate, the contest secretary Moses (Moyshe)

Kligsberg, at the time (and a subsequent, more substantial one by him published in 1974); they were "rediscovered" decades later by contemporary researchers.[22] Kligsberg's own biography, whose tragedy stands in sharp contrast to those he analyzed, is in many ways representative of a generation of YIVO associates who, their lives torn apart by the war and subsequent horrors, found community in the institute and meaning in pouring their energies into it.

A native of Warsaw, Kligsberg (1901–75) was raised in a traditionally religious family and pursued a secular education largely outside of formal academic institutions while engaging in political activism in interwar Poland. Active in Bundist circles before and after World War II, he was particularly attracted to the sociological study of Polish Jewish youth, a subject about which he published through the years in various YIVO publications. When the war erupted, he was obliged to leave behind his family in Warsaw as he joined the stream of Jewish intellectuals, along with religious and political leaders, who fled to Vilna in 1939. There he became a YIVO *aspirant* while remaining in contact with his wife and daughter in Warsaw. He managed to make it to the United States in 1941, but his attempts to bring them to join him there were repeatedly denied by authorities. Ultimately, his family perished in the Warsaw Ghetto.[23] For Kligsberg, a talented amateur musician and composer who never remarried, YIVO and Bundist circles functioned to a large extent as a surrogate family.[24]

As part of his analysis of immigrant autobiographies, Kligsberg challenged xenophobic claims, then widespread in the United States, that Jewish immigrants constituted, on the whole, an undesirable element in American society. He maintained, "The prevalence of the independent, vigorous type among the immigrants and their eagerness to adjust directly contradict the traditional anti-immigration argument that those who seek admission to our shores are the 'weak, unassimilable, ungrateful offscourings of Europe.'" Further, he rejected a trope common within American Jewish literature itself portraying the experience of immigrants, as the journal *Commentary* expressed it in 1948, as one of "frustration, disillusionment, and tragedy: the Golden Land turned out to be a hoax."[25]

In contrast with the pronounced tendency among youth participants in YIVO's autobiographical contests in interwar Poland to lament bitterly their circumstances and lack of a future, he found that Jewish immigrants overwhelmingly reported satisfaction with their lives and accomplishments in North America. They showed little disappointment despite acknowledging the travails of immigrant adjustment and, at times, the cultural estrangement they felt from their children. While they appreciated the material advantages that America offered, eastern European Jewish immigrants were not motivated primarily by the prospect of economic gain, he argued, but by a desire to achieve a measure of self-fulfillment and personal advancement denied them in an atmosphere of consistent discrimination in their native lands. This desire found its highest expression, he maintained, in the aspiration for socially beneficial and ethically meaningful careers such as lawyer, doctor, or teacher for them and their children.[26] Kligsberg thus presented Jewish immigrants not as greedy and vulgar materialists, as their detractors frequently maintained, but as carriers of values consistent with American individualism and civic-mindedness.

As Weinreich's assistant in charge of research projects, Kligsberg also organized and administered a YIVO essay contest about the wartime experiences of American Jewish soldiers in 1946 and used the occasion of his correspondence with fellow refugees around the world to convince them to donate books and materials to YIVO's collections. The second in YIVO's American essay autobiographical contests, this one followed a reverse trajectory from the first. It focused not on eastern European immigrants' path to and journey in a flourishing America but on American Jews' encounter with a destroyed Europe, including its surviving Jews. The experience of serving in the armed forces in Europe and encountering Hitler's victims, Kligsberg found, tended not only to activate a sense of sympathy and solidarity with European Jewry but to provoke reflection among American Jews—some, reportedly, for the first time—about the unique problems of Jewish identity and existence, including antisemitism. This translated into a heightened interest in Jewish subjects and their own identities as Jews among contest participants.[27]

Apart from Kligsberg's efforts, YIVO began aggressively collecting materials from America and around the world, rapidly expanding its library and archival materials through solicitations and thanks largely to donations from private and institutional libraries. Mendel Elkin (1873–1962), a fellow Bundist who had come to New York in the early 1920s, was chiefly responsible for the growth of the library beyond the recuperation of YIVO's Vilna collections after World War II (see next chapter). Elkin dedicated the last quarter century of his life to building one of the largest collections of Judaica in the United States. "The most energetic among us," as Max Weinreich described him, Elkin made up for what he lacked in professional training as a librarian with his commitment and resourcefulness.[28]

A former dentist and lumber merchant from what is today Belarus, Elkin had long been active in Yiddish literary and theater circles, including authoring stories and plays himself. His love of the Yiddish word led him to help found the Central Jewish Library, which he hoped would serve not only as a library but as a gathering place for cultural events. Like so many others active in YIVO, he was largely an autodidact in the humanities, not to mention library sciences. He implemented a cataloging scheme—conceived by a commission including Shatzky, Joffe, and others—whereby books, apart from serials, were shelved in the order of their acquisition rather than according to subject category. Despite its flaws, this system was maintained until a reorganization of YIVO's library was undertaken in the mid-1970s according to modern cataloging principles.[29]

The seemingly indefatigable Elkin also undertook multiple trips across North America to fundraise for the institute. Wherever he traveled, he collected books from elderly Jews or their children who had no need for them, crawling in attics and basements when necessary to retrieve them. He made good use of his personal charm, extensive friendships, and connections with Yiddish-speaking intellectuals and authors to persuade them to donate their personal collections or to gift first copies of their newest publications to what his successor as YIVO's head librarian, Dina Abramowicz, later dubbed "the national library of Yiddishland."[30] Elkin's mammoth collection efforts—and his very personal touch in engaging with donors of all walks of life—anticipated the efforts of Aaron Lansky, the founder of the National Yiddish Book Center, decades later.[31] On the occasion of his death in 1962, *Yedies* remarked that thanks to Elkin's efforts, "The institution grew from an indifferent assortment of some 10,000 books to a systematic and practically complete Jewish library of over 260,000 volumes—now one of the largest in the world."[32]

Rapid growth in collections and personnel since 1940 soon made YIVO's offices inadequate for its purposes. Without much fanfare in an issue already overflowing with information, *Yedies* reported in 1943 that

Mendel Elkin and Peretz Hirschbein, Bobruisk, 1910. Credit: YIVO Institute for Jewish Research the institute had relocated at the end of the preceding year to more suitable premises than the cramped and dusty space it had occupied in the HIAS building on the Lower East Side. Money had been quickly raised among the institute's supporters, which included individuals highly successful in the worlds of building and real estate, to acquire a four-story, twenty-six-room building that had previously belonged to the Jewish Theological Seminary. The new premises, located at 535 West 123rd Street in prestigious Morningside Heights, not only possessed ample space for a library, reading room, and exhibits but also boasted an auditorium, a 150-seat lecture hall, classrooms, and offices as well as a fireproof basement for storage of collections.[33] On the day of the building's dedication, 14 February 1943, H. Leivick entered a new poem, "Yiddishland," into the registration book.[34]

Weinreich would later point to the new residence as symbolic of YIVO's rootedness and the beginnings of its integration into mainstream American, as opposed to immigrant, life. Its original owner, he noted, was Jacob Schiff, a German Jewish grandee who had "loved eastern European Jewish immigrants but looked down upon them as subjects of charity who needed to be helped to dress correctly, speak a respectable language, etc."[35] The move uptown—and away from the immigrant Lower East Side, with its array of Yiddish-speaking institutions and the heart of Yiddish journalism—placed YIVO in proximity to such patrician American institutions as Columbia University, the Juilliard School, and the Jewish Theological Seminary, which trained rabbis for Conservative Judaism and had previously occupied the same building before itself moving on to new, larger premises.

The institute also intensified its research and publications beyond *Yivo bleter*, the institute's flagship multidisciplinary journal dedicated to research in the social sciences in Yiddish. Its expanding roster of publications included studies by historian Jacob Shatzky about the history of Jewish educational policy in Poland (*Yidishe bildungs-politik in poyln fun 1806 biz 1866*), the first volume of Tcherikower's planned five-volume history of the Jewish labor movement in the United States, and the launching of a new journal, *Yidishe shprakh*, devoted to questions in the standardization of Yiddish under the editorial leadership of language scholar and educator Yudel Mark. Refugee scholars who had not previously been associated with YIVO or Yiddish were invited to contribute to YIVO publications,

Chana Mlotek née Gordon and Zosa Szajkowski on stairs in front of the YIVO building, 535 West 123rd Street, 1945. Credit: YIVO Institute for Jewish Research

even if their articles needed to be translated into Yiddish. Plans were also taking shape for a language textbook aimed at adult learners of Yiddish as well as a dictionary of the Yiddish literary language.

In order to sustain a full-time staff, larger offices, and expanded publications and activities, more money was, of course, needed than the

Amopteyl had previously raised to sustain itself and the Vilna center. *Yedies* proudly reported on fundraising campaigns conducted across the United States, Canada, and beyond by associates such as Elkin, Shatzky, and Mark Uveeler. The latter, who was manager of the Yiddish Actors' Union (*Yidisher artistn-fareyn / Związek Artystów Scen Żydowskich*) in interwar Poland, had been active in YIVO in Warsaw since the 1920s and served on YIVO's Central Board while a refugee in Vilna during the critical period of October 1939 to June 1940. Having escaped to New York, he resumed his work for YIVO in 1941 and replaced the recently deceased Feinerman as its executive secretary in 1943.[36]

At its 1944 conference, YIVO approved an unprecedented budget of $150,000 for projects that would include the conversion of its Research Training Division into an independent YIVO Graduate School for Jewish Social Sciences, the production of a threefold dictionary (Yiddish-English, English-Yiddish, Yiddish-Yiddish), a new edition of Simon Dubnow's *Geshikhte fun yidishn folk* (History of the Jewish People) in ten volumes, and the organization of the proposed "Museum of Jewish Homes of the Past." It proudly reported that $11,000 alone had been raised at the conference banquet and that "the most active members of the Society of Friends of the Yiddish Scientific Institute in New York" had pledged to raise a third of the annual budget.[37] Still, while YIVO enthusiastically pursued ambitious plans for the expansion of its activities in America in the early 1940s, it could not—nor did it wish to—ignore events unfolding in Europe. On the contrary, the shadow of war and news of the fate of their brethren haunted its staff.

The Destruction of European Jewry

Following the German invasion of Lithuania in the summer of 1941, YIVO in New York definitively lost contact with colleagues in Vilna. Its offices kept abreast, however, as much as possible of developments affecting Jews in occupied lands by monitoring the international press and through contacts with a variety of networks and sources, enabling it to obtain reports smuggled out of ghettos and camps by the Jewish underground and conveyed abroad. In this way, it was at times able to provide information about the conditions of Jewish life and death in Nazi-occupied Europe not readily available elsewhere. Thus, for example, *Yivo bleter* carried news of the erection of the Warsaw Ghetto shortly after Jews were first confined there in October 1940.[38]

The institute also took steps to bring the plight of Jews to the attention of the larger Jewish and non-Jewish intellectual worlds by translating reports about the mechanisms of confinement and extermination into English and other languages. Indeed, YIVO was one of the first institutions to inform the American public of the horrors unfolding. Much information about the Warsaw Ghetto in particular was conveyed in speeches and publications by Shloyme Mendelson, a member of YIVO's administration active on behalf of Yiddish secular schools in Poland. A former Ger Hasid who had become a leading Bundist, Mendelson had himself fled from Warsaw with the German invasion of Poland in 1939 and taken refuge in Vilna. When the Soviets took hold of the city in the summer of 1940, he fled, first to Switzerland and then to the United States, where he arrived in the summer of 1941 with the help of the Jewish Labor Committee. At YIVO's annual conference in 1942, Mendelsohn delivered a report about conditions in the Warsaw Ghetto that was subsequently distributed in English translation in nine thousand copies under the title "The Polish Jews Behind the Nazi Ghetto Walls."[39]

Hoping to rouse the broad American public to action on behalf of European Jewry, YIVO distributed information about Nazi crimes and an appeal to American academics, especially professors in the social sciences, not to remain indifferent to Jews' slaughter. Some 283 scholars, many prominent in their fields and few of them Jews, answered YIVO's call by signing a petition to the American president in 1943 asking him to warn the German people of the guilt that would rest upon it for generations "unless the hands of the murders [were] stayed" and to "apply hitherto unused methods to save the millions of European Jews doomed to death by the enemy of civilization."[40] "We cannot know the practical results of this," a farsighted Weinreich noted, "but many of these academics—who will play a role in post-war administration in Europe—knew nothing about the slaughter previously." YIVO also appealed to the State Department to admit more refugees.[41]

While saving Jewish lives could hardly be viewed as a partisan position among YIVO supporters at the time, these efforts nonetheless represented a clear departure from YIVO's prewar avoidance of lobbying and political engagement. Nonetheless, they affirm YIVO's position of addressing the problems of contemporary life through the mobilization of scholarship. Such interventions, necessitated by absolute desperation, likely saved few lives. But they helped familiarize Weinreich with government channels, knowledge that would prove invaluable when he began the pursuit of surviving YIVO collections across Europe. Nor was he mistaken that academics would play a key role as advisers and in administering aspects of survivors' relief and rehabilitation following the war.

The following year, at YIVO's annual conference in January 1944, Mendelsohn read aloud a paper about the desperate rebellion of the remaining Jews in the Warsaw Ghetto against German forces bent on its final liquidation in the preceding spring. His stirring account of the uprising riveted an audience hungry for information about the fate of its brethren.[42] More than two thousand gathered in Hunter College's auditorium, many of them committed secularists and atheists, spontaneously took to their feet when someone in the auditorium prompted Rabbi Leo Reichel to recite *kaddish*, the traditional Aramaic prayer for the dead. In the words of *Yedies*, "It was an incomparable and unforgettable moment when all felt bound to their tortured brothers in the ghettos and experienced an echo of the courage and the holy rage that travelled from the ghetto to YIVO's conference."[43] Some thirty thousand copies of an English translation of Mendelson's report, "The Battle of the Warsaw Ghetto," were distributed to prominent scholars, university libraries, politicians, and public figures. A Spanish translation was made available by YIVO's Argentine branch in five thousand copies.[44]

Later that year, *Yedies* published the very last dispatch sent by historian Emanuel Ringelblum along with news of his capture and demise. The dispatch was a description of Jewish relief and cultural activity in the Warsaw Ghetto transmitted by the Polish government-in-exile in London. Rather than flee Poland when he had the opportunity, Ringelblum, a member of YIVO's Historical Section and a founder of its Young Historians Circle, remained in Warsaw out of a sense of duty to his fellow Jews. He directed the covert *Oyneg shabes* (Sabbath Delight) project, the largest effort to chronicle conditions in the Warsaw Ghetto. Employing YIVO methodologies for the collection of materials and their analysis, the project documented the functioning of a massive network of Jewish welfare, educational, and cultural institutions that had existed since the ghetto's inception.

Even after escaping from the notorious Trawniki work camp, Ringelblum returned to Warsaw, where he hid in a bunker, along with his wife, son, and other Jews. There he kept working, writing about Polish-Jewish relations and Jewish intellectuals, until the bunker was discovered and the Jews hiding in it were arrested and murdered by the Germans in March 1944. When he sent the coded note days before his arrest, Ringelblum was certain that some 95 percent of Polish Jewry had already been killed. But he assured his readers in the free world, as communicated on the pages of *Yedies* in November 1944, that Warsaw Jews' efforts to survive in the face of impossible odds had been no less than valiant: "The watchword of the organized groups of the Jewish community was 'To live with honor and die with honor!'"[45]

The same issue of *Yedies* also mourned the loss of two more historians of Polish Jewry at the hands of the Germans: Majer Bałaban, a pioneer of Polish Jewish historiography and the only person to occupy a position in Jewish history at a Polish university prior to the war, and Ignacy (Yitshok) Schipper, a Zionist politician, lecturer in economic history at Warsaw's Institute for Jewish studies, and member of YIVO's Historical Section who also participated in the *Oyneg shabes* project.[46] Such would be the fate of virtually all members of not one but two generations of Judaica scholars in Poland, making the burden of carrying YIVO's traditions in America all the more onerous.

By January 1945, YIVO was obliged to acknowledge publicly the devastating extent of Nazi Germany's genocidal project, even if its staff was not yet in possession of more or less precise numbers and had not abandoned all hope for European Jewry. At its annual conference, Abraham Joshua Heschel, the scion of an illustrious Hasidic line as well as a rabbi and professor at Hebrew Union College in Cincinnati, offered a eulogy for the martyred Jews of eastern Europe and their intensely spiritual civilization. His now-famous elegy would be subsequently published in English translation as "The Earth is the Lord's." In its fall issue that year, *Yivo bleter* published obituaries, most likely written by Weinreich, for its own: thirty-seven YIVO staff members and associates—among them Zelig Kalmanovitch, Zalmen Reyzen, and Noah Pryłucki. Reyzen, it was learned, had died in Soviet captivity; the rest had been murdered by the Germans and their accomplices.[47] A more complete picture of the fate of the institute and its collections would not be available, however, until after the war.

With a measure of reluctant pride, Weinreich delivered the message at the conference that YIVO "brought the news to hundreds of thousands of people" about not only how Jews had died under German oppression but also how they had *lived*—how they had shown remarkable resilience in upholding prewar Jewish society and cultural life as much as possible and in engaging in various forms of resistance to the occupier. The unbiased study of all aspects of contemporary Jewish life—even in extremis—was a hallmark of the YIVO scholarly tradition, he reminded his audience, that distinguished it from *Wissenschaft*'s preoccupation with the past.[48]

The Call to Youth

Turning his attention to the future, Weinreich next addressed what he deemed the urgent need for YIVO to serve as an institute of higher Yiddish studies that would bring an English-speaking American Jewish youth largely innocent of Jewish knowledge, both secular and religious, closer to eastern European Jewish civilization. Secular Yiddish culture and scholarship would help American-born youth to overcome the stigma of Jewishness and to develop a proud, modern—that is, secularized—Jewish identity that embraced the cultural heritage of eastern Europe without jeopardizing the Americanness it held so dear. It would provide an alternative to what he described as the equally uninspiring poles of immigrant "Hester Street" and the de-ethnicized "Reform Temple" favored by Jews of German origin.[49]

In order to achieve these aims, however, YIVO first had to become known to American Jewry. To do this, it would need to address American Jews in a language they understood, both literally and figuratively, and to adopt American methods. Once they knew YIVO's goals, he was confident, American Jews, especially the youth who flocked to universities, would turn to YIVO out of enlightened self-interest.[50] For Weinreich, the primary difficulty lay not in the absence of a native-born Jewish intelligentsia or even a Yiddish-speaking youth in America but in drawing it to academic functions in and about Yiddish. As he put it, "There is a Jewish academic intelligentsia in America. We just need to approach it and ungentile (*oysgoyish*) it."[51]

Lack of prestige for Yiddish and Yiddish scholarship in the eyes of virtually all sectors of the American population, above all its educated elites, was the first obstacle to overcome. An American Jewish youth would gain respect for Yiddish and begin to comprehend the relevance of YIVO's mission when he heard of it from a professor at Columbia University, not from his father, an immigrant tailor.[52] Dispelling misinformation and negative attitudes meant making available general information testifying to Yiddish's status as a literary language with a venerable history, such as contained in "Basic Facts About Yiddish." Prepared at the request of the B'nai Brith Youth Organization for distribution among its membership, the twelve-page booklet surveyed the development of the standard language promoted by YIVO and Yiddish's use in various modern cultural spheres such as literature, theater, and scholarship around the world prior to World War II.[53] It also meant acquainting the English-reading audience with Yiddish literature in translation. Bilingual editions published by YIVO, such as one of selected writings by Y. L. Peretz in the translation of Sol Liptzin—an American Jewish academic who was quick to embrace YIVO's mission—would communicate the message that Yiddish possessed a world-class literature (only one volume, however, was published).[54] Similarly, the high caliber of Yiddish-language scholarship on a wide range of subjects could be communicated through the publication of select articles from *Yivo bleter* in English translation in a new journal, *YIVO Annual of Jewish Social Science*, beginning in 1946. Eventually, Weinreich would welcome too original contributions in English as well as the idea of a YIVO journal of original scholarship entirely in English.[55]

Anticipating the protests of those who would claim that the foreignness of the eastern European milieu of much of Yiddish literature would be an insurmountable barrier to understanding and appreciation, Weinreich recalled his own experience as a child in eastern Europe who delighted in the translated works of Mark Twain and James Fenimore Cooper.[56] With the appropriate intellectual preparation, any work of literature, including a work so saturated with religious concepts as Peretz's "Tsvishn tsvey berg" (Between Two Mountains) about the contrasting approaches to spirituality of two rabbinic luminaries, could be approached and appreciated no differently than the works of Cervantes or Homer.[57] Moreover, Yiddish literature offered the contemporary Jew, he argued, something that virtually no other literature did: It addressed both universal and particularistic questions facing them from a uniquely Jewish perspective.[58]

Indeed, the stories and essays appearing in the bilingual edition of Peretz's work, such as "Escaping Jewishness" ("Vegn vos firn avek yidishkeyt") and "Advice to the Estranged" ("Tsu di tsurikgekumene geyrim an eytse") about Warsaw Jewish "Assimilationists" (Jews who considered themselves "Poles of the Mosaic Faith"), were carefully selected for what was perceived by its editors—Weinreich, Charney, and Liptzin—as being of contemporary relevance to American Jews. As Weinreich explained to Charney, they were meant to de-emphasize internal factionalism, such as the rift between Hasidim and their opponents—the *mitnagdim*—and to demonstrate "the calmness, harmony and ethical value of eastern European Jewish life."[59] As with Heschel's eulogy for the murdered six million, a process was already underway of sanctifying martyrs and idealizing the lost world of eastern European Jewry as a source of inspiration, edification, and the reinforcement of ethnic identity among postwar generations. To carry on its mission, however, YIVO needed to do more than awaken sympathy for the world of eastern European Jewry and demonstrate its relevance to American-born generations. It needed to train the next generation of scholars.

The *Aspirantur*

The presence of so many refugee scholars in New York City not only made possible the expansion of YIVO's research program and the swelling of *Yivo bleter* with articles; it also provided the faculty for the *aspirantur*, whose launching Weinreich announced in late 1940. Beginning in the academic year 1941–42, YIVO's Research Training program offered tuition fellowships and monthly stipends to promising students with either four years of undergraduate education for the *aspirantur* program ($30 per month) or two years for the *proaspirantur* ($15 per month).[60] Modeled on the Vilna *aspirantur* named for Weinreich's father-in-law, the well-known doctor and Vilna Jewish communal leader Tsemach Szabad, and the *proaspirantur* named for YIVO cofounder and Bundist activist Borukh Virgili Kahan, its courses were also open to nonfellowship students and the general public, including teachers and supervisors in public schools who could receive in-service credit with New York City's Board of Education for select courses. In 1946, YIVO reported, "At present there are 11 research associates and fellows, two of whom are in Shanghai and one in Switzerland. An additional 26 attend only formal courses."[61] As in Vilna, the *aspirantur* was meant to cultivate a Yiddish-speaking intelligentsia that would serve not only as scholars but as communal leaders. YIVO academic staff members and affiliates offered weekly evening courses focused on the history of Yiddish, the Hebrew language, and eastern European Jewish culture and literature, along with Jewish history and Jewish social studies more broadly.[62]

Instructors included Weinreich and the linguist and literary scholar Roman Jakobson (Weinreich's personal friend from outside Yiddish circles who had come to international prominence as a professor in Prague in the 1920s after leaving his native Russia) as well as YIVO philologists Yudel Mark, Judah A. Joffe, Shlomo Noble, and Nathan Süsskind; literature scholars Sol Liptzin and Samuel Charney; historians Jacob Shatzky, Raphael Mahler, and Rudolf Glanz; art historian Rachel Wischnitzer, formerly the curator of the Jewish Museum in Berlin; demographer Jacob Lestschinsky; pedagogy specialist and psychologist Leibush Lehrer; and Hunter College economist Nathan Reich. Reflecting YIVO's new emphasis on America, an additional course was proposed in English in 1945 about the Jewish community of the United States that would provide "a comprehensive survey of Jewish life in America, including its origins, social and economic characteristics, ideological groupings, and patterns of organization, as well as its interrelationships with the non-Jewish American community of which it is a part."[63] But it was one of several courses that were canceled because of inadequate enrollment.[64] At the same time, YIVO held two courses in Yiddish—one about the "Foundational Works of Jewish Literature" and one about "Jewish Intellectual Thought Since 1700"—for a group of twelve high school students at the request of the Yiddishist youth group *Hemshekh* (Continuation), whose members included Weinreich's sons Uriel and Gabriel.[65]

The faculty of the *aspirantur* program devoted what little free time it had to preparing the next generation of researchers, often teaching at YIVO in the evening for a meager honorarium. Highlighting YIVO's financial straits in 1947, Weinreich wrote to Yiddish poet and World War II partisan Avrom Sutzkever, then a refugee in Paris,

> It is materially extremely difficult for the time being. In order to conduct the work properly up until now and not fall behind, we

> would need another five or so permanent associates, new typewriters, card catalogues, and so on. That is, about another $30,000 per year. To build up our work seriously, we would really need to double our budget and that would soon also become little. Instead, we struggle for a penny. Last year there were enough weeks when, in Vilna fashion, we couldn't pay wages and this year we finished with a $30,000 deficit even though we deliberated every time whether we should send a letter by airmail or not. Nonetheless, we will not let up as long as we remain on our feet.[66]

Most YIVO affiliates relied on full-time jobs elsewhere—often as teachers or administrators in Yiddish schools and cultural organizations—or, as was often the case, multiple part-time positions for much, if not most, of their personal income. Their willingness to spend long hours preparing lectures, writing articles and books, and teaching in addition to their other activities testifies to their commitment not only to scholarship but to serving the Jewish people and the so-called *yidishe gezelshaftlekhkeyt*. The term referred to Yiddish-speaking political, educational, cultural, social, and mutual aid organizations primarily outside the Orthodox world, where secular Yiddishism found little sympathy and where YIVO did not programmatically recruit supporters. These included the Bund, the Labor Zionist Jewish National Workers Alliance, the Workmen's Circle, "Jewish" labor unions such as the International Ladies Garment Workers Union and the Amalgamated Clothing Workers of America, the various streams of Yiddish schools, *landsmanshaftn*, and the Yiddish press and theater organizations.

The American *aspirantur* hobbled along as a systematic training program a few years before it was obliged to relax its standards. Students were expected to have a BA or its equivalent in addition to fluent reading and writing skills in Yiddish and the ability to understand simple Hebrew texts (these requirements, especially the Hebrew requirement, were likely not strictly enforced, however, since some of the students did not know Hebrew). In addition to attending courses, participants pursued research projects under the supervision of faculty members and received stipends of $30–$50 per month to enable them to devote thirty hours per week to their studies. The "Research Training Program," as it was known in English, was, however, not a degree-granting program, and its courses were not eligible for credit in American universities. Further, several of its candidates were abroad or obliged to drop out when they were called up for military service.[67] To retain students, the program began to permit participants to attend classes alone.

Ultimately, the *aspirantur* did not survive the decade. Like its Vilna predecessor, it suffered from a lack of funding and opportunities for the gainful employment of its graduates, who were encouraged to enter social work, become teachers in Yiddish schools, or otherwise work in Jewish organizations. But whereas young people in Vilna often clung to the *aspirantur* as a lifeline because of the stipend it offered, American Jews were less financially desperate and possessed opportunities for study and work both within and without Jewish society that their Polish counterparts did not. Nonetheless, the American *aspirantur* helped shape a cadre of young men and women, some of whom—including Weinreich's son Uriel, Joshua (Shikl) Fishman, Lucy (Libe) Shildket (later Dawidowicz), and Zosa Szajkowski, a young refugee from Poland who had fought with the Free French—went on to careers in Yiddish scholarship and played crucial roles in YIVO. Nor was this the end of YIVO's attempts to revive the prewar *aspirantur*, a goal that Weinreich did not grow tired of championing for the next two decades in the face of naysayers who believed it too expensive or too fruitless an endeavor.

YIVO's Finances

YIVO was gaining a small but expanding foothold on the American Jewish scene and beginning to rise in prestige in the eyes of both Jewish and non-Jewish intellectuals. It remained, however, still far from a household name and woefully underfunded to meet its ever-expanding needs and ambitions to collect, research, and publish as well as host public events and mount exhibitions of its materials.

Repeatedly, *Yedies* pointed to the institute's lack of financial support as evidence of what it saw as the anglophone American Jewish Establishment's neglect of the vital interests of American and world Jewry. To highlight the alleged moral deficiencies of American Jewish organizations, *Yedies* shared with its readers the diagnosis of its fundraising problems offered in *The Reconstructionist*, the organ of Mordechai Kaplan's Reconstructionist Judaism. Kaplan's understanding of Judaism as an all-encompassing civilization accorded well with YIVO's secularist understanding of Jews as a world people united by language, culture, and history as much as by religion. *The Reconstructionist* linked YIVO's financial woes to its self-limiting use of Yiddish, the distance of America's wealthy Jews and their organizations from the institute's culture and cause, and the "fact" that American Jewry was "allergic" to intellectual movements. According to *The Reconstructionist*, however,

> Whose fault is it? Will time remedy this deplorable condition? Is there any future to a movement which dedicates itself with such steadfastness to the building of Jewish dignity and self-respect?
>
> Who knows the answers? This neglect is a sad omen for the future. What will survive? Only relief, only Judaism as a Yom Kippur religion, only Jewish philanthropic enterprises?[68]

The bulk of YIVO's annual income came from fundraising campaigns and membership fees from left-leaning organizations and individuals, overwhelmingly in the United States but with additional contributions arriving from Canada, Latin America (above all, Argentina), South Africa, and Palestine (subsequently, Israel). Neither *landsmanshaftn* nor the Council of Jewish Federations and Welfare Funds, a national body to coordinate federated charities across the United States, committed the large sums YIVO requested in the 1940s and '50s. In 1947, for example, it requested $140,000 but received less than $30,000 from Welfare Funds.[69] Repeatedly, *Yedies* expressed its profound disappointment in American Jewish communal bodies—even if their contributions represented its second largest source of income—for donating only a fraction of what YIVO believed it was rightfully due as a Jewish national institution. Gifts from organizations or individuals for specific research projects or technical facilities, such as bookshelves or an elevator, made up a small portion of its income. While annual income did rise in most years, it remained well below $200,000 into the mid-1950s and was exceeded by expenses almost every year. Typical of YIVO's spending habits was the year 1954, when it spent $200,000—of which some 80 percent went to scholarly work (research, training, editing, and publications) and maintaining its library and archives—despite only bringing in $175,000.[70] The result was a mounting deficit, painstakingly laid out in annual reports published in *Yedies*, with no clear path to liquidate debt other than through increased donations.

As a result of budgetary shortfalls, the institute was obliged to abandon or delay important projects, including publishing the remaining volumes of the *Geshikhte fun der yidisher arbeter-bavegung in di fareynikte shtatn* after its second volume appeared in 1945. The plan to create a "Museum of Jewish Homes of the Past"—what would have amounted to a pioneering Jewish heritage exhibit or museum—was never executed for most likely pecuniary reasons, despite that thousands of objects had been collected.[71] *Yedies* worried that it would not be able to execute a planned history of Jewish life in the United States in time for the three-hundred-year anniversary of Jewish life in America in 1954 (it did not). Similarly, it noted its concerns about Yiddish-language research that needed to be "completed without delay, while the generations that absorbed the wealth and color of the idiom are still among us." Monographs to commemorate destroyed Jewish communities were also a priority that could not be executed without adequate funding. While not specifically mentioned in *Yedies*, to this brief list could be added numerous other projects, including assembling materials for research about the recent "great catastrophe," such as bibliographies of sources.

Despite the repeated discrepancy between income and expenditures, *Yedies* sought to impress on its readers that the recurrent budgetary goal of $450,000—more than twice its usual annual income—was neither an unrealistic nor arbitrary figure. Rather, raising it was a moral imperative, one necessary to conduct the institute's essential work while there still remained a generation with the requisite linguistic and cultural background to undertake this work.[72] More than a generation of Jewish scholars had been murdered, making for a cultural rupture between pre- and postwar Jewry, between eastern Europe and America, of unprecedented abruptness and profundity.

Weinreich pressed the case for financial support at YIVO's annual conference in 1950 even more forcefully by linking it directly to what he depicted as the existential needs of American Jewry. He rejected the idea of a smaller, more financially modest YIVO, as some urged. He argued instead that the fulfillment of YIVO's aspirations was an urgent necessity for the welfare of American Jewry, even if American Jewry had not yet come to embrace the need for Jewish social research in the YIVO tradition or to appreciate the role played by the Yiddish language and literature as a transmitter of Jewish heritage. "We are not tired of stressing," he elaborated, "the Yiddish language and literature, just as Kabbalah and Hasidism and Midrash and Gemara, are not elements of the past. They are for us not merely topics—topics could wait—but they are an approach: a prism through which we see that our addressee is the entire Jewish America and that building *yidishe visnshaft* is the immediate, urgent task of today."[73]

YIVO not only had an impressive record of publications in America, he offered. It had also experienced the tremendous growth of its collections—books, periodicals, images, letters, manuscripts, Holocaust testimonies, folklore, and more—thanks to the efforts of its researchers and donations by selfless collectors the world over who understood it as their duty to the Jewish people to send materials to New York, especially those items that YIVO could not afford. In fact, so much had YIVO's collections grown since 1940, Weinreich explained, that twenty or more full-time workers were needed just to catalog new acquisitions, to advise researchers visiting its library and archives in their use, and to publish collections of documents. Material from Vilna that the Germans had seized and that YIVO had subsequently recuperated (to be discussed in the next chapter) was itself of sufficient size to justify an institute of its own. But rather than expand its staff, YIVO had recently been obliged to let go of workers for financial reasons. And the remaining full-time workers—one archivist (Lifschutz) and two librarians (Elkin, Abramowicz)—were not only overtaxed in their proper functions but also seconded for other YIVO tasks of a purely technical nature. Meanwhile, a dozen or more finished or nearly finished studies remained unpublished for lack of funding, and important work such as that about the destroyed Jewish communities of eastern Europe could not yet be begun.[74]

It was therefore the duty, he concluded in his conference address, of all those present—of all those who understood and believed in YIVO's mission—to recruit additional financial contributors. Quite simply, YIVO's survival and hence the future of American Jewry—and with it, a world Jewry that would look to it for guidance—depended on it.[75] He presented New York as a new Yavneh, where according to Jewish tradition ancient rabbis created the first yeshivah to preserve Jewish learning (and thus ensure the survival of the people as a collective) after great calamity—the Romans' destruction of the Second Temple in Jerusalem in the first century of the Common Era. It was necessary for YIVO—the secular embodiment of the Jewish tradition of learning—to impress American Jewry with the scope and quality of its diverse activity in order to win its attention and allegiance.

YIVO did not limit itself, however, to exhortations of its constituency to increase contributions. One proposed solution, at least in part, to the financial woes of YIVO and of other research institutions concerned with American Jewry was to pool resources in what Weinreich called the creation of a "central clearinghouse for documentation and planning."[76] The idea was an outgrowth of a conversation between Weinreich and Harry Lurie, executive director of the Council of Jewish Welfare Funds, at a conference hosted by the Jewish affairs journal *Commentary* in 1948. Lurie had piqued Weinreich's interest with his comment that American Jewry's lack of interest in scholarship itself merits academic investigation. Together they organized a symposium in 1950 about the state of Jewish Social Science research in America under YIVO's auspices. The symposium brought together members of YIVO's Academic Council with other social scientists in the country and leaders of Jewish institutions interested in the organizational problems of scholarship.[77]

At the symposium, YIVO's executive secretary Mark Uveeler proposed the creation of "the proper milieu for the scholar—a centralized library and archives, a consultation exchange and clearing house, assistants, contact with scholars and communities on a world-wide scale, and the opportunity to earn a living in one's chosen field of work."[78] Not surprisingly, Weinreich, who wished for his institute to play a leading role in research about American Jewry, supported YIVO as the locus for such activity. Others present, including Harvard's Oscar Handlin and Nelson Glueck, president of Hebrew Union College in Cincinnati, were less enthusiastic about centralization, pointing to differences in approaches, techniques, and orientations between institutions. Ultimately, discussions held under the auspices of the National Conference of Jewish Communal Service in 1951 between YIVO, the American Jewish Historical Society, the American Jewish Archives, and Yeshiva University about centralizing Jewish archival collections did not result in the pooling of resources. Too much divided the institutions despite each wishing the others well; nor was any one institution willing to be subordinate to the others.[79] YIVO announced its own intentions in late 1950 to create a "Central American Jewish Archive" to gather materials about the neglected eastern European chapter in American Jewish history and to document contemporary Jewish life. But this initiative, which would have relied on the efforts of *zamlers*, seems to have been stillborn.[80]

Whither YIVO?

Despite its financial limitations, YIVO produced in the 1940s an impressive array of publications on diverse topics in the areas of modern Jewish history, demographics, sociology, Yiddish linguistics and literature, and psychology as well as works concerning more general topics such as language and race relations in the United States. It hosted exhibitions about aspects of American and eastern European Jewish life, including the Holocaust and its aftermath. Its public lectures, adult education courses, and other events drew enthusiastic participation and acquainted a broad audience with the latest in scholarship about contemporary Jewry. Four-day annual conferences—held usually in January—were more than professional meetings of academic specialists or gatherings of Yiddish-speaking intellectuals. They were communal events that routinely drew crowds well in excess of one thousand people (and sometimes as many as two thousand) to hear prominent lecturers reflecting on topical matters such as the recent Nuremberg Trials at their opening nights in Hunter College's auditorium. The opening night's orations as well as the more specialized academic talks given over the following days were discussed for days in the global Jewish press—above all, in Yiddish and Hebrew.[81]

YIVO also managed to transport the archives of its Historical Section, carefully curated by the Tcherikowers since after World War I, from France to New York City and to reclaim a large part of its Vilna collection of books and archival materials that had miraculously survived the Germans and Soviets. Its expanded archival and library holdings, enhanced through systematic collection and increased donations of materials, necessitated its relocation to a regal new home in Upper Manhattan. Further, YIVO's small staff of full- and part-time workers grew despite occasional layoffs, in part through the postwar absorption of recently arrived Holocaust survivors and their employment with government funding.

Among them were such future pillars of the institution as librarian Dina Abramowicz (1909–2000). A graduate of Vilna's Yiddish secular schools and the city's Stefan Batory University, she worked as an assistant librarian in the Vilna Ghetto Library (1941–43) during the German occupation before escaping and joining a partisan unit, where she helped care for the wounded. Following the war, Abramowicz joined her father, the Bundist writer and educator Hirsz Abramowicz. He was visiting the United States when the war erupted and was unable to return to his family (his wife was murdered in Treblinka following the liquidation of the Vilna ghetto). After working briefly as a librarian assisting with Slavic collections at Massachusetts's Smith College, she joined YIVO's staff as assistant librarian in 1947 with aid granted by the United Service for New Americans. With YIVO's sponsorship, she graduated with an MS from Columbia University's School for Library Science in 1953, making her one of its few full-time staff members at the time to have received professional training and accreditation in her field of expertise.

Known for her no-nonsense style, Abramowicz became an accomplished bibliographer and reference librarian who helped expand the institute's collections. Her intimacy with YIVO's long idiosyncratically organized collections and her erudition—especially in the fields of Yiddish literature, the Holocaust, and eastern European Jewish history and culture more broadly—made her legendary among generations of visitors to YIVO's library. Scholars, writers, and laypeople alike relied on her precise answers to even the most recondite queries.[82]

The institute drew not only praise in the Jewish press for its achievements and service to visitors, however, but also withering critiques questioning whether it was fulfilling its historic mandate. The extent of these critiques, which spanned the political spectrum, testifies to the degree to which YIVO was considered a public institution responsible to the *yidishe gezelshaftlekhkeyt*. Their critiques also reflect the porous boundaries in the Yiddish intellectual world, with many of the articles written by professional writers or journalists who were themselves engaged in YIVO activities or who sat on its various commissions and boards.

Complaints heard in New York recalled prewar ones, such as that YIVO neglected Hebrew, Yiddish's prewar rival for the title of "Jewish national language" and a language associated with both religious tradition and the Zionist movement. YIVO was also accused of discriminating against communist and pro-Soviet elements along with their schools and publications. These included members of the Jewish Cultural Association (*Yidisher kultur-farband*, IKUF) and of the International Workers Order, a mutual aid society that broke off from the more social democratic Workmen's Circle after World War I. The pro-Soviet daily *Morgn frayhayt* (*Morning Freedom*) charged "the old embittered Bundists" Weinreich and Shloyme Mendelsohn as well as Lestschinsky, Shatzky, Charney, and Liptzin with ignoring or unfairly evaluating Soviet Yiddish scholarship and communist contributions to the struggle against Nazism and antisemitism in their conference addresses and publications.[83] Meanwhile, *Morgn frayhayt* failed to acknowledge that both the Bund and Zionism had long been suppressed in the Soviet Union or the precipitous decline in Yiddish cultural institutions there even before the war.

Most of the dissatisfaction centered, however, around YIVO's relationships to eastern Europe and to Yiddish in the wake of the Holocaust. Some critics objected that YIVO had lost its way by devoting too much attention to the United States when its primary duty ought to be documenting and preserving the legacy of a murdered eastern European Jewry. Other voices, to the contrary, protested that YIVO should not dwell on the past and ought to make ever greater accommodations to an English-speaking Jewry both in order to remain relevant and to raise funds desperately needed for its survival among donors for whom Yiddish was a relic of the immigrant experience. And yet other voices complained that by moving to Morningside Heights, in using a snobbish "YIVO Yiddish" not readily accessible to the average reader (a subject for a later chapter), and in seeking to attract an uninterested American youth, YIVO had turned its backs on the immigrant "East Side"—the working-class Jews and labor organizations whose contributions kept YIVO afloat and who were the primary audience for Yiddish culture in America. In short, critiques in the press centered around the question of who represented YIVO's present and future constituency: eastern European Jews wherever they were to be found in concentrated masses, an increasingly English-speaking American Jewry, or those groups within American Jewry that explicitly supported Yiddish culture. Less prominently, they also touched upon the degree to which YIVO should devote itself to research or work of a more popular nature—such as exhibits and adult education programs—to meet the cultural needs of its audience.[84]

Similar complaints were also heard within YIVO. An experienced Yiddish educator in eastern Europe and New York, Yudel Mark urged the institute to leave work about American Jewry to more qualified parties and not to place such high hopes on drawing in American youth, since this was, in his view, a largely futile pursuit. At the annual conference in January 1946, Mark rebuked YIVO for not focusing exclusively on eastern Europe and the cultural creativity of eastern European Jews in other parts of the world as well as for contemplating compromises with English.[85] Asserting the primacy of Holocaust research, Mark argued that it was YIVO's duty to continue the kind of work that their ill-fated colleague Emanuel Ringelblum and others had undertaken in the *Oyneg shabes* project to chronicle life in the Warsaw Ghetto and to analyze the conditions of Jewish survival and death in extremis. Moreover, only by setting clear goals and sticking to its principles, not by Americanizing the institute in its themes and language (beyond issuing occasional translations of publications), would YIVO draw youth—to the extent that this was possible—to its mission.[86]

In a private letter to essayist and literary critic Shloyme Bikl, a member of YIVO's Board of Directors who criticized Mark's views in the Yiddish press, Mark defended his outspoken critique at the conference not as a personal or public attack on YIVO itself but as the expression of the collective will of members of the YIVO circle who disagreed with the "two or three people who have led it recently on dangerous paths."[87] Presumably, Mark had in mind Weinreich or Executive Director Mark Uveeler, both of whom supported building bridges to English-speaking Jews, although to differing extents and in different ways.

Weinreich was little moved by Mark's concerns, even if he had no desire to abandon YIVO's commitment to Yiddish or its past. With palpable irritation, he wrote to his son Uriel, then a soldier in the US army in Germany, that Mark sought to "erect a tombstone for eastern European Jewry."[88] Similarly, Shlomo Noble warned that Mark's perspective neglected the reality of a still-living Jewish nation in America and around the world and would transform YIVO scholarship into something akin to that of *Wissenschaft des Judentums*, which was built "on the ruins of Jewish peoplehood in Emancipation-era Germany."[89]

Mark's views were echoed, however, by those of Jacob Lestschinsky, who had previously expressed his lack of faith in a Jewish future in

America. Lestschinsky maintained that YIVO's main objective ought to be the preservation of eastern European Jewish culture and not the study of American Jewry or the promotion of Yiddish culture among American-born Jews. He also expressed dissatisfaction with what he considered an excess of philological studies by YIVO scholars when more important topics—presumably, historical and sociological analyses—awaited. Yet despite increasingly dissociating himself from the institute, Lestschinsky continued to work there until 1950 and to participate in its events. He eventually found his intellectual home not in YIVO but in the Institute for Jewish Affairs, a research institute founded and headed by international legal expert Jacob Robinson under the auspices of the World Jewish Congress and American Jewish Congress to study the situation of postwar Jewry and to secure its rights and freedoms around the world.[90] Ultimately, Lestschinsky fulfilled his Zionist aspirations by moving to Israel in 1959.[91]

Needless to say, such pessimistic attitudes, particularly when expressed by YIVO insiders, not only threatened to preclude a future for YIVO as more than an institute for the recording and study of the eastern European Jewish past; they also suggested that the institute itself should not continue after the passing of the eastern European–born and raised generation. The mission of YIVO would necessarily end with their generation because its language and values—above all, a sense of belonging to a national collective—could not be adequately transmitted to American Jewry.

In contrast, in 1950, YIVO's twenty-fifth anniversary year, the Jewish socialist party the Bund emphasized the institute's alleged neglect of the contemporary needs of the American Jewish working class. Since its founding, many Bundists counted themselves among YIVO's staff, associates, and supporters, contributing to the party's sense of ownership over the institute. "Under the pretext of scientific objectivity"—a reference to Weinreich's insistence on YIVO's nonpartisan position—YIVO had in America "compromised too often with its ideological principles." Not only did YIVO accord insufficient attention to the contributions of immigrant Jewish workers and the ideological founders of Yiddishism in its scholarship. It was insufficiently committed to the preservation and advancement of the Yiddish language and had failed to establish "sufficient contact with the Yiddish-speaking masses in the United States, with the Jewish Labor Movement, with the Jewish secular educational system, its teachers or its graduates." And yet, for all its manifold faults, the Bund declared, "[YIVO] still remains *our* Jewish Scientific Institute."[92] Ironically, the Bund, which did not shy away from the pragmatic use of Polish before World War II, offered its critique in English, suggesting some awareness of the need to use the language to reach a broader audience despite its criticism of YIVO for doing so.

The Bund's critique repeated prewar accusations that YIVO was an elitist organization that, in its attempts to remain above party politics, projected aloofness from the Yiddish-speaking working-class Jews who formed the lion's share of its constituency and the educational institutions they supported. Yet it failed to take note of some of the significant differences between the Yiddish secular schools in prewar noncommunist eastern Europe and the United States. Those in eastern Europe were full-day institutions and part of a robust and integrated network of Yiddish-speaking political, cultural, and economic organizations functioning in a Jewish society that was itself predominantly Yiddish speaking in all generations. Less than 10 percent of children enrolled in Jewish day schools in Poland attended the *TSYSHO* network of Yiddish secular schools closely associated with YIVO. Indeed, Zionist schools teaching in Hebrew (or Hebrew and Polish) and Orthodox schools teaching chiefly in Yiddish were more popular private options even as most Jewish children attended tuition-free state elementary schools. But at their peak in the late 1920s, some twenty-four thousand students were enrolled from kindergarten through high school in the *TSYSHO* network in addition to the Vilna Jewish Teachers' Seminary, where Weinreich taught. In many ways, the *TSYSHO* schools, which were harassed by state authorities for their association with socialism, provided a safe haven for Jewish life to flourish culturally and psychologically intact apart from a largely hostile majority culture in a time of declining economic and physical security.[93]

In contrast, in the United States, Yiddish secular schools existed only as supplementary schools and in the postwar era drew a shrinking percentage of Jewish youth, who were primarily shaped by American public schools. They were also divided according to ideological orientation into discrete networks ranging from internationalist communism (International Workers Order; other school networks generally avoided cooperation with it because of its support for the USSR) and social democracy (the Workmen's Circle) to socialist Zionism (Labor Zionist Farband) and nonpartisan Yiddishism (Sholem Aleichem Folk Institute). The schools reached the height of their enrollments in the United States with almost twenty thousand students (10 percent of all children receiving a Jewish education) in the mid-1930s but saw enrollments fall to about fourteen thousand by 1950 and to twelve thousand by 1961.[94] Even with the arrival between 1940 and 1952 of some 137,450 Jewish refugees and Holocaust survivors, many of them Yiddish speakers, the number of Yiddish secular schools was in rapid decline in the post–World War II era. This contrasted with the exponential growth of Orthodox all-day schools, including those established by the some twelve thousand *Haredim* who had settled in New York and were often intent on preserving Yiddish as part of the reconstruction of their prewar communities.[95]

Nor was it accurate to describe YIVO as wholly turning its back on Yiddish schools and Yiddish-speaking children in America. On the contrary, it invited students to its exhibitions, offered essay prizes, and supported the creation of Yiddish clubs in New York high schools. But in the postwar world, YIVO's educational outreach would aim above all at the university level (a subject for later discussion), and in contrast with Europe, school-age children were seldom a subject of YIVO's study. As Yudel Mark was painfully aware, the Yiddish secular school movement in America, despite its achievements in shaping Jewish identity and appreciation for Yiddish culture, had thus far failed to launch a significant cadre of youth whose primary language was Yiddish and who sought employment in the schools or Yiddish-speaking organizations after graduation. Indeed, even before World War II, a large and growing proportion of pupils had no knowledge of Yiddish prior to enrollment.[96]

A rather different critique of YIVO's activities than that of the Bund came from Polish-born historian Bernard Dov Weinryb, a professor at Yeshiva University. Reviewing an issue of the English-language *YIVO Annual*, Weinryb also found YIVO's efforts to awaken interest among American-born Jews a dismal failure. Most of the articles in the *Annual*, he pointed out, were translations from *Yivo bleter* that did not take into account the differing perspectives and intellectual background of an American audience. They were too focused on Yiddish language and culture to be of interest to an English-reading public, he concluded. Like others, he urged YIVO to concentrate its research on the "now vanished past in Eastern Europe rather than in the American scene for which it is hardly equipped."[97] But whereas other critics condemned what they perceived as YIVO's declining commitment to Yiddish and Yiddishist ideology, Weinryb instead emphasized what he considered the unavoidable problem of waning enthusiasm for Yiddish and Yiddishism in postwar America—a problem for which he saw no solution.

Yet in perhaps the most trenchant part of his critique, Weinryb reproached YIVO with having failed to uphold its commitment to *visnshaft*. Its research profile had fallen victim to budgetary shortfall, and its limited funds were spent on almost anything but fostering new scholarship:

> Administrative offices, maintenance of a library and archives—with, incidentally, meager salaries—fund raising, public relations, printing and publication, are actually the main expenditures of the organization. In some years minor sums from the regular budget were spent on research, in other years perhaps nothing at all. Most of the research workers from time to time associated with Yivo received stipends from outside institutions (JDC, United Service for New Americans, etc.) as refugee scholars. Or they were employed on some particular project financed by a special group (History of the Labor Movement, for instance). Thus Yivo became rather a publication organization for articles and studies written by scholars mostly on their own initiative and on topics in which they were interested.[98]

YIVO found Weinryb's remarks especially provocative, if not defamatory, to an institute that prided itself on its research tradition. The characterization of its publications as eclectic or haphazard, the work of individuals laboring without coordination rather than the fruit of a concerted research program executed by a collective, was no doubt especially perturbing to Weinreich, its research director. As was the case before the war, YIVO's main problem was not the ill-advised use of funds but the sheer lack thereof. But YIVO decided not to publish a rebuttal in the Yiddish press, as it was wont when it felt inaccurate or slanderous information had been published about it.[99] This avoidance of polemics showed unusual restraint for an institution that embodied eastern European Jewish culture, which perhaps valued contention more than consensus. It also perhaps reflects that this critique resonated at some level with Weinreich, who was disappointed by YIVO's research profile and scholarship, which he felt did not meet "Vilna standards" regardless of its impressive volume.

YIVO's Self-Study Commission

In late 1951, YIVO's Board of Directors announced the results of a self-study commission to determine whether reorganization and a change in focus were needed. Appointed to the commission were Weinreich, Charney, Uveeler, Lehrer, and other members of YIVO's Executive and Board of Directors. The institute essentially endorsed Weinreich's position, calling for YIVO in New York to remain the center of a world organization, to continue efforts to win new supporters, and to create a graduate school for the training of a new generation of social scientists and communal leaders.[100] It would endeavor to expand the scope of its research to give greater attention to topics related to Latin America and Israel while continuing to focus on eastern European Jewry and its contributions to newer centers of Jewish life.[101]

Indeed, while New York was YIVO's world center, by 1952 there also existed YIVO branches, committees, and Friends of YIVO societies not only in larger cities in the United States and Canada but also in Latin America (Argentina, Brazil, Uruguay, Chile, Mexico, Cuba and Central American countries), Australia, South Africa, Europe (England, Belgium, Denmark, and France), and Israel. These local bodies, some of which predated World War II, organized fundraising events, solicited materials for YIVO's archives in New York, purchased and sent books for its library, and held public events such as exhibitions (such as about the Holocaust) and lectures—often held by touring YIVO representatives from New York. At the same time, the American YIVO's publications made it to universities, Jewish organizations, and individuals in fifty-four countries, exclusive of the United States and Canada.[102] Thus, despite occasional statements and gestures to the contrary, YIVO remained in theory dedicated to the global legacy of Yiddish-speaking eastern European Jewry.

In practice, however, it was extremely difficult for YIVO to preserve its global character after World War II. YIVO relied on financial support coming overwhelmingly from the United States, including from Welfare

Funds whose main focus was American Jewry, and experienced pressure from its English-speaking environment. These factors, combined with the fact that YIVO scholars were most concentrated in the New York area, intensified tendencies to concentrate its activities on America. YIVO's branches abroad, which looked to New York for financial support it could not provide, were relegated to the periphery of its concerns.[103]

The exception to this New York-centric model of organization was YIVO's branch in Buenos Aires, which maintained contact with New York but remained autonomous after World War II. Serving Latin America's largest Jewish community, the Argentine YIVO established its own archives and collections, as well as produced its own publications, about which *Yedies* periodically reported. It served a Jewish community where Yiddish was proportionately much stronger than in New York despite its smaller size. This was thanks in part to uninterrupted immigration by Polish Jews in the 1920s and '30s and the dominant place of secular rather than religious institutions, including Yiddish schools, in the infrastructure of communal life.[104]

At the same time, YIVO continued to collect and accept materials about Jewish life everywhere, as reflected in the acquisition of Holocaust documentation from across Europe, including about non-Ashkenazic Jews, and the Ladino materials donated in 1956 following the death of Dr. William Milwitzky, a YIVO supporter and member of its Linguistics Circle.[105] Indeed, even if preserving the cultural legacy of non-Ashkenazic Jews was never expressed as an explicit goal, photos and announcements on the pages of *Yedies* throughout the postwar era, particularly the 1950s, reflect an interest in non-Ashkenazic Jewish communities in North Africa, Ethiopia, the Balkans, and elsewhere. These communities had often come into closer contact with Ashkenazic Jewry as a consequence of the recent war and immigration, particularly to Israel. Moreover, YIVO journals had never limited themselves to writing about Ashkenazic or Yiddish-speaking Jews, and this policy did not change.

If anything, the Holocaust and the birth of Israel affirmed for YIVO's staff, as for many Jews everywhere, a sense of interconnectedness and a common fate. Weinreich was himself deeply affected by the arrival in YIVO of songs written in Auschwitz in Greek and Ladino, and he wrote articles for the *Forverts* about Ethiopian Jews and the challenging encounter of Ashkenazic and Middle Eastern Jewish communities in

Israel.[106] *Yedies* published images in 1948 from its press collections of Jewish underground organizations in British Mandate Palestine, and YIVO's Historians Circle devoted a symposium in 1949 to Jewish life in the Muslim World that included a paper about the position of Jews after the proclamation of the State of Israel.[107] In recognition of the country's role in postwar Jewish life and its growing importance for many American Jews by the 1950s, YIVO invited Israeli scholars and topics to appear at its conferences and symposia, such as one about "State and Religion in Israel" held in 1952.[108]

Nonetheless, it would be a mistake to conclude that postwar realities and an intensified interest in non-Ashkenazic Jewish languages and cultures reflected deviation from YIVO's Diaspora-focused, Ashkenazic-centric worldview in a period when Yiddish remained the most widely spoken language among Jews and their largest concentration, who were overwhelmingly Ashkenazic, was to be found in the United States. At least in its official proclamations, YIVO envisioned a global future for Yiddish as a language that united Jews around the world. It was therefore imperative for YIVO to affirm its support for Israel as an emerging Jewish center while also expressing its hope that Yiddish had a future there. At its January 1948 conference, it resolved,

> We have full faith in the ability of Eastern European Jewish spirituality to create a new synthesis and to inspire the Jewish communities all over the world with Jewish creativity. . . . Fully conscious of the significance of this fateful hour, we appreciate the resolution of the United Nations that places Palestine on the threshold of Jewish statehood. Our hearts are with the Yishuv in its struggle to convert this decision into living reality. We are confident that in a free Jewish state all forms of Jewish culture will be able to develop freely.[109]

The "Coup" in YIVO

As impressive as its accomplishments in the 1940s may appear in retrospect—particularly in light of the circumstances—Weinreich was profoundly disappointed by YIVO's failure to execute adequately what he considered the institute's two primary functions: research and teaching. In his view, YIVO's relative neglect of these functions could no longer be justified by the exigencies of the war years and their immediate aftermath, during which it was essential to establish YIVO on firm footing in America and to reclaim what had survived of its Vilna collections. As he expressed to his friend Leibush Lehrer in 1948, he saw great opportunities for YIVO in America, particularly following an experience teaching Yiddish folklore and linguistics to graduate students as a visiting professor at UCLA that summer. "But," he continued, "I cannot bring YIVO to the level to do this work. And the way the work is going, I have a feeling that I am wasting my energy. That is the most bitter feeling in the world. And I won't be able to bear it much longer."[110]

Weinreich felt that he had neither time to conduct his own research nor the opportunity to guide others to do meaningful academic work. The consequence was that "a generation of young people in their mid-30s [was] coming up (of the type of Shikl Fishman and Hershl Gelpart) that any intellectual organization would welcome," but YIVO was neglecting the cultivation of heirs of its academic tradition. He also was convinced that spending most of his time with library and archival matters or proofreading *Yivo bleter*, which he felt reached an undifferentiated audience and did not stimulate further research, did little to promote the institute or scholarship.[111]

Dismayed by circumstances in New York City, Weinreich seriously weighed an offer from the Hebrew University in Jerusalem to occupy a proposed chair for Yiddish language and literature. He was very much flattered by the academic honor and relished the opportunity to train graduate students, eager to convey as much as possible of the eastern European tradition to Israeli youth. Coupled with the debut in 1949 of *Di goldene keyt*, a highbrow Yiddish literary and cultural journal sponsored by the *Histadrut* labor federation, a quasi-state agency, the proposed position represented for him the hope of a fundamental reorientation in official Zionist circles that would result in the allotment of resources for the preservation and promotion of Yiddish and other diasporic Jewish cultures in the new state.[112] Some twenty-five years earlier, an attempt to create a Yiddish chair in Jerusalem with funding provided by the editor of the liberal Zionist daily *Der tog* in New York had been defeated by an anti-Yiddish faction in the faculty.[113] Now, after the Holocaust had brought about the destruction of Yiddish culture in its heartland, there was a greater openness to the idea of a

Yiddish chair as long as it was not used as a platform for political agitation on behalf of Yiddishism.[114]

But after six months of negotiations with the university, Weinreich declined nomination to the position, citing his obligations in New York. Beyond a sense of responsibility to YIVO, he was deterred by the expectation of debilitating political battles that his hire as a former Bundist and ideological Yiddishist would likely occasion among the faculty in a Hebrew-speaking Zionist state. He also wished to continue his work on a comprehensive history of Yiddish—a lifelong project whose foundations he had laid with his doctoral dissertation in 1923—without the burdens of designing new courses and mastering a new language, spoken modern Hebrew, in his mature years.[115] His decision to remain in America made possible the hiring of Dov Sadan, a longtime Zionist activist and talented journalist and literary critic lacking, however, formal academic training. Under Sadan's leadership, the development of Yiddish studies in Israel assumed a more literary focus than perhaps Weinreich, a rigorously trained philologist best known for his linguistics contributions, would have chosen.[116]

Beginning in the summer of 1950, Max Weinreich took a leave of absence from his administrative duties at YIVO to devote himself to work on what would become his magnum opus, *Geshikhte fun der yidisher shprakh* (*History of the Yiddish Language*). So satisfied was he with his time away from the institute and the renewed pleasure of long days devoted to research rather than administration that he extended the leave for an additional year in 1951–52. As he wrote to his son Uriel, he had no desire to return to organizational work and was frustrated by the lack of money available for research purposes in YIVO.[117] Meanwhile, during his absence from formal duties, opposition to his return as research director hardened among his opponents.

Following further discussion by its self-study committee, YIVO's administration voted in 1952 for the institute's reorganization. Weinreich, who resolutely objected to proposals to change YIVO's English name to attract more supporters and pushed for the creation of a graduate school, was outvoted by the majority seeking to take the institute in a different direction. Feeling outmaneuvered, he resigned from his position as research director, and the position was replaced with a nine-member Committee on Research (*visnshaftlekhe kolegye*) that would choose projects and conduct research under the guidance of a coordinator serving limited hours.

Opponents of the decision in the Yiddish press framed this as little more than a calculated purge: under the guise of democratizing the institute's leadership, a mutinous faction had ousted Weinreich from his position because he insisted on Yiddish as the language of the institute's operations and privileged research and training above the expansion of archival collections and scholarly popularization efforts. They complained bitterly that YIVO had strayed from "the path of Vilna" embodied by Weinreich and the "old guard" of scholars active in Europe until the war, and instead embarked upon the "path of New York" represented by YIVO Executive Secretary Mark Uveeler. Seeking to attract nonelite and English-speaking audiences, Uveeler urged investing more heavily in publicity around conferences and holding an annual conference in English to accommodate the one-third of YIVO's membership he estimated was dominant in English. He also proposed reducing the number of copies of *Yivo bleter* produced and publishing a more accessible Yiddish journal since the average Yiddish reader, he maintained, resented that he did not understand the contents and language of *Yivo bleter*.[118] These policies, his critics warned, would lead YIVO away from research about eastern Europe and cause it to diminish the role of Yiddish, which they feared it would eventually discard.[119] One anonymous commentator even pronounced the "coup" as the definitive end of the Vilna era in YIVO's history.[120]

While there certainly existed tensions in the organization around its direction and factions gathered around Weinreich and Uveeler, the divisions were more of degree than of kind. No one in YIVO seriously supported abandoning its eastern European legacy or Yiddish. Nonetheless, its members were divided—at times bitterly—about how much to engage America and the use of resources. In the estimation of Joshua Fishman, long an intimate of both Weinreich and his son Uriel, the conflict between Weinreich and Uveeler was more personal than ideological and practical. Weinreich sensed that Uveeler, a highly ambitious and talented administrator with a showman's eye for self-promotion, sought to unseat him as the institute's leader. Weinreich was not only disinclined to cede control of the institute, convinced as he was of the rectitude of his own positions. As a scholar and acknowledged expert who had guided the institute from its earliest days, he also could not abide a nonresearcher dictating the path of the institute he had cofounded and built.[121]

According to folklore and music scholar Chana (Eleanor) Mlotek, who succeeded Lucy Shildkret as Weinreich's secretary after World War II, the sentiment was mutual: Uveeler maintained that Weinreich, an impractical scholar, was unsuited to direct an institute.[122] Further, despite their admiration for Weinreich as a capable administrator and brilliant scholar, many in the institute perceived him as domineering. At least privately, they reproached him with near dictatorial control of virtually all aspects of the institute's functioning—including policing the language of YIVO publications (to be discussed in a later chapter)—and his need to subordinate others' will to his own.

Weinreich, for his part, did not publicly complain about the turn of events, but his bitterness and disappointment were unmistakable. It is true, he explained to Abraham Golomb, a YIVO cofounder and the former director of Vilna's Jewish Teachers' Seminary, that frustration had led him to retreat from the "community council room" of YIVO to the "study house" to pursue his private research. He did not believe he could persuade "a circle of people unable to understand and evaluate logical proofs" of his conviction that YIVO must be foremost a research institute. Despite his disappointment, however, he was certain that he had made the right decision for the collective well-being of his community and for future generations: "Without scholarship, we will certainly not be a community." As he wrote his friend, now active in Mexico City's Jewish schools, "I am preparing spiritual weapons for those who will come [after me]."[123]

Weinreich's resignation as research director was not the only change contested in YIVO's organization at this time. The question of renewing the institute's lapsed sections also divided members of the Commission on Research, which had replaced Max Weinreich as the institute's coordinating body for scholarship. While formally existing in America, YIVO's prewar sections had effectively ceased to function as such by the 1950s, if not sooner. With the exception of the Philological Section, the other sections were decimated even if their leaders had made it to America. The full reasons why the sections fell into abeyance await, however, further investigation.

Philologist Yudel Mark was the chief proponent of the idea of renewing the sections, an act that he argued would intensify YIVO's commitment to research. But others questioned whether sections, which relied on a secretary to direct them and conduct their administrative work, had ever been a successful means of organization. Further, they warned that reviving them—which effectively meant introducing new structures—would only multiply administrative burdens for the already understaffed institute and unavoidably manufacture new conflicts within the Commission on Research itself.[124]

Rather than revert to its prewar model, the postwar YIVO relied primarily on the various structures that functioned alongside and gradually supplanted its prewar sections in order to fulfill its mandate of research and dissemination. Among these was the Y. L. Cahan Folklore Club, founded in 1948 by Weinreich's students in honor of the pioneering folklorist. The club, dedicated to collecting, cataloging, and analyzing folklore, hosted in its first year a systematic course by Max Weinreich about the history of folklore as well as lectures by such figures as Ruth Rubin, Shmerke Kaczerginski, and Mark Zborowski (then an assistant librarian in YIVO) about aspects of folklore. Active into the 1950s, it produced a number of publications, including a journal (*Yidisher folklor*) whose three issues featured songs, stories, Purim plays, riddles, jokes, children's folklore, and the like that were collected by its members or previously unpublished.[125]

Beyond the folklore club, the most important among these internal bodies were the informal "circles" of linguists, historians, and social scientists that held regular (usually monthly) meetings at which members presented their work for discussion among peers. (A proposed literature circle never materialized.) The first to be formed was the Historians' Circle, which was led from 1945 to 1949 by Mark Wischnitzer. A professor of Jewish History at Yeshiva University, Wischnitzer had arrived in New York in 1941 from Paris, where he had worked since 1938 as a researcher for the American Joint Distribution Committee after fleeing Berlin. Previously, he had served as secretary general of the German Jewish relief organization *Hilfsverein der deutschen Juden*.[126] Reorganized under the leadership of Philip Friedman in 1954 (who was in turn succeeded by Isaiah Trunk following his death in 1960), it remained quite active into the 1960s, organizing symposia that yielded articles for *Yivo bleter*.[127]

The Social Science Circle, dedicated to research about American Jewry, was the last to be formed in 1956. Its Executive Board consisted of both YIVO insiders, such as Leibush Lehrer, head of the prewar Psychological-Pedagogical Section, and rising stars of American Jewish sociology and social psychology, such as Marshall Sklare and Nathan Glazer. The prewar Section had relied on close cooperation with Yiddish schools for its research and large numbers of Yiddish-speaking children for its subjects (a resource that was regrettably not widely available in postwar America).[128] In contrast, the new circle studied primarily English-speaking adults. Perhaps more than any other YIVO circle, it drew participation from individuals active in both Jewish and general American academic life, a trend almost certainly nurtured by investment by the American government and universities in the social sciences—above all, economics, sociology, and political science—as a means to address social concerns arising from World War II and the Cold War as well as to develop policy for national development.[129]

While the Linguists Circle was not formed until 1952, its founding twenty members included many who were or would become YIVO stalwarts—among them Jean Jofen, Judah A. Joffe, Max and Uriel Weinreich, Chaim Gininger, Nathan Süsskind, and Mordkhe Schaechter.[130] Indeed, the character of the American YIVO in these years was very much shaped by the presence of so many philologists in its ranks, as is reflected in its extensive work on behalf of language research and standardization that remains one of YIVO's most enduring and recognizable achievements. Their presence is also reflected in debates about changing YIVO's name.

What's in a Name?

Weinreich vehemently objected throughout the 1940s and early 1950s to proposals made by members of YIVO's Executive Board to change its English-language name from "Yiddish Scientific Institute" to "Jewish Scientific Institute" in order to draw a broader audience of interested parties and financial backers. Such a change, proponents such as Samuel Charney argued, did not mean a change in YIVO's purpose but would emphasize that the institute's focus encompassed all things Jewish. It was intended to convey that YIVO was not exclusively concerned with Yiddish philology, as was often assumed by English speakers. The philologist Judah A. Joffe—who was among the founders of the Amopteyl—took a squarely contrary position despite his animosity toward Weinreich, who barely concealed his insultingly low opinion of Joffe as a scholar.[131] He testified that the choice of YIVO's English name by Amopteyl founders had been deliberate and not simply a poor translation. It was meant to make clear that Yiddish was the language of its operations and publications.[132]

Weinreich acknowledged that replacing *Yiddish* with *Jewish* would disentangle the semantic overlap inherent in the word *Yidish*, which means both "Yiddish" and "Jewish" in Yiddish. He also recognized that "Yiddish" was hardly conducive to fundraising because of its still largely negative associations among most American Jews.[133] But as he and others opposed to the change pointed out, YIVO was called into being foremost for the purpose of conducting research about Yiddish-speaking Jewry. Changing its name, while philologically justifiable, represented to his mind a capitulation to the prejudice that all things Yiddish were inherently inferior. It would be followed by the removal of Yiddish signage, such as *shtupn* (push) and *tsien* (pull) on the doors.[134]

Removing Yiddish from YIVO's name, Weinreich argued, betokened a radical reorientation of the institute, one which would lead it away from its historic mission as the academy of a global, Yiddish-speaking Jewish people and transform it into an English-language "Jewish Research Institute" focused on American Jewry.[135] Moreover, it would likely do nothing to expand YIVO's audience since it was YIVO's fundamental program—its emphasis on Jewish distinctiveness and the European roots of American Jewry—that was the main obstacle to finding a welcome place among the mass of contemporary American Jews. Above all, however, Weinreich warned of the ultimate betrayal of the institute's founders: the disappearance of "YIVO" from the institute's name because it served as a reminder of Yiddish. "YIVO" was for him not merely an acronym. It was a sacred inheritance from Vilna that expressed an approach to Jewish life.

Conclusion

While a new chapter in YIVO's history began with the transfer of its center to America, this did not mean that YIVO had yet become an American institution. In its earliest decades in New York, YIVO relied on a mixture of eastern European immigrants and recently arrived refugees for its vitality. At the same time, it struggled with financial deficits, a lack of qualified permanent staff to carry out its ambitious research and collection projects, and the chilly reception of much of American Jewry. It also wrestled with the question of its own relevance and the feasibility of translating its mission of diasporic Jewish nation-building and the pursuit of self-knowledge as a tool for collective survival into the idiom of its new American reality, literally and figuratively. Given the status of English as the primary language of American Jews and their self-conception as foremost a religious community, Yiddish could not serve the same role as Yiddishists had championed for it in Europe. But this did not mean that YIVO or Yiddish had lost relevance, Weinreich argued. On the contrary, he maintained that American Jewry, especially its younger generation, needed Yiddish and the scholarly tradition of YIVO now more than ever.

Following renewed debate between proponents and opponents of greater Americanization within the Committee on Research, YIVO did indeed change its name in 1955—briefly to the "Jewish Scientific Institute" and then permanently to the "YIVO Institute for Jewish Research," a decision provoking acrimonious exchanges in the Yiddish press.[136] A humbled Weinreich, who previously had a hand in almost all matters, kept at a remove from day-to-day administrative functions for roughly the next decade. The drastically reduced presence of the institute's dominant figure, who seldom took a break from work, had a noticeable effect on the execution of research. The Committee on Research, which replaced the office of research director, met usually once a month and exercised only loose control over projects. With Weinreich gone, there was no one present on a daily basis to oversee research operations, to provide authoritative guidance in scholarly questions that arose, and to ensure coordination between associates working on collaborative projects.[137] Deprived of its main pillar, the institute was, in linguist and archivist Chaim Gininger's apt description, "a ship without a rudder."[138]

But Weinreich never truly left YIVO. Nor did the association of the institute with his persona diminish in popular perception. Apart from teaching at City College, where he found stable employment as the university's first Yiddish professor in 1947, and conducting his private research (with the help of YIVO grants), he continued to sit on YIVO's Executive Board and helped organize, as well as participate in, its conferences and various academic projects for years to come.[139] Moreover, his opinions still mattered, especially to influential members of YIVO's Board of Directors, such as his friends Julius (Yudel) Borenstein and Leah M. (Manya) Eisenberg, wealthy patrons of the institute. He also had the ear of Leibush Lehrer, who became the secretary of YIVO's newly formed Committee on Research.[140] Mark Uveeler, in contrast, resigned from his position as the institute's executive secretary in 1956 to pursue a career working for the Conference on Jewish Material Claims against Germany and the Memorial Foundation for Jewish Culture. Eventually, Uveeler moved to Israel, where he assumed a position in the administration of the Hebrew University.

In retrospect, it seems difficult to imagine that YIVO (or Weinreich, for that matter) could have fulfilled so many mandates at once. But Max Weinreich was, as Mordkhe Schaechter later described him, a "maximalist" who believed that only by aspiring to the highest standards could YIVO make modest accomplishments.[141] Further, he was possessed of an iron will and deep conviction in the rectitude of his own vision. Even in the moment of his greatest frustration and in times of depression, he did not surrender the conviction that American Jewry—if only a small elite—needed to be shaped by YIVO to ensure that not only YIVO but the Jewish people would have a future worthy of its intellectually distinguished past. As he did not tire of repeating in public addresses, the survival of the Jewish people depended on the transfer to New York City of as much as possible of the spirit of Vilna—a spirit of self-sacrifice for the communal good and commitment to learning not only as a value in itself but for the betterment of Jewish life. It also meant reclaiming what remained of YIVO's Vilna past—its archives and library—and bringing it to America to unite it with the Vilna YIVO's other survivors.

3
YIVO AND THE HOLOCAUST

When the City of New York slated buildings on West 123rd Street for destruction as part of a plan for the construction of a cooperative housing complex, YIVO was obliged to relocate. With proceeds from the sale of the Schiff mansion in 1954, it purchased what had once been the residence of Cornelius Vanderbilt III's socialite widow on Manhattan's posh Upper East Side.[1] In all, some $480,000—a bit more than the amount paid by the City to YIVO—was spent to buy what the Yiddish press described as the "palace" on Fifth Avenue at the corner of Eighty-Sixth Street and to transform its ornate rooms into a research institute that could better accommodate YIVO's expanding collections.[2] Its impressive new home in proximity to the city's "Museum Mile" boasted twenty-five offices on six floors as well as eleven halls and rooms for use by the library, archives, reading room, conference room, and more. The basement contained mechanical installations, storage space for publications, and part of the archives.[3] One of the first actions of the "Vanderbilt YIVO" following its dedication in the summer of 1956 was the transfer of dozens of crates of books, survivors of prewar Vilna, that had been awaiting cataloging for nearly a decade in a local warehouse.[4]

The books' transfer highlights a tragic paradox of YIVO's history. The destruction of eastern European Jewry, the very civilization that defined its purpose, not only hurried its American branch toward self-sufficiency but also fueled the dramatic growth of its collections and strengthened its sense of purpose in America. The near miraculous recovery in the ruins of Vilna of materials concealed by YIVO associates, the recuperation of books and documents confiscated by Germans and Soviets, the seizure of incriminating Nazi documentation, and the collection of survivor testimonies and of materials produced in ghettos and Displaced Persons (DP) camps swelled YIVO's archives and library into the 1950s and beyond.

Recovering YIVO materials was no mean feat, however. It required Weinreich and his associates to engage in a complex mixture of salvage work, diplomacy, and sometimes legally dubious actions in the immediate postwar period, when laws regarding the restitution of heirless cultural property had not yet been firmly established. It also required mobilizing the assistance of extensive networks of individuals associated with YIVO or sympathetic to its mission. Weinreich rightly feared that even if Jewish cultural treasures were secured against widespread looting and destruction during those chaotic years, YIVO's property might be claimed by rival institutions or countries that did not recognize its claims to it. Efforts to recuperate the cultural treasures of eastern European Jewry were further complicated by the international rivalries of the emerging Cold War as well as the symbolic contest for cultural leadership of the postwar Jewish world between the United States and what would become the State of Israel.

Cataloging books and processing archival collections linked to the war took years and required special funding to hire additional staff that could not be covered by YIVO's meager budget. The materials made YIVO a world center not only for the study of the life and culture of eastern European Jewry—YIVO's founding mission—but also for the destruction of the entirety of European Jewry. Moreover, through their individual and collective scholarship, YIVO's associates helped lay the foundations of the contemporary field of Holocaust studies in America in a time before English-language scholarship gave much attention to the genocide of European Jewry. Above all, their experiences reckoning with the trauma reinforced a sense of shared identity among those gathered around YIVO and helped define the institute's agenda for research, publications, and public events for decades to come.

The Plunder of YIVO

A week after German troops arrived in Vilna in the summer of 1941, Johannes Pohl and Herbert Gotthardt of the Einsatzstab Reichsleiter Rosenberg (Reichsleiter Rosenberg Taskforce, ERR) arrived with a list of Jewish scholars and cultural institutions. Named for its leader, chief Nazi party ideologue Alfred Rosenberg, a Baltic German who had settled in Germany following the Bolshevik Revolution, the ERR's teams were deployed throughout Nazi-occupied Europe to seize valuable items, including books, archival materials, cultural artifacts, and artwork.

Looting was also conducted in the early months of the German occupation of Vilna by Heinrich Himmler's Reichssicherheitshauptamt (RSHA, Reich Security Main Office). YIVO's building, located outside the city's Nazi-imposed Jewish ghetto, was used as a depot and sorting grounds for materials seized from a number of Vilna Jewish institutions as well as Jewish and non-Jewish libraries and museums from throughout the region.[5]

The contents of ransacked Jewish libraries and archives were invaluable to German scholars engaged in so-called *Judenforschung*—research about Jews and Judaica conducted from an unabashedly antisemitic perspective. Jewish scholars, they maintained, had self-servingly falsified the historical record in order to present themselves to the world in a positive light. These sources were deemed invaluable for creating a body of scholarship about Jews, even if the books and documents needed to be treated with appropriate suspicion because of their authorship. It was the task of German scholarship to make judicious use of them in order to illuminate Jews' long history of "crimes" against non-Jews, who had foolishly emancipated this dangerous foe in European countries in the name of false humanitarian ideals. In short, scholarship about Jews and Judaism by Jewish authors was to be turned in Nazi hands into a weapon against Jews to justify German policy against them. Ultimately, what remained of the vanquished Jewish race would be its books, securely preserved in Nazi research institutions such as the Institute for Research on the Jewish Question, which sought to amass the world's largest collection of Judaica. Nonetheless, not all materials were to be preserved. The Germans designated up to 30 percent for integration into the collections of their research institutes, while the rest was to be destroyed—usually to be burnt for warmth or converted into pulp for sale to paper mills, thereby enriching German coffers.[6]

Dr. Pohl, a former priest who had studied at the Hebrew University in Jerusalem, served simultaneously as Hebraica expert for the unit and chief librarian of the Nazis' Institute for Research on the Jewish Question in Frankfurt am Main. Soon after his arrival in Vilna, he went looking for key figures knowledgeable about the city's Jewish book collections: Max Weinreich; the lawyer, Folkist politician and philologist Noah Prylucki; and the scholar Khaykl Lunski, longtime librarian of the city's famed Strashun Library. A Vilna landmark, the Strashun Library was eastern

Europe's first Jewish public library and known for its impressive collection specializing in Hebrew and rabbinic literature.[7] Weinreich was, of course, not present in Vilna in the summer of 1941, but the others were easily found. Pryłucki, a member of YIVO's Philological Section, had been placed in charge of YIVO and occupied the Yiddish chair at the University of Vilnius since the Soviet takeover of the city the preceding summer. He was escorted daily from his cell in a Gestapo prison to the Strashun Library to prepare lists of early printed books in preparation for their shipment to Germany. Pryłucki was assisted in his labors by Eliyohu Yankev Goldshmidt, a Yiddish journalist and director of the Ansky Jewish Ethnographic Museum in Vilna, with whom he shared his prison cell. Infirm after repeated beatings and abuse, Pryłucki was "liquidated" in German custody, apparently in August 1941. Goldschmidt was found dead in his cell not long after. Lunski avoided their grim fate for the time being but was pressed into service as part of a team of workers furnished by the ghetto's Judenrat (Jewish council) at the behest of the ERR to sort books and artifacts.[8]

The workers, many of them YIVO employees, were permitted to leave the ghetto daily to report for duty at YIVO. The spotless, state-of-the-art building on Wiwulski Street symbolized the institute's commitment to a modern, secular future for Yiddish-speaking Jewry. It had been a source of pride and tourist attraction for Jews from throughout the region since its dedication in 1929. Now it was converted into an entrepôt where the fate of cultural treasures was to be decided. At its entrance, where previously there had been a world map titled "YIVO and Its Connections in the World," the Germans had painted a German eagle with the inscription "Deutschland wird leben und deshalb wird Deutschland siegen" (Germany will live and therefore Germany will be victorious).[9] Herman Kruk, librarian of the Bund's Grosser Library in Warsaw prior to the war and now chronicler and director of the Vilna Ghetto's library, noted in his diary that "YIVO is dying; its mass grave is the paper mill."[10]

Led by poets Avrom Sutzkever and Shmerke Kaczerginski, members of the "Paper Brigade" risked their lives to keep the most valuable books, manuscripts, and cultural artifacts out of the hands of the enemy. The somewhat derisive sobriquet was given to them by Jewish guards at the ghetto gate because their work consisted of sorting and compiling lists rather than hard physical labor. Defying German orders, members of the Paper Brigade both engaged in passive resistance by reading books aloud rather than sorting them and in active resistance by hiding them. They secreted thousands of items in the attic and basement of the YIVO building itself, smuggled them on their persons for concealment and burial within the ghetto, or entrusted them to sympathetic Gentiles such as the Vilna university librarian Ona Šimaite in the hopes that they would be returned after the war or at least be preserved for the benefit of future generations of sympathetic readers.[11]

Some members of the Paper Brigade were also in contact with the Jewish underground, for which they procured books about weapons and even stored arms for transfer to fighters. Fellow ghetto inmates were bemused by their choice of contraband when others burned paper for warmth or smuggled necessary provisions such as food for physical, not cultural, survival into the ghetto. Not all among the workers approved of such methods, however. Kalmanovitch, for one, believed that items stood a better chance of surviving under German protection than being exposed to wartime bombings. He hoped to impress on members of the ERR the scholarly or even financial value of individual items in the hopes that they would be included in shipments to Germany.[12]

The survival of a large part of the cultural inheritance of Vilna Jewry is due to the heroism of the city's intellectuals, Jewish and non-Jewish, who risked their lives to preserve Jews' cultural heritage even if they themselves would not survive the war. Kalmanovitch, who died in the Klooga concentration camp in Estonia, did not err, however, in his evaluation: an even larger part of YIVO's collections survived due to Nazi Germany's obsession with studying a people and culture it had marked for destruction. YIVO's building itself was destroyed in a bombing, and the largest cache buried beneath the Vilna ghetto was discovered and destroyed by the Germans before their departure from the city. But hundreds of thousands of books seized by the ERR from Jewish institutions across Europe were discovered following the war in 1945 by the American army in the basement of the Institute for Research on the Jewish Question and various locations—including a cave, a castle, and a barn—in Hungen, some fifty kilometers northeast of Frankfurt, where the Germans had relocated them to protect them from Allied bombings.[13] Additional YIVO materials taken by the RSHA, above all the Vilna institute's press collection, were subsequently identified in a castle in Czechoslovakia by an agent of the Hebrew University in Jerusalem.

The discovery and securing of YIVO materials in eastern and central Europe was not sufficient, however, to ensure that they would reach New York City. It was not even guaranteed that these items would be deemed the property of the American YIVO. The restitution of YIVO collections was a historical drama that unfolded over decades, "in acts," as historian Bilha Shilo has aptly described in her painstaking reconstruction and analysis of these events. Fortunately, several works of recent scholarship, including hers, have reconstructed these rather complicated developments. They permit us to describe the main features of efforts to reclaim YIVO materials in the American zone of occupied Germany and in Czechoslovakia, a state reconstituting itself after dismemberment and occupation by Nazi Germany.[14]

Reclaiming YIVO Collections

By early 1942, Weinreich and colleagues in New York City had learned via underground sources and indirect channels that YIVO collections in Vilna were being transferred to Nazi institutions, specifically to the Institute for Research on the Jewish Question (Institut zur Erforschung der Judenfrage) in Frankfurt and the Institute for German Work in the East (Institut für deutsche Ostarbeit) in Kraków. Anticipating a future international process for the restitution of cultural materials, Weinreich lost no time in informing US officials of their plunder and describing the scope and character of YIVO collections in case they were found.[15]

Benefiting from the counsel of various parties working for Jewish organizations and the American government, Weinreich understood well that the restitution of cultural assets could be a very complicated and protracted affair. Without a state of its own, the world Jewish community lacked standing in an international legal system founded on the rights of nation-states. Therefore, it could make no claims as a collective on the cultural property of heirless murdered European Jews and of Jewish cultural institutions. YIVO materials were liable, he feared, to be returned in accord with the conventions of international law to their country of origin—either Poland, to which Vilna had belonged until the German invasion in September 1939, or to Soviet Lithuania, whose capital was made Vilnius until the German military arrived there in the summer of 1941.

Weinreich labored to demonstrate to American officials that YIVO's Vilna collections were not heirless, however. On the contrary, he asserted that the American YIVO was YIVO Vilna's legitimate successor. It was thus entitled to whatever could be salvaged of YIVO's European collections. Not only had New York City been declared the institute's world headquarters during the war; several of its European staff members had taken refuge in New York since the late 1930s, heightening the continuity between the institute's branches. Since YIVO's birth in 1925, the American branch had supported the center in Vilna with financial contributions that made up a large part of its operating budget. It had also collected archival materials and publications on behalf of Vilna. However, its role was not limited to that of a subservient auxiliary, he argued. YIVO scholars in New York had also contributed articles to and edited the institute's books and journals. Equally important was that the Amopteyl had been founded by American citizens, was supported by the contributions of American taxpayers, and was recognized as a public body under US law. Hence YIVO was an American organization, Weinreich maintained.[16] Historian and literary scholar Shlomo Noble (1905–86), assistant to the research director and *Yedies* editor, vividly expressed this continuity between the two cities in a different context. In an article explaining the importance of the institute for American readers, he wrote, "From Vilna to New York—in this passage the Yivo symbolizes the timelessness and universality of Jewish life and Jewish learning. Vilna and New York! Vast is the distance separating these two cities, and the bond uniting them is Yivo."[17]

After a lull of more than a year without news of the fate of YIVO's collections, Weinreich was roused in the spring of 1944 to seek information from the American government about the whereabouts of Jewish cultural property. Weinreich's intervention was precipitated by the publication of two articles in *The New York Times* relevant to the fate of YIVO's collections. The first article related that discussions were underway in Palestine to establish a central body to coordinate the retrieval of European Jewish cultural materials. It included mention of a proposal by Dr. Leo A. Mayer, Dean of the Hebrew University, to bring YIVO's library and collection, then presumed to be in Munich, to Jerusalem.[18] The second article offered the first news of Avrom Sutzkever, whose miraculous survival evoked elation in YIVO's New York community. A member of the prewar literary group *Yung Vilne* (Young Vilna), Sutzkever had been a member of *Di Bin* (The Bee), the Yiddishist youth group Weinreich directed until the late 1930s.

Sutzkever brought the devastating news of the murder of seventy-seven thousand of the city's eighty thousand Jews. But he also offered firsthand evidence that a portion of YIVO's collections had survived in Vilna, giving hope for the recovery of further materials there. Sutzkever had survived the liquidation of the Vilna ghetto by escaping through its sewers and was fighting as a partisan when his poetry, smuggled out of the ghetto and transported to Moscow, brought him to the attention of Soviet officials. He was airlifted to Moscow by the Red Army to meet with members of the Soviet Jewish Anti-Fascist Committee who were documenting Nazi atrocities against Jews. There he delivered news of the horrors that had unfolded in Vilna, as well as told the tale of his and his colleagues' remarkable commitment to rescuing Jewish and non-Jewish cultural treasures from the Germans.[19]

The September 1944 issue of *Yedies* shared news of Sutzkever's survival and the fate of its collections. A brief notice, "What Is Left of the YIVO in Vilna?," conveyed that while the YIVO building had been destroyed by the Germans as they retreated from the city, a portion of its collections had escaped this fate—either because items had been dispatched to Germany or because they had been buried by the Paper Brigade. It cited Sutzkever, who shared that he and a small group of other Jews had returned to the site of the ghetto and unearthed what remained of the materials they had concealed there.[20]

Sutzkever also managed to send proof of the survival of Vilna Jewish materials to Weinreich personally in New York a few months later. He used the occasion of an interview with Ella Winter, a pro-Soviet correspondent for the *New York Post*, in Moscow that December to recruit the reporter's assistance in conveying a package to his mentor. Once contacted by Winter, Weinreich ran to meet her personally, intuitively understanding what the package she bore likely contained. In January 1945, in the presence of his YIVO colleagues Mendel Elkin, Jacob Shatzky, and Leibush Lehrer, he carefully unwrapped the envelope containing a document from Simon Dubnow's archive, an issue of the newsletter

Avrom Sutzkever stands beside the ruins of YIVO in Vilna, 1945. Credit: YIVO Institute for Jewish Research

of the Vilna ghetto administration, and other items whose survival—a symbol of continuity with a world lost—inspired reverent tears among them. The envelope also contained a note from Sutzkever informing of the death of Weinreich's mother-in-law, Stefania Szabad, noting that she had died in her bed—a fiction most likely intended to spare the Weinreich family further pain. (Stefania Szabad had actually been deported to Maidanek, a fact likely already known to Weinreich through Warsaw channels. As a US Army soldier in Germany later that year, his son Uriel began a poem, "I came to Germany to avenge my tortured grandmother.")[21] Fearful that drawing attention to Sutzkever's relationship with YIVO in New York, an American institution, would imperil him in the Soviet Union, Weinreich cautiously refrained from writing to him in Moscow.[22]

While news of Sutzkever's survival and feats was very much welcome, the interest expressed in Palestine in YIVO's collections was cause for profound concern. It reflected yet another question that would complicate

Leibush Lehrer. Credit: YIVO Institute for Jewish Research

the restitution process: who was entitled to speak on behalf of a murdered European Jewry and represented its legitimate heir? Surviving Jewish communities in Europe could be expected to assert claims to cultural property. Meanwhile, the *yishuv*, the six-hundred-thousand-person-strong Jewish community of Palestine, believed that it represented the natural and most suitable home for the remnants of European Jewish life—including its cultural patrimony—in fulfillment of the ideal of *kibbutz ha-galuyot*, the ingathering of the dispersed Jewish people from around the world.[23] As the academic instantiation of the Zionist interpretation of Jewish history, the Hebrew University represented the main rival to YIVO's Diaspora Nationalist conception despite good relations between scholars in the institutions. Acquiring surviving European Jewish collections would further cement the Zionist claim to constituting the rightful inheritor of prewar Diaspora Jewry, a claim that YIVO obviously contested.

At the Yalta Conference, held in the Crimea in February 1945, leaders of the "Big Three" Powers—America, the USSR, and Britain—agreed to divide a Germany near defeat into American, Soviet, British, and French occupation zones. In the ensuing months, Allied soldiers advanced across Germany from east and west, culminating in its unconditional surrender on 8 May 1945. By mid-April 1945, the media carried news of the discovery of cultural treasures secreted in castles and neighboring buildings near Frankfurt. Writing to American officials in Washington in early 1945, Weinreich described the destruction and plunder of YIVO's collections by the Germans in Vilna and called for Jewish cultural assets to be transported to the safety of the democratic United States, where they could be properly cared for and made accessible to researchers.[24]

In June 1945, encouraging news reached YIVO from an American military chaplain. Rabbi Abraham Aaroni, a YIVO supporter, wrote his wife that he had found part of its Vilna library in Frankfurt. He saw what he estimated were one thousand boxes filled with volumes from private libraries and a number of institutions, including those of YIVO, the École Rabbinique in France, the Rabbinical Seminary of Amsterdam, and the Jewish student organization of the University of Königsberg. Additional sightings of YIVO books were reported by American soldiers with ties to the institute, including Zosa Szajkowski. Confirmation subsequently arrived from the State Department that a significant part of YIVO's library had indeed been recovered in the American zone.[25]

Rescuing Materials in Vilna

Following Vilna's liberation by the Red Army in July 1945, six surviving members of the Paper Brigade returned to the city. Led by Avrom Sutzkever and Shmerke Kaczerginski, a fellow member of *Yung Vilne* and partisan, they began the difficult work of salvaging whatever was possible of Jews' cultural legacy—reclaiming materials entrusted to Gentiles for safekeeping and locating and excavating buried caches that had not been destroyed by the Germans or Allied bombs. Working closely with Abba Kovner, a socialist Zionist and partisan leader, they created what would effectively become the world's first Holocaust museum. The Museum of Jewish Art and Culture was subsequently renamed the "Commission to Collect and Process Documents of Jewish Culture" when approval for a museum was not forthcoming from Soviet Lithuanian officials. It was, however, in many ways more of an archive, library, and research institute than a museum devoted to conventional displays, although these were also part of its work. Though lacking a budget, its staff collected whatever remnants it could of Jewish cultural life in the destroyed Jerusalem of Lithuania as well as eyewitness testimonies and documentation relevant to recording the recent genocide and prosecuting war criminals.[26]

Within months, however, it became clear that Soviet policy dictated in Moscow would not tolerate indefinitely an independent Jewish cultural life in Lithuania despite the continued existence of the Jewish Anti-Fascist Committee and a Yiddish press in Moscow. Book and newspaper publication in Yiddish was prohibited in Soviet Lithuania, and the local Jewish school was harassed and eventually restricted to teaching only to the fourth grade, with the expectation that Jewish children would thereafter study in Russian or Lithuanian. Soviet ideology encouraged Jews' assimilation into one of the dominant cultures of the region or their relocation to Birobidzhan, the Jewish autonomous oblast created by Soviet authorities in faraway central Asia, where relatively few Jews actually resided. The increasing administrative ill will that met Sutzkever and Kaczerginski, a convinced communist, in response to their petitions to Soviet Lithuanian officials caused them to fear that the museum, which focused on the unique experience of Jews during the German occupation, would be shut down as an expression of bourgeois Jewish nationalism and its contents confiscated. They consequently worked hard to find practical solutions to ensure that the museum would continue to function in the face of bureaucratic obstructionism.[27]

At the same time, Jews were beginning to leave Vilna, including members of the Paper Brigade and Abba Kovner, who was involved in *Bricha*, the clandestine transfer of Jews to Palestine in defiance of British immigration restrictions. Over a million Jews had taken refuge in or been exiled to the Soviet interior as "hostile" parties in the framework of general Soviet policy in the course of the war. Citizens of prewar Poland were granted a limited window for return there. Fearful of anti-Jewish violence and pessimistic about their future under Soviet rule, some 175,000 Jews took advantage of the opportunity between 1944 and 1948 for repatriation from Soviet held territory. Most would eventually make their way to Germany, where some two hundred thousand Jews lived in DP camps awaiting an opportunity for emigration. The American occupation zone would prove the safest place for Jews in postwar Europe.[28]

Sutzkever and Kaczerginski again risked their lives as it became all too clear to them that Jewish cultural treasures were once more in danger of disappearing into warehouses or, worse, being destroyed—this time on Soviet orders. Such was the case when some thirty tons of paper reclaimed from the ruins of the city's ghetto—archival materials, manuscripts from YIVO's autobiographical contests, Yiddish plays, books, and more, making up but a small part of the surviving heritage of YIVO and Vilna Jewry—were sent by the local trash administration to a paper mill for recycling. Sutzkever and Kaczerginski's pleas to officials in Vilna and Moscow to reverse this callous decision, which was justified by a lack of space to store them, were to no avail. Consequently, they began surreptitiously sending packets of materials from the museum both to Weinreich in New York and to the Hebrew University in Jerusalem, entrusting them to the personal care of Jews departing for Poland and agents of the Zionist underground directing Jews to Palestine. Some of the items they recovered had belonged to the collections of the prewar YIVO; others had belonged to private individuals, other institutions, or had been produced in the Vilna Ghetto itself during the war.[29]

When tipped off by a colleague at the museum of his imminent arrest by Soviet officials, Kaczerginski fled in November 1945 to Poland, where many survivors were already gathering in Łódź. Sutzkever followed suit in May 1946 and then continued on to Paris, where he could send materials more freely and via regular post. By smuggling books and papers out of Vilna on their own persons or entrusting packets of materials to couriers, Kaczerginski and Sutzkever managed to convey a large portion of the materials they had unearthed or collected to Weinreich in New York by August 1947.[30]

Sutzkever and Kaczerginski's alarm about the future of the museum and its collections proved justified. The museum created by Jewish survivors in Vilna to document their wartime experiences and commemorate the destroyed world of the region's Jews was definitively closed by Soviet authorities in 1949. Its dissolution was linked by this time to the larger Soviet policy of anti-Zionism, despite that most of its contents had little, if anything, to do with Zionism. The Soviet Union and its allies had been among the first countries to approve the partition of Palestine into Arab and Jewish states in the United Nations in 1947 and to recognize the new State of Israel the following year—largely because Stalin saw in it a potential ally and thorn in British Middle East policy. In Stalin's paranoid and calculating worldview, however, widespread enthusiasm expressed by Soviet Jews for the creation of the Jewish state was a provocation, an indication of disloyalty to the Soviet fatherland. All manifestations of Jewish culture, including the Jewish Anti-Fascist Committee and the remaining Yiddish press, were to be liquidated as expressions of Jewish national chauvinism or as tools of Zionism, which was itself condemned as a tool of American espionage. Hundreds of Jewish cultural activists were arrested for treason; some were executed, including members of the Jewish Anti-Fascist Committee (leading Yiddish cultural figures were later executed in 1952 following a show trial, an event commemorated annually as the infamous "Night of the Murdered Yiddish Poets"). The largest part of the Vilna Jewish Museum's materials—books and documents—were dispatched to the Lithuanian National Book Chamber, where knowledge of their existence remained a tightly guarded secret among the staff for decades to come. Thus, unbeknownst to YIVO in New York, some fifty thousand Jewish books, hundreds of periodical sets, and about 170 boxes of documents—chiefly materials from the Jewish Museum but also materials collected by devoted staff members in Vilnius and across a Lithuanian countryside now depleted of Jews—were gathered in a former church that belonged to the Book Chamber for protective concealment.[31]

Yedies acknowledged the rescue of materials—including manuscripts and rare books, both religious and secular—from Vilna. In particular, it drew attention to the recovery of Theodor Herzl's diary and the wartime diaries of YIVO leader and administrator Zelig Kalmanovitch and of Herman Kruk, the librarian of the Vilna Ghetto.[32] Kruk's diary had special meaning not only as an invaluable chronicle of Jewish life in the days of destruction but also because its author was the brother of YIVO board member Pinchos Schwartz, an adopted name for Shmuel Kruk (Schwartz later succeeded Mark Uveeler as YIVO's executive secretary from 1955 until 1963). Both wartime diaries were later published with introductions and notes by YIVO.[33] The gripping story of how these items were recovered and subsequently smuggled to New York was initially concealed, however, and in fact would not be reconstructed and revealed in full for decades. Not only did Sutzkever and Kaczerginski fear that drawing attention to their role would result in charges of complicity being leveled at remaining museum employees. Publicizing the connection between the two men and the institute, Weinreich worried, raised the danger of Soviet interference in YIVO's attempts to reclaim its materials discovered in the German zone or elsewhere. In the summer of 1948—a year after it had regained most of what it could from its collections—YIVO did publicly acknowledge, albeit without much fanfare, the role of the partisan poets by announcing the "Abraham Sutzkever-Shmerke Kaczerginski Historical Collection" of prewar materials retrieved from caches and items created during the years bearing on life in the Vilna Ghetto.[34]

The Restoration of YIVO's Library

Weinreich engaged every connection at his disposal to assist him in his efforts to locate and regain YIVO materials. He wrote to officials in the US government and military agencies and established contact with Jewish bodies such as the American Jewish Committee. He also mobilized the assistance of sympathetic parties across Europe, including US servicemen with ties to YIVO. He asked them not only to be on the lookout for YIVO materials but also to procure Nazi documentation and German books that would be useful to it. At a time when the seizure of German books and documents, while technically forbidden by American authorities, was widely tolerated, Weinreich was eager for YIVO to gain as much material relevant to the wartime experiences of Jews as possible, not to mention incriminating German documentation. He also desired to acquire for YIVO surviving books and Judaica collections that were not necessarily part of its prewar collection. This included his own personal collection and others from Vilna that had been integrated into YIVO but had not yet been cataloged.

Weinreich felt particularly indebted to Zosa Szajkowski (the pen name of Polish-born Szajke Frydman), who was accepted to YIVO's *aspirantur* for 1938 to 1939 under a special agreement permitting him to work from Paris under Elias Tcherikower's supervision. Szajkowski had fought first with the Free French and then, after coming to the United States as a refugee in 1941, joined the American *aspirantur*. He was, however, impatient to rejoin the fight and volunteered for the US Army, where he served as a paratrooper and translator. When he returned to Europe in an American military uniform, he possessed the explicit goal of collecting materials of historical-cultural value. These included a large portion of the archives of YIVO's Historical Section that he had hidden in France on behalf of his friend and mentor Tcherikower during the war, which he subsequently recuperated and had shipped in crates to YIVO in New York with the help of the American army. Szajkowski also gained access to a trove of Nazi publications and archival documents, many of them classified, that had been captured by American forces.[35]

In a letter to Weinreich, Szajkowski described his daily work on behalf of YIVO in mid-September 1945:

> I haven't written you in a few days but, forgive me, I was busy sending books and documents for YIVO. The day before yesterday I sent ten big and small packages. Yesterday another six and today I am sending another few. In the packages that I sent there is a rich collection of Nazi publications about the Baltic countries. In a separate package, I sent the anti-Jewish bulletin from Vilna (purchased from a German for a piece of chocolate, a pack of chewing gum, and two cigarettes). The bulletin is a bit wet. So when you receive it, you should dry it immediately. Other books are also a bit wet.
>
> Of all the affairs—sending books is not one of the easiest things. They aren't lying on shelves but in destroyed buildings. A few days ago, I almost broke a foot crawling in the ruins of the Ministry of

> Propaganda. But the hardest thing is bringing the books home and then to the post office.[36]

Weinreich expressed tremendous gratitude to Szajkowski for rummaging in the ruins of Berlin on YIVO's behalf in his free time. From there, he hoped Szajkowski would be able to travel throughout Europe in further pursuit of books and documents to send to New York. He cautioned Szajkowski to keep his eyes open for books not readily identifiable as belonging to YIVO because they lacked the institute's ex libris stamp, but he did not provide a comprehensive list of collections:

> Keep in mind that from the beginning of the war (until June 1941), a large number of private libraries came over to YIVO, although they probably didn't manage to inventory them. Among them is the private library of the undersigned—more than 6,000 books (apart from manuscripts and photostats), including series of dictionaries, periodicals, and so on.
>
> All that must, of course, come back to us—the sooner, the better.[37]

By the spring of 1946, Weinreich learned that Jewish books found in the American Occupation Zone had been transferred by the US Army to a depot in Offenbach in the vicinity of Frankfurt under the authority of the Office of Military Government of the United States (OMGUS). Appropriate steps to preserve, sort, and catalog them were to be undertaken at the Offenbach Archival Depot (OAD) by the experts of the Monuments, Fine Arts and Archives (MFA&A), specialists in art, archives, and libraries attached to field commands. Millions of volumes stolen from over four thousand libraries and private collections across Europe awaited restitution there.[38] At Weinreich's request, the American Jewish Committee wrote to Secretary of State Burnes on YIVO's behalf, and Rabbi Judah Nadich, General Eisenhower's adviser on Jewish affairs in Europe, wrote directly to the General. "We can't know what the reaction will be," Weinreich wrote to Uriel, then a US Army soldier in Germany, "but there can't be any better pull (*protektsye*)."[39]

As noted previously, many YIVO books lacked its ex libris. Chronic underfunding and understaffing meant that YIVO had not been able to catalog all its holdings even prior to the war. Moreover, the American YIVO's claim even to books and documents readily identifiable as belonging to YIVO's Vilna collections had still not been accepted by US authorities. It was thus imperative for Weinreich to represent YIVO in the Commission on European Jewish Cultural Reconstruction (subsequently established as Jewish Cultural Reconstruction Inc.—JCR—in 1947), a consortium whose purpose was to collect and redistribute heirless Jewish cultural property found in the American zone of occupied Germany. Founded in 1944, it included representatives of the World Jewish Congress, American Jewish Committee, the Hebrew University, and other major Jewish groups. Apart from Weinreich, who sat on its advisory board, its membership included such leading Jewish intellectuals as Salo Baron, the eminent professor of Jewish history at Columbia University who led the Commission, and the political theorist Hannah Arendt, who had herself fled Nazi Germany in 1933.[40]

The Commission sought recognition by the United States government as a trustee responsible for all Jewish books, manuscripts, and ritual objects found in the American occupation zone of Germany on behalf of a global Jewish people. One of the Commission's first tasks was to draw up a list of cultural treasures that had been pilfered by the Germans in order to facilitate their location and identification. According to the information compiled by YIVO's staff for the "Tentative List of Cultural Treasures in Axis-Occupied Countries" published by the Commission, prior to the outbreak of war in 1939 the institute possessed eighty-five thousand books (of which only twenty thousand had been cataloged), seventy-five thousand handwritten documents in manuscripts, over one hundred thousand folklore items, and over fourteen thousand volumes of Jewish periodicals in various languages.[41]

While the Commission aimed to distribute items to Jewish communities around the world, it resolutely opposed returning Jewish cultural property to Germany, which it maintained had forfeited its moral right to care for Jewish cultural property, and to Poland, whose Jewish community had been decimated and whose future viability was in question. Indeed, Jews who had emerged from hiding there or returned after the war were fleeing the country in droves after a pogrom in Kielce in July 1946 took the lives of forty-two Jews and injured forty more.[42]

Despite his membership in the Commission, Weinreich was loath to see YIVO collections entrusted to it alongside books belonging to heirless institutions and private individuals. This could delay their return to YIVO until a general restitution policy was formulated for the American zone—or worse, it could lead to their being assigned to other institutions. In his communications with American government and military authorities, Weinreich insisted that the restitution of YIVO possessions represented a clear-cut case of returning property to its rightful owner and should therefore be treated separately from the fate of the 1.5 million books in Jewish languages and on Jewish themes gathered at Offenbach.[43] While the State Department eventually recognized YIVO's exclusive claim to its Vilna collections, the US War Department was unwilling to deviate from the policy of restitution to nation-states rather than individual owners or organizations. It was reluctant to budge on the issue of YIVO's property until the larger question of heirless Jewish books, for which it was inclined to name the Commission as trustee, had been resolved (only in 1949, in fact, did the Commission conclude an agreement with the State Department and War Department to this effect).[44]

While US officials took Jewish parties' opposition to restituting cultural treasures to Poland to heart (and Poland had yet to make any claims on Jewish cultural assets), the Offenbach Depot still complied with requests from other countries looted by the Germans for the restitution of materials. Weinreich long feared that the governments of Lithuania and the Soviet Union would make claims on its Vilna collections. Recognizing that the transfer of materials into Soviet hands was likely irreversible, he even formulated a contingency plan as early as September 1944 for this eventuality: to make eventual arrangements for the exchange of documents, microfilm, and photocopies of YIVO materials in Soviet custody.[45] Fortunately for Weinreich, American officials would not countenance the return of books to Lithuania or any of the other Baltic States. The United States refused to recognize them as part of the USSR, which had integrated them as Soviet Republics during World War II in circumstances it deemed illegitimate.

But the possibility still remained, Weinreich feared, that YIVO materials would be handed over to the Soviets, perhaps in exchange for other materials in Soviet hands. Following a visit by a Soviet restitution officer to Offenbach in June 1946, seven hundred and sixty cases—more than 230,000 books, including Jewish library collections from Odessa and Kyiv seized by the ERR—were prepared for shipment to the Soviet Union. Further, the Jewish Museum in Vilnius, aware of the disappearance of its materials after Kaczerginski and Sutzkever's flight, urged Soviet officials "to take all necessary steps so that Soviet property be returned to its true owners."[46] A visit of Soviet and Polish representatives to the OAD was announced for July 1946, provoking further anxieties in New York.

An unexpected windfall came to YIVO in the form of growing discord between the Western Allies—the US, Britain, and France—and the Soviets. Negotiations in the Allied Control Council, the governing board for occupied Germany, yielded no agreements about restitution policy, not even about the definition of the term *restitution* itself. By the fall of 1946, it was evident that each occupying authority would decide on its own how to approach the question of restitution within its zone. As political tensions mounted in the Allied Control Council, American interim policy regarding restitution to the Baltic States became permanent policy. The US was also disinclined to allow for the further transfer of cultural materials to the USSR from Offenbach.[47]

In summary, YIVO, recognized as an American organization by the US government, benefited from the alignment of its own interests with those of American policy in the emerging Cold War. YIVO's "Americanness," at least in a geographic and legal sense, helped it to secure the support and later material aid of the victorious superpower for the restitution of pilfered eastern European collections housed in occupied Germany to an institution run by Yiddish-speaking refugees and immigrants in New York. The apparent irony in this accomplishment was, however, only superficial, as US sympathies at the time did largely lie with Hitler's victims, and YIVO's staff was coming increasingly to understand America as home. Indeed, to achieve YIVO's goals, Weinreich had relied heavily on its associates with connections to government and military offices as well as those serving in the US forces. Showing remarkable foresight, Weinreich himself had applied for US citizenship only a few months after arriving in New York in the spring of 1940.[48]

Still, while the return of YIVO materials to eastern Europe was thwarted, it took several additional months of negotiations before the bureaucratic impasse between US agencies affecting the restitution process was resolved. In March 1947, the War Department authorized OMGUS to release YIVO's collections to the Library of Congress Mission in Germany, which could then facilitate their transfer to YIVO in New York. By releasing them to a US government institution, the War Department was able to uphold its policy of restituting cultural property exclusively to states—in this case, the United States.[49]

"Ownerless" Books

Lucy Shildkret took up the position of Weinreich's personal assistant once he arrived in New York in the spring of 1940, working closely with him through the remainder of the war and becoming intimately familiar with his investigations and diplomatic forays in pursuit of YIVO collections in Europe. They grew closer during those desperate years than they had been during her year as an *aspirant* in Vilna. Nonetheless, tensions arose between them. Weinreich found her highly competent and possessing brilliant ideas but also bossy, capable of acting impetuously, and frequently clashing with colleagues.[50] She, in turn, found him unwilling to allow her to grow. In retrospect, it seems clear that Shildkret had ambitions for independence and a career that could not be satisfied as long as she remained under Weinreich's tutelage. Reflecting back on this time, she wrote in her memoir that she felt "restless" at YIVO in New York and did not wish to serve "the life term of discipleship he [Weinreich] demanded." Weinreich, she recalled, took her departure as "a form of apostasy" but held out the hope she would return.[51] Eager to help Holocaust survivors and refugees, Shildkret traveled to Germany in the fall of 1946 to work for the Education Department of the JDC in Munich at the urging of Koppel S. Pinson, who served as the department's director.

The Vilna-born Pinson, a professor of German history at Queens College and member of YIVO's Academic Council, secured the permission of US authorities to select twenty-five thousand books deemed of lesser value, especially textbooks, from among those in Offenbach for distribution among Jewish DPs in the American Zone. While this plan alarmed Weinreich, who feared that YIVO books would likely never be returned, he sympathized with DPs' desperate need for reading material after years of deprivation and understood that for many, a connection to YIVO had tremendous emotional resonance.[52] Pinson also convinced US officials to appoint a restitution officer trained in Judaica to direct the Offenbach Archival Depot. To Max Weinreich's satisfaction, Seymour Pomrenze was placed in charge of the installation. Pomrenze, a former archivist at the National Archives in Washington, DC, now serving as an MFA&A officer, possessed the requisite facility in Yiddish, German, and Hebrew to oversee the work of sorting and identifying the large number of books in Hebrew script. He also happened to be the brother of Israel Chaim Pomrenze, who sat on YIVO's Executive Board. Weinreich was consequently confident that he had in Offenbach an ally who would do all in his power to facilitate the reclamation of YIVO's possessions.[53]

Arriving in Munich in October 1946, Shildkret spent her early months in Germany securing basic materials for DPs' educational institutions and facilitating the publication of a Yiddish newspaper by procuring the necessary permission and typesetting for it. In regular contact with Weinreich, she learned that her Vilna friends, the poets Chaim Grade (who had spent the war as a refugee in Soviet Central Asia), Avrom Sutzkever, and Shmerke Kaczerginski, had made their way to Paris, and she hurried to meet them in January in JDC offices there. Following an emotional reunion, during which she learned of the efforts of the Paper Brigade firsthand, Shildkret returned to Germany to resume the work begun by Pinson at Offenbach, who had distributed some twenty thousand books prior to his return to the United States. In February 1947, she began the work of choosing the remaining five thousand books for distribution.[54]

Shildkret's own displeasure at being in the "land of Amalek" (a reference to the perpetual enemy of the Israelites in the Hebrew Bible), as she called it in her memoir, was allayed to some extent by the elevated station and imperious authority her US uniform permitted her to exercise over the defeated Germans, whom she held in contempt. She supervised a team of twelve German civilian workers sorting piles of Hebrew and Yiddish books considered ownerless. Unable to decipher the Hebrew alphabet, they were trained to recognize an assortment of ex libris stamps from a catalog prepared by the OAD's director, Captain Isaac Bencowitz, a Russian-born chemist who replaced Pomrenze as OAD director in April 1946.

Shildkret personally sorted and cataloged tens of thousands of Hebrew and Yiddish books in search of volumes that could be assigned for the cultural rehabilitation of Displaced Persons. Not surprisingly, she found the work of examining dusty and often damaged books not only monotonous and uncomfortable. It was also emotionally exhausting. She described the Offenbach Depot as a "mortuary of books," with each one a reminder of the tragic fate of its unknown owner and past readers. She later recalled that the "smell of death emanated from these hundreds of thousands of books and religious objects."[55]

Shildkret's familiarity with YIVO's collections from her time as an *aspirant* in Vilna led her, however, to a discovery that evoked an unanticipated sense of quasi-religious exultation, "a feeling akin to holiness, that I was touching something sacred."[56] Among the mass of books lacking an ex libris, she found familiar signatures and other indications that they had belonged to YIVO's collection or private libraries of individuals closely associated with the institute, including Weinreich's. While she had initially sought not to conflate her JDC assignment with her YIVO loyalties, Shildkret found herself compelled to act on YIVO's behalf. Naturally, she conveyed her discovery to Weinreich in New York, with whom she conferred about how to proceed to expedite the return of YIVO materials. With difficulty, she obtained permission from the JDC to focus her efforts on identifying YIVO materials. By late May 1947, Shildkret had examined more than 160,000 identified volumes in Hebrew and Yiddish at the Offenbach Depot. Of these, she managed to identify close to thirty-three thousand—of which 75 percent belonged to YIVO or the Strashun Library. A month later, Shildkret sorted an additional twenty thousand books.[57]

During his tenure as OAD director, Pomrenze had not explicitly acted on YIVO's behalf despite Weinreich keeping him informed of his negotiations concerning the collections. Upon his return to the US, however, he became purposefully engaged on YIVO's behalf, providing Weinreich with invaluable advice about how to navigate official government channels to reclaim YIVO materials. While Dawidowicz urged Weinreich to come to Europe to arrange the shipment of the books himself, he had no desire to come to Germany even if Uveeler could raise the money for the trip. Burdened with survivor's guilt, he felt uncomfortable with the very idea of traveling to Germany, anticipating that he would not be able to restrain himself from looking around out of curiosity. The contrast between nostalgia for his student years in Germany and the suffering he would encounter there in the present among Holocaust survivors and Displaced Persons was too much for him to bear. As he wrote to Uriel, "[I am] filled with the pain of the Jews in the ghettos, of death, and of the materials that come to us for the exhibit about Jews in Europe 1939–40, and today in the camps and everywhere."[58] Moreover, he soberly appreciated that Pomrenze would be far more valuable than he in ensuring that the operation—which placed US government money (in addition to YIVO's own), personnel, and resources at YIVO's disposal—proceeded without a hitch.[59]

Pomrenze returned to Germany in June 1947 at Weinreich's request as part of the Library of Congress Mission charged with collecting Nazi publications. He oversaw the loading of 420 crates of materials containing close to eighty thousand items—more than thirty-two thousand books as well as newspapers, brochures, music, and archival material—into freight cars and accompanied them as they were transported under military supervision to the port of Bremen, whence they were shipped across the Atlantic.[60] YIVO lacked the space to store so many books, which significantly expanded its collections. Fortunately, Pomrenze's brother Israel Chaim, an executive for the Manischewitz Matzo company, made arrangements for the crates to be stored in a company warehouse in Jersey City, New Jersey, free of charge for two years. A special room was subsequently equipped in YIVO's library to accommodate the collection.[61]

Associated Vilna Libraries

Ultimately, YIVO managed not only to recover a significant part of its own prewar library but also to acquire surviving books originating in a number of other collections that were designated by OAD director Isaac Bencowitz as YIVO's "Associated Libraries." Most of these were the private collections of individuals who worked in or had close ties to the institute. They included not only Weinreich's own collection but those of Zalmen Reyzin, Zelig Kalmanovitch, Pinchas Kon, Alfred Landau, and Moyshe Lerer as well as educator and folklorist Shloyme Bastomski; folklorist Yehudah Leib Cahan, an Amopteyl cofounder; and the Vilna Jewish Teachers' Seminary.[62]

Reclaimed books being sorted in YIVO in New York, 1947. Credit: YIVO Institute for Jewish Research

Included among the "Associated Libraries" were also a large number of books belonging to the Strashun library and the Jewish Ethnographic Society. YIVO affirmed in affidavits that these institutions, with which it had collaborative relationships prior to the war, had concluded formal agreements in the early months of the war to incorporate their collections into YIVO's once efforts were taking shape to transport YIVO's collections to safety in New York City. As Weinreich explained, YIVO, with its specialization in modern scholarly literature, and the Strashun library, with its focus on traditional rabbinic and Hebrew-language scholarship, complemented each other. Moreover, the two institutions enjoyed cordial relations, with YIVO directors sitting on the Strashun Library's Board of Trustees and loans made between the institutions.[63] Similarly, YIVO explained that the Ethnographic Society, which lacked adequate space for Ansky's collection, had already entrusted to it a part of the collection's books and archives in the mid-1930s.[64]

It is difficult to assess YIVO's claims to parts of the "Associated Libraries" based on the paucity of surviving documentary evidence from Vilna from the relevant period. It stands to reason, as YIVO asserted to American officials, that YIVO employees or their relatives transferred collections to the institute when they could no longer be certain of their own personal safety, especially when they were forced into the Vilna Ghetto. Some of the material had also been bequeathed or donated to YIVO prior to the war. This was certainly the case for historian Simon Dubnow, whose bequest of his collection to YIVO in the late 1920s was well publicized in the press and was affirmed by his daughter, Sofia Dubnow Erlich, then residing in New York, in an affidavit submitted by YIVO to US authorities.[65] But almost all the trustees of the Strashun Library and the Ethnographic Society had perished during the war (the only surviving Strashun trustee, Rabbi Isaac Rubinstein, who escaped from Vilna in 1940, died in New York in 1945), leaving no one among them to corroborate YIVO's account of an institutional merger.[66]

It does not seem implausible that discussions were held at a time of great panic between representatives of the two institutions and YIVO to save their collections jointly, since YIVO offered the safest location. Indeed, one of the first acts of YIVO's staff in Vilna when the war began in September 1939 was to move its collections into a fireproof basement and to recruit all members of the administration, staff, and *aspirantur* to stand guard over the building around the clock.[67] The Amopteyl was also very much interested in transferring invaluable materials from Vilna to New York in late 1939.[68] But no further steps to transfer them to America were taken once conditions in Vilna under Lithuanian rule had stabilized, bringing an end to panic—at least in Vilna—about the future of these institutions, and when the conditions of war made travel between New York and Vilna impossible. Moreover, as we have seen, communication was greatly impaired once World War II began between New York and Vilna, where YIVO staff members differed in their fluctuating appraisals of the situation not only from colleagues in New York but among themselves.

Whatever the case may be, American officials supported YIVO's claims.[69] Weinreich and YIVO colleagues, as well as several other parties sympathetic to them, believed that YIVO represented the spirit and legitimate heir of prewar Vilna Jewry. They sought to lay claim to as much as possible of the heritage of Vilna Jewry for YIVO as well as to prevent it from falling into Soviet hands or even rival Jewish ones. Given Sutzkever and Kaczerginski's experiences and the fact that much of YIVO's collections had not been cataloged, these anxieties were not unjustified. To avoid arousing suspicions surrounding the books in case a formal inspection was made by US officials upon their arrival in New York, Shildkret equipped Weinreich with a copy of the Vilna YIVO's *ex libris* from Bencowitz's catalog and advised him to begin stamping books whose belonging to YIVO was not obvious.[70]

Shildkret and Weinreich exchanged private congratulations for their achievement in 1947. It was not until 1951, however, that YIVO publicly celebrated the event, wary in the intervening years of drawing attention to its accomplishment while competing claims could still be made or questions raised about the legitimacy of some of its actions. Nonetheless, material continued to arrive: More than ten thousand more books and documents arrived from the JCR from 1949 to 1952.[71]

Nor did YIVO's possession of rescued books go wholly uncontested. In particular, the matter of the Strashun collection brought to the fore not only the question of to whom does possession of the Jewish past—and hence claims to leadership in the Jewish future—belong: the Jewish Diaspora or the State of Israel and their concomitant ideologies? It also raised the question of who was the proper inheritor of the vast body of Hebrew and religious literature produced by eastern European Jewry—a secular nationalist institution whose scholars and patrons would likely view them as relics of a venerable past or an Orthodox one, where the books would be received as part of a living tradition.

Tzvi Harkavy, a grandnephew of Mattias Strashun, claimed that the largely Hebrew and rabbinic library belonged not in the collections of a Yiddishist organization in New York but instead in a religious institution in Israel, where he was director of the Central Rabbinical Library of Heichal Shlomo in Jerusalem. Despite possessing no real claim to be the heir of what was a communal rather than private institution, Harkavy came to a settlement with YIVO in 1958. In return for the "gifting" of duplicates of rabbinic volumes bearing the Strashun Library stamp (some five hundred tomes) to the Central Rabbinical Library, Harkavy renounced his right to further claims on YIVO's holdings from the Strashun Library.[72]

To this day, the bulk of the Strashun Library's collection remains in YIVO in New York, a reflection of Weinreich's understanding of the American YIVO as the inheritor of the entirety of the Vilna Jewish intellectual tradition. Nonetheless, the presence of so many scholarly volumes in rabbinic Hebrew and Aramaic posed a unique challenge for an institute staffed almost exclusively by prewar members of left-wing, ideologically secular Jewish parties. Despite all being polyglots, few possessed the requisite knowledge of traditional sources to process the books competently, with the exception of Shlomo Noble, a yeshiva graduate who was already overburdened with YIVO tasks that were not his regular duties.[73]

It was therefore the institute's good fortune that Chaim Liberman, the Lubavitcher rebbe's secretary and curator of that Hasidic dynasty's own impressive collection in Crown Heights, Brooklyn, volunteered to help with the cataloging of rabbinic literature in YIVO's collections. A *haredi* polymath, Liberman was an admirer of the institution who regularly attended its conferences and contributed works about Hasidism, publishing history, and the Yiddish language to its publications. Moreover, he was uniquely suited for the task: he had worked with Strashun librarian Khaykl Lunski to prepare an inventory of the Strashun Library's holdings in prewar Vilna.[74]

It is a telling reflection of the degree of religious observance among YIVO's staff that the mezuzah that Liberman, who scrupulously avoided contact with secular Hebrew and *maskilic* books from Vilna, affixed to the doorframe of his workroom was the only one in the building. "Reb Chaim," as he was fondly called among staff members, was treated with respect and very much made to feel welcome in an institute that did not shy away from holding meetings on the Sabbath.[75] While Liberman's contributions represent those of a tiny Orthodox minority active within YIVO at the time, they testify to the openness of the institute to include religious Jews in its activities as well as Liberman's own tolerance for the institute's secularist worldview. Beyond a reflection of individual personalities, this collegiality and mutual cordiality between representatives of world views in often bitter opposition prior to the war was itself likely an outgrowth of the shared trauma of eastern European Jewry.[76]

Failure in Czechoslovakia

In contrast with YIVO's great success in reclaiming materials located in the American occupation zone of Germany, Weinreich met with frustration in recuperating cultural treasures found in Czechoslovakia. During the war, YIVO's press collection, along with some books belonging to the Strashun library, was looted not by the ERR but by the German military for use by the library of the Reich Security Main Office in Berlin. Along with other cultural objects, these items were eventually evacuated to the territory of prewar Czechoslovakia that had been incorporated into the German Reich in order to protect them from Allied bombing.

After the war, the more than one million plundered volumes from Jewish and non-Jewish sources secreted in Bohemian castles by the German occupier were entrusted to the country's National and University Library and other Czech institutions, including the Jewish Museum. Prof. Hugo Bergmann, former director of the National Library in Jerusalem and rector of the Hebrew University, was dispatched from Jerusalem to convince Czech officials to allow for the shipment of Jewish cultural treasures there. Bergmann encountered newspapers and books clearly belonging to YIVO in Niemes and other castles in Mimoň in northern Bohemia, and dutifully informed Weinreich of his discoveries in late June 1946.[77]

YIVO and other Jewish organizations found themselves obliged to negotiate not only with the Czech government but also with the local Jewish council about the possession of looted property, even materials that patently originated outside the territory of the prewar state. Weinreich authorized the Council of Jewish Communities in Bohemia and Moravia to represent YIVO in negotiations about its collections and requested that the American Embassy in Prague assist it as necessary. He soon found himself at odds with his colleague Salo Baron, who, as head of the Commission on European Jewish Cultural Reconstruction, sought to discourage YIVO from pursuing an independent claim to its materials. Baron feared that doing so might jeopardize or delay the overall restitution of Jewish cultural property. He had already requested that the State Department recognize the Hebrew University as trustee for looted Jewish property and that it approve the transfer of Jewish cultural property from Czechoslovakia to Jerusalem, where future decisions about its distribution among Jewish bodies around the world could be made. Weinreich, for his part, grew increasingly mistrustful of the Commission, fearing that its goal was to impede YIVO in New York from reclaiming what he believed rightly belonged to it despite the State Department's recognition of it as the legal heir of YIVO in prewar Vilna.[78]

A second impediment to YIVO's operations in Czechoslovakia was growing Soviet pressure, which was vividly reflected in the country's rejection of the Marshall Plan for American aid in the reconstruction of Europe, despite expressing initial inclinations to the contrary. The country's increasingly communist-controlled regime was resistant to sending cultural materials to the West and impeded the efforts of YIVO agents to gain access to them. Lucy Shildkret, dispatched by YIVO from Germany with full authority to represent its interests in March 1947, was unable to achieve anything during her stay in Prague. Similarly, Seymour Pomrenze, sent by YIVO in July to negotiate the return of YIVO's newspaper collection, met with insuperable bureaucratic obstacles during his stay in the city. This included being denied access to Niemes Castle despite assurances of aid from the Jewish Museum and the local Jewish council.[79] In the atmosphere of the emerging Cold War, YIVO's New York location and postwar associations with American government offices and military authorities—so beneficial to its obtaining books from Offenbach—proved a detriment in relations with eastern European countries.

Moreover, YIVO was likely outmaneuvered by representatives of the Hebrew University in Jerusalem. They could circulate more freely in Czechoslovakia due to the personal connections of its agents, Prague natives like Bergmann and his brother Arthur, to local Jewish communities. Individuals in the Hebrew University expressed hope that YIVO itself could be persuaded to relocate to Jerusalem for incorporation into the university when Weinreich's name was suggested in discussions surrounding the creation of a Yiddish chair at the University in the late 1940s.[80]

Agents of the *va'ad le-hatzalat otzrot ha-gola* (Committee for Saving Treasures of the Diaspora), the university's team dedicated to bringing the remnants of European Jewish civilization to the Jewish national home in the *yishuv* (and, later, Israel), themselves met with obstacles. But they were able to arrange for the shipment of tens of thousands of Jewish books—including numerous Yiddish collections—to Jerusalem through a combination of connections to local Jewish communities and bribery of officials. Indeed, as Bilha Shilo, who has produced the most extensive account of the complicated matter of the postwar restitution of YIVO's materials, has argued, it is possible that Ze'ev Scheck, the envoy who replaced Arthur Bergmann, deliberately misled or provided justification to the Committee's leadership to conclude that Weinreich had shown little interest in recovering these materials, thus opening a path for the Hebrew University to proceed unilaterally. Unlike Hugo Bergmann, who apprised Weinreich of the whereabouts of YIVO's collection, Scheck did not inform YIVO when its collection was evacuated from the castle on orders of the military and moved to a warehouse by the Jewish Council. More gravely, the letters he claimed to have sent to Weinreich to inform him that payment and a direct appeal were required by Czech officials to effect the shipment of YIVO's materials to New York apparently never arrived.[81]

The fate of YIVO's press collection ultimately remains unknown. Some of it may have been sent, Shilo speculates, via the Israeli Legation in Prague in diplomatic packages to avoid arousing suspicion and was subsequently absorbed into collections of the Hebrew University; some of it may have become part of Czech library collections or simply sold on the open market.[82] While not reporting on the debacle in Czechoslovakia, *Yedies* enthusiastically reported in 1951 that with the help of Jewish Cultural Reconstruction Inc. as well as "numerous friends and correspondents in Europe," it had managed to replace many items from its Vilna press collection.[83]

Hitler's Professors

During the war years, Weinreich read everything concerning Nazi activities and the fate of European Jewry that he could get his hands on. He distilled much of this information into his regular articles in the *Forverts*. As early as 1942, he also began to summarize his findings about Nazi Germany's policies toward Jews in *Yivo bleter*. There he published studies of Nazi scholarship that detailed the contributions of scholars such as Heinz Peter Seraphim, an expert on eastern Europe who visited YIVO in the 1930s "with strong recommendations from the Polish government" and "played a fatal role in familiarizing German scholars and political leaders with Eastern Jewry and, ultimately, in mapping out the 'removal' scheme."[84] These studies helped Weinreich to lay the groundwork for *Hitler's Professors: The Part of Scholarship in Germany's Crimes Against the Jewish People*, his study of German academics' role in furnishing the moral and intellectual legitimization for the Final Solution.[85] Materials that Zosa Szajkowski uncovered in the ruins of Nazi offices in Berlin—hundreds of boxes making up some twenty-five linear feet—and had shipped to New York provided Weinreich with thousands of Nazi documents and publications that complemented his project.[86]

Weinreich was very much aware of the painful irony that Nazi Germany had condemned the entirety of the Jewish people to death while enabling a selection of its books and documents to survive. Anticipating Daniel Goldhagen's controversial thesis about the uniqueness of an "eliminationist antisemitism" in Germany culminating in genocide,[87] he maintained that the "burning of six-million men, women and children" was a specifically German phenomenon for which there was little contrition among a population bearing collective guilt. The involvement of scholars lay not merely in the nature of the totalitarian state, as the Austrian Jewish philologist Leo Spitzer, a personal friend and member of YIVO's Academic Council, argued in a letter to Weinreich.[88] He countered, "The Germans are the only nation in the world to produce scholarship . . . that contributed more to annihilation than required of it." While he accepted that there were also what he called "decent Germans," they were vastly outnumbered in his estimation by those who had participated in murder or given their tacit consent.[89]

Weinreich produced *Hitler's Professors* during a six-month leave of absence from his duties at YIVO, writing the study with breakneck speed with the hope that it would be available to the prosecution at the upcoming Nuremberg Trials for Nazi war criminals in the summer of 1946. Leibush Lehrer replaced him as director during this time. While the book was ultimately not ready in time for the trials, YIVO did, however, share documentation with members of the American legal team for this and subsequent trials of war criminals.[90] The book itself also proved directly useful in trials such as that of the Nobel Prize–winning physicist Johannes Stark, an early Nazi supporter who attacked Einstein's theoretical physics as "Jewish" and stressed the need to purify German science of Jews and their ideas.[91]

In a time before widespread access to Nazi archival materials, Weinreich reproduced select documents and quoted them extensively in *Hitler's Professors*, rendering their ponderous language into lucid English in order to provide a clear picture of the activities of individual scholars and institutions. Somewhat impractically given his greater facility in Yiddish, he wrote the original manuscript in English—a reflection of his appreciation of the power of that language in the American and international spheres. He availed himself of the help of a Hunter College English professor recommended by Lucy Shildkret to polish his language and then translated his own words for the Yiddish edition.[92] As he explained to Uriel, he worked very hard on the book, learning a great deal of English in the process. At times, he found himself spending a few hours refining a ten-sentence paragraph in order to ensure that the language adequately and clearly conveyed his attitude toward German scholars: "coolness, agitation, sarcasm, and disdain."[93]

Weinreich's feat—researching and organizing so much information about dozens of scholars in so short a time—was mammoth, a reflection not only of his incomparable work ethic but of the rage that drove him. His basic argument was, however, quite simple:

> This murder of a whole people was not perpetrated by a comparative small gang of the Elite Guard or by the Gestapo, whom we have come to consider as criminals. As is shown by Hitler's threats, afterwards frequently repeated by himself and his henchmen, as the literature of the Nazi Party, the Reich government, and the Wehrmacht shows, the whole ruling class of Germany was committed to the execution of this crime. But the actual murderers and those who sent them out and applauded them had accomplices. German scholarship provided the ideas and techniques which led to and justified this unparalleled slaughter.[94]

For Weinreich, these scholars, who included some of Germany's most respected figures in the natural sciences and humanities prior to the Nazi era, had willfully perverted the purpose of scholarship by subverting it to an immoral ideology that predetermined its conclusions.[95] Jurists, biologists, and physical anthropologists had, in his estimation, played the leading role. But he held in special disdain those who had contributed to the Nazi field of *Judenforschung*. They had transformed the study of Jewish life and culture from an instrument for the sake of improving Jewish lives, which was YIVO's explicit mission, into one for the express purpose of destroying them.

Thanks in large part to the availability of significantly more Nazi documentation since the 1940s, contemporary historians have a more extensive, nuanced, and in some ways more accurate understanding of the decision-making process that led to the Final Solution than the one presented in *Hitler's Professors*. The volume nonetheless represents a pioneering contribution—the first and for decades only systematic study of complicity by academics in Nazi genocide—and a reflection of the information available in the immediate postwar era. When first published, it was considered one of the few meticulously documented studies of Nazi Germany. Scholars today recognize Weinreich's contribution in emphasizing the crucial role of academics in making racial antisemitism respectable among broad segments of the population in a country that prided itself on the renown of its universities.[96]

Among those Weinreich identified as having collaborated with the Nazi regime were individuals to whom YIVO had provided intellectual and moral support. Two in particular stand out: the linguists Heinz Kloss and Franz Beranek. While the former only receives brief mention in *Hitler's Professors* and the latter is completely absent (perhaps because Weinreich did not have sufficient evidence about him at the time), the actions of both would preoccupy Weinreich for years to come because of their extensive interactions with the prewar YIVO and their continued postwar engagement with Yiddish and linguistics scholarship. Moreover, they had an actual command of Yiddish and extensive familiarity with its sociology—a rarity among German scholars. For Weinreich, who had previously hailed both scholars as examples of Gentile allies to the cause of Yiddish in a time of rising Jew hatred, their conduct was a form of personal betrayal as much as one of YIVO, the Jewish people, and humanistic scholarship itself.[97]

Prior to the war, Weinreich described the paper that Beranek delivered about Yiddish dialects in his native Czechoslovakia at YIVO's world conference in 1935 (subsequently printed in *Yivo bleter*) as a "revolutionary" contribution to the study of Yiddish dialectology. He and colleagues welcomed Beranek during a visit to Vilna the following year on his way back from a research trip in the Baltic region. Beranek, in turn, approached YIVO as late as 1940 to publish his study of Yiddish in sub-Carpathian Ruthenia, the southeastern tip of pre–World War II Czechoslovakia that is today part of Ukraine. When this did not work out for financial reasons, Beranek—who was, unbeknownst to YIVO, a Nazi party member since the German annexation of Czechoslovakia's Sudetenland in 1938—published the study instead with the help of a Nazi institution, the Institute for the History of the New Germany.[98]

Kloss had also relied heavily on assistance from YIVO offices—in Vilna, Berlin, and New York—in gathering data about Yiddish and Jewish organizations in the 1920s and '30s. He used it to write a study of YIVO as a model research institute and language authority for a national minority lacking a state of its own and as part of a campaign to create a university-affiliated institute dedicated to German and cognate languages (including Yiddish) in the closing years of Weimar Germany. During the war years, he was promoted through the ranks of the nazified Institute for Germans Abroad (*Deutsches Ausland-Institut*) and became a leading figure in the network of researchers, to which Beranek also belonged, involved in plans for the ethnic "re-ordering" of Europe.[99] A copy of his 1944 guide to North American Jewry and its organizations (labeled "For official use only!" on its cover), acquired in 2018 by Library and Archives Canada from Hitler's personal library, leaves little doubt about his utility to the regime.[100]

Both scholars published about Yiddish after the war, including calls for German academics to study Yiddish in order to preserve the remnants of that culture as a means to promote reconciliation between Germans and Jews. But only Beranek, who founded a journal devoted to scholarship about Yiddish in German-speaking lands, dared to renew contact and seek collaboration with YIVO. In 1947 he sent a letter to YIVO in New York inquiring about the welfare of Zalmen Reyzen, Zelig Kalmanovitch, and YIVO *aspirant* Berl Schlossberg—the former a victim of the Soviet Union, the latter two of Germany. Weinreich opted to ignore Beranek's overtures until news reached him of Beranek's creation of a Yiddish studies journal and his efforts to create an academic position for Yiddish for himself in postwar West Germany.

Relying on documentation found in YIVO and materials he gathered through international connections, Weinreich demasked Beranek in a series of sardonic articles in the *Forverts* in 1956 as a Nazi party member who had published a Yiddish dialect study he originally submitted to YIVO with the help of a Nazi institute and then had the gall to attempt to renew his contacts with Jewish colleagues. In his rebuttal, also published in *Forverts*, Beranek portrayed himself as a victim of the Nazi regime who could not advance professionally because of his pro-Jewish attitudes. He neglected to mention occupying a prominent position in a Nazi research institute in Slovakia for more than a year before being approved for an academic position at the University of Prague. Nor did he mention that his "philosemitic" scholarship had benefited from access to Jewish informants at a time when they were being ghettoized and deported from Slovakia.[101]

YIVO's College Yiddish Association, created to promote the spread of Yiddish instruction in universities, refused to have anything to do with Beranek. Nonetheless, his postwar career only benefited from its association with Yiddish. He eventually obtained a position in German Philology, specializing in Yiddish, at the University of Giessen. His colleague Kloss went on to even greater prominence, becoming an internationally renowned scholar of minority language rights. While aggrieved by these developments, Weinreich felt he had neither the time nor the resources to continue his case against them further. Moreover, YIVO Yiddish scholars could not ignore their contributions to the field. Uriel Weinreich, for example, did not shy away from citing Beranek's work but was careful to announce Beranek's tainted past in his articles, and Max Weinreich continued to read Kloss's work despite his disdain for him.[102]

Weinreich, like his son Uriel, regarded all German researchers who approached him with undisguised suspicion, questioning them directly about their activities during the war if they wished to have any business with him or YIVO. His seething rage at Germany for its crimes against the Jewish people—the destruction of the people and civilization to which he had dedicated his life—was magnified by his sense of betrayal by German culture. A native German speaker who had received his doctorate in 1923 after studying at the Universities of Berlin and Marburg, Weinreich had been a great admirer of the German academic culture, above all its renowned commitment to precision, organization, and systematic inquiry, even if he was not blind to the antisemitism of that same culture. His own work sought to achieve a fusion of the German tradition of objective scholarship with the eastern European Jewish populist ideal of scholarship as a tool for social engagement.[103] He refused contact with any who could not demonstrate to his satisfaction their distance from the Third Reich's institutions or the regnant antisemitic ideology.[104]

Most YIVO colleagues shared Weinreich's reluctance to have contact with Germans and German institutions, believing it necessary to conduct independent inquiries before engaging in any exchanges of materials or information.[105] So great was the hatred of Germany among many YIVO associates that the question of accepting German reparations to fund much-needed projects to document and commemorate the destruction of eastern European Jewry repeatedly proved bitterly divisive and at times undermined larger scholarly goals. Yet in what was an especially cruel irony, YIVO depended on German reparations monies for roughly a decade to fund many of its most important, Holocaust-related projects.

The Birth of Holocaust Studies

Even before reparations enabled YIVO to expand its work significantly, the institute began to lay the material basis for what would become the field of Holocaust studies. As early as the end of 1945, YIVO began a campaign to collect personal letters, diaries, and photographs produced in lands under German occupation. With the destruction of so much documentation produced during the war and the very limited opportunities for Jews to commit their experiences for posterity, personal documents depicting the horrors of Jewish life under Nazi rule were needed as a safeguard, as *Yedies* warned, against a future "time when the Germans and their accomplices will attempt to minimize the whole matter or cast it on the shoulders of a few 'irresponsible persons.'"[106] Building on prewar practice, YIVO mobilized surviving *zamlers* living in DP camps in addition to American military and relief and rehabilitation workers to gather materials and to interview survivors in close to six hundred locations from Bergen Belsen to Shanghai for its "Archives of Jewish Life Under the Nazis." Efforts to collect documents created in ghettos, records from Nazi agencies as well as from wartime Jewish organizations, and materials such as publications from DP camps continued until 1954, by which time the last DP camps were closed except for one.[107] YIVO thus accumulated some two thousand survivor testimonies along with collections from several ghettos, most notably Warsaw (Hersch Wasser Collection), Łódź (Nachman Zonabend Collection), and Vilna (Abraham Sutzkever-Shmerke Kaczerginski Vilna Ghetto Collection). It also opened its archives to researchers seeking to memorialize communities, such as in the *yizker-bikher* (community memorial books) produced by *landsmanshaftn*, and to produce radio and television programs about the Holocaust.[108]

While Emmanuel Ringelblum did not survive the war, much of the trove of writings that he and colleagues engaged in the *Oyneg shabes* project buried beneath the Warsaw Ghetto did. A year after the war's end, in the fall of 1946, YIVO announced an agreement with the Central Jewish Committee of Poland, the representative body of postwar Polish Jewry, for the exchange of documents and archival materials with the Central Jewish Historical Commission of Poland as well as for collaboration in the area of publications. It also agreed to share the costs of exhuming what was the first cache of the archive buried by Ringelblum and colleagues from underneath the ghetto's ruins. A second of the three caches of materials, famously contained in milk jugs and providing invaluable insights into daily life in the ghetto, was discovered in 1950; the third remains to be found if still extant. While Ringelblum and the project's executive committee had decided at the height of the Great Deportation from the Ghetto in August 1942 that the eventual destination of the archive should be YIVO in New York City in the case of their deaths, the collection remained in Warsaw. It is preserved in the Jewish Historical Institute (Żydowski Instytut Historyczny), located in a reconstructed building that was the home of the city's Institute of Judaic studies prior to the war and that was named in Ringelblum's honor in 2009.[109]

In 1952, the State of Israel concluded an accord with West Germany for the transfer of three billion Marks (close to 714 million USD) over fourteen years as compensation for material damages to Jewish property. A further 450 million Marks (about 107 million USD) was given to the Conference on Jewish Material Claims Against Germany for distribution to Jewish cultural and rehabilitation organizations in the Diaspora. A storm of controversy arose in the Jewish press around the world over what was widely condemned as accepting "blood money" to expunge German guilt. In Yiddishist circles, for example, several writers (among them Aaron Zeitlin and future Nobel Prize winner Isaac Bashevis Singer) refused to be included in the *Leksikon fun der nayer yidisher literatur*, a new biographical dictionary of modern Yiddish writers, despite the fact that the project employed Holocaust survivors as researchers and writers. The project, which built upon and extended Zalmen Reyzen's prewar *Leksikon fun der yidisher literatur, prese un filologye* (Biographical Dictionary of Yiddish Literature, Press, and Philology), was conducted under the auspices of the Congress for Jewish Culture. It employed several YIVO associates (including Charney and Shatzky as its first editors) and made use of YIVO collections in its completion.[110]

At a YIVO symposium titled "Relations Between Jews and Germans at Present," Yudel Mark no doubt expressed the feelings of many when he protested against YIVO accepting reparations. He argued that while contact with individual Germans was to be permitted, accepting compensation from the German state would permit Germans as a collective to feel that they "had made adequate amends to the Jewish people."[111] Perhaps out of deference to Yiddish readers, *Yedies* failed to convey Mark's remarks in its Yiddish section. Nonetheless, its Board of Directors resolved in late February 1952 to request inclusion among the organizations allotted funds by the Claims Commission.[112] Freeland League (Frayland-lige) secretary general Isaac N. Steinberg, a YIVO cofounder known for his efforts since the late 1930s to establish an autonomous settlement for Jewish refugees outside of a Jewish state, resigned from the board in protest.[113]

Yet despite the emotional revulsion that reparations elicited, it was difficult to reject the pragmatic case for their acceptance. Without them, it would be impossible for YIVO to conduct precisely the work for which it not only was uniquely qualified but also felt a deep moral responsibility. Louis H. Sobel, a prominent social worker and the board's chairman, therefore submitted a memorandum with a detailed budget in 1953 for close to $4.5 million for projects "designed to serve those European Jewish scholars, teachers, students in the fields of Jewish social, community leaders and teachers who survived the Holocaust."[114]

YIVO requested money for a series of projects connected to the restoration of its collections and the documentation of the Holocaust. The work was anticipated to continue for at least a decade, and YIVO stipulated that it would employ Jewish victims of Nazi Germany as much as feasible. The tasks outlined included (1) the restoration of the Vilna YIVO

Library (the purchase of available books to replace losses, restoration of tattered and scattered materials brought to New York, and preparation of a catalog), (2) a similar reconstruction of the Vilna YIVO archives, (3) training a new generation of Jewish studies scholars and the continuation of the work of an older generation, (4) reprinting destroyed publications of the Vilna YIVO, (5) the publication of works by murdered scholars, and (6) the publication of a history of several of the largest Jewish communities that were destroyed. Mark Uveeler, YIVO's executive secretary, stressed that administrative expenses would be covered out of YIVO's regular budget. Moreover, while money from the Claims Conference represented a significant contribution that would enable YIVO to undertake important projects, these monies would not contribute to the institute's regular functioning and projects, which remained grossly underfunded.[115] YIVO was thus not only a victim of Nazism deserving of just compensation to restore its prior functioning as much as possible and to enable it to conduct the important work of documenting and analyzing the recent catastrophe; it was also to use reparations monies to engage in the rehabilitation of surviving scholars and the training of future ones.

The restoration and cataloging of YIVO's Vilna collections was begun almost immediately. The largest deployment of resources went, however, to a joint project with Yad Vashem, the Holocaust Authority established in Israel in 1953, to produce a series of bibliographies of literature about the Holocaust. While Yad Vashem's official operating language was Hebrew, much of its correspondence with YIVO about joint projects was in Yiddish, the language best understood by YIVO workers, who often lacked a good command of Hebrew. Naturally, Yiddish was well known to many at the Israeli Holocaust authority, who themselves originated in eastern Europe and frequently had personal ties to YIVO colleagues dating to before the war. Indeed, YIVO was first approached to join the project by Ben-Zion Dinur (formerly Dinaburg), Israel's Minister of Education and Culture, who knew Weinreich from their university days in St. Petersburg and Weinreich's trip to Palestine as a *Forverts* correspondent in 1935.[116] Addressing YIVO's annual conference in 1954 on Dinur's behalf, Israeli Consul-General Avraham Harman announced that ensuring the continuity of Jewish spiritual creativity and preserving the cultural treasures of Jewish life was a mission shared by YIVO and Yad Vashem. Theirs was a "consecrated mission" that united Jews throughout the world, first and foremost in "the two major Jewish centers: the great American Jewish community and those Jews building the state in Israel."[117]

Work on the joint YIVO–Yad Vashem project was led by Dr. Philip Friedman, a historian and YIVO associate who had lectured for its Vilna *aspirantur* and contributed to its publications. Following the war, Friedman, who had himself survived in hiding on the Aryan side in Lwów but lost his wife and daughter, was appointed head of the Central Jewish Historical Commission (created by the Central Committee of the Jews in Poland) dedicated to gathering material for the prosecution of Nazi war criminals. Along with fellow survivor scholars, he was active in the collection of survivor testimonies and documentation as well as the publication of studies about the recent genocide. During this period, Friedman grew alarmed by increasing ideological pressures exerted on the Soviet-dominated Commission to abjure foreign sources of funding and conform to communist ideology in the writing of history. After providing testimony at the Nuremberg Trials, Friedman, accompanied by his second wife, Ada, opted not to return to Poland. He spent the years 1946–48 serving as educational director of the JDC in the American occupation zone of Germany, where he worked with Shildkret as well as heading the research department of the Centre de documentation juive contemporaine in Paris. He then immigrated to the United States on the invitation of his mentor during his doctoral studies in Vienna, Columbia historian Salo Baron.[118]

The YIVO–Yad Vashem project arose from Friedman's personal collection of 30,000 bibliographic references and employed several of his fellow survivor scholars, both lay and professional historians, who had relocated to the United States and Israel after the war.[119] So important were his contributions to what is today called Holocaust studies that Baron dubbed him the "chief founder" of a new field in Jewish studies. Under his guidance, YIVO's revived Historians Circle also devoted attention to bibliographies and Holocaust research alongside such subjects as American and eastern European Jewish history. At the time, the journal *Jewish Social Studies*, under Baron's editorship, was the only English-language scholarly journal in the United States to give significant attention to Holocaust scholarship. In contrast, *Yivo bleter* not only already had a track record of writing about Jews' experience during the war years; it contributed to the professionalization of the emerging field by devoting two issues to Holocaust subjects—one in 1947 focusing on survivor testimony and the other in 1953 emphasizing research by survivor scholars such as Friedman and Isaiah Trunk.[120]

YIVO historians also participated as researchers and writers in Yad Vashem's *Pinkas ha-kehilot* (Encyclopedia of Communities) project commemorating the destroyed communities of eastern Europe, which was also supported by Claims Commission money.[121] Prior to Friedman's death in 1960, the project produced three volumes under his editorship.[122] More than a dozen additional volumes about the Holocaust were undertaken with funding from the Claims Commission through the combined efforts of YIVO, Yad Vashem, the Centre de documentation juive contemporaine in Paris, and the Wiener Library in London.

Isaiah Trunk succeeded Friedman as the head of YIVO's Historians Circle. Born into a prominent rabbinical family, Trunk received both a traditional religious education and completed a Polish-Hebrew gymnasium in Łódź. After receiving an MA in Jewish history under the direction of Meir Bałaban at the University of Warsaw, he taught history and Latin in Jewish schools in Warsaw and Bialystok and was active in YIVO's Historian's Circle. Following the joint German and Soviet invasions of Poland in 1939, Trunk fled eastward from Bialystok in Soviet occupied Poland. He spent the war years clearing forests as a slave laborer in the Soviet Far East and returned to Poland after the war, where he joined Friedman working in the Historical Commission. He too, however, left Poland, relocating first to Israel in 1950 and then Calgary, Canada, where he spent a year before coming to New York in 1954.[123]

Trunk won acclaim for his 1962 study of life within the Lodz Ghetto, a continuation of work begun by Friedman that was largely based on materials found in YIVO's Zonabend Collection (named for Nachman Zonabend, a Ghetto survivor who donated this large collection comprising material from the Nazi-imposed *Judenrat* or Jewish Council, secretly taken photographs, diaries, and more that he managed to preserve).[124] Nearly a decade later, Trunk's mammoth volume on the *Judenrat*, whose English translation won the National Jewish Book Award in 1973, revealed in excruciating detail the multiplicity of behaviors exhibited by the heads of hundreds of Jewish Councils operating under pain of death for themselves and their fellow Jews in German-controlled territory.[125]

The question of Jewish leaders' complicity with their Nazi overlords, a subject of raging public debate since the publication of Hannah Arendt's *Eichmann in Jerusalem* in 1963, was also the subject of the "Colloquium on German-Imposed Jewish Representations" convened by Weinreich in 1967, in the words of *Yedies*, "[t]o bring the light of scholarship to bear on the various facets of this problem in calmer perspective."[126]

Indeed, the overall approach of YIVO historians to the Holocaust was to be scientific and not sentimental, no matter how much they mourned privately and collectively the loss of their closest relatives and indeed of an entire civilization. It was an unquestioned assumption—a moral imperative—that YIVO scholars document and dispassionately analyze the lives and deaths of millions of Jews under extreme conditions using the same social science techniques that characterized YIVO's approach to researching prewar Jewish life. Above all, it was necessary to combat what Isaiah Trunk characterized as the post-Holocaust Jewish demand for "emotional history" and "history written cum ira et cum studio (with anger and with bias)."[127]

YIVO scholars' work situated the Holocaust in the context of centuries of Jewish history and responses to oppression and adversity, eschewing the notion that it represented a "master rupture" caused by a breakdown in civilizational norms that would come to characterize much early English-language scholarship on the subject. Before it became fashionable among scholars working in Western languages, their work also focused on the experiences and perspectives of victims rather than perpetrators. They consequently emphasized the use of internal Jewish documentation in multiple languages less familiar to Western researchers (such as Yiddish and Slavic tongues) and eyewitness testimonies (albeit treated with extreme methodological care) rather than relying exclusively on the perspective presented in the trove of German sources that had been discovered and seized in the aftermath of the war.[128] (Weinreich's *Hitler's Professors*—with its focus on perpetrators and reliance on German documentation—is here the exception). Moreover, YIVO historians' exploration of subjects such as Jewish resistance, physical as well as cultural and spiritual, and the dilemmas facing the leadership of ghetto councils helped undermine notions of Jews as passive victims. Their scholarship was consistent with YIVO's overall emphasis on how Jews *lived* rather than how they died.[129]

Conclusion

Long before the term Holocaust had become a household word in American Jewish homes or Holocaust studies had become an accepted part of the academy, YIVO scholars invested tremendous energies in amassing documentation about the crimes committed against the Jewish people and how it withstood them. They also managed to reclaim much of the surviving cultural heritage of eastern European Jewry from its ruins. "The myth of silence" in American Jewish circles surrounding the Holocaust prior to the trial of Adolf Eichmann in 1961 is very much disproved by the institute's active engagement to document and draw attention to the suffering and murder of Europe's Jews. In fact, YIVO provided material for researchers and journalists preparing for the Eichmann trial, including for the Israeli prosecution.[130] In the evaluation of historian Hasia R. Diner, the primary figure associated with debunking this myth, "No institution on the postwar American Jewish communal landscape did more to foster the presentation of the Holocaust than YIVO."[131]

Projects to document and study the *khurbn*, as the destruction of European Jewry became known among Yiddish speakers, were a very public endeavor that began early in the war years. In the early aftermath of the war, particularly when goodwill persisted among the victorious Allies, the endeavor encouraged international collaboration and thereby reinforced YIVO's identity as a global organization. Moreover, it relied on the efforts of survivors and refugees displaced from their prewar homes and uncertain where they would ultimately build their postwar lives. Prewar YIVO *zamlers* and associates again became active contributors wherever they were to be found, particularly in survivor communities. When the Iron Curtain fell by the end of the 1940s, much collaboration and communication with Jews and agencies in the communist world—most notably Poland—came to an end. Indeed, YIVO's communications with Jewish organizations and scholars in Poland would be extremely limited for decades to come. Meanwhile, new opportunities for institutional collaboration arose with the nascent State of Israel, particularly with Yad Vashem, its Holocaust authority.

In contrast, the recovery of a substantial part of YIVO's library and archives—the remnants of a destroyed civilization—was accomplished chiefly within a couple of years and thanks in great measure to the help of the US government and military officials. Moreover, these efforts unfolded largely behind the scenes—through diplomatic channels and the intervention of key individuals acting according to their moral intuitions against the backdrop of the emerging Cold War. They also occurred in competition with other organizations and states seeking to lay claim to the heritage of European Jewry. In particular, the rivalry between Diaspora Nationalist and Zionist ideologies and scholarly commitments played itself out in the competition for possession of the Jewish past in order to assert leadership for the Jewish future. YIVO was ultimately successful in its efforts in occupied Germany thanks to its new identity as an American institution; that same identity served as an impediment in dealings in a Czechoslovakia increasingly subject to Soviet influence.

As Holocaust consciousness grew in America, so too did public support—moral and financial—for YIVO's Holocaust-related collections, scholarship, and public events such as its annual commemoration of the Warsaw Ghetto Uprising and its exhibition "Life, Struggle, and Uprising in the Warsaw Ghetto," which drew more than ten thousand visitors and toured Jewish communities and universities around the country in 1964.[132] Perhaps more than any other factor at the time, YIVO's work on the Holocaust brought it to the increasing attention of an English-speaking audience consisting of both Jews and non-Jews and enhanced its status among them.[133]

For roughly a decade, however, much of this essential work would not have been possible without German reparations, monies whose acceptance was the subject of bitter division in the global community of Yiddish-speaking intellectuals as well as the larger Jewish world. Meanwhile, YIVO's activity in the area of publications, particularly of journals, necessarily slowed due to a lack of adequate personnel and funding, even as its archival holdings continued to swell with donations of materials from aging immigrant organizations and individuals seeking a home for their private legacy.

No expansion of YIVO's activity or its collection, however, could compensate for the loss of life. At least two generations of scholars engaged in creating the scaffolding for the study of Yiddish and eastern European Jewish culture and society in the YIVO social sciences tradition were gone. These losses added urgency to two other key areas of YIVO's activity: the preservation and standardization of the Yiddish language itself and the training of a new generation of scholars capable of perpetuating YIVO's traditions.

4
YIVO YIDDISH

Of the six million Jews murdered by Nazi Germany and its accomplices, as much as 85 percent were Yiddish speakers, making for what has been described as linguicide. If there were some eleven million Yiddish speakers on the eve of World War II, there remained an estimated five to six million after the war.[1] While Yiddish was still the most widely spoken language among Jews, these numbers could be expected to decline further due to the rapid pace of linguistic assimilation in postwar centers of Jewish life, particularly in the United States, Israel, and the Soviet Union—home to the vast majority of Ashkenazic Jews. As *Forverts* writer Boris Smolyar lamented in 1966, the year of YIVO's fortieth anniversary conference in New York, "Grey haired women in Jewish neighborhoods now speak mainly in English, not Yiddish like forty years ago."[2]

YIVO's critics in America long denounced what they perceived as its aloofness from its primary constituency—Yiddish-speaking Jews from eastern Europe and the secular cultural institutions they had built—and reproached it with the betrayal of its Yiddish "soul" through its use of English and engagement with American subjects in pursuit of an elusive audience of American-born Jews. Despite often being the implied target of such criticisms, Weinreich shared their conviction that a YIVO without Yiddish was no YIVO at all. Better than others, however, he understood that if YIVO were to have a present as well as a future, it would need to find a way to meet the diverging needs of two groups—or generations—who lacked literally and metaphorically a common language: an aging cohort of eastern European–born Yiddish speakers and a rising American-born generation of Jews (and non-Jews) for whom Yiddish was increasingly to be acquired not at home and in community but as adults in the classroom. The Yiddish language itself would need to become a bridge linking the generations rather than the chasm dividing them.

Beginning in World War II, Yiddish found a modest but growing place in the North American university thanks principally to the interventions of YIVO scholars and their supporters and the creation of a chair for Yiddish at Columbia University in New York. At the same time, YIVO scholars initiated epoch-making projects to preserve and perpetuate the prewar language and its culture, both recording Yiddish in all its diversity and codifying a standardized variety of it. Prominent among these initiatives was *College Yiddish*, the first Yiddish-language textbook for adult English speakers, along with dictionary projects and a language and cultural atlas.

Such efforts brought to the fore conflicting understandings both within the institute and broader Yiddish-speaking circles of how best to serve the remnants of the eastern European folk while ensuring that its legacy would have a future among generations that did not intimately know eastern Europe or its vernacular, the *folkshprakh*. At the center of discord was "YIVO Yiddish"—a catchall term for language norms associated, rightly or wrongly, with the institute and, above all, the Weinreichs, especially Uriel. The younger Weinreich occupied a central role as author and architect of some of YIVO's most important projects that have shaped the field of Yiddish studies and ensured the dominance of its language standards in the contemporary academic world.

Yiddish in the University

While YIVO's *aspirantur* was not a great success in the 1940s and the creation of an independent graduate school remained a distant goal, new opportunities and horizons for studying eastern European Jewry and Yiddish language and literature emerged as the language entered American academia. The presence of a significant number of Yiddish scholars, many of them recent arrivals from Europe, and increasing sympathy for the language of Germany's victims in influential liberal circles helped pave a way for its introduction in the form of courses taught by YIVO scholar Judah A. Joffe at the École Libres des Hautes Études (the French University-in-Exile) and the Introspectivist poet and literature critic N. B. Minkoff at the New School for Social Research during the war years. These classes complemented literature courses already given at the University of Massachusetts Extension School since 1929 by Abraham Aaron Roback. A psychologist by training, Roback was a YIVO affiliate who wrote extensively about Yiddish philology, including an English-language work about the history of Yiddish literature (*The Story of Yiddish Literature*, 1940) that YIVO commissioned to acquaint an English-speaking audience with the subject. University-level Yiddish literature courses were typically taught in English, even if some students understood Yiddish (but could not read it).[3]

It was at City College in New York City (CCNY), however, that the first regular position in Yiddish language and literature offering for-credit courses emerged in an American university. In 1947, Max Weinreich was appointed to its Department of Germanic and Slavic Languages, where he occasionally taught Russian and German as well. He thus received his very first academic appointment not as the chair for Yiddish in Vilnius, to which he never returned, but as chiefly a language instructor in an American university with a Jewish enrollment of nearly 90 percent in the interwar period.[4]

Weinreich enthusiastically announced the introduction of evening courses in Yiddish at Brooklyn College that same year as further proof of a growing tide of interest in the language, in part as a response to the

Max Weinreich and Sol Liptzin with students in Yiddish class at City College in 1947. Credit: YIVO Institute for Jewish Research

identity questions engendered among Jewish youth by the Holocaust and the war. He also hailed the preparation of a textbook under YIVO's auspices—the first of its kind—by his elder son for university instruction in Yiddish.[5]

Instrumental in launching Weinreich's integration into American academia at a time when Jewish studies of any kind was not widely recognized by it was Sol Liptzin (1901–95), the secretary of YIVO's Academic Council. Despite widespread reluctance to hire Jews for faculty positions, Liptzin was a respected literature scholar who headed City College's Department of Germanic and Slavic Languages from 1943 to 1958. Having arrived in the United States as a child from Ukraine in 1910, Liptzin followed a common immigrant pattern of ceasing to speak Yiddish with his parents as he became more comfortable in English.[6] But his encounter with Weinreich in 1933, when Weinreich was a fellow at Yale University, awakened an interest in his mother tongue. Deeply impressed by YIVO's mission, he became one of its first American academic supporters. Almost a decade later, Liptzin managed to convince City College officials not only that Yiddish was a Germanic language with a literature worthy of study but that Max Weinreich was the ideal scholar to teach it.[7]

Liptzin sought to create the material conditions—such as a more substantial salary and pension—not only for Weinreich to pursue his research but to transform YIVO into a diasporic Jewish university parallel to the Hebrew University in Jerusalem. He shared Weinreich's vision of training a new generation of American-educated scholars—a "vidervuks" (regrowth) in Liptzin's words—to replace the heavy intellectual losses sustained by Yiddish culture and to salvage and reinvigorate eastern European Jewish studies after the destruction of European Jewry.[8] Together, he and Weinreich conceived plans to obtain accreditation from the New York State Board of Regents for a fully independent, degree-granting YIVO graduate school.

Liptzin was painfully aware that American Jews perceived YIVO scholars as "impractical idlers" (*batlonim*). Disabusing them of their ignorance about Yiddish and drawing support for YIVO's mission meant not only making use of English but also adopting American methods of fundraising. This included providing scholarships to promising students and appealing to wealthy individuals who were personally very far from

Yiddish. He even met with Hollywood moguls while a visiting professor in California in the hopes of cultivating them as donors and suggested hiring a public relations firm to improve YIVO's image to compete more successfully with American Jewish organizations for donations. YIVO, like Yiddish itself, Liptzin insisted, must escape its association in the United States with the uneducated and aging and find a more lucrative financial base than the working-class immigrants and large relief organizations that had previously funded it in Europe.[9] It had to cease being perceived as a pathetic charity recipient outside of or on the margins of mainstream American Jewish life and instead be seen as a future-oriented American and world institution. Weinreich had misgivings, however, about such an approach. He believed that YIVO could not compete with the "big noise" (*groyser tararam*) that other institutions made. It would need to compete, he argued, with the clarity of its goals and the importance of its publications, not with aggressive public relations campaigns that it could scarcely afford.[10]

A big break for Liptzin's plans came when he managed with the help of non-Jewish folklorist Wayland D. Hand, the head of the UCLA German Department, to arrange for Weinreich to come to Los Angeles in the summer of 1948 to teach advanced courses in Yiddish linguistics, ethnography, and folklore at the university. The participants—forty in the folklore and ethnography course and twenty in the linguistics course—were a mixture of native-born Americans and promising youths drawn from elsewhere, including some relatively recent arrivals from Europe. Most were active in Yiddishist cultural work and youth organizations, and eleven attended with the aid of YIVO scholarships.[11] Indeed, Weinreich devoted great energy to what his student Joshua Fishman years later compared to "collecting butterflies"—recruiting and cultivating intellectually minded, Yiddish-speaking youth for the cause of Jewish scholarship.[12]

While in California, Weinreich's students served as ambassadors for Yiddish and YIVO on the campus and in the larger community. Their outdoor Yiddish sing-alongs drew interested passers-by, for example, and they also performed a marionette version of a Yiddish play in a local Yiddish secular school.[13] Their attendance proved historic in more ways than one. Weinreich emerged energized from the summer, convinced that he could achieve great things with a small cadre of highly motivated youth in America. In fact, six students emerged as prominent, lifelong contributors to Yiddish culture and scholarship (and to YIVO) under Weinreich's tutelage: linguist Uriel Weinreich, Workmen's Circle Educational Director Joseph (Yosl) Mlotek, folklorist Beatrice (Bina) Silverman (subsequently Silverman Weinreich after her marriage to Uriel in 1949), musicologist Chana (Eleanor) Gordon (later Gordon Mlotek after her marriage to Joseph in 1949), sociolinguist Joshua (Shikl) Fishman, and folklore collector and bibliographer Leonard (Leybl) Kahn. Notably, the latter four were all born in America and educated in its Yiddish secular schools, where Uriel also received a part of his education, in addition to public schools. Bundist journalist Joseph Mlotek fled Warsaw for Vilna after the outbreak of World War II. There he collected testimonies from Jewish refugees under Noah Pryłucki's guidance and enrolled in YIVO's *aspirantur*. Fortuitously, he fled to Shanghai, where he spent most of the war as a refugee, prior to arriving in Canada in 1947.[14]

Despite the success of Weinreich's visit to UCLA, he was well aware that Yiddish would not experience a revival on American soil—at least not to the extent of what was lost in Europe—by activating the passive competence of those who study it in a university classroom. "But we must not deceive ourselves about how well those who do not speak Yiddish understand it," he cautioned at a 1951 symposium devoted to problems facing the Jewish people and their survival. For the vast majority of Jews under twenty-five, he estimated, knowledge of Yiddish was limited to a few mangled words and expressions. And even those raised in homes in which much Yiddish was spoken, he noted, could seldom produce grammatical utterances.[15]

While some non-Jews elected to study Yiddish at the university level, Jewish undergraduates formed the vast majority of students who took Yiddish-language courses introduced into universities beginning in the 1940s. Some had studied in Yiddish supplementary schools. Most, however, came from homes where some Yiddish was spoken but where the attenuation of linguistic, religious, and cultural traditions was accelerated by a lack of formal Jewish education.[16] As reflected in course evaluations written by Max Weinreich's students at City College in the early 1950s, students had typically enrolled in the course not so much to attain fluency—although that certainly was desirable—but as a means to expand their understanding of Jewish history and culture, topics seldom represented in other university courses, and to make sense of the world of their parents and grandparents.[17] For many, an interest in Jewish identity and questions of Jews' relationship to the non-Jewish world had been awakened by the recent war. Whether they understood this consciously or not, Yiddish drew them, as Weinreich had argued in several of his YIVO addresses, as the key to unlocking their collective past and as an aid in understanding contemporary Jewish problems. Some students might have found practical value in learning Yiddish in order to pursue a career in social work within the Jewish community or to work for a Yiddish-speaking cultural organization, but a journey of personal discovery was often their primary motivation.

College Yiddish

In facilitating this journey, a new textbook uniquely suited to the needs of a postwar American-educated audience proved invaluable. Without a doubt the most influential work of modern Yiddish pedagogy to date, Uriel Weinreich's *College Yiddish* has gone through six editions (and more than twenty print runs as well as appeared in Hebrew translation) with only slight changes—chiefly to update demographic statistics—since it first appeared in 1949.[18] Its author embodied a unique fusion of the scholarly traditions of YIVO and of American academia and in many ways represented the institution's best hopes for future leadership and direction.

Born in Vilna in 1926, Uriel Weinreich was raised in the atmosphere of YIVO and Vilna's secular Yiddishist intelligentsia. He attended the city's Sophia Markova Gurevitch Yiddish secular school, where his mother, Regina, was a teacher, and the city's Yiddish Real-gimnazye (secondary school emphasizing math and natural sciences). Uriel completed the first year of the Real-gimnazye's six-year program prior to leaving Vilna with his parents in the summer of 1939. Fluent in both his native Yiddish and Polish, he acquired Danish as a pupil in a local school during the six months he spent with his father in Copenhagen after the outbreak of World War II. He arrived in the United States in the spring of 1940 as an almost fourteen-year-old refugee and enrolled in George Washington High School in Upper Manhattan, where he quickly mastered English and graduated as salutatorian in 1943. He also attended the Sholem Aleichem Folk Institute's *mitlshul* (high school) near Union Square on weekends and was active, along with his younger brother

Gabriel, in *Hemshekh*, a Yiddishist youth group uniting Jewish refugees from Poland with American-born Yiddish speakers.[19]

With the help of a Pulitzer Free Scholarship, Uriel pursued a BA at Columbia until he was drafted into the US Army in the summer of 1944. He served in army intelligence in Germany and learned Russian while working in the Allied Control Commission in Romania. During this period, he also began composing what would become *College Yiddish*.[20] After his discharge from the military, Uriel resumed his studies at Columbia in the latter half of 1946. There he earned a Bachelor of Arts degree in 1948 and a Master's in linguistics the following year under the guidance of prominent scholars André Martinet and Roman Jakobson.[21]

In writing *College Yiddish*, Uriel Weinreich went far beyond furnishing students with a systematic grounding in vocabulary and grammatical structures on par with textbooks used in first- and second-year courses for other modern languages in university classrooms. He sought to distill between its covers the essence of a civilization as well as to present

Uriel Weinreich (right side of table, center) and Beatrice Silverman (later Weinreich, left side of table, center) in a YIVO seminar led by Jacob Shatzky, 1947. Credit: YIVO Institute for Jewish Research

a comprehensive, if brief, overview of the field of Yiddish studies. Each chapter's readings offer a lesson in some aspect of Yiddish-speaking society: its history, literature and theater, schools, religious philosophy, folk culture, and general way of life. Decades later, it remains a remarkable cultural artifact not only as an expression of Yiddishist ideology but as an early response to the Holocaust.[22] The book's memorable opening sentences in Yiddish are themselves as much a matter-of-fact summary of Jewish demographics in 1949 as an affirmation of national survival and the enduring relevance of Yiddish as a language that "unites Jews in all countries": "Jews are today a people numbering eleven million. Jews live on all continents: in America, in Europe, in Asia and in Australia. . . . In the United States, Jews speak Yiddish and English. In Argentina and Mexico, Jews speak Yiddish and Spanish. In many countries, Jews speak Yiddish. Yiddish is the language of Jews in many countries."[23]

Characteristic of the book's unflinching approach to the Holocaust are frank depictions of conditions such as starvation and epidemics in ghettos (accompanied by photos of the Warsaw Ghetto and its 1943 uprising from YIVO's archives) and descriptions of Germany's antisemitic rampage that teach the vocabulary of murder (e.g., *umgebrengt*, "killed," and *der gaz*, "gas").[24] No doubt the choice of reading selections featured in the book, many of which are original compositions by the author about families affected by war and displacement, was influenced by the author's own experience reading letters from family friends and relatives who were refugees in the immediate postwar years as well as by his personal encounters with surviving European Jews while serving in the US military. Further addressing key aspects of both traditional and modern Jew hatred, the book offers folklore passages about Elijah the Prophet rescuing medieval European Jews from a blood libel (chapter 15) and a chapter (chapter 23) titled "Di yidishe noz" ("The Jewish Nose") dispelling notions of Jews' racial homogeneity.

Nonetheless, the overwhelming impression conveyed by *College Yiddish* is not a depressing litany of bigotry and loss. It does not present the recent genocide of European Jewry as a final rupture in the millennium-old life of the Yiddish language and Ashkenazic civilization. On the contrary, the book emphasizes continuity, presenting Yiddish as a living language and its culture as that of an unfolding, if severely reduced, *global* civilization. Peppered with good-natured humor, proverbs, folklore, riddles, and moralistic tales drawn from the Jewish tradition, the book is dedicated as "a gift to all in whose children's mouths Yiddish will live"—a reference to both native speakers (who may be turning to the book to learn standard grammar and pronunciation or to teach it to their children) and novice language learners who, it may be hoped, will adopt it as their own.

Channeling the collective preoccupations of scholars eager to demonstrate the autonomy of Yiddish and the value of its high culture, *College Yiddish* also goes to great lengths to correct common misperceptions about Yiddish as a deformation of contemporary German. It does so in part by explaining how both Yiddish and modern German share a common ancestor in medieval German dialects—"just as present-day man and ape may be said to be descended from a common pre-human, pre-simian ancestor"—but developed in parallel and under different influences into distinct literary languages.[25] At the same time that its distance from German is asserted, Yiddish is placed in the context of a larger and ancient phenomenon of Jewish-language creation beginning with Hebrew that has resulted in analogous vernaculars among non-Ashkenazic Jews such as Judezmo (Ladino) and Judeo-Arabic that can be studied in comparison to shed light on "what is specific in Jewish life and culture, as well as to trace similarities and contrasts between various Jewish communities." Of all diasporic Jewish languages, however, "Yiddish is most richly developed and is furthest removed from its origins."[26]

Yiddish is presented throughout the book as "a key to Jewish life"—that is, a tool for understanding the unique cultural history of Ashkenazic Jewry.[27] Students thus learn about the history of Jews in central and eastern Europe, including their persecution, through explanations of idioms reflecting earlier times (such as *meylekh sabetskes yorn*, "in the olden days," i.e., in the days of Poland's King Sobieski in the seventeenth century, and *me zol im afile brenen un brotn*, "even if he should be burned and roasted," as an indication of someone's unstinting commitment).[28] They also learn about differences between Yiddish dialects, their geographical distribution, and the language's standardization, including the prominent role played by YIVO in this process (ch. 2).

The work of a young man raised in an agnostic, if not atheist, home where Jewish dietary laws and religious practice were absent, the textbook nonetheless displays a respectful attitude toward religious culture and informs readers about aspects of traditional practice, such as the observance of Sabbath and holidays.[29] The Hasidic movement (ch. 27) is singled out not as an archconservative and coercive force, as was common in the literature of the *Haskalah* and among much of the Jewish Left prior to World War II, but for its important contributions to Yiddish culture, including the development of modern Yiddish literature. Students also learn about important Jewish historical figures—prominent rabbis such as Rashi (ch. 19) as well as secular political and cultural leaders—and the basics of the Jewish calendar and holidays (ch. 22).

Perhaps also unexpectedly for the work of a scholar raised in circles associated with the Bund, explicit endorsements of socialism or left-leaning ideologies are absent. There are, however, comments about the historical role of the Bund and illustrations of folk wisdom disapproving of materialism as well as anodyne references to the shared brotherhood of peoples, as expressed, for example, in Y. L. Peretz's poem "Ale mentshn zaynen brider" ("All People Are Brothers," ch. 5). Further, in keeping with widespread sentiments among Jews after the Holocaust, Israel is treated positively as a home that has welcomed many Yiddish-speaking immigrants and their children. Indeed, one chapter's reading is exclusively devoted to the career of Theodor Herzl, the "father" of political Zionism (ch. 2).

Nonetheless, *College Yiddish* unambiguously conveys the message that Israel has not supplanted the Diaspora either in demographic terms or in its significance for the future of Jewish life. True to the Dubnowian model of multiple hegemonic centers of Jewish civilization, Israel is depicted—alongside the United States, whose Yiddish culture also receives attention—as an emerging but not exclusive center of Jewish life. At the same time, *College Yiddish* posits traditional religious culture as the antecedent of modern secular Yiddish culture, by which it has been implicitly supplanted. These views are consistent with those of the author's father, who expressed profound respect after World War II for religious tradition as the foundation of Yiddish culture and accepted Israel, albeit ambivalently, as a modern Jewish society despite never relinquishing his secularism or commitment to Jews as a world people.[30] They also reflect the general orientation of YIVO in America, which emphasized commitment to Jewish peoplehood (including non-Ashkenazic Jews) alongside the Yiddish language and literature as the primary factor uniting Jews on all continents. Indeed, *College Yiddish* does not mince words in expressing a conception of Jews as a transnational *folk* (translated in the glossary as "people" or "ethnic community") despite the widespread understanding in the United States of Jews as foremost a religious community.

Reviews of *College Yiddish* in English-language periodicals were generally positive, such as the one in *Commentary*, a Jewish intellectual journal favorably inclined toward YIVO's mission of engaging with the recent eastern European Jewish past while constructing an American Jewish future.[31] The journal celebrated Uriel Weinreich's work as "the first textbook in Yiddish or Hebrew which can compare favorably both in content and organization with the best textbooks in the other modern languages." The book was a huge success in the reviewer's appraisal for both its historical-cultural content and its approach to grammar, even if "the number of words and grammatical details introduced in *College Yiddish* is much higher than one finds in first-year texts in the other modern languages."[32] The author of a review in the professional journal *American Speech*, himself an English dialect specialist, similarly observed that "unlike many introductory language texts, this one has been produced by a competent linguist."[33] Nonetheless, at least one reviewer expressed a more patronizing view of its ambitions:

> A measure of admiration is due the small heroic band of devotees which, with a gesture likely to prove quixotic, is laboring to bolster up the waning interest in Yiddish. The stronghold of Yiddish speech and culture was destroyed with the Nazi extermination of East-European Jewry. In this country, children of Yiddish-speaking parents are increasingly drifting away from Yiddish as a medium of speech or literary pursuit.
>
> That this quantitatively imposing volume with the grandiloquent name (whatever "College Yiddish" may mean) will succeed in reversing the trend is hardly to be expected.[34]

While the reviewer was correct in an absolute sense—the textbook did not stem, of course, the tide of language shift—he underestimated the role the textbook would play in not only transmitting the language but awakening and deepening interest in its culture for generations to come as university attendance increasingly became the norm among American Jewish youth.

The Atran Chair for Yiddish at Columbia University

While Max Weinreich's position for Yiddish at City College added to the language's prestige in American Jewish circles, a much greater boost for the language and YIVO's activities came through association with Columbia University. Weinreich first learned in May 1950 from the Bundist journalist Tsivyen, pen name of Ben-Zion Hoffman, that a "good friend" sought to endow a Yiddish chair at Columbia University. While the notion that Columbia would accept money for such a position struck him at the time as "fantastic," Weinreich was assured by Jakobson and Martinet in Columbia's Linguistics Department that a Yiddish chair was indeed feasible if adequate funds could be found.[35] Tsivyen's "good friend" turned out to be Frank (Efroym Zalmen) Atran, a Bundist from Poland who was the chairman of an international hosiery manufacturing concern prior to World War II. Atran fled in 1940 to the United States, where he had extended family, and became wealthy in real estate and property management. During the war years, he was active in the Jewish Labor Committee's efforts to help underground movements and to rescue Jews and others being persecuted in Europe. In 1945, he founded the Atran Foundation, which aided Jewish refugees in Europe as well as supported medical philanthropy and the furtherance of Yiddish culture in the United States. Weinreich himself later joined the board of the foundation, which has remained a generous supporter of Yiddish and YIVO to this day.[36]

Max Weinreich was apparently the desired candidate for the Columbia chair, but he had no personal interest in the position other than to ensure that it did indeed materialize—ideally, with Uriel as the occupant.[37] Opposition initially existed to Uriel's appointment because of his youth and lack of experience, but few could deny that he possessed tremendous talent.[38] He also enjoyed the support of respected scholars, including his dissertation adviser at Columbia and his influential father. Any lingering doubts dissipated within a few years as he rose with lightning speed through academic ranks.

While he was not obliged to compete with other candidates for the position, Uriel began his appointment in Columbia with the relatively lowly rank of "associate in Yiddish Language, Literature, and Culture" in 1952. By the following year, however, he had been promoted to Assistant Professor—the first step on the normal path to tenure in a university.

In 1956, he received tenure as an associate professor of linguistics and Yiddish studies on the Atran Chair. Finally, in 1960, he became a full professor and bore the title of Atran Professor of Yiddish Language, Literature, and Culture.[39] Despite his extremely busy schedule as a researcher, teacher, and administrator outside of YIVO, Uriel remained active in the institute throughout his short adult life—including as editor (together with Beatrice Weinreich, Chana Mlotek, and Wolf Younin) of the journal *Yidisher folklor* produced by YIVO's Y. L. Cahan Folklore Club, as a member of its Linguistics Circle, as a frequent lecturer at its events, and eventually, as a member of its Committee on Research Planning.

Beyond his contributions as a researcher, administrator, and mentor, Uriel's extraordinary breadth as a teacher is reflected in the courses he offered during his fifteen years of activity as a Columbia faculty member. He taught a total of fifteen different courses for MA and PhD candidates in Yiddish studies: six in linguistics, six in literature, two straddling literature and linguistics, and one on folklore. These included such topics as the formation of the Yiddish literary language, topics in the pre-nineteenth-century language and literature, the Germanic component of Yiddish, Y. L. Peretz and his world, and contemporary Yiddish poetry. In 1954, he edited *The Field of Yiddish*, the first of a series of English-language collections of studies about Yiddish linguistics, folklore, and literature with contributions from YIVO and non-YIVO scholars alike that helped both to conceptualize the contours of Yiddish studies as a field and to integrate it into American academia.[40] At the same time, he also taught general linguistics, served as editor of the influential linguistics journal *Word*, and chaired Columbia's Department of Linguistics from 1957 to 1965.[41] As his doctoral student William Labov, founder of the field of variationist sociolinguistics, recalled, Uriel Weinreich's name inspired well-nigh universal respect in general linguistics circles.[42] His scholarship in general linguistics artfully made use of Yiddish to illustrate phenomena or insights of universal relevance.

While an independent YIVO graduate school remained a desideratum, the presence of a foothold for Yiddish in the graduate linguistics program at a leading American university met some of the need for training a new generation of Yiddish teachers and scholars (notably at Columbia's, not YIVO's expense) and afforded YIVO through Uriel's person a degree of access to Columbia's infrastructure and resources. Further, the association with Columbia provided an immeasurable boost in prestige for both YIVO and Yiddish, especially in the English-speaking world. Among Uriel's students who went on to become leaders in the field (and active in YIVO) were the Toronto-born and bred linguist Marvin (Mikhl) Herzog and Israeli literature scholar Dan Miron (who completed his literature study with Max Weinreich after Uriel's death). Another prominent literature scholar, Ruth Wisse—also a Canadian (born in Czernowitz but raised in Montreal)—studied Yiddish literature one-on-one with Max Weinreich, who substituted for Uriel at Columbia during his sabbatical in Israel in 1959–60.[43]

It is not clear why Columbia's administration was receptive to the offer of Frank Atran, a Jewish refugee with a socialist past turned real estate mogul, to fund a chair for a language long held in low esteem by Jews and Gentiles alike in the United States. Columbia already possessed the privately endowed Nathan L. Miller Chair in Jewish History, occupied since its inception in 1929 by renowned scholar Salo Baron, himself an import from eastern Europe via Vienna (born and raised in Galicia in Austria-Hungary).[44] But it remained an institution known, like other Ivy League schools, for its lack of enthusiasm for Jews as either students or faculty members, as reflected in a quota and other measures to limit Jews' enrollment implemented during the long tenure (1902–45) of President Nicholas Butler.[45]

Perhaps in the wake of the Holocaust, as the stigma attached to the language began to recede, Columbia hoped to atone for a history of institutional antisemitism as elite American universities began to become more hospitable to Jews and/or to inspire contributions from additional Jewish donors for other purposes. There can be no question, however, that the presence of a Yiddish chair at an Ivy League school occupied by a scholar of Uriel Weinreich's caliber set a precedent for other institutions. For-credit courses in Yiddish were introduced in a growing number of universities, including Brooklyn College, Georgetown University, and Brandeis University (where money was donated to establish a Yiddish chair in 1960).[46] Equally, if not more, important in fueling Yiddish's expansion in the American university was the general "ethnic revival" in American society that arose in the context of 1960s counterculture.

The post–World War II era saw Jews' widespread movement out of densely populated immigrant and second-generation urban neighborhoods to suburbs in which synagogue membership became the major barometer of Jewish affiliation (even if religious observance was not on the rise)—what sociologist Nathan Glazer described as a move from Jewishness to Judaism.[47] Despite affluence and acculturation, the discrediting of antisemitism by Nazi atrocities, and the growth of civil rights measures to guard against racial and religious discrimination, many Jews still felt ill at ease in their new environments. In particular, they worried about the attenuation of community and ethnic culture, as well as the persistence of Jew hatred in neighborhoods from which Jews had often been excluded until recently. Malaise and the search for "authentic" content and meaning for their middle-class Jewish identities were expressed in articles in English-language Jewish intellectual journals exploring the "decline" of Jewishness and seeking strategies, including drawing upon select elements of eastern European Jewish culture, to address it. Growing interest in Yiddish culture among English speakers was reflected in the popularity of translated works of Yiddish writers such as Sholem Aleichem and Isaac Bashevis Singer in, for example, Irving Howe and Eliezer Greenberg's *Treasury of Yiddish Stories* (1954) and of *Life Is with People* (1952), an anthropological study offering a composite picture of the "lost world" of shtetl culture. Nonetheless, Yiddish and its culture were still both too close and too foreign—and hence menacing to their sense of Americanness and social integration—to inspire widespread appreciation among the vast majority of American Jews.[48]

It was not until the mid-1960s that a more sizable interest was kindled, especially among young people more distant from Yiddish and ethnic neighborhoods than their parents' generation. By then, changes in American society that fostered the strengthening and public expression of other minority identities, foremost Black and Hispanic, not only made the reclamation of ethnic identity and culture socially acceptable among acculturated American Jews but also encouraged its public celebration. Holocaust consciousness and the trauma engendered by Israel's wars in 1967 and 1973, which were widely understood as struggles for Jews' collective survival, provided further impetus for the renewal of Jewish identity, both religious and secular, in the United States. This trend often found expression in the pursuit of Jewish studies in universities, where middle-class Jewish students enrolled in record numbers—often in private colleges that had restricted their admission not long before. This interest extended to courses for both Modern Hebrew and Yiddish.[49]

College Yiddish became the default textbook in the university, holding an effective monopoly in the field for decades in the absence of serious rivals. The ready availability of a well-designed textbook published with YIVO's imprimatur also made it possible for virtually anyone with knowledge of the language to become an instructor in informal settings, such as in classes organized by the network of Hillel houses on campuses and in Jewish community centers. Through its influence in training generations of Yiddish teachers, YIVO's conception of "Standard Yiddish" (*klal-yidish*) has reached countless language learners.

Standard Yiddish

Prior to World War II, YIVO scholars worked assiduously—parallel to Soviet Yiddish-language planners—to codify the norms of an already emerging Yiddish *kultursphrakh*, a register for cultured use. This variety was not meant to be identical with any one dialect and could therefore be shared by all Yiddish speakers, especially for formal purposes such as publications, schools, and academia. It was widely agreed that the basis for this Yiddish was the literary language that had emerged largely thanks to the writings of leading Yiddish writers in the late nineteenth and early twentieth centuries. In its grammar, "literary Yiddish" favors forms derived from southern dialects (central or "Polish"/"Galician" and southeastern or "Ukrainian" Yiddish) employed by writers such as Mendele Moykher Sforim, Y. L. Peretz, and Sholem Aleichem. Its pronunciation, in contrast, was based on the northeastern ("Lithuanian") dialect—or, to be more precise, the pronunciation of secular Vilna intellectuals such as those gathered around YIVO.

Independent of YIVO's efforts, so-called literary pronunciation was widely used by the 1920s in the Yiddish secular sector in Europe, North America, and elsewhere—for example, in schools, in speeches at political gatherings and union meetings (although not in theater and film, where "Ukrainian" Yiddish was typically used outside the Soviet Union). It derived its prestige from the Vilna area's reputation as a center for both traditional and modern Jewish learning as well as the city's important role in the development of modern Jewish intellectual and political movements such as the Bund and Zionism.[50]

Following World War II, the need for a standardized, prestige-bearing variety of Yiddish that transcended all dialects and united Yiddish speakers around the world took on even greater importance for YIVO linguists in response to what they considered alarming trends. Writing in 1941, Max Weinreich described Yiddish as being in a "state of disintegration" in the mouths of American-born speakers unaccustomed to speaking it outside the home.[51] To the extent that school-age children heard Yiddish, they often heard multiple dialects from family members originating in different regions in the limited context of home life (so-called kitchen Yiddish) without the reinforcement of Yiddish as a language of the broader community or as a literary language.[52] Beyond the noticeable impact of English phonology, grammar, and vocabulary (all of which impeded communication with Yiddish speakers outside the anglophone world), dialect mixing could be commonly heard among them.[53] Since most youth principally spoke English in their daily lives, there was little expectation among YIVO language scholars of the formation of a distinctly American variant of Yiddish that would arise through a fusion of influences, stabilize in terms of grammar and pronunciation, and be transmitted further in the way that eastern European dialects had crystallized over time and been passed across generations.

Optimists placed their hopes on the small minority of children who were being educated in the networks of Yiddish secular schools to form the next cohort that would speak and be culturally creative in Yiddish. But not only were enrollments in the schools declining by the 1950s. It could not be assumed by the 1940s that most children attending Yiddish supplementary schools, such as those of the Workmen's Circle, came from Yiddish-speaking homes or would become fluent in the language through regular instruction.[54]

The erosion of linguistic norms made it all the more important in Uriel Weinreich's evaluation to impart not only standardized grammar but also standardized pronunciation to Yiddish learners. As he wrote in 1951 in *Yidishe shprakh*, YIVO's journal for language standardization launched in 1941, "If, however, the school organizations and teachers will cooperate in the matter, the generation growing up will at least know that there is a standard (*klal*) pronunciation and will use it—to the extent that it will speak Yiddish in general."[55]

While painfully conscious of the decline of Yiddish in secular circles, like most YIVO linguists, Uriel seems then to have been little aware of developments in the *haredi* ("Ultra-Orthodox") sector, whose organized presence in the United States was negligible prior to World War II.[56] The language was now being passed on in many *haredi*, especially Hasidic, communities as an integral part of Jewish identity—indeed, often with greater intentionality than in those same communities in the prewar era. Nowhere does this characterization apply more than among Holocaust survivors and refugees from the pre–World War I Hungarian cultural sphere who built tight-knit communities in Brooklyn neighborhoods such as Williamsburg and Boro Park.

While YIVO linguists' neglect of *haredi* society despite their geographic proximity may strike contemporary observers as an oversight, it must be borne in mind that YIVO scholars were not only preoccupied with their own circles, which they deemed linguistically normative.[57] Transplanted *haredi* communities, which were busy reconstituting themselves after their decimation during the Holocaust, were themselves wary of secular Yiddishists. The latter outnumbered them significantly and presented a formidable ideological danger in the early postwar decades precisely because they operated large cultural institutions, including multiple daily newspapers, and shared a language and cultural heritage with other eastern European Yiddish speakers.[58] Nor were Yiddish-speaking *haredi* communities receptive to notions of linguistic "purity," let alone to YIVO's brand of linguistic prescriptivism that eschewed anglicisms and Germanized spelling conventions (if they were indeed aware of it).[59]

Uriel did by the early 1960s anticipate the growth of a Yiddish based on the dialect spoken in eastern Transcarpathia (the basis of the Yiddish spoken by most "Hungarian" Hasidim in America today and the subject of Franz Beranek's Nazi-supported study). Indeed, sociologist Solomon Poll reported to YIVO's Social Science Circle in 1962 on the expanded use of Yiddish in all spheres of life among recently arrived "Hungarian Hasidim" in Williamsburg in comparison with Hungary, "where Yiddish was only used among small and isolated groups of orthodox and Hasidic Jews."[60] But Uriel likely did not foresee the exponential demographic growth in Yiddish-speaking *haredi* circles in America and elsewhere after the Holocaust.[61] And even if he had, it is unlikely that an encounter with the evolving features of this dialect would have dissuaded him or other YIVO scholars from efforts to complete the codification of Yiddish based on the norms of the prewar secular sector. The codified language receives its most explicit elaboration for English speakers on the pages of *College Yiddish*. There Uriel Weinreich explains the grammatical and phonetic norms of *klal-yidish* (as YIVO usually called its conception of a Standard Yiddish in publications after World War II; here, *klal* means "common" in the sense of the common or shared possession of all Yiddish speakers).[62]

The advancement of Lithuanian dialect as the basis of a standard pronunciation met with opposition—both before and after the war—from proponents of other dialects as well as from opponents of the very idea of a standard pronunciation. The most trenchant critique was offered by Solomon Birnbaum, the lone *haredi* (although not "Hungarian") Yiddish linguist operating in a field dominated by ideological secularists. In particular, he opposed the Lithuanian-based standard for introducing vowel mergers not occurring in any natural Yiddish dialect and which, he argued, created homophones (e.g., *toyb* for both "deaf" and "dove," whereas Yiddish dialects distinguish between the two) that mirrored German (*taube* and *Taube* for "deaf person" and "dove"). Years later, he would sharpen his critique, arguing that such a pronunciation was limited to YIVO circles—"convinced democrats" who, ironically, wished to impose their will on the majority (three-quarters in his estimation) of Yiddish speakers, who were speakers of southern dialects. His views were shared by YIVO's own Chaim Gininger, who publicly objected to declaring any pronunciation normative or "superior" to others. While continuing to work in YIVO, for personal and professional reasons, Gininger grew increasingly disgruntled with the institute and privately shared Birnbaum's rejection of Yiddishism as a secularist distortion of traditional *Yidishkeyt*.[63]

The chief postwar opposition in America to YIVO's linguistic prescriptions was, however, in the areas of spelling and vocabulary. These too were controversial matters in Europe, where rival spelling systems engineered by YIVO, Soviet scholars, and Birnbaum all competed to unseat older, German-influenced conventions common in Yiddish publications. But whereas European critics in the prewar Yiddish secular sector were inclined to fault YIVO's spelling reforms with not being radical enough—especially YIVO's rejection of a scheme to spell elements of Hebrew origin phonetically—they were typically rejected as too radical in postwar America.[64]

"YIVO Yiddish"

The American Yiddish press was, in the eyes of Yiddish scholars, fraught with lexical, orthographic, and even syntactic *daytshmerizms* (as modern German borrowings were derisively called in contrast with elements of medieval German origin considered native to Yiddish). Since the *Haskalah*, Yiddish spelling was subjected to Germanizing influences (despite the use of different alphabets) as part of efforts to "ennoble" the language by bringing it closer to German, which enjoyed great prestige among eastern European Jews as a language of humanism, commerce, science, and social progress prior to the Nazi era. Since the nineteenth century, many German words were also borrowed for aesthetic reasons or simply to express new realia and concepts—for example, *tsaytung*, "newspaper," from German *Zeitung*. In America, these tendencies were reinforced by the formative influence of the German socialist movement and its press on the early immigrant Yiddish press.[65]

In its embrace of *daytshmerish*, the American Yiddish press compared unfavorably in the eyes of YIVO scholars with much of the interwar Yiddish press in noncommunist eastern Europe, where reformist measures encouraged "purifying" Yiddish of "barbarisms," whether they be borrowings from German, Russian, or Polish. Still, many Germanisms had penetrated since the late nineteenth century into the spoken language on both sides of the Atlantic.[66] While disagreements were not lacking either before or after World War II among YIVO scholars about what constituted *daytshmerish* and to what extent Germanisms should be purged from the language, there existed a consensus that their presence represented a distortion of the language.[67]

YIVO's efforts to fashion a scholarly idiom in Yiddish that eschewed Germanisms as much as possible and cultivated Yiddish's native resources to express new and complicated ideas won it frequent criticism. With some important exceptions—such as leading poets and writers H. Leivick (1888–1962), Joseph Opatoshu (1886–1954), and Jacob

Glatstein (1896–1971), who served on various committees and/or its Executive Board through the years—Yiddish literary figures in America generally kept a distance from YIVO's administration and seldom spoke at its conferences. Hungering for an audience, they may have been put off and their egos wounded by the relative lack of attention that YIVO gave to contemporary belles lettres, as was the case prior to World War II too, in its publications.[68] Their coolness to the institute also derived from their sense of its academic elitism, which was manifest, for example, in linguistically puristic campaigns they deemed as having gone too far. Complaints abounded in the American Yiddish press of "YIVO Yiddish," a "contrived" language that its detractors considered a distortion of the language as it was actually used by native speakers and used in Yiddish literature. The language of YIVO publications, they complained, was difficult to parse for the average reader and full of awkward neologisms that frequently went unacknowledged as such. Max Weinreich himself proudly coined hundreds of new words over the course of his career in addition to employing neologisms introduced by others and dialectal forms that were often unfamiliar to readers.[69] Writing under his usual pseudonym, Yitskhok Varshavski, in the *Forverts*, I. B. Singer lamented, for example, "not knowing whether to laugh or cry" upon hearing such bizarre terms as *kadmen-yidish* and *bereyshis-yidish* ("Proto-Yiddish" and "Early Yiddish," words coined by Max Weinreich to refer to phases in the history of the language) at a YIVO lecture.[70]

Similarly, the veteran *Forverts* columnist Tsivyen, a YIVO supporter who would later serve on its Board of Directors, complained in a discussion on the pages of *Yidishe shprakh* that the average Yiddish reader's comprehension was strained by the artificiality and snobbishness of the language in YIVO publications. This was marked above all by the avoidance of Germanisms that had taken deep root in the language such as *forshlog* ("recommendation"), a taste for highfalutin Hebraisms, the rejection of useful anglicisms such as *beybi* ("baby") and *trobl* ("trouble"), and the use of a spelling system that departed from the norms of the American Yiddish press. "For whom do they write in this way?" he asked. "Only for a small number of scholars? But our language is not for scholars."[71]

While an admirer of Yiddish literature who invited authors to read aloud from their works at soirees in his own home, Weinreich seldom treated contemporary writers as arbiters of linguistic correctness.[72] For his own writing in the *Forverts*, he consciously used a language more accessible to the average reader (and acceptable to editors). But his focus in YIVO publications was on his own needs and the needs of those like him, even if this meant a small avant-garde that would contribute to the growth of the language and make use of it in the future. He thus responded—not without a measure of condescension,

> For Mr. Tsivyen the question of Yiddish ends with the current generation, but for me it is a question of future generations. The second difference is that Mr. Tsivyen writes for a newspaper, but I need a language for all areas of life. I am therefore not obligated to avoid words that are difficult; if one needs those difficult words, one has to learn them. One learns language. Only among Jews do some think that one does not need to learn.[73]

The Spelling Debate

It would be an understatement to say that Weinreich's hand could be felt in virtually all YIVO endeavors while he was research director. Despite not being the official proofreader for YIVO publications—a task that would fall to Szymon Dawidowicz, a Bundist refugee who arrived in the US in 1940 (and future husband of American Jewish historian Lucy Dawidowicz née Shildkret)—he strived to ensure that all YIVO's publications met with "Vilna standards." They were to be written in a similarly high caliber, correctly employ YIVO's Standard Yiddish Orthography, and not stray too far from what he considered acceptable vocabulary. The time he invested in reading not only scholarly articles but internal communications was great, and his interventions, both in terms of language and style, were frequently perceived as meddlesome, if not controlling and condescending. Jacob Shatzky, for one, was so angered by Weinreich's editing of the first two volumes of his (unfinished) monumental study *Geshikhte fun yidn in varshe* (History of the Jews in Warsaw) that he launched a formal complaint against him that had to be settled by an internal adjudication commission consisting of Mark Wischnitzer, Abraham Joshua Heschel, and Samuel Charney.[74]

Even after his resignation as de facto head of the institution, Weinreich continued to exert great influence, particularly on language matters, through both his personal influence and the engagement of his "disciples" within the institute. Beginning in 1955, for example, YIVO initiated a letter-writing campaign, organized by linguist Mordkhe Schaechter with Max Weinreich's support, for the implementation of its orthographic system in the New York Yiddish daily press.[75] The result was a public debate about spelling reform, particularly in the *Forverts*, with the participation of YIVO associates, teachers, writers, newspaper editors, and readers.

In general, the debate pitted those who taught or mentored youth and saw them as future producers and consumers of Yiddish culture against those who had little hope for a Yiddish readership beyond their own generation. Representative of this debate were the remarks of Chava Rosenfarb, later to earn acclaim for her novels about the Holocaust, who was then teaching in a Yiddish secular school in Montreal. Rosenfarb complained, for example, that her students were perplexed that the YIVO orthography they were learning in school was not used in the Yiddish press. She asked the editors of the *Forverts* to account for the presence of so much "chaos"—the absence of a single standard for spelling in the Yiddish press, which she and other educators complained discouraged students from reading Yiddish newspapers.[76] A contrary position was taken by the American reader M. Smits, who countered that there was no point in trying to accommodate students since "school children are not future readers of the Yiddish press." Adopting YIVO spelling in the *Forverts* for the benefit of youth unlikely ever to read Yiddish again after bar-mitzvahs (and with it often the completion of their formal Jewish educations) was, he advanced, guaranteed only to alienate older readers who were comfortable with the existing system.[77]

In January 1956, a delegation of educators—Mordkhe Schaechter (representing the Sholem Aleichem Folk Institute), Yosl Mlotek (for the Workmen's schools), L. Rubinstein (for the Labor Zionist Farband schools), and Uriel Weinreich (representing Yiddish courses in universities)—met with the editors of the New York dailies *Forverts* and *Der tog*. The delegation presented a sixteen-page memorandum authored by Schaechter proposing spelling reforms in keeping with the system outlined in YIVO's *Takones fun yidishn oysleyg* (Rules of Yiddish Spelling), the YIVO spelling codex.[78]

In addressing the memorandum on the pages of the *Forverts*, the newspaper's editor, Shimen Weber, pointed out that some measures proposed by YIVO had already been adopted by the newspaper in previous years, such as dropping a silent *hey* in many words, modeled on the use of a silent *h* in German orthography. More changes were possible, he acknowledged, but only on the condition that they demonstrably represented improvements. He objected to a variety of elements of the YIVO spelling system—such as the dropping of a silent *ayin* that he did not consider silent—on the grounds that they achieved the contrary, making reading more difficult or even distorting the language.[79] He concluded that "there is no reason why students, who possess education, cannot read a Yiddish newspaper because of the so-called silent *ayin*. For American young people, that certainly ought not to be an obstacle. Even if the *ayin* were entirely silent, they are accustomed to such things. The English language has many silent letters. . . . But if they don't read any Yiddish newspapers, throwing out the *ayins* will not help at all." The best way to encourage Yiddish readership among youth, he concluded, was not for the Yiddish press to reform its spelling in accord with YIVO norms but for Yiddish professors to teach proper (i.e., non-YIVO) Yiddish.[80] As far as Weber was concerned, Yiddish linguists should take their cue from Yiddish writers and not the reverse.[81]

Looking past the frequent exchanges of personal slights, there can be little doubt that the issue of Yiddish spelling was one of greater symbolic than practical import for adult native speakers of the language already accustomed to a given system. For them, the spelling conventions that dominated New York's daily Yiddish press presented no difficulties outside of perhaps unfamiliar words such as neologisms and internationalisms that they were encountering for the first time. The need for a near-perfect spelling system—one with an almost one-to-one correspondence between grapheme and phoneme—struck many as not only an affront to tradition but as wholly unnecessary, especially when a language such as English fares quite well with so imperfect a system (or rather, multiple systems, e.g., British and American orthographies). The adoption of YIVO's system meant to its champions, however, not only distancing Yiddish from selective dependence on Germanized norms—a sign in their minds of subservience to a more powerful language, one with which Yiddish speakers now often held particularly negative associations. It also meant asserting the authority of the institute's scholars—rather than that of Yiddish writers or editors—in matters of style and linguistic correctness. Finally, it announced solidarity with the perspective that Yiddish's future in America beyond the eastern European-born generations—to the extent that it had one—resided among Jewish youth learning Yiddish in secular schools and, above all, universities, where YIVO norms were taught.

The Campaign for YIVO Spelling

It was of the utmost importance to Max Weinreich that Standard Yiddish Orthography (known in YIVO publications as *der eynheytlekher oysleyg*—uniform spelling—and popularly as "YIVO spelling") be adopted by as many publications and institutions as possible. In 1958, an international academic Yiddish conference, the first of its kind in the United States, was held through the cooperation of YIVO, Columbia University, City College, and the Hebrew University. The four-day conference drew the participation of some forty scholars active in areas of Yiddish linguistics, literature, folklore, and more from around the world and was accompanied by an exhibit about the history of the language and its study curated by Ezekiel Lifschutz and Zosa Szajkowski.[82] One of its outcomes was the formation of an international Commission for the Implementation of Standard Yiddish Orthography that included Max and Uriel Weinreich, Mordkhe Schaechter, Avrom Sutzkever (editor of the *Goldene keyt* in Israel), the journalist Mordkhe Tsanin (editor of the newspaper *Letste nayes* in Israel), and writer and Argentinian YIVO leader Samuel Rollansky in Buenos Aires.[83]

As a language instructor in a number of New York area institutions, most notably the Jewish Theological Seminary and the Jewish Teachers Seminary, Schaechter played a leading role in the campaign to spread YIVO orthography. Schaechter (1927–2007) attended Yiddish secular schools in his native city of Czernowitz (which belonged to Romania in the interwar period), including during the city's Soviet occupation during World War II. A DP in the immediate postwar years, he became one of YIVO's European correspondents while earning a doctorate in linguistics at the University of Vienna with a dissertation about verbal aspect in Yiddish. At the same time, he agitated for the creation of a

Yiddish-speaking agricultural territory in Surinam under the auspices of the *Freeland League*.[84] His territorialist aspirations unfulfilled, Schaechter immigrated to the United States in the early 1950s, where he found a warm welcome in YIVO circles. Weinreich enthused about the new arrival, describing him as a "grandson" since he had studied in Czernowitz with Weinreich's own prized student in the Vilna *aspirantur* Chaim Gininger.[85]

In many ways, Schaechter was the perfect lieutenant to Max Weinreich in his campaign for standardized Yiddish and to reach youth. Although a native Yiddish speaker, like Weinreich, he had been raised in the German cultural sphere, making him highly sensitive to Germanizing influences on the language. As editor of *Afn shvel*, the organ of the *Freeland League* (subsequently the *Yidish-lige*, the League for Yiddish, once it relinquished its attachment to territorialist ideology and focused exclusively on Yiddishism), Schaechter saw his own Yiddish frequently attacked in the New York Yiddish press for what were denounced as excessively puristic tendencies and a penchant for antiquated and dialectal forms, as well as neologisms, that exceeded that of even the Weinreichs.[86]

With Max Weinreich's assistance, Schaechter compiled an updated guide to YIVO orthography containing some eight thousand words and expressions. *The Guide to Standardized Yiddish Orthography* (known in Yiddish as the *Ortografisher vegvayzer*), a spelling dictionary for YIVO's orthographic system with an introduction by Weinreich outlining the principles of the system, clarified many questions that had not been settled in the *Takones*. While the guide was published not by YIVO but by the independent Committee for the Implementation of the Standardized Yiddish Orthography, *Yedies* emphasized its continuity with YIVO's prewar work: "Thus a project initiated by the YIVO in Vilna has now been realized."[87] Delighted with the results, Weinreich wrote Yiddish writer Meylekh Ravitch in Montreal that "the cleanliness and the purposiveness recall the best years of YIVO. And it's a pleasure to see that young people (among them our beloved Schaechter) basically did it."[88] Over eighty individuals enrolled in a course about the history of Yiddish spelling and the practical use of YIVO's system that Schaechter taught in a cycle of ten two-hour lectures that ran evenings from late November 1965 until January 1966. In conjunction with the course, archivist Zosa Szajkowski created an exhibit about the history of Yiddish spelling and its reform from the sixteenth century until the YIVO *Takones*, which was first published in 1937.[89]

The Great Dictionary of the Yiddish Language

Ironically, the conflict over YIVO spelling found its sharpest expression not on the pages of a conservative Yiddish press but within YIVO itself. It took the shape of a controversy surrounding the publication of *Der groyser verterbukh fun der yidisher shprakh* (The Great Dictionary of the Yiddish Language) that would divide the institution into rival camps, poisoning relations between longtime friends and colleagues and undermining the execution of one of YIVO scholars' most ambitious language projects.

The need for a Yiddish-Yiddish dictionary, already acute before World War II when there existed networks of Yiddish schools and an audience of millions of Jews for the Yiddish literary language, took on new urgency after the war. Even before the war had ended, I. B. Singer chided YIVO for prioritizing what he considered nonessential projects, such as a history of the Jewish Labor movement in the United States, and "putting off from year to year" the duty of recording and preserving the language as spoken in the Old Country. A wealth of words and expressions, as well as customs, he lamented, were fading into oblivion with the travails of immigration adjustment and the encroachment of new coterritorial languages such as English and Spanish.[90]

A step in the direction of creating a comprehensive dictionary for Yiddish speakers was Nahum Stutchkoff's *Oytser fun der yidisher shprakh* (Thesaurus of the Yiddish Language), a Yiddish thesaurus published by YIVO in 1950 that includes as many as 175,000 entries. This was intended, however, not as a defining dictionary but rather as a collection of near synonyms and related terms, expressions, idioms, folk sayings, and the like, arranged according to semantic category. It was also not the work of a trained scholar or team of scholars, as detractors were fond of pointing out, but of a single dedicated autodidact. Its compiler was a radio broadcaster and theater writer who frequently worked during bouts of insomnia. In the absence of a comprehensive Yiddish dictionary, Stutchkoff had gathered tens of thousands of words in the course of more than a decade, often by scouring Yiddish literature late into the night, and then classified them for his thesaurus. While the book received YIVO's imprimatur, Stutchkoff was responsible for raising the $30,000 necessary for the thousand-page book's publication through a combination of contributions, subscriptions, and his own money.[91]

The work was generally praised in the Yiddish press but nonetheless faulted by some for its lack of discrimination, as reflected in the inclusion of naked Americanisms (such as *krostaunbus*, "cross-town bus"), Germanisms, and unmarked neologisms.[92] As a matter of fact, however, many of the neologisms were not Stutchkoff's but the work of Max Weinreich. In his introduction to the work, Weinreich emphasized the importance of making distinctions between words that were suitable for use in the Yiddish *klal-shprakh* under construction and ones best left for more casual registers or only in certain contexts. But despite employing various abbreviations and symbols to mark the suitability of words, Weinreich failed to indicate which words were only recently coined by him or others. As editor of the thesaurus, Weinreich also drew criticism in the press for marking some borrowings from the German literary language with a wedge to indicate that they were undesirable (to him, at least) in the *klal-shprakh*.[93]

Stutchkoff subsequently approached YIVO with the idea of creating a proper dictionary on the basis of the thousands of words he had already collected and found an enthusiastic response among members of its Committee on Research. YIVO pledged to facilitate the project by providing working space and access to its library and collections, as well as to help in selecting editors for the proposed dictionary. But it was unwilling to cover the cost of its publication, leaving the financial responsibility for the project to an organizing committee.[94] Given its own financial straits, YIVO was little inclined to take on a project of such magnitude, especially one likely to drag on longer than anticipated. Several YIVO projects had already been abandoned or were indefinitely delayed for lack of means to pay a suitable staff to complete them. Indeed, echoing conditions in prewar Vilna, YIVO at times strained even to pay salaries to its regular staff, necessitating the letting go of employees. Archivist Ezekiel Lifschutz recalled, for example, staff members voluntarily accepting a 10 percent reduction in their already meager salaries in the late 1950s in order to save their colleague Moyshe Kligsberg's position.[95]

Such expressions of solidarity were hardly unheard of among YIVO's staff, whose largely socialist sympathies and common experiences as refugees from eastern Europe dictated a large degree of collegial solidarity and mutual support regardless of interpersonal frictions and conflicts.

The dictionary's editorial board included Stutchkoff alongside veteran YIVO philologists Yudel Mark and Judah A. Joffe. Neither of the latter two was particularly disturbed by the degree of the Dictionary's independence from YIVO, however.[96] On the contrary, they likely preferred to preserve their autonomy—most likely to stave off interference by Weinreich. Unlike Joffe, with whom Weinreich shared thinly, if at all, veiled mutual contempt, Mark maintained good relations with Weinreich through the years despite numerous disagreements. Not only had the two known each other since their university days prior to World War I in St. Petersburg, where their friendship began in the Jewish students' organization; Mark also participated in YIVO's organization and proudly titled himself its "first donor" for contributing twenty-four dollars (the honorarium he received for a lecture) toward realizing Nokhem Shtif's vision for a Yiddish academic institute in 1924.[97] Having played a significant role as a YIVO representative in his native Lithuania, Mark likely anticipated a leadership role for himself in the American YIVO and was sorely disappointed when this did not materialize. He was, nonetheless, deeply loyal to YIVO. He described his role within the institute with respect to Weinreich as being that of "His Majesty's Opposition."[98]

Despite widespread enthusiasm among both Yiddish scholars and the Yiddish press for this conception of the project, the dictionary project was almost immediately hobbled by two major conflicts. The first arose around the question of accepting payments from the Claims Commission, which Mark and several others in the Committee equated with accepting "blood money" to acquit Germany of the crime of the murder of six million Jews.[99] Stutchkoff, in contrast, saw German funding as a practical necessity since contributions from individual donors did not make for sufficient sums to execute the project. When he appealed for financial support to the Claims Conference through YIVO's Administration in 1954, Yudel Mark condemned his action as not only a brazen overstepping of his authority as administrative secretary of the project. It was also a morally reprehensible act in wealthy America to request money from Germany that had "the smell of burnt bodies and the feeling that you are taking up a handful of ash from Majdanek."[100]

Mark was joined in his opposition by Joffe and assistant editors Mordecai Kosover, a professor of Hebrew literature at Brooklyn College perhaps best known for his book on spoken Yiddish in British Mandatory Palestine, and Isaac Rivkind, a librarian at the Jewish Theological Seminary who was the author of a study that YIVO published in 1946 about gambling among Jews as reflected in literary sources.[101] Meanwhile, the journalist M. Mratshni called on American Jews to fund the project themselves, denouncing it as "immoral" for YIVO (which, strictly speaking, did not finance the dictionary but whose associates staffed it) to accept money for cultural projects when it should be going to ease the burden of Holocaust survivors.[102]

During the ensuing controversy, Stutchkoff not only took umbrage at remarks accusing him of impetuousness and a lack of social responsibility; he also objected to the fact that as both administrator of the project and secretary of its editorial board, he bore the bulk of responsibility for its day-to-day operations such as correspondence, management, and fundraising as well as the execution of its scholarly aspects. Stutchkoff was wholly committed to the project, devoting most of his week outside of his radio work to its administration in addition to conducting research for dictionary entries—all without remuneration. He was undoubtedly the most productive member of the editorial staff in those years. His contributions could not be matched by those of Joffe, a man in his eighties often sidelined by his or his wife's illnesses, or Mark, who was burdened by his full-time responsibilities as an educator and administrator in the city's Yiddish secular schools in addition to his duties as editor of the YIVO journal *Yidishe shprakh*. The journal, which expanded its original mandate beyond language standardization to include folklore and dialectology, never knew more than a few hundred subscribers and was appearing with decreasing regularity by the 1950s due to a lack of funding. Nonetheless, it relied heavily on Mark, who wrote much of its content.[103]

Stutchkoff resigned from the project in November 1955, depriving the project of its most industrious worker. His pragmatic approach was, however, soon vindicated. In the absence of adequate funding, more than once, work had to be suspended on the dictionary and staff members let go. Only a few years later, Mark saw little choice but to accept

German reparations beginning in 1958. As was the case with other Yiddish cultural and historical projects funded at this time with German monies, such as the *Nayer leksikon fun der yidisher literatur* and the *Algemeyne entsiklopedye* (a project that was begun before the war to produce an encyclopedia of Jewish and general knowledge in Yiddish; many of its contributors were associated with YIVO or conducted research in its collections), the employment of Holocaust survivors provided necessary funds and hands for the work, even if, as nonphilologists, these hands were not always qualified for the undertaking.[104]

The second conflict undermining the dictionary project also had precedents in the recent experience of YIVO. It revolved around the delicate issue of spelling, pitting camps gathered around Mark and Weinreich against one another and ultimately leading to the project's dissociation from YIVO. Long critical of the *Takones fun yidishn oysleyg*, Mark wished to deviate from YIVO spelling in a number of instances. However, the controversy surrounding the silent *alef*, traditionally used to disambiguate the reading of certain consonant and vowel combinations, is likely best remembered today as the impetus for the parting of ways between YIVO and the *Groyser verterbukh* project. Indeed, it remains to this day the most commonly recognized shibboleth separating YIVO and non-YIVO spelling systems.[105]

The struggle over spelling in a larger measure reflected not only the simmering rivalries and resentments of Yudel Mark and Judah A. Joffe against what they perceived as Weinreich's unwillingness to compromise and his penchant for dictatorial control. As Leyzer Burko has argued in his thorough reconstruction and analysis of the *Groyser verterbukh* debacle, the more Mark came to conceive the dictionary as a memorial to the victims of the Holocaust, the more the matter of spelling rankled him.[106] The same could no doubt be said for Weinreich too but from a different perspective. Both men had escaped the catastrophe by sheer luck—Mark having come to the United States on a fundraising trip on behalf of YIVO in 1935 and settled there permanently the following year,[107] and Weinreich finding himself in Copenhagen when the war erupted. Beyond their shared rage at Germany, each experienced an intense sense of survivor's guilt, albeit each in his own way.

For Mark, the drive to make the *Groyser verterbukh* as comprehensive as possible (including even extremely low-frequency internationalisms

Yudel Mark. Credit: YIVO Institute for Jewish Research

and ephemeral words) was a way to honor the memory of millions of murdered Yiddish speakers as well as previous generations "who expressed their joys and sorrows, their thoughts and aspirations, in Yiddish." It was a testament, he explained, not only to the martyrs but to the "language of martyrs," a term he attributed to Israeli president Dr. Chaim Weizmann.[108] Using a spelling system he associated with an assault on tradition not only served to promote division in the surviving community of Yiddish speakers; it also represented a desacralization of the memory of past generations. For Weinreich, in contrast, to challenge the standards of the prewar YIVO not only undermined what remained of the institute's authority in Yiddish-speaking society. It was an impious act that broke faith with the legacy of his Vilna colleagues, whose idealism and expertise he venerated and could not be equaled—certainly not in the present and likely not in any future generation.

Years later, Yudel Mark wrote in his obituary for Weinreich that he had avoided the topic of orthography in conversations with him in the last fifteen years of Weinreich's life. Mark's position seemed to cause Weinreich, who considered YIVO's spelling one of his greatest achievements, physical pain.[109] Similarly, as Joshua Fishman later recalled, Weinreich always retained his public composure and conveyed a sense of strength and scholarly purpose—so much so that many questioned his capacity for emotions. Only once did Fishman see Weinreich cry: in connection with a dispute about Yiddish spelling with YIVO colleagues.[110]

The first volume of the *Groyser verterbukh* appeared in 1961 with a declaration by Weinreich that the dictionary did not bear YIVO's imprimatur because of its unauthorized departure from YIVO's orthographic rules, "the result of long years of work standardizing and codifying . . . [which] therefore symbolize in the present day the continuity of the Yiddish *kulturshprakh* beyond the Holocaust."[111] The dictionary's introduction includes a section outlining and explaining its deviations from YIVO orthography. It offered a compromise, however, between Mark's and YIVO usage with regard to the silent *alef*.[112]

After seeing a prevolume sample, the poet and essayist Jacob Glatstein criticized what he considered an overly tolerant policy of admitting internationalisms unfound even in richer languages—what he derided as "shmentilgente verter" ("shmintellectual" words) included for the sake of making Yiddish seem more sophisticated—and foreign words used by uneducated Jews that had never entered widespread use.[113] Solomon Dingol, editor of the Yiddish daily *Der tog*, complained of the projected size of the dictionary, one that was supported by funds from everyday Jews but would, with its many unnecessary words, be suitable primarily for future academics. What was truly needed, he argued, echoing other voices, was not a large and inclusive dictionary but a smaller, practical one for immediate use: "If a good Yiddish dictionary for the folk is not published now, I doubt there will be enough people in a generation who need a ten-volume dictionary." The emphasis, he elaborated, "should be placed not so strongly on *great* as on *Yiddish* dictionary."[114]

But while Mark's expansive ambitions had previously been subject to much criticism, reviewers in the Yiddish press were on the whole rather enthusiastic, impressed as they were with the thoroughness of the attractive and authoritative volume and the promise of subsequent ones. Nonetheless, this compulsion for comprehensiveness—an ambition that could never be fully satisfied—would impede the dictionary's completion within the lifetime of the remaining generation of eastern European–born Yiddish speakers for whom it was primarily intended. A second volume did not appear until 1966, with further ones published in 1971 and 1980. Work on the dictionary continued after Mark's death in 1975 under the editorial supervision of Professor Wolf Moscovitch (Hebrew University) and Meyer Wolf in Jerusalem (although Marvin Herzog in New York was formally editor in chief), but publishing ended once funding was exhausted to complete the project. As of 2025, only four volumes of an anticipated twelve or thirteen have appeared in print—the work of decades by hundreds of volunteers who submitted words and citations in addition to a professional staff that compiled them, found illustrations, and wrote definitions. These published volumes, which cover the letter *alef*, represent roughly a quarter of the 250,000 words in the dictionary's corpus because of the particularities of Yiddish spelling. Further, the entries can often be used to deduce the meaning of related terms, expanding the utility of the existing volumes significantly. Typewritten manuscripts for two additional volumes covering the letters *beyz*, *gimel*, *daled*, and *hey* were, however, scanned and published online in 2024 by Dmytro Tyshchenko, the author of Yiddish-Russian and Yiddish-Ukrainian dictionaries.[115]

The Language and Culture Atlas of Ashkenazic Jewry

Dialectology had long been a subject of great interest among Yiddish scholars. Influenced by the Romantic currents that dominated the field of linguistics in nineteenth-century Germany, where historical linguistics first came to the fore in European universities, Yiddish scholars sought not only to document and interpret the diversity of Yiddish speech forms but also to demonstrate the underlying unity of a historically Yiddish-speaking—that is, Ashkenazic—Jewish people across the boundaries of nation-states across Europe and beyond. Moreover, the collection of data about dialects—a practice in which both Soviet research institutes and YIVO engaged prior to World War II through the work of individual scholars and through the engagement of *zamlers*—could be applied to YIVO's language standardization work in, for example, creating lexicons of specialized terminology and making normative decisions about gender and pluralization in the standard language under construction.

Uriel Weinreich's own experiences studying dialectology while conducting research for his doctoral dissertation about languages in contact in Switzerland inspired him to conceptualize a Yiddish atlas that would go far beyond the study of linguistic geography (e.g., mapping the differing pronunciations of a word or where variants exist for the same lexical item to understand how barriers to communication such as rivers and political boundaries shape the differentiation of dialects) to include cultural information that was in danger of disappearance due to dislocation and genocide. *The Language and Culture Atlas of Ashkenazic Jewry* (*LCAAJ*) was envisioned as an ethnographic storehouse that would help researchers to understand processes of cultural as well as linguistic diffusion. Thus, it would identify, to give but some culinary examples, where gefilte fish was preferred sweet or savory, where potato pancakes (latkes) were eaten during Channukah, or where tomatoes were deemed unkosher. The diffusion of words, pronunciations, and cultural practices would also help in attempting to track the settlement history of Ashkenazic Jewry and to shed light on other historical questions, as well as to gain insight into Jews' linguistic and cultural relations with their neighbors. The *LCAAJ* would also provide a model for the field of bilingual dialectology more broadly, as Yiddish had, since its inception, always been coterritorial with other languages. Hence it would serve as a resource for present and future generations of scholars whose questions and methodologies had not yet even been imagined.[116]

The possibility of gathering such information through the interviewing of informants at a physical remove from their original location had already been made evident through YIVO's own work in New York and by individuals with ties to it. Immediately after the war, interviews were conducted in Upper Manhattan's Hotel Marseille with recently arrived refugees under the auspices of the Stonehill project, in which Uriel's future wife, Beatrice, had participated.[117] Together with professional writer Elizabeth Herzog, anthropologist Mark Zborowski, who was briefly employed as a librarian in YIVO (and years later revealed as an NKVD agent), also produced *Life Is with People*, a study of shtetl culture for which dozens of interviews were conducted on the basis of Margaret Mead's notions of salvage ethnography.[118] Moreover, Jean Jofen, herself a refugee from Vienna, produced an atlas as a PhD thesis at Columbia in 1953 based on interviews with refugees—the first attempt in America at a Yiddish-language atlas.[119]

As a world-class linguist, however, Uriel Weinreich conceived the project not only to serve the community of scholars of Yiddish and eastern European Jewry but to possess a dimension of theoretical interest to scholars outside of the field of Yiddish. He also anticipated the computerization of data to facilitate analysis and the production of linguistic and cultural maps. He received expert advice on the subject from Mendel Hoffman, an Auschwitz-Birkenau survivor who assisted with the shipping of books to YIVO while a DP and subsequently learned about the emerging field of information technology while serving in the US Army in the early 1950s. Hoffman, who became an amateur YIVO book cataloger and later board member, was also the husband of Miriam Hoffman, the Yiddish writer, dramaturge, and educator who would later teach the language at Columbia University.[120]

Uriel began interviewing subjects during a sabbatical spent in Israel in 1959–60. Strictly speaking, the *LCAAJ* was a Columbia rather than a YIVO project, but it relied largely on the labors of YIVO associates—above all, Mordkhe Schaechter, the chief interviewer, and Marvin Herzog, the associate director until Uriel's death—in addition to those of Columbia undergraduate and graduate students. Funded by substantial grants from the US National Science Foundation and other agencies, it represents a brilliant example of how its architect was able to make the concerns of Yiddish studies methodologically and theoretically relevant to a wide audience of language researchers, adding prestige to the language and to scholarship about Yiddish. The project grew to include a team of several researchers, including eighteen fieldworkers, working chiefly in the United States and Israel until 1972 to elicit information about language use and cultural practices from native informants from locations identified on a map stretching from western to eastern Europe (including data about vestigial Western Yiddish, the dialects of Yiddish spoken in central and western Europe that had effectively died out by the late nineteenth century), as well as the prestate Ashkenazic *yishuv*. The heightened sensitivity to linguistic and cultural diversity that the project fostered also shook the foundations of Uriel's own Lithuanian bias, opening him to greater consideration for forms from other dialects in producing a normative work perhaps better known to the general public, his *Modern English-Yiddish Yiddish-English Dictionary*.[121] The work—the most complete expression of "YIVO Yiddish" so far—was near completion by the time of YIVO's fortieth anniversary in May 1966.

YIVO's Fortieth Annual Conference

In keeping with an annual press ritual, journalist A. Varshever (likely a pseudonym of Moyshe Elboym) tallied YIVO's impressive accomplishments in connection with the annual conference to highlight the distance it had traveled since the days of the Amopteyl. The new YIVO center, he noted in *Der tog*, had begun in 1940 "with the credit of a prestigious father but with a meager estate: a library of about 15,000 volumes, only the beginnings of an archive, and some very worthwhile academic publications that were, however, few in number." But it had outdone its Vilna parent over the next twenty-five years. In comparison with the 210 books and journal volumes (including fourteen of *Yivo bleter*) produced in the institute's first fifteen years in Vilna, the American YIVO had produced some 337 books, journal volumes (including twenty-nine of *Yivo bleter* and twenty-five of *Yidishe shprakh*), brochures, and the like. These were overwhelmingly published in Yiddish, but some fifty publications—among them *Hitler's Professors*, *YIVO Annual*, and *College Yiddish*—were in English. Together with materials rescued from Europe, the ones gathered in America amounted to a "cultural pedigree for American Jewry, which previously possessed no such thing."[122]

The journalist concluded his survey with a pointed refutation of those critics "who have deluded themselves and want to delude others in thinking that YIVO 'puts on airs,' that it 'cuts itself off from the masses.'" "What is the textbook *College Yiddish*," he asked rhetorically, "if not a means to teach Yiddish to a mass audience (and which has achieved this goal to a large extent)?" But even beyond the success of the textbook, how could one dismiss the many exhibits YIVO mounted about such themes as the Holocaust and *shtetl* life, its courses about Yiddish literature and Jewish life in America introduced that year that drew some two hundred New York City public school teachers, or the large public conferences it held with lectures by recognized experts on diverse topics?[123] The courses, for which teachers obtained in-service credit from the Board of Education, received a renewed subsidy from the Workmen's Circle and were to be expanded in the coming year with the addition of a cycle of courses about Jewish history.[124]

Rather than enumerate YIVO's proud accomplishments, Shlomo Noble, chair of YIVO's Committee on Research, addressed a packed auditorium in Hunter College at the conference by reverently recalling those colleagues who were no longer alive. Beyond those lost to Soviet repression and the Holocaust, the institute mourned the deaths of leading figures active in the still-unfolding American chapter in its history—among them, Elias Tcherikower (1881–1943), Samuel Charney (1883–1955), Jacob Shatzky (1893–1956), Leibush Lehrer (1887–1964), and only a few months prior, Jacob Lestschinsky (1876–1966).[125] Seventy-two-year-old Max Weinreich was the last of YIVO's original section heads to remain alive.

Weinreich nonetheless struck an optimistic tone in his conference address. Speaking on the subject of "YIVO in its Fifth Decade," he announced, "We are here and we stand today more firmly than ever since we came to America twenty-five years ago." He acknowledged how much progress had been made since 1940 in overcoming negative attitudes toward the Yiddish language and its literature, as well as the cultural legacy of eastern Europe more broadly, despite the institute's persistent financial deficit. Hopeful for the future, he detected the beginnings of a "reorientation" in American Jewish life that would bring increasing numbers of youth into YIVO's orbit. This was reflected, for example, in the success of the recent Broadway musical *Fiddler on the Roof*, based on the stories of Sholem Aleichem, and of Yiddish literature in translation. "We know that the true Tevye sings *zmires* [Sabbath songs] and not English arias," he added about the performance, which debuted on the New York stage in 1964 with Zero Mostel in the lead role, "but that doesn't matter." It could be seen too in the popularity of *College Yiddish*, which had sold some eight thousand copies, and the demand for the forthcoming English-Yiddish Yiddish-English dictionary.[126]

Even an ever-pessimistic Ezekiel Lifschutz noted in his diary, "A novelty is seeing in recent years a number of students or young instructors with an interest in Jewish academic matters."[127] Not only did promising undergraduate students present their prize-winning contributions to YIVO's annual contests for best student essay in Jewish studies at YIVO conferences. Scholars who had come of age after World War II were also increasingly counted among featured conference speakers. Papers were delivered, for example, about such topics as the history of the Bund and of Labor Zionism in eastern Europe and America at YIVO's 1964 conference on "Jewish Participation in Social Progress Movements" by Abraham Ascher, Ezra Mendelsohn, Jonathan Frankel, Moses Rischin, and Henry Tobias—all of whom went on to prominent careers as historians in the United States and Israel.[128] While most students delivered their papers in English at YIVO conferences, many did so in Yiddish—to the delight of YIVO stalwarts, even if critics occasionally faulted them for linguistic peccadillos.[129]

Highly symbolic too was the appointment of American-born Executive Secretary Shmuel Lapin, the son of a Yiddish poet and himself a scholar of Yiddish literature with a history of communal engagement in Canada and the United States.[130] Lapin, then in his mid-thirties, had written a master's thesis about Yiddish literature at Columbia under Uriel Weinreich's supervision and previously served as the executive director of the Canadian Labor Zionist movement.[131] His immediate predecessor was Isidore David Passow, another American, who had assumed the position following Pinkhos Schwartz's retirement in 1961 due to illness (Schwartz passed away in 1964).[132]

The appointment of someone so young as Lapin pointed to a lack of suitable candidates and financial resources to draw a more experienced applicant to manage the institute. But it also represented an infusion of youthful energy into an institution dominated by men in their sixties and seventies and, occupying less prestigious but no less important roles, by women in their forties and fifties. These included not only librarian Dina Abramowicz but also research assistants such as Shoshke (Rachel) Erlich, who specialized in Yiddish language and literature, and Hannah Fryshdorf, a veteran of the Warsaw Ghetto Uprising who then served as Weinreich's secretary.[133] Notably, Uriel Weinreich and Joshua Fishman (now dean of Yeshiva University's School of Education), young scholars whom Weinreich had personally cultivated, were appointed to the institute's Committee on Research Planning (*visnshaftlekhe planir-komisye*), formed in 1962 to approve and coordinate its projects. They sat on the committee alongside Columbia University economist Alexander Erlich, a more senior scholar who was not only the son of Bundist leader Henryk Erlich (who died in Soviet captivity during World War II) but also the grandson of revered historian Simon Dubnow and Shoshke Erlich's husband.[134]

For all his eagerness to encourage American Jewish youth interested in pursuing and celebrating their "roots," Weinreich also acknowledged that interest was no substitute for real knowledge of Jewish subjects:

> In YIVO we constantly encounter quite grotesque examples when Jews who are general scholars want to take on Jewish themes and don't know where to begin. The last case is with a young man who really appears to be a fine fellow and he wants to write a monograph about a famous Yiddish poet. The young man knows no Yiddish but he has a good friend who does and this helper translated various poems into English.
>
> It's as if someone with a screw driver were digging coal from the earth. But is it fair to laugh at the young man or to blame him? We have here to do with tasks that exceed the resourcefulness of an individual. No rising generation will come up on its own. We have to raise it with a cool head and a loving heart.[135]

The way forward, Weinreich asserted, lay in the creation of an independent YIVO graduate school that would recruit students and grant stipends—first to five or ten students, eventually to a hundred—to study in a four-year program to become independent researchers qualified to serve the Jewish community. Of course, public support was needed to make possible a graduate program emphasizing Yiddish language and culture and the YIVO tradition of research in the social sciences. But once it was secured, said Weinreich, "Then I can guarantee you that in 1975, at the beginning of its sixth decade, YIVO will bring you a much more self-confident perspective than I have brought you tonight."[136]

Conclusion

The works discussed here represent but a fraction of the projects in which YIVO scholars engaged in the post–World War II period in fulfillment of the institute's commitment to the fostering of Yiddish as a living language and civilization. Between 1940 and 1970, they made tremendous contributions to Yiddish-language pedagogy, lexicography, dialect research, and the growth and standardization of the language in ways that have defined the subsequent history of Yiddish studies and Yiddish-language pedagogy. At the same time, the conflicts and travails surrounding these projects and their execution once again reflect the personal rivalries and intellectual conflicts dividing YIVO's staff as they struggled to maintain continuity with the prewar past while seeking to engage an American—and, to a lesser extent, world—Jewry for whom Yiddish and the legacy of eastern Europe could not mean the same things as to them.

As Burko has observed in his insightful study of the YIVO Linguistics circle, its members were very much focused on documenting and standardizing the Yiddish of the last generations of eastern European-born Yiddish speakers. Such efforts were meant as much as an act of pious loyalty and commemoration for their murdered brethren as an effort to complete work begun prior to the Holocaust to preserve, codify, and propagate the *kultursphrakh* before its treasures had been irretrievably lost. But apart from those active in teaching in Yiddish secular schools or camps and producing resources for them—an area in which Yudel Mark, who supervised dozens of Yiddish schools as the head of the Committee for Yiddish Schools (a division of the Jewish Education Committee of New York), and Leibush Lehrer, who directed the Sholem Aleichem Folk Institute's Camp Boiberik, distinguished themselves—YIVO scholars were, for the most part, little attuned to the needs of early childhood learners and the means to maintain Yiddish as a multigenerational language of home and community.[137]

Yiddish secular schools and camps, where children increasingly encountered Yiddish as a foreign language, were not enough to ensure the intergenerational transmission of the language. Weinreich himself bemoaned this fact in a speech on the fiftieth anniversary of the Czernowitz Conference in 1958, when he pointed to the lack of attention given by Yiddishists as a collective to preparing age-appropriate learning materials for use by preschool children and by older children outside the framework of schools.[138] As Burko notes, "Except for J. Fishman in his later years [beginning in the late twentieth century], none of the YIVO linguists had a deliberate, thought-out strategy for language maintenance—which is not surprising, since the field of language revival had not yet been created."[139]

Instead, the university—an inherently elite institution—increasingly became the locus of language and cultural transmission of a language associated with folk, family, and community. There it was typically taught from textbooks and dictionaries conceived for English speakers that were authored or inspired by Uriel Weinreich. Even more than his father, Uriel found recognition beyond Yiddish circles and forged a bridge between YIVO and American and global academia, helping the institute to become the recognized authority for Yiddish in the scholarly world. It is one of the cruelties of history that the shrinking of the Yiddish secular sphere by the latter part of the twentieth century has meant the disappearance of most voices challenging YIVO norms.[140] But even in the contemporary *haredi* world, which ignores YIVO's authority, less *daytshmerish* spelling norms approaching that of the YIVO system have become increasingly common.[141]

Normative language resources directed at an adult audience have—seen with the benefit of hindsight—proven some of YIVO's most successful and enduring contributions to the transmission of the legacy of an eastern European Jewish folk to its "estranged" children and grandchildren, as well as to any others interested in learning about it. In doing so, YIVO succeeded against the odds. It could not reverse language shift among American Jews. But it transformed what was long considered by many its greatest liability for continued relevance in America—namely, its commitment to the preservation and promotion of a language associated with poverty, parochialism, foreignness, and the immigrant experience—into one of its greatest assets in drawing a segment of American Jewry, especially young adults, into its orbit. When a wave of interest in Yiddish language and culture arose among American Jewish youth in the late 1960s and '70s, YIVO was ready to meet the folk and teach them *their* language.

5
A GENERATION GOES, A GENERATION COMES

In late 1966, Uriel Weinreich received news that a previous cancer, for which he had been asymptomatic following treatments, had returned to his lymph nodes and brain. Understanding that he had little time left, he concentrated his energies on proofreading his *Modern English-Yiddish Yiddish-English Dictionary* and spending time with his family and children. Although weakened by chemotherapy, he also continued teaching at Columbia until almost his final day. On 30 March 1967, Uriel succumbed to his illness, fewer than two months shy of his forty-first birthday.[1]

The deaths of members of the older generation of eastern European–born scholars were a painful inevitability that sapped YIVO's strength incrementally since it transferred its center to New York in 1940. The death of one so young and the personal embodiment of continuity between Vilna and New York was, however, a crushing blow to the institute and the broader Yiddish cultural world. At his funeral, Abraham Joshua Heschel eulogized Uriel Weinreich, the scion of Vilna Yiddish "aristocracy," as "the prince who remained true to his mother, the Queen [Yiddish]," when so many of her children had been murdered and those who remained had forgotten her.[2]

Max Weinreich had taken enormous comfort in the presence by his side of his elder son, who had been raised since an early age to follow in his footsteps and with whom he had a powerful bond intensified by their shared exile from Vilna and flight from Europe. His unmistakable pride was reflected in the tears of joy he shed when Uriel delivered his first academic addresses at YIVO conferences.[3] Having already lost so much, including his "firstborn"—the Vilna YIVO—the loss of Uriel was too much to bear even for one so disciplined in restraining his emotions. Max Weinreich survived his son by little more than a year.

Although not the last of the generation of Eastern European–born scholars, the deaths of the two Weinreichs effectively mark the end of an era in YIVO's history. YIVO was deprived of its leading personality, a polymath scholar and talented if domineering administrator, and left without a clear successor to steward it into the next generation. In other ways, however, their demise accelerated changes that were already underway within the institute and facilitated the arrival of a young generation of scholars that would lead the institute in new directions more suitable to an American Jewry ignorant of its collective past but eager to reclaim those aspects of it compatible with its late-twentieth-century sensibilities and commitments. Ultimately, Weinreich and Sol Lipzin's concept of *idervuks*, "regrowth," would come to fruition, although not wholly in the way they had envisioned it. By the mid-1970s, a new YIVO began to emerge, one that was on its way to becoming, if it was not already, more American than eastern European in personnel and character but also relevant in ways reflecting what was, by this time, American Jewry's greater confidence in its leadership role among Diaspora Jewry.

The transition to a new generation of scholars and scholarship was most strikingly reflected in the creation of a long-anticipated graduate program and an intensive Yiddish summer program that laid the groundwork for new directions in YIVO's pedagogic activities. These were complemented by the posthumous publication of Uriel Weinreich's dictionary, an essential resource for both language learners and fluent speakers, and Max Weinreich's *Geshikhte fun der yidisher shprakh* (*History of the Yiddish Language*), a sociocultural history of not only the language but the civilization that had produced it. The far-reaching effects of these endeavors, whose launching coincided with the demise of their main authors and initiators, beyond the institute and its circles of loyal supporters, would only become apparent with time. They ensured the transmission of scholarship and the tools for learning that would likely have otherwise become exceedingly rare, if not disappeared.

The YIVO Center for Advanced Jewish Studies

A sorrowful cloud hung over YIVO's annual conference, held only a week after Uriel Weinreich was laid to rest in a New Jersey cemetery. Conference chair Israel Knox, a Russian-born professor of philosophy at New York University who had long been active in YIVO and the Workmen's Circle, began his address to the over one thousand people gathered in Hunter

College's auditorium by recalling Uriel's remarkable scholarly accomplishments and all that he had done for YIVO in the less than two decades that he had been professionally active. The next speaker, Uriel's doctoral student Marvin (Mikhl) Herzog—only one year his junior—focused his remarks on his mentor's profound commitment to friends and family as well as his unstinting support for colleagues and students.[4]

The four-day conference thereafter offered its usual bounty of lectures, including a special focus on the American Jewish community. Presentations embraced topics of both historical and contemporary relevance as well as emphasized themes in Yiddish language, literature, and culture. Speakers included YIVO conference veterans and, as the Yiddish press emphasized, a number of early career scholars. These included the Hebrew University's Khone Shmeruk, whose annotated edition and study of Y. L. Peretz's play *Bay nakht oyfn altn mark* (A Night at the Old Market) was soon to be published by YIVO, and the Weinreichs' student Ruth Wisse, then a lecturer in English at Montreal's McGill University.[5] To the astonishment of many, Max Weinreich showed up at the conference banquet in the Commodore Hotel to deliver scheduled remarks to honor his personal friend Yudel (Julius) Borenstein (1889–1975) on the occasion of his eightieth birthday.[6]

Weinreich's appearance at the banquet despite being in mourning was likely motivated by more than a personal sense of duty to the institute or appreciation for a friend who had contributed much, financially and otherwise, to YIVO. It was also the opportunity to share an announcement of utmost importance to him: the raising of $250,000 in Borenstein's honor that would serve as the nucleus of a one-million-dollar fund for a YIVO Center for Advanced Jewish Studies that Weinreich would direct.[7] The center would provide both assistance to established scholars with their research and training to students already enrolled in university graduate programs. American-born Jewish educator and Labor Zionist organizer Dr. Judah Shapiro was appointed secretary of the newly founded YIVO Center for Advanced Jewish Studies. Shapiro, a member of YIVO's Board of Directors, had previously served as director of Cultural and Education Reconstruction for the JDC in postwar Europe and as secretary of the National Council for Jewish Culture.[8] With his assistance, YIVO succeeded the following year in obtaining a long-sought-after charter from the State University of New York for a graduate program.[9]

Lacking both financial resources and New York State certification to grant degrees, YIVO's *aspirantur* had functioned in the 1940s as a supplement to the education of students already enrolled in New York universities. In the late 1950s, the idea arose to create a Yiddish university by uniting YIVO with the Jewish Teachers Seminary and People's University in New York, whose main task was to train teachers for Yiddish secular schools. Within YIVO, the chief proponent of the concept was Yudel Mark, who worried about the lack of qualified faculty to staff Yiddish schools once European-born educators were no longer available. He championed the merger as a means to combine the strengths of the two institutions and rescue both from decline. In his view, YIVO would benefit from the Teachers Seminary's existing student pool, its larger social base, and the capacity granted it by the State Legislature to confer Bachelor's and Doctor of Jewish Literature degrees. The Teachers Seminary, which no longer occupied its own premises, would benefit from YIVO's building, prestige, expansive library, and accomplished staff. Characteristically, Weinreich was skeptical that the necessary funds could be raised (he estimated $100,000 would be needed for the first five years alone) and reluctant for YIVO to share control over the proposed university. For reasons that require further investigation—likely because YIVO did not wish to compromise its autonomy or its elite status as much as its cost—such an arrangement never came to fruition. The seminary, which merged with the Herzliah Hebrew Teachers' Institute in 1967, nonetheless pursued the goal of creating a university. It drew on several YIVO associates for its faculty, including Yudel Mark, Leibush Lehrer, Nathan Süsskind, and Mordkhe Schaechter. Uriel Weinreich, Sol Liptzin, and Mordecai Kosover were also recruited to its Academic Advisory Council.[10]

After nearly thirty years of effort, Weinreich finally saw the realization of his vision for an independent YIVO graduate center on the horizon, even if degree-conferring privileges had not yet been granted by the New York State Board of Regents.[11] Two seminars were announced for the inaugural academic year 1969–70: "The Social and Cultural Background of Yiddish Literature in Eastern Europe 1800–1950" taught by Dov Sadan, chair of the Hebrew University's Yiddish Department, and "The Sociolinguistics of Yiddish Speech Communities in the United States" offered by Joshua Fishman, chair of YIVO's Research Planning Committee and research chair of Social Sciences at Yeshiva University.

The New York Yiddish press rejoiced in the graduate center, signaling it as yet another reason middle-class American Jewry bore a moral responsibility to support YIVO financially. If the New York Jewish Federation had only recently made a $30 million gift to Columbia University's School of Social Work, one journalist reasoned, it was only appropriate that American Jewry collectively support YIVO, a Jewish "national" institution, with similar largesse.[12] The fact that those American Jews who made large donations to general American institutions were, with some notable exceptions, unlikely to share an eastern European conception of Jewish nationhood and its responsibilities—let alone to read their chastisements—did not deter Yiddish journalists from expressing their disappointment with the state of American Jewish philanthropy.

The Uriel Weinreich Summer Program

Even before introducing its first seminars, the newly formed Center for Advanced Jewish Studies announced that plans were underway for an immersive Yiddish-language and cultural summer program to be held

Khone Shmeruk's seminar at the Max Weinreich Center with I. B. Singer as guest, 1978. Credit: YIVO Institute for Jewish Research

under its auspices at Columbia University in 1968. The idea for a "High School Yiddish Language Program" was proposed to Max Weinreich in the summer of 1967 by linguist Robert Austerlitz, Uriel Weinreich's successor as chair of the Columbia University Linguistics Department. Austerlitz, himself a multilingual Jewish refugee from Romania, conceived of the idea as a way to help prepare candidates for Columbia's graduate Yiddish program, which suffered from low enrollments.[13]

The high school Yiddish program was inspired by and modeled on a language and cultural immersion program for Mandarin Chinese that Columbia hosted each summer with support from the Carnegie Foundation.[14] In his proposal for the program, Judah Shapiro noted that Chinese's practical utility in areas such as government service, translation, academia, and commerce was evident. Yiddish, in contrast, did not offer a wide range of career options. But cultivating competence in it among nonnative speakers was, he argued, an urgent task to ensure that future generations would have direct access to source materials in the language. Competent instructors were already hard to find, and even competent translators, Shapiro warned, would likely be scarce in the future. Such a situation "would represent catastrophic aspects for future Jewish learning and responsible Jewish institutions cannot accept the prospect of the distortions of future interpretations of the past when Yiddish sources are eliminated a priori from Jewish scholarship."[15]

The summer program was heralded with much fanfare in *Yedies* and the Yiddish press. Doubts existed nonetheless whether a sufficient number of students would be willing to forgo summer job earnings to study the language, especially when it brought no clear practical reward.[16] Apart from a $100 enrollment fee, the cost of mounting the eight-week program—$11,000—was borne almost entirely by the Atran Foundation. While organizers were disappointed when enrollments fell short of the twenty-five-student target, they were pleased with the results of the program and anticipated greater enrollments in the future. Eleven students traveled daily to Columbia's Morningside Heights campus from throughout the New York / New Jersey area to attend courses from early July through August. Most of them were Jewish high school seniors, although one was a non-Jewish Columbia graduate student in Linguistics.[17] In his report to the Atran Foundation, Shapiro emphasized, perhaps with some exaggeration, the high academic caliber of the students who had applied to study at Columbia despite safety concerns that summer.[18] Its campus had only recently been convulsed by student demonstrations protesting the Vietnam War and the proposed construction of a new university gymnasium on public land in Morningside Park that would have offered separate floors for use by Columbia undergraduates and Harlem community residents, respectively. Violent clashes between students and the New York City police made for, in the words of YIVO associate Mordecai Kosover, "a devastation such as Columbia has never seen in its 215 year existence."[19]

In contrast with much of YIVO's activity, the summer program's day-to-day operations were run by a youthful staff, most of whom had been educated in North America. At barely forty years old, the program's director, Marvin Herzog, was one of the oldest. The Toronto native was by this time an associate professor of Linguistics who succeeded his mentor in the Atran Chair for Yiddish at Columbia and as director of the *LCAAJ*. He was also appointed to YIVO's Research Planning Committee, adding, alongside sociolinguist Joshua Fishman and historian (and later Jewish Theological Seminary chancellor) Gerson D. Cohen, another North American under the age of fifty to the committee's composition.[20] Boston native James Matisoff, also an associate professor of Linguistics at Columbia (who later specialized in Asian languages), brushed up on his childhood Yiddish to teach beginners' grammar. Mordkhe Schaechter, then an associate professor of Yiddish at the Jewish Teachers Seminary–Herzliah, covered more advanced Yiddish-language topics. Lessons from Uriel Weinreich's textbook *College Yiddish* were complemented by visits to the language lab, where students used dialogues specially developed for the program by Schaechter and Matisoff and recorded by veteran Yiddish actor Deborah Rosenblum Mielnik.[21]

The day was divided between formal language instruction from 9 a.m. to 12 p.m. daily and a cultural program featuring lectures and events lasting until 4 p.m. three times a week. Afternoon programs, which drew on the contributions of younger and seasoned Yiddish scholars and cultural figures alike, introduced students to Yiddish folk creativity and literature, the eastern European Jewish way of life, and Jewish history. There were also conversation groups, a folk song circle, movie screenings, a historical tour of the Lower East Side, and visits to Yiddish cultural institutions and projects such as the *LCAAJ*, the YIVO Library

Instructors and students in YIVO Summer Program, 1970. Credit: YIVO Institute for Jewish Research

and Archives, the Atran House (home to the Bund Archives, the Congress for Jewish Culture, the CYCO Yiddish book store, and Yiddishist camp *Hemshekh*), and the editorial boards of the newspapers *Forverts* and *Tog morgen-zhurnal*.[22]

The program thus offered a thorough introduction to secular Yiddish culture and its institutions in New York. In Shapiro's evaluation, "The course began as a study program in Yiddish and ended as a program in *Yidishkeyt*."[23] However, as befitting a secular university and in conformity with Yiddishist conceptions, this *Yidishkeyt* eschewed active engagement with growing Hasidic communities, where Yiddish was widely spoken, or the religious tradition of Yiddish speakers, despite that this culture permeated its texts and folkways. *Yedies* proudly reported that members of the audience gathered in YIVO's auditorium for the summer program's graduation were impressed by speeches delivered in correct, fluent Yiddish using the "literary pronunciation" (i.e., Standard Yiddish pronunciation) by students who had never spoken the language prior to that summer.[24] Given Uriel Weinreich's centrality to Yiddish pedagogy, his role as a bridge between YIVO and Columbia, and his recent demise, it was only natural that the program be named for him.[25] The Uriel Weinreich Yiddish Summer Program was deemed a success worth repeating, with YIVO requesting additional funding from the Atran Foundation to expand the number of students enrolled in 1969.[26]

This was not the only posthumous honor bestowed upon Uriel, however. A one-day conference uniting more than forty representatives of American Jewish cultural and social organizations, as well as Yiddish studies scholars, was convened that same year to celebrate the publication of his *Modern English-Yiddish Yiddish-English Dictionary* and to discuss efforts to promote Yiddish among youth.[27] The dictionary was an outgrowth of a project for which Uriel was contracted while writing his dissertation in 1948—a concise dictionary for use in the Yiddish secular schools that was never published, likely because political differences between communist and noncommunist schools led to the dissolution of the committee that had commissioned the work. Some fifteen years later, work on the dictionary was resumed and expanded thanks to grants from the Atran Foundation to YIVO and a $10,000 bequest from YIVO supporter Solomon Bogorod.[28]

The bidirectional dictionary, first published in 1968 (and subsequently reissued multiple times), was a critical success whose significance was readily appreciated by journalists and scholars alike. Intended to bring Yiddish vocabulary into the twentieth century, it included many words and expressions that had entered the language since the last publication of an English-Yiddish dictionary by amateur lexicographer Alexander Harkavy close to forty years prior. At the same time, it represented a careful culling of the language, balancing the ambition to provide readers with a comprehensive, albeit selective lexicon of the language with the prescriptive aspiration to furnish a guide to the cultured use of a standardized language—all in a clear and concise one-volume format. Through the application of an ingenious system (albeit one daunting to novice users) of symbols and abbreviations, the dictionary furnished readers with a tremendous amount of grammatical information (such as about the gender of nouns and how to conjugate and form the past participles of verbs, pluralize nouns, and pronounce Hebraisms in Standard pronunciation) as well as made recommendations about register and stylistic usage.

Criticisms of the work focused on its avoidance of vulgarisms, its occasionally inadequate or misleading explanations of religious concepts and terminology, the unannounced presence of neologisms, and the eschewing of *daytshmerish*. But scarcely a reviewer failed to marvel at the virtuosity of a work that was, in the words of one of them, "a model of concision and precision"—the first up-to-date Yiddish dictionary in decades and a milestone in general as well as Yiddish lexicography.[29] As one reviewer explained, Alexander Harkavy published a dictionary in 1925 for Yiddish-speaking immigrants in America; Uriel Weinreich produced a work for the benefit of American Yiddish speakers and Yiddish learners in the late twentieth century.[30]

History of the Yiddish Language

Following Uriel's death, Max Weinreich practiced his usual antidote to depression: He poured himself into his work, immersing himself in the institute's affairs and relentlessly revising and polishing his *Geshikhte fun der yidisher shprakh* to his satisfaction.[31] Even before Uriel's death—around the time of his retirement from City College in 1964—Weinreich had begun to appear regularly again in the YIVO building. By now, Weinreich had become so involved in YIVO's daily business that Executive Secretary Shmuel Lapin reproached him in 1968 with usurping his authority, using his influence to become the institute's de facto director. Lapin found himself obliged to obtain Weinreich's approval for virtually all decisions—big and small. "According to the current system," Lapin complained, "you actually conduct YIVO's administrative work and I bear the responsibility for it to the administration even when I don't agree with our actions regarding certain matters."[32]

Weinreich, assisted foremost by Liptzin, had formulated plans to cultivate a small elite trained in Yiddish and YIVO's approach to the social sciences to provide leadership and inspire a cultural renaissance among American Jewry through the transmission of eastern European knowledge and values. He also set out to leave "spiritual weapons" for future generations in the form of his own research contributions. His *Geshikhte fun der yidisher shprakh*, represents the culmination of a lifetime of scholarship and the fulfillment of an ambition he first set for himself while a university student in tsarist Russia. Nearly blind in his damaged eye by the end of his life, Weinreich relied on the assistance of YIVO research associate Shoshke Erlich to read sources aloud to him,

Zosa Szajkowski to check his notes, and Shlomo Noble to proofread the three-thousand-page manuscript that he presented to YIVO in early 1967 after more than fifteen years of near-daily labor on the book.[33] Ironically, he likely would never have completed the work without a decade of "exile" from the institute's day-to-day affairs.

A four-volume linguistic and cultural history of the Yiddish language and its speakers, Weinreich's *Geshikhte fun der yidisher shprakh* is perhaps best known among contemporary scholars for its elaboration of Weinreich's theory of the language's genesis and development. There he locates Yiddish's origins roughly a millennium ago in the interaction of local urban German dialects with Jewish correlates of Old French and Old Italian transported by Jewish migrants from today's eastern France and northern Italy to the Rhineland in Germany. As such, Yiddish is coterminous with Ashkenazic Jewry, which came to form a distinct cultural unity in this period. Contrary to generations of derogatory theories of the language's origins, Weinreich describes its evolution as a *shmeltsshprakh* (fusion language) combining and recasting medieval German, Semitic, Romance, and Slavic linguistic elements into an organic whole that developed parallel to rather than from modern German.

For Weinreich, each diasporic Jewish vernacular, such as Yiddish or Ladino, builds upon a previous one, inheriting its Hebrew-Aramaic as well as other elements in a chain of linguistic continuity and creativity stretching back to antiquity. Yiddish, he argued, was the product not of German-speaking Jews' compulsory segregation from Christian society in the medieval era, as was often advanced. Rather, it was a distinct language from its inception that arose out of Jews' desire to express their unique needs stemming from *Yidishkeyt*. By this term, he meant not the modern concept of secular Yiddish culture (*yidishe kultur*) that had been championed by the Yiddishist movement in eastern Europe but an outlook on life shaped by the pervasive influence of religion in all spheres of thought and activity in premodern Ashkenazic society.

Yiddish had not only selectively integrated linguistic and cultural elements from surrounding non-Jewish societies without sacrificing any of its Jewish character; it was also the vehicle and repository for thousands of years of accumulated Jewish tradition and learning. This perspective reflected Weinreich's postwar appreciation for the role of Judaism as an all-embracing religious culture in shaping Jewish life and preserving Jewish distinctiveness through the millennia, even if he, an ardent secularist, still clung to the prewar Yiddishist hope that language alone could sustain—if only for a small, culturally creative elite—Jewish life in the Diaspora in a secular age. Weinreich argued in his *Geshikhte fun der yidisher shprakh* for pride of place for Yiddish as the leading Jewish diasporic vernacular, one possessing the largest number of speakers as well as the most developed in terms of its social and cultural functions. He hoped that the lessons of Yiddish might serve as a blueprint, even if indirectly, for Jewish survival in a new, unfolding chapter in the history of Ashkenazic civilization on American soil.[34]

Weinreich was, however, also a pragmatist who understood that the mass revernacularization of Yiddish was not obtainable and that an exclusive concern with the eastern European past would yield no future for the institute or the Jewish people. While he struggled to convince YIVO's administration to spend the necessary funds to publish his *Geshikhte fun der yidisher shprakh* in full, he also insisted on having it translated into English in order for his ideas to reach a wider audience, especially linguists.[35] YIVO's Board of Directors, always in a panic over YIVO's financial distress, balked at publishing the work in its entirety, preferring to consign its two volumes of footnotes to the archives. Weinreich protested bitterly. Although he was convinced that his work would find few qualified readers, he was certain that precisely those readers could not do without the notes. Fortunately, the poet Avrom Sutzkever, who was then visiting New York, managed to convince the Board of Directors to accede to his friend's wishes. He had, in the words of Ruth Wisse, "berated the members for basking in the glory of their office while nickel-and-diming the man who earned it for them."[36]

Weinreich's magnum opus was published posthumously in 1973, a fitting testament to a life of singular devotion to Yiddish language and culture. Its first two volumes were subsequently translated into English as *History of the Yiddish Language* by Shlomo Noble with the help of Joshua Fishman, appearing in 1984. Only in 2008 was a full translation published, including its two volumes of notes meticulously translated by Paul (Hershl) Glasser, then the Dean of the Max Weinreich Center (as the Center for Advanced Jewish Studies was renamed after Weinreich's death).[37] This work that he believed would find few readers assured both Weinreich's legacy as the most important Yiddish scholar of his generation and YIVO's position as the academy of the Yiddish language for decades to come. Although aspects of Weinreich's theory of the origins of Yiddish are today contested, Weinreich's *Geshikhte fun der yidisher shprakh* remains a classic with which all must reckon who are engaged in studying the history of Yiddish or the field of Jewish interlinguistics, the comparative study of Jewish languages.[38]

YIVO After Weinreich

Max Weinreich did not live to see more than the firstfruits of many of his labors. He did not witness further iterations of what would evolve into one of YIVO's most successful and celebrated educational endeavors, an annual "ritual" affectionately known as the *zumer-program* by its graduates that has drawn scores of students to New York from around the world each summer since then. Nor was he present for the inaugural year of YIVO's Center for Advanced Jewish Studies or the publication of his own *Geshikhte fun der yidisher shprakh*. In late January 1969, Weinreich, one of the first and last of the Vilna YIVO's founders and builders, died following a brief bout of illness.[39]

Like Uriel, Max Weinreich worked assiduously until his final days to complete his life's work, preparing plans for the graduate program he had intended to direct. As per his instructions, Weinreich's funeral proceeded in stoic silence apart from the chanting of the haunting *El male rahamim*, the reading of psalms, and the recitation of *kaddish* by his son Gabriel at his grave in the Workmen's Circle cemetery in Cedar Park, NJ—a surprisingly traditional funeral for an "old Bundist" who lived most of life far away from religious observance. Abraham Joshua Heschel, the sole religious thinker to maintain a longtime affiliation with YIVO, exhorted the hundreds assembled to use this silence to reflect on what Weinreich had preached throughout his lifetime: the preservation of the Yiddish language, its culture, and its values.[40] Only during the *shloshim* ceremony marking thirty days since his passing did colleagues commemorate him in public speeches.[41] Reflecting on his role in the institute, *Yedies* noted, "It was Dr. Weinreich who from its beginning staked out its field, established its character and directed its work. In all its activities there was the guiding hand of Dr. Weinreich. His departure marks a turning point in the history of YIVO. He will be sorely missed, but the spiritual legacy left by him is so ample, so brilliant that it will continue to guide the way."[42]

Not surprisingly for so consequential a figure, opinions of Weinreich varied. Some experienced him as formal and imperious—the epitome of a "cold Litvak," as Jews from today's Lithuania and adjacent regions are known in Yiddish culture, convinced of his own rectitude and callous about the feelings of others, particularly those subordinate to him. Others found him warm and caring, even sentimental, beneath a very formal, "Teutonic" exterior. His students and secretaries recalled him as a patient and nurturing teacher and mentor.[43] But none doubted his historic importance for the institute or the depth of his passion for it. No single figure associated with YIVO commanded his influence or possessed his force of personality; nor had he groomed a successor, perhaps because he deemed no one other than Uriel his equal and wished to retain as much authority as possible for himself despite his preoccupation with the future of YIVO and Yiddish scholarship.

Following Weinreich's demise, the institute was further destabilized by the passing in 1973 of its Executive Secretary Shmuel Lapin, who, like Uriel Weinreich, died in the bloom of youth. After unsuccessful efforts to find a replacement on YIVO's constrained budget, Lapin was succeeded briefly in late 1974 by Joseph Berg, who had retired from a career in the chemical industry, and then in 1976 by Morris Laub, a long-term officer of the JDC and member of YIVO's administration. Laub's ability to work was, however, severely impaired by a stroke, and he continued to work only part-time until he retired from the position in 1979.[44]

Even with hiatuses in formal leadership, however, the institute continued to function thanks to the efforts of its dedicated staff, many of whom played multiple roles in its administration, and the largesse of the US government, whose grants provided a lifeline. In particular, Hannah Fryshdorf (1920–89), a lifelong Bundist like several other YIVO associates, played a leading role in ensuring continuity. Despite her official title as Assistant Executive Director, Fryshdorf, who had risen through the ranks since joining YIVO's staff as a research associate in 1954, supervised the institute's daily operations. Though she was not wont to preside over YIVO's public events, her office received regular visitations from staff, and her presence was deeply felt at internal meetings as the institute's de facto administrator. She made a deep impression on Joshua Fishman's adolescent son (and future Jewish historian) David as a woman directing the male-dominated institute. As he later recalled, “Her days consisted of cigarettes, coffee, telephone, typewriter.”[45]

Meanwhile, scholarships furnished by individual donors for the summer program and the Max Weinreich Center enabled them to expand their enrollments and activities, making students and student-centric activities once again a vital part of the institute. Students and fellows joined circles (*krayzn*) newly formed under faculty supervision in history, linguistics, and literature as well as in folklore and terminology—the latter being areas that had been relatively overlooked since the 1950s.[46] Their research in and between multiple disciplines appeared—in Yiddish and in English—in a new series edited by Shoshke Erlich and Joan Bratkowsky (“Working Papers in Yiddish and East European Jewish Studies,” which debuted in 1974 and continued until 1982) as well as in other YIVO publications.[47]

On the eve of YIVO’s fiftieth annual conference in 1975, YIVO’s transition from Europe to America had proved a success to judge by the usual metrics of publishing, collections, and events. Not only was YIVO one of the few European Jewish institutions alongside yeshivas to survive the war and transplant itself to new soil. It had also greatly expanded its collections and activities during its first thirty years in America, winning it academic recognition in North America, Europe, and Israel. It had become an indispensable resource to students and researchers of the Jewish past while not neglecting the Jewish present. It also served as *the* authority for the Yiddish language for those who sought such an authority. Yet despite an infusion of youthful energy and government funding for projects at the time of a landmark moment in the history of any institution, anxiety about the institute’s future was palpable.

YIVO at Fifty

At its annual conference in 1975, most speakers offered talks summarizing and evaluating YIVO’s ample academic achievements since 1925, as could be expected at an event feting the “golden jubilee” of the institute’s founding. Notably, these talks overwhelmingly focused on the European era in its history. In contrast, Joshua Fishman, recently returned from three years of research and activity promoting Yiddish and other Jewish languages in Israel, concentrated his remarks on YIVO's American era. Citing his mentor Weinreich's admonitions, Fishman warned about the potential for what he described as the "routinization" of scholarship and the "deethnicization" of the institute. A specialist in the sociology of minority languages, Fishman noted how cultural societies founded by immigrants often surrendered their language and particularist identity in order to attract younger generations. He expressed fears that Yiddish would—to what would be Weinreich's horror—one day play at best a perfunctory role in YIVO's daily operations and that the production of scholarship would become divorced from a connection to a vital Jewish community, making YIVO "just another knowledge factory—a university 'kekhol hagoyim' [as among the nations], even a Judaica Study center like others, without active Jewish purpose, active Jewish responsibility, and active Jewish mission." In doing so, Fishman highlighted the ongoing tension between YIVO's popular and academic missions that was exacerbated by the disconnect between generations in its audience. "YIVO's ultimate purpose," he declared in what likely was received more as a reproof than an admonition, "is to rebuild, to strengthen and to enrich, and not just to teach and to publish and to research."[48]

Speaking in Montreal later that year, historian Isaiah Trunk, who replaced Ezekiel Lifschutz as head archivist upon his retirement in 1972, offered his own assessment of YIVO's accomplishments in America thus far. Addressing an audience at Montreal's Jewish Public Library, the seat of that city's secular Jewish intellectual life, he noted that YIVO had struck deep roots in America despite its struggles since the 1940s to draw the interest of American Jews possessing little desire to be associated with Yiddish or eastern Europe. In his analysis, World War II and the Holocaust had triggered a process of awakening Jewish national consciousness and feelings of solidarity with Jewish communities around the world among a segment of American Jewry. Together with the weakening of "cosmopolitan and assimilationist illusions," he advanced, came a desire to commemorate and understand the world of eastern European Jewry. This development was reflected in university enrollments in Jewish studies courses and student interest in YIVO.[49]

The Max Weinreich Center, he continued, had modestly begun with only two courses in the 1968–69 academic year but boasted eleven courses in 1975–76. The faculty included not only veteran YIVO associates but also several young, American-born or trained academics. The 103 registered students could take courses taught by a team of recognized experts from North America and Israel from multiple disciplinary angles in subjects such as Introduction to Yiddish Studies, Yiddish Folklore, Jews in the Soviet Union, Polish Jewry in the Nineteenth Century, the Jewish Community in Modern Times, and the Sociology of Jewish Life. They could also take Jewish studies courses at Columbia, the Jewish Theological Seminary, and other universities belonging to its academic consortium. Some of the center's graduates, Trunk announced, had even already gone on to become professors of Yiddish language and literature. Meanwhile, the Uriel Weinreich Yiddish Summer Program continued to attract dozens of students each year to the Columbia University campus.[50] YIVO thus represented the only place in North America—and perhaps the world—to find such a rich concentration of courses about the eastern European Jewish experience.

YIVO's rootedness and expansion in American soil were also reflected in its growing holdings and publications. Trunk counted some 350,000 volumes—chiefly Judaica—in more than twenty languages in its library, with Yiddish and Hebrew predominating. Its archives contained more than ten million pages about Jewish life around the world, especially the last two hundred years in eastern Europe and the last century in North America; some one hundred thousand photos dating since almost the invention of photography; the world's largest collection of Jewish theater materials; and a rich art collection that included music, paintings, prints, and more. Among its publications, he enumerated more than 450 books and articles, including 60 in English in the *YIVO Annual*, and 15 volumes of essential Holocaust bibliography produced in close cooperation with Yad Vashem.[51] To this list, he could have added 30 annual volumes of *YIVO bleter*, 15 volumes of *YIVO Annual of Jewish Social Science*, and 34 of *Yidishe shprakh* that had appeared since 1940.

But the Vilna YIVO, he emphasized, could not be transferred to a new environment with complete success in the absence of similar social conditions, even if surviving collections and personnel had been brought to America. Trunk concisely summarized the situation for his audience of chiefly eastern European immigrants, many of them avid YIVO supporters, when he noted that "In Poland, YIVO was the roof over a great Jewish culture in Yiddish. In America, such an edifice does not exist."[52]

Trunk did not explain this assertion, but its meaning was likely self-evident to his audience.

Despite having undergone secularization in adolescence and early adulthood, YIVO scholars in Europe possessed—with few exceptions (particularly among Bundists born in the interwar period)—a background rooted in the traditionally religious culture of the Jewish lower middle and working classes of pre–World War II eastern Europe. They belonged to different parties but shared a sense of belonging to a Jewish nation as defined by secular criteria and embraced identities organized around participation in political parties, vocational and commercial associations, educational institutions, sporting clubs, musical societies, newspapers and publishing, social clubs, and more in which the Yiddish language occupied a central role and was considered a force for shaping a progressive Jewish future. They were part of a Yiddishist intelligentsia that exercised a leadership role in political and culture life beyond the world of scholarship and enjoyed the eager support of a broad social base—the so-called folk masses and their organizations—for whom scholarship in and about Yiddish, their mother tongue, was not only a tool for self-recognition and self-improvement but a source of pride in being Jewish in the largely hostile environment of interwar Poland and neighboring states.

In America, in contrast, YIVO operated with the support of a sympathetic government that applied its resources generously to help it reacquire its collections and even provided substantial grant monies for its projects. But YIVO lacked here a comparably large and appreciative base—formal and informal networks of social, political, cultural, educational, and professional organizations functioning in Yiddish. Many such organizations existed in America in the early decades of the twentieth century, especially when immigration continued to flow unimpeded from eastern Europe. However, rapid acculturation and Jews' aspirations for participation in the English-speaking American mainstream, which were increasingly fulfilled in the post–World War II era, ensured the decline, if not disappearance, of most institutions committed to Yiddish and the heritage of eastern European Jewry by the last quarter of the twentieth century.

Most importantly perhaps, YIVO lacked in America a symbiotic relationship with youth and the hopes for a Yiddish-speaking future for them comparable to what they knew in Europe, where tens of thousands of children attended schools (both secular and religious) and participated in social and political organizations functioning in Yiddish in Poland alone. YIVO not only played a role in training teachers in prewar eastern Europe, further cementing its relationship with the *TSYSHO* school network with which it conceived its spelling system. The schools themselves stimulated the need for pedagogic materials in Yiddish. They also produced graduates who were to be the future consumers and producers of highbrow Yiddish culture as well as an audience for YIVO's research and language planning activities.[53]

YIVO did seek to cultivate the interest of students in New York's Yiddish secular schools in its activities, and several of its leaders (especially Leibush Lehrer, Yudel Mark, and Samuel Charney) contributed as writers and editors to the production of children's literature and publications employed in the various streams of Yiddish schools. However, such efforts were largely independent of YIVO. More importantly, American Yiddish schools and camps drew smaller numbers than in Europe and, as supplementary educational and cultural institutions, could not provide the linguistically immersive environment of full-day schools and Yiddish-speaking communities. They did not produce a sizable cadre of committed youth readers who would become adult producers of Yiddish culture in the United States. The proportionately sizable presence of Yiddish-speaking Canadians (including Marvin Herzog, Barbara Kirshenblatt-Gimblett, David Roskies, and Ruth Wisse) among the younger generation of scholars associated with YIVO, especially in the 1970s, may itself reflect the greater longevity and more intensive nature of Yiddish schooling there than in the United States—a reflection of distinctly Canadian nationality politics as well as of a pattern of generally later immigration from eastern Europe in the twentieth century.[54]

As was predicted during discussions of moving YIVO's center from Vilna to New York during the war, the relatively favorable conditions that America presented Jews in comparison with eastern Europe—especially comparatively low levels of antisemitism (particularly in the postwar era, when expressions of Jew hatred reached historic lows even if they remained cause for anxiety),[55] advanced acculturation, greater political freedom, unprecedented career and social opportunities, and affluence—would in some ways prove detrimental to YIVO's work, including its ability to attract and retain promising youth to its staff. Not only were full-time staff positions unavailable for lack of sufficient funding, but YIVO salaries were often inferior to those of jobs elsewhere. In his resignation letter in 1975, for example, future historian Steven Lowenstein expressed profound regret that despite how meaningful and compelling he found his work as an archivist at YIVO, he simply could not sustain his growing family with YIVO's wages. He accepted a more financially rewarding position—as archivist and assistant to the director of the "rival" German Jewish Leo Baeck Institute—while expressing his wish to continue teaching in the Max Weinreich Center.[56]

Young Jews' success in integrating into general academia further contributed to this "problem." Weinreich himself had encouraged this phenomenon, which was hardly conceivable in Poland, among his own students and saw it as fostering the productive cross-fertilization of American and YIVO scholarly traditions. His leading students and disciples did not pursue careers focused on YIVO. Instead, several—among them Lucy Dawidowicz, Ruth Wisse, Dan Miron, and Joshua Fishman, not to mention his son Uriel—pursued careers in Jewish cultural affairs or in Jewish studies in general academia. They remained, however, active in YIVO in various capacities through the years—as committee members, project leaders and researchers, and Max Weinreich Center scholars. Chana Mlotek and Beatrice Weinreich too remained crucial to the institute as archivists, teachers, publication editors, and researchers—becoming more active as their children matured—but were likely not encouraged to occupy higher positions in the institute precisely because they were women.[57] Perhaps under different circumstances—such as a stronger commitment to Yiddishism and Yiddish as the language of its operations and, most importantly, larger budgets to employ them full-time—figures such as Mordkhe Schaechter and Joshua Fishman would have played a more central role in YIVO in the closing decades of the twentieth century. But these are questions concerning finances, ideology, and interpersonal dynamics within the institute as well as external factors that require further investigation.

On the other hand, Weinreich's death—and the decline of the eastern European generation more broadly—opened up new opportunities for YIVO as an institution whose focus was increasingly on preserving and interpreting the world of Yiddish-speaking Jewry for the benefit of an English-speaking audience, chiefly Jewish but also non-Jewish. YIVO never relinquished its commitment to the concept of a global Jewish people. But the inevitable passing of generations accelerated YIVO's transformation from a Diaspora Nationalist research institute staffed by native Yiddish speakers and serving the remnants of the eastern European Jewish folk into an American ethnic organization that functioned as custodian of the documentary record and cultural legacy of Ashkenazic Jewry for the benefit of primarily postwar generations. Further, while YIVO never abandoned its interest in contemporary Jewish life—on the contrary, research about post–World War II topics continued to be presented at its conferences through the years—social science research about matters such as contemporary Jewish demography, economic structures, sociology, psychology, and education that had largely defined YIVO's pre–World War II agenda declined by the 1960s, especially following the deaths of scholars such as Lestschinsky and Lehrer who specialized in those areas. YIVO publications—whether in the fields of history, literature, or language studies—also became concerned primarily with the Holocaust and the pre–World War II world of European and American Jewries. That is, YIVO publications focused on the past more than the present, even if annual conferences offered more of a balance of pre- and post–World War II topics, including about Israeli and Soviet Jewries.

A World or American Jewish Institution?

Prior to the war, not only did there exist YIVO Committees and Friends of YIVO Societies in major cities around the world. YIVO's academic sections were housed in multiple cities—Vilna, Berlin, Paris, and New York—and often maintained their own libraries and archives, even if operations were coordinated from Vilna. After World War II, YIVO Committees and Friends of YIVO Societies continued to exist (to what extent is a question for a future researcher) in many locales outside of continental Europe. But while these affiliates were a great source of pride to YIVO in New York, sustaining them was not among its priorities. YIVO effectively relinquished ambitions in the post–World War II era to exist as a truly global organization with branches wherever Yiddish-speaking Jewry was to be found in significant numbers.

Moreover, given that American monies had historically made up a large part of YIVO's budget prior to World War II, the model of YIVO's global periphery supporting its center financially quickly lost its relevance. Whereas in the prewar era, YIVO's various branches sent what money they could to sustain the center in Vilna, poorer branches and branches in countries with weak currencies, such as in Latin America, were not able in the postwar era to do the same for New York.[58] On the contrary, they often looked to New York for assistance, struggling to maintain themselves financially, even if they occasionally held local fundraising drives on behalf of YIVO in New York, often with visiting speakers from there. They hosted cultural events such as lectures and exhibits into the late 1960s as long as interest and adequate funding were to be found locally among eastern European immigrants.

On the other hand, the tradition of the periphery collecting materials on behalf of the center was upheld. YIVO affiliates and private individuals sent items they collected—such as books and documents—to New York. Indeed, they seldom produced original scholarship or possessed their own archives. Even the YIVO Committee in London, which sponsored an immigrant essay contest of its own and produced a collected volume of articles (*Yidn in england*, 1966) about Jewish life in England among Yiddish-speaking immigrants, sent its materials to New York. First organized in 1937, it finally closed its doors in 1971 because YIVO's center in New York was not willing to contribute enough funding to supplement the little that it raised on its own, and—more importantly—several of its key figures passed away.[59]

The significant exception to the rule of New York centrism and dwindling branches by the 1960s was the YIVO branch in Argentina. Since its founding in 1928, it had maintained its own archives and museum, as well as produced its own scholarship and publications, including the important hundred-volume *Musterverk* (Masterpieces) of Yiddish literature series edited by its director Shmuel Rollansky. The YIVO in Buenos Aires (la Fundación IWO–Instituto Científico Judío en Argentina) operated (and continues to operate thirty years after the 1994 terrorist bombing of the Jewish community center building that housed it), however, as an independent organization despite remaining in irregular communication with New York, with which it has exchanged books, materials, and visits of personnel from time to time.[60]

YIVO continued nonetheless to play a vital social and cultural role among eastern European Jews in the United States, Canada, and sometimes beyond. Annual conferences, at which noted Yiddish-speaking intellectuals presented, were held in Los Angeles and Chicago, and the YIVO Forum in Miami drew the participation of New York–based Yiddish writers, actors, and intellectuals who spent the winter months in this mecca for Jewish retirees.[61] The operations of these YIVO affiliates, while helping disseminate Jewish learning and Yiddish secular culture and useful for fundraising, did little to further YIVO's primary scholarly mission. But they did reinforce YIVO's territorial rootedness and its identity as an organization active across the American Jewish population and its cultural centers, even if YIVO's activities were concentrated in New York City. By the late 1970s, YIVO even began to draw greater attention in mainstream American and American Jewish intellectual communities, as evidenced by the increasing appearance in publications such as *The New York Times* of not only obituaries for members of its staff, administration, and Board of Directions—itself a recognition of the prominence of the institute—but also articles about its role in preserving Jewish history and promoting Yiddish culture for an American audience.

An Old World Institution in America

Descriptions of YIVO and its building between the 1940s and '60s in the Yiddish press focused on prestigious addresses with up-to-date technical installations hosting conferences and producing reams of scholarship as a sign that Yiddish culture and scholarship had "arrived" in America despite the indifference of a broad swath of American Jewry. YIVO boosters then regularly complained about the lack of attention given to the institute in the influential English-language press (brief articles frequently appeared, however, in small Jewish communal publications). In contrast, as Jewish history and culture, including Holocaust commemoration, found wider acceptance in American society, YIVO was increasingly portrayed as a haven for the survivors of a vanished world and a storehouse for its cultural treasures worth visiting by researchers and nostalgic tourists alike.[62]

English-language sources in the 1970s—as well as retrospective pieces written years later—often emphasized the faded grandeur of the repurposed Vanderbilt mansion and its "European" atmosphere. They fostered an image of YIVO as an idiosyncratic Old World institution tenaciously clinging to life with much good humor and little money for its daily operations.[63] Together, the two dozen or so staff members were depicted as engaged in Sisyphean efforts to process a backlog of archival collections for which there was never adequate time or resources and to catalog an unrelenting flow of new acquisitions: books, photographs in need of identification before the names of their subjects were forgotten, artwork, music, and archival collections.[64]

Grants from both private organizations such as ORT, an international Jewish educational and vocational training organization, and from US government agencies, above all the National Endowment for the Humanities (NEH), provided a lifeline for the institute throughout the 1970s and into the 1980s as individual contributions, the institute's main stream of revenue for years, receded with donor deaths and regular expenses increased. NEH funding made possible such important projects as microfilming books and periodicals to preserve them, cataloging unprocessed books from the pre–World War II Vilna YIVO and Strashun collections, producing record guides for archival collections, and modernizing library systems to embrace the use of computers.[65]

Obtaining a steady stream of government grants reflected the staff's skill in writing grant applications and the impressive vision of its projects, making possible the hiring of additional temporary workers to execute several multi-year undertakings otherwise unrealizable in the absence of adequate funding in YIVO's regular budget. But these grants did not cover the basic operating costs of the institute, which were constantly on the rise. Moreover, government matching grants set a high bar, obliging YIVO to intensify its own fundraising efforts among the public. Thus, for example, the Max Weinreich Center alone received a five-year NEH grant of $675,000 for the period 1974–79 with the expectation that YIVO itself would raise an additional $470,000 for supplementary support in that five-year period from its circle of donors and the broader American Jewish community. An additional $100,000 was pledged by the NEH on the condition that YIVO could match it with money it raised itself.[66] As Zachary Baker, a YIVO librarian in this era, recalls, "A perfunctory level of fundraising and a Herculean effort in creative bookkeeping ensured that grant funds were ostensibly matched."[67]

Meanwhile, upon assuming duties as YIVO's new executive secretary in 1980, thirty-two-year-old Samuel Norich discovered that the payment of staff wages was weeks overdue.[68]

YIVO's chronic underfunding was evident not only in its understaffing and payroll delays but also in the increasingly cramped and antiquated nature of its physical installation. To make more space to process collections, shelves were constructed in a former ballroom already used for archival processing. Meanwhile, the system for delivering books to the reading room, while functional, had not been updated over the years. A journalist observed that "books come down on the dumbwaiter from stacks on the third and fifth floors by way of a striped shopping bag, and call slips go up safety-pinned to its handles."[69] This was, however, but a quaint curiosity, while climate control represented a genuine problem. In the absence of air conditioning, the oppressive summer heat and humidity penetrated reading rooms and offices where staff and visitors worked. In the winter months, in contrast, steam heat from the subbasement overheated those same rooms, frequently obliging staff to keep windows open to compensate.[70]

The climatic conditions were not only disagreeable to people, however. They presented a pressing danger for fragile books and documents, especially those stored in the hot and humid subbasement, where the building's heating system was also located. Repeating the dire admonitions first issued by her predecessor, Ezekiel Lifschutz, a decade earlier, head librarian Dina Abramowicz warned about the fragility of rare books, especially those printed on cheap, acidic paper in interwar Europe. YIVO could not afford to let these books, many of them saved from Hitler's clutches, disintegrate; new editions of popular works and classics, let alone rare works, she warned, could not be expected.[71] Abramowicz's calls for the introduction of modern conservation techniques before it was too late added to archivists' concerns about the lack of space for ever-expanding collections, as organizations that formerly jealously guarded their records now sought a place for them to be preserved for posterity. Meanwhile, the children of Yiddish actors and literati, unable to read the language in which their parents made their careers, sought a home for their papers. Sizable additions to the archives from major American Jewish organizations since the 1950s included papers of the Hebrew Immigrant Aid Society, the Joint Distribution Committee, the Educational

Alliance, and the records of numerous *landsmanshaftn* collected in a concerted effort by YIVO in the 1970s to stimulate the writing of the history of Jewish immigrants in the United States and of their hometowns in eastern Europe.[72]

What the Vanderbilt YIVO lacked in space and state-of-the-art functionality, it made up for in the character of its collections and the unique experiences it offered staff and visitors alike. Once the playground of New York socialites, the grand building was decorated with the priceless artifacts of Yiddish culture and its personalities that had accumulated over the decades: plaques honoring donors, photographs and busts of famous cultural figures and YIVO associates, donated paintings, theater posters and marionettes, remnants of YIVO exhibitions and more—in short, a museum of Yiddish-speaking Jewry in itself. Even "Leivick's tree," a plant sitting in a corner of the reading room, recalled the celebrated Yiddish poet and member of the YIVO administration who bequeathed it.[73]

Moreover, the physical condition of the installation belied the tremendous vitality of the personnel. Staff members in the 1970s could be seen (and heard) conducting their business as well as eating, drinking, and conversing in multiple languages on the periphery of the reading room while visitors conducted their research seated at wooden tables in its center. Visitors recall the older generation of archival and library workers who knew the collections intimately offering guidance in direct measure to their degree of confidence in the abilities and seriousness of, as well as affection for, students and researchers who requested access to them. The extreme case of this institutional eccentricity was archivist Zosa Szajkowski, a notoriously difficult personality who seemed to take a perverse pleasure in denying access to materials that he carefully guarded as if his private fiefdom.[74]

Avoided by colleagues after a rupture in relations in the 1950s, Szajkowski was "exiled" to his fourth-floor office, where he organized collections and exhibitions. He nonetheless continued to circulate throughout the building, informing himself of activities elsewhere. Though Szajkowski was reviled by many of his colleagues for his penchant for gossip and insulting others, Weinreich valued his contributions and felt a sense of obligation toward him for his role in reconstituting YIVO collections and acquiring Nazi documentation. Consequently, Weinreich interceded at times on his behalf, privately rebuking him for his conduct but helping him to preserve his job for his own sake and that of his wife and child.[75]

Szajkowski's life took a darker turn when he was caught stealing in 1961 from the Strasbourg Municipal Archives in France, whose Jewish communities were the major subject of his postwar scholarly publications. Indeed, it was later revealed that Szajkowski had for years absconded with books and archival materials from research institutions in Europe and the United States—often initially for his own personal use and later for sale to libraries and research institutions to supplement his meager income. As his biographer Lisa Leff explains, Szajkowski's actions highlight not only the connivance of those institutions that asked few questions about the provenance of materials he acquired. They also draw attention to the shift in attitudes that occurred between the latter half of the 1940s, when the acquisition of materials amid the rubble and legal chaos of postwar Europe was widely seen as a heroic act of rescue and a fitting response to the Holocaust, and years later, once institutions and law had resumed their normal functioning. Such behavior was then condemned as wanton acts of theft and "an affront to the norms of historical and archival practice."[76] Barred from French archives, Szajkowski was eventually arrested for pilfering rare pamphlets closer to home—in the New York Public Library—in 1978. He resigned from YIVO and took his own life in disgrace.[77]

A New Generation

Many of YIVO's staff members and associates, as well as members of its Board of Directors, in the latter half of the 1970s belonged to a generation born in Europe in the 1920s, if not earlier. Not only did they include native Yiddish speakers in their fifties and older raised in milieus in which the language dominated; some had received their educations in whole or in part in Yiddish secular schools, where Yiddish literature and secular culture were stressed as the bases for a modern Jewish identity. Their American-born peers of roughly the same generation—such as Joshua Fishman, Chana Mlotek, and Beatrice Weinreich—were those exceptional graduates of Yiddish supplementary schools and American public schools who devoted themselves to Yiddish culture. Largely absent was a generation born in the 1930s and '40s—European Jews destroyed by the

Holocaust and their American coevals who, though largely spared the horrors of war, did not embrace YIVO's purpose or see it as an attractive or viable career option in the postwar era.

At the same time, however, the institute also drew to its staff idealistic, academically minded young people in their twenties and early thirties who had often neither attended Yiddish schools nor grown up in Yiddish-speaking milieus. Many had only recently completed their undergraduate degrees, often after studying at the Uriel Weinreich Yiddish Summer Program and/or enrolling in YIVO's Max Weinreich Center. In contrast with eastern European–born generations of YIVO workers, whose intimacy with Yiddish culture they could not replicate, these youthful employees had typically not only received an undergraduate but sometimes also a graduate education. Some had also obtained certification in areas such as archival and library sciences, contributing to greater professionalization and familiarity with up-to-date techniques among YIVO's staff. They also contributed to the diversification of YIVO's staff in terms of their degrees of religious observance.

Illustrative of this phenomenon is Minnesota native Zachary Baker, who enrolled in the *zumer-program* while an undergraduate at the University of Chicago in 1971. Having acquired an ability to read Yiddish with the help of his grandfather, a rabbi, Baker pursued rigorous study of Yiddish language, literature, and culture with Mordkhe Schaechter and David Roskies, then a twenty-three-year-old graduate student in Jewish literature at Brandeis University. He enrolled in 1976 in a librarian internship program funded by the National Endowment for the Humanities conducted at the Max Weinreich Center by Dina Abramowicz and assistant librarian Bella Hass Weinberg. Baker subsequently became a YIVO librarian himself, working there until he left to pursue an opportunity as chief librarian at the Jewish Public Library in Montreal in 1981. He returned, however, a few years later to replace Abramowicz as head librarian when she stepped down from the position in 1986 (although she continued to work as a reference librarian in YIVO until her death in 2000). Together with Hass Weinberg, who had herself begun working at YIVO in 1972 fresh from librarian graduate school, he helped rationalize YIVO's complicated cataloging system and bring contemporary methods of organization and preservation into the library, including the eventual computerization of the catalog.

Hass Weinberg, who came from a Yiddish-speaking family, was herself not only one of YIVO's young, American-born staff members but also one of its first Orthodox employees. By the late 1970s, the institute not only closed for Jewish holidays but also shut its doors early on Friday afternoons in the winter in advance of the Sabbath even if many of its staff were ideological secularists.[78] A mezuzah was eventually affixed—not without controversy—to the entrance of the temple of secular Yiddishism out of respect for Jewish custom and the religious sensitivities of a part of its staff and the broad American Jewish public.[79]

Another young arrival (as well as Orthodox Jew) was Fruma Mohrer, herself from a *haredi* home in Montreal. She came to YIVO in 1978 with a BA in history and graduate diploma in education from McGill University (she subsequently earned a JD from New York Law School). Working closely in the archives with Marek Web, she helped preserve and catalog collections (including materials recovered from Vilna in the 1990s), produce the indispensable *Guide to the YIVO Archives* (1998) describing YIVO's immense archival holdings and their history, and usher YIVO's archival management into the twenty-first century.[80]

The experience of working with the last generations of Yiddish-speaking Jews who had come of age in prewar eastern Europe was itself an education for this younger generation that had grown up in such radically different circumstances. Performer and music scholar Henry Sapoznik (himself the child of Holocaust survivors and founder, with ethnomusicologist Mark Slobin, of YIVO's Max and Frieda Weinstein Sound Archives in 1982), recalls, for example, remarkable conversations about prewar life and wartime experiences with colleagues such as building manager Bolek Ellenbogen, a veteran of the Polish and Jewish undergrounds. Ellenbogen, a lifelong Bundist from a working-class family and highly learned autodidact, had survived the war working first in the Medem Sanatorium for children and then on the "Aryan side" of Warsaw.[81]

Yet while members of the older generations were most often native Yiddish speakers, they did not necessarily uphold the institute's insistence on the language's monopoly in YIVO affairs. To be sure, Yiddish remained the dominant language of daily operations into the mid- to late 1970s but English could be increasingly heard—a moral outrage to committed Yiddishists such as Joshua Fishman and Mordkhe Schaechter.[82]

Schaechter complained in a letter addressed to the entirety of the administration and personnel that only a handful of twenty or so employees spoke Yiddish in their daily business. He estimated that 80 percent of conversations proceeded in English. Even worse, he maintained, was that YIVO hired employees who did not know Yiddish and had the temerity to hold meetings in English to accommodate them.[83] While Schaechter's appraisal was perhaps exaggerated, the linguistic trends were clear. Such a betrayal of Yiddishist ideals was hardly conceivable as long as Weinreich's presence was still felt and indicated that the Yiddishist ideology that had launched the institute was becoming increasingly symbolic. Although YIVO had no intention of surrendering its ethnic particularity or wholly jettisoning Yiddish, this particularity was increasingly expressed in American Jewish terms, most notably via the English language and the ethnoreligious symbolism (such as holiday closures and a mezuzah) embraced by most American Jewish institutions, religious and secular.

The linguistic situation in YIVO was, however, far more complicated than described above. Visitors and staff recall the existence of a seeming hierarchy of languages, with each one reflecting increasing degrees of intimacy and proximity to the eastern European Jewish world. English, used for encounters with the broad public, was the language of the first and largest circle. It was heard among visitors and in interactions with American-born staff members and sometimes even between European-born ones who knew Yiddish better than English. Yiddish, the language to which YIVO was dedicated, continued to function as a language of administration, minutes, archival descriptions, and correspondence alongside English into the 1980s and in interactions with dedicated Yiddishists and members of the Yiddishist youth group *Yugntruf*.[84] Finally, Polish and Russian—languages many staff members knew fluently or even natively from their countries of origin—were reserved for the smallest and most intimate circles belonging to those who had grown up in prewar Europe or more recently arrived following the "anti-Zionist" purge in 1968. It caused some twenty-five thousand Jews to flee Poland, reducing its Jewish population to between five and ten thousand individuals.[85] In this way, YIVO's connection to Poland, with which it had little formal contact in the 1950s and '60s, was refreshed, if to a very limited extent.

Among the recent refugees from communist Poland were Marek Web (1938–2021) and Lucjan Dobroszycki (1925–95). Web obtained an MA in history from the University of Łódź and worked as a history teacher in a Jewish school in Wrocław and a journalist for a Jewish newspaper in Warsaw prior to leaving his native land. Having already made contact with YIVO prior to his arrival in America in 1969, he began working in the archives and enrolled in graduate study at the Max Weinreich Center the following year. He developed an affinity with the institute, where he worked first as a junior archivist and eventually succeeded Trunk as head archivist in 1980.[86]

A survivor of the Lodz Ghetto and multiple concentration camps, Dobroszycki had already completed his doctorate in Russia and established an academic career in his native country prior to 1968. He joined YIVO's staff in 1970, teaching at both the Max Weinreich Center and Yeshiva University. Making use of YIVO collections, he continued to write about Nazi-occupied Poland, contributing most notably studies about the collaborationist Polish press during World War II, life in the Lodz Ghetto, and the postwar reconstitution of Jewish communities in Poland.[87]

The frequency with which Polish was heard caused some employees jokingly to refer to the institute as PIWO, the Polish Scientific Institute (and the Polish word itself for "beer"). This bit of merriment contained, however, a sad truth—at least for Yiddishists. In the interwar period, Yiddishists aspired to make eastern European Jewish society effectively monolingual, functioning chiefly in what was for them Jews' diasporic national language—Yiddish—rather than relying on additional, non-Jewish languages to conduct aspects of their daily lives, especially those related to higher prestige activities such as scholarship and politics. They vehemently condemned the growing Polonization of Jewish society as a threat not only to the Yiddish language and its culture but to Jewish national survival. Now the Polish language, previously an idol in the temple of Yiddishism, was at home alongside Yiddish and other languages in the mouths of graduates of the very Yiddish secular schools and youth movements Weinreich's generation had struggled to found and sustain. YIVO's ideological Yiddishism had yielded to a practical multilingualism, if not a linguistic polysystem in which each language served distinct but complementary functions.[88]

A Victim of Its Success?

The Max Weinreich Center never became the wholly independent degree-granting institution of which Weinreich dreamed. It nonetheless fulfilled much of the role he had envisioned by providing training in YIVO's areas of strength: Jewish life and culture in central and eastern Europe, the period of mass settlement of Jews in the United States, and Yiddish language, literature, and culture. In its Julius Borenstein Graduate Program, YIVO staff members and qualified faculty from various universities provided graduate students with courses in such areas as Jewish history and Yiddish language, literature, linguistics, and folklore. The center's Panel of Consultants offered expert mentoring and YIVO's unparalleled library and archival resources were made accessible to graduate students and faculty members conducting research in these fields.[89]

The center served in the 1970s and '80s as a hub for innovative and interdisciplinary work in Jewish studies in fields such as ethnography and cultural anthropology, as well as more traditional ones such as history, language, and literature, under the guidance of figures such as folklore and performance studies scholar Barbara Kirshenblatt-Gimblett, linguist Marvin Herzog (who became the acting dean of the Max Weinreich Center in 1975), and American Jewish historian Deborah Dash Moore (first an instructor in the late 1970s and later research director and the center's dean beginning in 1988).[90] It also provided invaluable opportunities to young people to gather experience and launch academic and academic-adjacent careers.

This model of cooperation between the Max Weinreich Center and select universities, whereby students received credit in their home institutions for courses taught by local and visiting faculty offered virtually nowhere else, proved extremely fruitful. If the *zumer-program* offered the rough equivalent of an undergraduate degree in Yiddish studies, the Max Weinreich Center enabled a generation or more of scholars to acquire the necessary training to anchor eastern European Jewish studies in universities in North American and beyond.[91] It helped to mitigate the irreparable loss of knowledge and disruption in cultural transmission occasioned by the war and Holocaust. The list of instructors and students (many of whom later became instructors themselves) of the two programs reads like a Who's Who in the contemporary field.[92]

The center's success was, however, in some ways a double-edged sword. The expansion of Jewish studies into general academia meant that YIVO's priceless collections became ever more important for a growing academic research culture in fields such as eastern European Jewish History, Holocaust studies, Yiddish and Hebrew literatures, and Jewish folklore and ethnography. This brought greater opportunities to publish scholarship in English (as well as the practical necessity of doing so to reach a wider audience and to advance one's career) in journals dedicated to the burgeoning field of Jewish studies instead of in Yiddish in YIVO journals.[93]

The decline in the number of scholars capable and willing to produce scholarship in Yiddish (as well as staff qualified and available to undertake the mammoth task of editing) coupled with a severely limited publications budget resulted in new issues of *Yivo bleter* and *Yidishe shprakh* appearing with decreasing frequency. This downward trend was already noticeable in the late 1950s, by which time *Yivo bleter* ceased to appear more than once a year, but culminated in ever longer hiatuses

The "Vanderbilt Mansion," YIVO's home at 1048 Fifth Avenue at the corner of Eighty-Sixth Street in 1982. Credit: YIVO Institute for Jewish Research

between issues in the 1960s. The journal finally ceased publication in the 1980s (it was briefly revived in the mid-1990s in a new series edited by historian and Jewish Theological Seminary professor David Fishman, who joined the faculty of the Max Weinreich Center).

While *Yidishe shprakh* continued to appear regularly until 1977 (and irregularly until 1986), its editor Mordkhe Schaechter, who succeeded Yudel Mark in the role in 1971, complained of the journal being treated in a "stepmotherly" fashion by a YIVO administration that made little effort to publicize each new issue. As further signs of the institute's neglect of Yiddish, he noted that it was the only YIVO publication denied office space and its contributors were paid less than those of the English-language *YIVO Annual*, which itself had by then long ceased to appear annually. In 1986, *Yedies* itself ceased publishing its issues half in Yiddish and half in English and adopted a new format with overwhelmingly English articles. But even English-language publications were hard to staff with seasoned editors. Hence, YIVO relied on the appointment of a recent PhD, a young assistant professor of Jewish literature at the Jewish Theological Seminary, David Roskies, as the editor of *YIVO Annual* in 1976 when Shlomo Noble stepped down from the position to dedicate himself to translating Weinreich's *Geshikhte fun der yidisher shprakh* into English. The journal ceased publication in 1983 but was briefly revived in the 1990s under the editorship of Deborah Dash Moore.[94]

Further, as universities became well-funded and prestigious sites for Jewish studies courses and programs, they began to offer similar courses in undergraduate and graduate programs, duplicating some of the work of the center. Still, the Max Weinreich Center offered highly specialized courses taught by world renowned experts, both local and visiting scholars, unavailable elsewhere. Into the late 1990s, center scholars continued to work closely with graduate students, in particular offering private tutorials with students enrolled in Columbia's Yiddish studies graduate program. The reduction in the number of courses offered by the center in the 1990s and its ultimate decline in the new century has deprived aspiring scholars of a centralized location for systematic training in many advanced subjects of Yiddish and eastern European Jewish studies.[95]

Finding an American Audience

As the folk that YIVO initially sought to serve receded in the postwar world, YIVO's staff, like the audience drawn to its educational programs and cultural events, increasingly resembled American Jewry itself—or at least a substantial segment of it: predominantly American-born or raised, university educated, middle class, and seeking to embrace its ethnic heritage while remaining socially integrated and firmly grounded in American culture and society. In an era when Jews came to play a prominent role in virtually all aspects of New York City politics and culture, YIVO received accolades for its achievements not only in surviving Yiddish newspapers—above all, the *Forverts*—but in *The New York Times*, the paper of choice among the city's intellectual elite boasting a large Jewish readership. A particular success was the exhibition *Image Before My Eyes*, which enjoyed the support of the New York State Council for the Arts and the National Endowment for the Humanities among its funders. It presented a careful selection of some four hundred images gleaned from YIVO's special collection of ten thousand photos about Jewish life in Poland from the nineteenth century to the eve of World War II, many of them recovered from the Vilna YIVO. The exhibition, which included documentaries and art films as well as lectures, was curated by YIVO associates and Max Weinreich Center faculty members Lucjan Dobroszycki and Barbara Kirshenblatt-Gimblett. It sought to represent the diversity, vibrancy, and complexity of prewar Polish Jewish community in order to counter the distorted image of it as a "a community wracked with poverty and living on the edge of destruction."[96] The exhibition traveled around the country after its March 1976 debut at New York's Jewish Museum, and served as the basis for both an eponymous photo album with extensive commentaries published the following year as well as an award-winning documentary film directed by independent filmmaker Joshua Waletzky that played in arthouse cinemas.[97]

YIVO associates also contributed to the invigoration of American Jewish cultural life by helping found and lead the klezmer and Jewish folk arts revival in the 1970s and '80s. Not only were several artists, musicians, and performers who played a foundational role in the revival active as employees and scholars working at YIVO in those years.[98] YIVO's Folk Arts Program ("KlezKamp"), directed by its founder Henry Sapoznik in the 1980s, acquainted thousands of music enthusiasts, scholars, and performers with the world of Yiddish popular music, which had fallen out of vogue, if not into virtual oblivion, among most American Jews post–World War II. While disappointing some veteran YIVO supporters who reproached such pursuits as frivolous in comparison with conventional scholarship, the younger generation of YIVO's staff and circles thus served as bridge between the world of the older generation and an American Jewry that did not know Yiddish well (or at all) and for whom its Yiddish past and its values needed to be presented in an American idiom or the language of music and art.

Looking back, the 1970s and '80s appear to have been the "golden age" of the Max Weinreich Center and for experimentation with new initiatives and directions for YIVO despite ongoing challenges. It did not lack critics then, however, who saw in it further confirmation of the American YIVO's deliberate drifting from its historic mission and constituency. Yiddish journalist Sh. L. Schneiderman exemplified this trend when he, along with other officers of the Yiddish PEN (Poets, Essayists, Novelists) Club, published a protest letter in the *Forverts* in 1976 accusing YIVO of neglecting its "familial ties" with "the Yiddish writers, teachers and in general the Yiddish-speaking folk intelligentsia [that] shaped the character of the institution and gave its work vibrancy" in its early years in America. In accusations similar to those heard in the 1950s, he alleged that YIVO focused its energies on its archives and library and failed to invite Yiddish writers to participate in its conferences, literary colloquiums, or the activities of the Max Weinreich Center.[99]

Only a year later, Schneiderman complained that the majority of the Max Weinreich Center's courses were conducted in English for students who "in most cases" lacked contact with the Yiddish-speaking community. They produced research on what he deemed arcane and marginal topics while failing to mark milestones in Jewish history and culture such as the birthday of pioneering historian of Polish Jewry Majer Bałaban or the centennial of Yiddish literature in America. Such engagement not only reflected a disparaging attitude toward contemporary Yiddish cultural creativity, he maintained, but was more inclined to "mummify" Yiddish language and literature than to stimulate it.[100]

Such accusations of disrespect, if not disdain, for Yiddish-speaking society, not to mention the trifling and obscurantist nature of research conducted by students and scholars affiliated with the center, were grossly exaggerated but contained a kernel of truth. Beyond an expression of the usual gap between scholarship and contemporary letters, they reflected the unmistakable anxiety about their continued relevance so keenly felt in surviving circles of secular Yiddish writers and cultural activists faced with dwindling audiences for their creative endeavors. In contrast with YIVO's early decades in America, Yiddish culture and its carriers were now being unapologetically studied as an inheritance of the past rather than as contributors to a living, vernacular civilization by young staff members and students conducting their personal and professional lives mainly in English.

Toward a New Century

Naturally, YIVO would continue to evolve over the years in ways that Weinreich's generation both anticipated and could never have imagined. Beyond significant technological advances that allowed for the improved conservation of collections on digital media and enhanced access to resources, the 1990s saw the reopening of eastern Europe for free scholarly inquiry and cultural exchange after the dissolution of the Soviet Union. Previously, YIVO's contact with post–World War II Soviet Jewry was almost exclusively limited to scholarship and exhibitions about Soviet literature and the repression of Jewish identity and heritage.[101] Among them was a *Century of Ambivalence*, an exhibit of photographs of Russian and Soviet Jewish life largely donated to YIVO's archives by Soviet emigres that drew more than 50,000 viewers at New York's Jewish Museum and culminated in a historical volume by cocurator Zvi Gitelman in 1988.[102]

Unforeseeable political developments soon afterward in the historic heartland of Yiddish culture infused the whole of eastern European Jewish studies and YIVO in particular with fresh energies and expertise, including new staff members who immigrated to the United States. Political changes also sparked the creation in 1991 of Project Judaica in collaboration with the Jewish Theological Seminary in New York and the Russian State University of the Humanities in Moscow "to bring to light long-hidden Judaica collections across the Commonwealth of Independent States, and to train aspiring archivists in Jewish history, culture and languages so that they may properly care for these collections."[103] The program, which was founded by David Fishman, brought Western scholars to teach courses in Jewish studies, including Yiddish language and eastern European Jewish history and culture, to Russian university students, both Jewish and Gentile—a dramatic inversion of the relationship between American and eastern European Jewish scholarship that YIVO so rued in the 1940s. Through initiatives such as this one, YIVO, which had served as a chief guardian of the eastern European Jewish academic tradition since the destruction of that world, helped restore Jewish learning to eastern Europe after the Cold War.

At the same time, some four decades after a plan was proposed by Weinreich and colleagues to unite American Jewish research institutions under a single roof, ground was broken for YIVO's present home in the Center for Jewish History on Sixteenth Street in New York City (YIVO found temporary residence on West Fifty-Seventh Street between 1994 and 1999, when the center opened its doors). While the institutions retained their independence, the pooling of resources—above all a reading room, staff, and amphitheater—as well as a common address highlighted YIVO's integration into the mainstream American Jewish scholarly and communal scene, if not its place as *primus inter pares* among its smaller partners—the American Jewish Historical Society, the Yeshiva University Museum, the Leo Baeck Institute, and the American Sephardi Federation.

Indicative of YIVO's growing embrace among American-born Jewry by the late twentieth century was also a change in its sources of income. If YIVO benefited in the 1940s from its connections to largely immigrant and refugee Jews—including ones playing prominent roles in the US military and government institutions—by the late 1980s, it benefited increasingly from connections to Jews of eastern European origin established not only in the worlds of business and scholarship but also in the arts and entertainment. In particular, the support lent by the theater impresario Joseph Papp, whose Public Theater occupied the space of YIVO's original headquarters in the HIAS building, brought YIVO into unprecedented realms. Gala evenings featuring performances by Broadway stars brought not only hundreds of thousands of dollars in donations to the institute. It also introduced YIVO to new audiences of Jews and non-Jews.[104] This trend of substantial giving by wealthy patrons and corporations—a far cry from reliance on small contributions from working-class immigrants—expanded in the 1990s.

The 1990s also brought a project to create an authoritative *YIVO Encyclopedia of Jews in Eastern Europe*, the collaborative work of some 450 scholars active in sixteen countries that appeared in print in 2008 and soon after online. The size of its academic staff and the range in the stages of their careers—from recent PhDs to veteran professors—testifies to the staggering growth of Yiddish and eastern European Jewish studies since the last third or so of the twentieth century. The two-million-word reference volume in English (contributors' entries in other languages, including Yiddish, were translated as necessary) represents the best in the traditions of YIVO in both Vilna—a dedication to high-caliber nonpartisan scholarship about the Yiddish-speaking folk—and in its postwar American incarnation, namely the practice of making this knowledge accessible and intelligible to the contemporary inheritors of the folk who are separated by time, space, and language from eastern Europe. It aims to educate its readers not only about the Holocaust, the subject with which the American lay reader is likely most familiar, but about all aspects of Jewish life and culture in the region prior to the Holocaust and, as much as possible, in the post–World War II world.[105] As in the case of *Image Before My Eyes*, its inclusion of figures active in multiple languages and spanning the ideological spectrum from Orthodoxy to Communism testifies to its broad conception of eastern European Jewry as an internally diverse, multilingual civilization whose dominant, but not exclusive, language was Yiddish into the twentieth century—a stark departure from YIVO's foundational emphasis on secular Yiddish culture and its proponents.

In the words of its editor in chief, the late historian of eastern European Jewry Gershon D. Hundert (McGill University), in the preface to the encyclopedia,

> It is filiopietistic *and* dispassionate precisely in the sense that in describing the civilization of our forebears it seeks to present East European Jewish life in a dispassionate manner, as accurately and fully and precisely as possible—not to celebrate or eulogize but to recover and represent. That is, the piety—our obligation to our ancestors—is expressed in our determination to present East

> European Jewish civilization without bias and without nostalgia but as comprehensively and as objectively as possible. . . . *The YIVO Encyclopedia* is intended to be an ecumenical work: nondenominational, nonideological, and nonconfessional. Nothing Jewish is considered foreign. One can see this encyclopedia as a massive work of *translation*. This is meant both simply—the language of that culture was chiefly Yiddish, together with Hebrew and vernacular tongues—but also in a more metaphorical way, making the culture comprehensible to our readers, most of whom live in quite different circumstances today.[106]

Further, in a modernized version of the YIVO tradition, the encyclopedia seeks to represent the everyday experience of not only elites but also the Jewish masses, including women and children, and all aspects of Jewish culture—from economic life, criminality, folklore, popular culture and entertainment to religious and secular education, high and low brow literature and theater, political activism, rabbinic creativity, and more.[107] As a reflection of the current state of knowledge about the Jews of eastern Europe—defined here as those who historically lived on the territory corresponding roughly to today's Romania, Poland, Hungary, Czech Republic, Slovakia, the Baltic states, Finland, Moldova, Ukraine, Belarus and Russia—the *YIVO Encyclopedia of Jews in Eastern Europe* in some ways represents a more fortunate successor to the volumes dedicated to Jewish life and culture in the ill-fated *Algemeyne entsiklopedye* series, a Yiddish-language encyclopedia project begun prior to World War II to which many YIVO associates contributed. It saw its completion only in the mid-1960s, however, by which time much of its intended audience was no longer alive and the information it contained was considered outdated for contemporary readers (although not for historians).

Yet, perhaps most staggering of all developments of the late twentieth century was the rediscovery of additional surviving parts of the Vilna YIVO's archives and library in the late 1980s. While Weinreich foresaw the possibility of exchanging photocopies of surviving Vilna archival materials with Soviet research institutes, never could he have imagined millions of dollars being raised for materials residing in Vilnius to be "reunited" digitally with other Vilna materials in New York in the twenty-first century. This process would in a sense bring the saga of the transfer of YIVO's center from Vilna to New York City in 1940 to its conclusion almost eighty years later.

Conclusion

Max Weinreich's death after nearly thirty years of intensive activity in the United States represents not merely the end of a transitional era in YIVO's American history still dominated by the goals and memory of Vilna; it also marks the beginning of a truly American one. During the Weinreich years, YIVO contended with the tension between its commitments to the eastern European past, its sense of duty to the remnants of a Yiddish-speaking folk in America and abroad, and its desire to be relevant to American Jewry in the present and future. After years of debate about its direction and purpose, the passing of generations accelerated its passage from an eastern European Jewish nationalist institution serving a global Yiddish-speaking diaspora whose origins were in eastern Europe into a primarily English-speaking, American Jewish institute focused on preserving, interpreting, and transmitting the language and culture of pre-Holocaust eastern European Jewry for the benefit of future generations in the USA and beyond. While Vilna continued to represent for YIVO associates the symbolic heart of Yiddishland, New York had replaced it for them as the functional center of YIVO and the Jewish Diaspora.

Modest signs of the longed-for *vidervuks*—the emergence of an academically trained cadre of young scholars, librarians, archivists, and administrators to serve the institute and American Jewry more broadly—could be seen by the 1960s among the children of immigrants and immigrants who had arrived as children. This phenomenon did not truly begin to take root, however, until the 1970s. Thanks to a number of initiatives focused on the training of youth for which Max Weinreich had worked persistently through the decades and the arrival of a new generation of primarily North American–born staff members, YIVO underwent a period of creative rejuvenation following his death that sustained it into the late twentieth century. Paradoxically, however, precisely Weinreich's death and the passing of much of his generation—a cause for so much disorientation in the 1970s—freed the institute from many of its prior linguistic and other constraints, allowing it to become more responsive to the sensitivities and needs of late-twentieth-century American Jewry. The Uriel Weinreich Yiddish Summer Program and the Max Weinreich Center for Advanced Jewish Studies stand out in particular for their role in fostering a new cadre of academically and culturally creative forces, many of whom would work not only to continue and expand the institute's primary activities but also to launch eastern European Jewish studies in American universities and to create a popular revival movement centered on the folk culture of eastern European Jewry.

While the American YIVO did not find a welcoming milieu among American or New York Jewry to the same degree that it knew in prewar eastern Europe, by the 1980s it had made significant strides toward becoming a mainstay of the American Jewish academic and societal landscape. The postwar incarnation of the Vilna-centric institute ceased to be referred to as "the YIVO in America" or "the American YIVO"—a reference to the USA, Canada, and to a much lesser extent, Mexico, where it found its main financial supporters and contributors of materials. Instead, it became simply known as YIVO: an institute firmly grounded in New York City that drew visitors from around the world, including Israel, as the foremost repository and interpreter of the eastern European Jewish past.

CONCLUSION

In 1988, an article in *Sovetish heymland*, the only Yiddish journal then published in the Soviet Union, announced the discovery of 20,705 books in Hebrew and Yiddish housed in the Book Chamber of the Lithuanian Soviet Socialist Republic. An emotionally shaken Dina Abramowicz, the institute's last surviving link between the YIVO in wartime Vilna and in present-day New York, brought the staggering news to the attention of colleagues. Executive Director Samuel Norich contacted the article's author, Emanuelis Zingeris, a graduate student in comparative literature at the University of Vilnius, whom he had met at a conference in Warsaw some months prior. Back then, Zingeris confidentially revealed to Norich that he had encountered YIVO materials while conducting his doctoral research in Vilnius. But Zingeris, who was active in the movement for Lithuanian independence from the Soviet Union, cautiously offered few details. Now, in response to Norich's letter, he invited Norich to attend the inaugural conference of the Jewish Cultural Society in Lithuania. The organization's recent founding after a forty-year hiatus in Jewish public life testified to greater freedom of speech for citizens under Mikhail Gorbachev's policy of *glasnost*.[1]

Recognizing a once in a lifetime opportunity to reclaim YIVO materials, Norich and Chief Archivist Marek Web traveled to Vilnius to attend the conference. But an even bigger find awaited them. While visiting the Book Chamber, they were shown not only books but archival documents clearly belonging to the Vilna YIVO's collections. The materials had been recovered by surviving members of the Paper Brigade after the war and included in the Vilna Jewish Museum that they established. After being confiscated by Soviet security officials, they were hidden for nearly four decades in the recesses of a former Catholic church and monastery repurposed as the Book Chamber of the Lithuanian SSR since 1945. They owed their survival to Antanas Ulpis, a courageous Lithuanian librarian and humanist who dared to defy Stalinist orders for their destruction after World War II and entrusted his secret to precious few. The revelation of their survival was earthshattering news not only for YIVO in New York but for Jewish studies scholars around the world. Researchers

Dina Abramowicz, 2002. Credit: YIVO Institute for Jewish Research immediately recognized the materials' value for present and future generations of scholars writing the history of Jewish life in eastern Europe.[2]

Political liberalization in Lithuania and the subsequent dissolution of the USSR created the circumstances in which Lithuanian parties informed YIVO of the discovery of additional caches in the 1990s. Norich and Web, who made multiple visits to Vilnius, were astonished to find troves of dirty, damaged, and unsorted materials stored in the book repository as well as in a library and archives—much of it bearing YIVO stamps and other markings indicating their belonging to prewar collections housed in YIVO. Some of these turned out to be papers that completed fragments of documents found in YIVO's New York collections. Despite the materials' dismal state, their discovery was cause for rejoicing in New York. The existence of further surviving materials from YIVO collections had been suspected through the decades by Weinreich and others, but their reclamation was a cause that had been largely abandoned during the Cold War.[3] The announcement of their survival held out the tantalizing possibility of achieving what he had dreamed of years earlier: making whole again what remained of YIVO's prewar collection—materials that had been separated for some eighty years between eastern Europe and America.

Years of strenuous negotiations between YIVO and Lithuanian officials ensued. They were rendered even more difficult by the frequent changing of governments and the consequent replacement of heads of libraries and archives in Lithuania's early postcommunist years. Echoing disputes about the ownership of heirless cultural treasures after World War II, negotiations in the 1990s centered around the question of to whom the books and documents—largely but not exclusively originating in prewar YIVO collections—today belong: the Lithuanian people as a whole, a postwar Lithuanian Jewish community then numbering some twelve thousand Jews (the vast majority of them in Vilnius, where they composed less than 2 percent of the city's population),[4] or YIVO in New York? They also focused on the costs of processing, conserving, and photocopying books and documents to preserve and share them. Claiming the materials as part of its cultural patrimony, Lithuania was disinclined to grant YIVO possession of them.[5] Having only recently emerged from decades of communist rule, the country lacked, however, adequate funding to conduct the necessary work. Nor did it have the facilities and sufficient personnel possessing the requisite linguistic, cultural, and historical knowledge about prewar Jewish life to do so.

In an editorial ostensibly supporting the position of Lithuanian officials, *The New York Times* urged that the books and papers remain in Vilnius. It wrote in November 1996, "Keeping the material in Vilnius would give the Jewish community there a sense of continuity, and serve as an inspiration to a city still struggling to overcome decades of repression and enforced denial of its own history. The texts themselves would be enhanced if they could be studied in the place where they were produced."[6] In the spirit of his predecessor Max Weinreich, historian Alan Nadler, YIVO's Director of Research (a position revived in the late 1980s in connection with the Max Weinreich Center), penned a scathing open letter to the newspaper's editor in which he condemned the proposal as ignoring "historical and legal facts": "Your suggestion," he wrote, "that keeping the books in Lithuania would serve as 'an inspiration to a city still struggling to overcome decades of repression' is naive. Their content—Rabbinic Law and Jewish History—is in no way connected with Lithuanian history or culture. . . . After more than a half century of abysmal neglect of the Judaic treasures that remained hidden in Europe, this remarkable collection must be re-unified, for the sake of both justice and scholarship."[7]

In contrast, Columbia University historian Michael Stanislawski urged caution in determining the future home of Jewish cultural treasures after years of concealment and neglect. While decrying the material's treatment as a "scandal" and calling for researchers to have access to it, he noted, "Jews are in an awkward situation. We constantly protest that they write history in countries like Lithuania that excludes the Jews. Yet we are always trying to take Jewish material away from there." Meanwhile, Lithuanian Jewish leaders were themselves torn between the desire to hold on to what remained of their violently destroyed heritage and the recognition that their tiny community's future was uncertain—especially as many Jews immigrated to Israel and elsewhere. The items, many local Jews as well as scholars agreed, would find their best use in a major Jewish center such as New York or Jerusalem, where they would be properly cared for and find readers familiar with Yiddish and Hebrew.[8]

Eventually, after many frustrations and disappointments, including a contract abrogated due to the transfer of materials between Lithuanian institutions, an agreement was concluded in 1995 whereby materials would be temporarily transferred to New York. There they would be identified, repaired, chemically treated, and photocopied by YIVO's staff prior to returning them to Lithuania. YIVO did not initially budget enough time for the project, which was of unprecedented scope and nature. Its delays in returning materials fueled Lithuanian suspicions that it intended to hold on to them indefinitely (it did not). The project was finally completed in 2001.[9]

Years followed without any major breakthrough in relations between YIVO and Lithuania to provide for the restoration and custodianship of materials. Only in 2012 did a rapprochement begin as a result of meetings between YIVO's recently appointed director, Jonathan Brent, and Emanuelis Zingeris, then a member of the Lithuanian parliament and a leading Jewish figure in the country. In 2014, a pragmatic compromise was reached: A plan for "sharing" materials was conceived, taking advantage of extensive technological advancements that had emerged since their initial discovery. The Edward Blank YIVO Vilna Online Collections Project, named for the lead donor, would bridge the physical distance between New York and Vilnius by scanning surviving books and papers in the two cities and joining them in a single digital collection, thereby circumventing discord around their ownership and physical possession. In 2017, an additional 170,000 pages of documents were discovered in the church basement, adding to the scope of the project. Finally, in January 2022, YIVO announced that the digital reunification of the two surviving parts of its collections, dating from prior to the German invasion of Vilnius in the summer of 1941, was complete. Thanks to the seven-million-dollar project, more than four million pages of scanned books and documents are now accessible to researchers and the general public via the institute's website. The conserved and cataloged originals remain, however, physically divided between YIVO in New York and three institutions in Vilnius—the Lithuanian Central State Archives, the Wroblewski Library of the Lithuanian Academy of Sciences, and the Martynas Mažvydas National Library of Lithuania. Among the archival items are pages from YIVO's administrative files; the archives of schools and yeshivas, the Vilna Jewish community (*kehilah*), and other organizations; research projects undertaken by students in YIVO's *aspirantur*; submissions to YIVO's youth biographical contests; literary and theater manuscripts; folklore, such as children's songs and games collected by *zamlers*; artwork, including sketches by Marc Chagall; testimonies from pogrom victims; and much more.[10]

While a major feat, the project also aroused controversy and bitter feelings toward YIVO. Critics accused YIVO of collaborating with the Lithuanian government and its institutions, whose only interest in Jewish cultural heritage was allegedly in its value for drawing Western, especially Jewish, tourist dollars. Its treatment of Jewish cultural treasures was described as tantamount to extortion: It had effectively insisted that YIVO pay a ransom for the rehabilitation and processing of its very own materials and then refused to surrender them to their proper owner.[11] Worse, others argued, YIVO was burnishing the international reputation of a government that was engaged in the deliberate obfuscation of the role played by members of Lithuania's wartime generation in the persecution of the very people who had created and risked their lives for these treasures.[12]

The subject of collaboration with the Germans remains politically sensitive in Lithuania. Some 95 percent of its Jews perished in the Holocaust, many at the hands of their countrymen—thousands even before the arrival of the Germans. And some who allied themselves with the virulently anti-Bolshevik Germans and contributed to the killing of Jews are celebrated as national heroes who valiantly resisted the imposition of communist rule—an act still associated in many minds with Jews as a collective, despite that Jews too suffered under the Soviets. As historian Jelena Subotić observes, "A long period of Communism has eclipsed the four years of Nazi occupation and is broadly felt as a more pervasive collective trauma." Indeed, some state institutions and commissions present the decades of communist rule as a genocide on par with the Holocaust, an equivalence scholars widely reject as a gross distortion of history, despite acknowledging the suffering of the Lithuanian people.[13]

Ultimately, the virtual "reunification" of YIVO materials admirably solves a practical problem by making the materials available to present and future generations of researchers. But it does not resolve the moral question of to whom the cultural patrimony of Vilna Jewry belongs today—the Lithuanian state, a Vilnius Jewish community numbering a few thousand, or the American YIVO, the successor of that prewar Vilna institution that gathered or produced much of this material in the service of a global, Yiddish-speaking Jewish people.[14] Nor can this question likely be resolved in any satisfying way to all parties. Barring the discovery of additional materials, the Edward Blank Project brings a practical end to the drama of the reclamation of YIVO collections that began some eighty years ago. Of course, given the extent of the destruction of prewar collections, any reunification would remain necessarily incomplete, even as it reinforced the association of YIVO with the legacy of Vilna Jewry in its entirety. As such, it serves as an apt metaphor for the unhealable rupture suffered by the institute as a whole.

At the same time, the tale of the reunification highlights not only the concrete but also the figurative distance YIVO has traveled since World War II. For the founding generation of scholars who established the Amopteyl and then YIVO's center in New York City, there would always be an unbridgeable gap between the idealized past of "the Vilna YIVO" and present reality of "the American YIVO." The former was the bustling center of a global organization centered in a relatively sleepy provincial town, possessing tremendous significance for Jewish culture in both its traditional and modern forms but located on interwar Poland's economic and political periphery. The latter signified the organization's postwar headquarters in New York, a metropolis that was the cultural and economic capital of a global superpower but whose Jewish community, despite its massive size, lacked the cohesiveness of a culture that had crystallized over centuries.

Weinreich and his colleagues remained mindful of the difficulties faced by YIVO in its first period—above all, the crippling poverty, the struggle with a hostile environment, the hopelessness of much of Jewish youth over its future, and the internal political divisions that sought to pull YIVO away from its goal of serving as a "big tent" organization for Yiddish-speaking Jewry. But they were also very painfully aware of what they had lost and could not be replaced: a spirit of collectivism that was bolstered by a Yiddish-speaking social milieu into which YIVO was organically integrated and that enthusiastically supported its activities with seemingly inexhaustible energies that vastly exceeded material resources. In a city as large as New York—with its eight million inhabitants, including two million Jews—Yudel Mark lamented in 1951, "The cozy intimacy (*heymishkeyt*) and warmth of the Vilna center and of the YIVO circles in the city (and even the shtetls) of the old country are lacking."[15] Even if its financial burden could be lightened over time, the American YIVO suffered in the postwar decades from the indifference of much of American Jewish society and a cool relationship on the part of Yiddish writers, teachers, and cultural activists who had various gripes about its direction and its treatment of them. Nonetheless, it persisted in its mission, all the while seeking to balance its commitments to eastern Europe and Yiddish culture with a program of outreach to American-born generations.

Weinreich stewarded YIVO for more than four decades and on two continents, presiding over the institute's contested transition from Vilna to New York and the Amopteyl's transformation into the institute's world center in the direst times. He also played a leading role in orchestrating the reclamation of a large part of its European holdings and oversaw the rapid expansion of its collections and publications by a staff consisting overwhelmingly of immigrants and refugees like himself—many of them Holocaust survivors—united in shared grief and loss. Perhaps most significantly, he articulated a vision for YIVO's future in a new environment deemed by many to be unconducive, if not hostile, to the institute's mission, and he saw through its implementation. This vision called for maintaining the Vilna YIVO's three foundational pillars—research, training, and collecting—while allowing for selective adaptation, linguistic and otherwise, to the environment of the postwar United States. While not all his YIVO colleagues shared this vision in its entirety or disagreed with aspects of its implementation, they understood themselves as engaged in a common project to preserve and commemorate the lost world of eastern European Jewry and to convey as much as possible of the "spirit of Vilna" to future generations in America and elsewhere.

As before the war, Weinreich remained dedicated to the YIVO ideal of scholarship in the social sciences for the betterment of Jewish life. He was convinced of the necessity of the institute to serve not only as a guardian of the Jewish past but as a tool for the construction of the Jewish future—to provide, as he was fond of saying, not merely *visnshaft* (scholarship) but *visn vos shaft* (knowledge that creates).[16] Under his leadership, YIVO conferences and publications embraced a wide array of subjects, including contemporary Jewish life in America and Israel, even if the institute's focus remained on centuries of Yiddish-speaking Jews in eastern Europe and its diaspora. Indeed, the American present and what he diagnosed as its pathology and weaknesses were always very much in his mind, even if his early ambitions for YIVO to become a leading archive and center for the study of contemporary American Jewish problems went unfulfilled.

As soon as he arrived on American shores, Weinreich insisted that it was YIVO's mission to prepare American Jewry for a leadership role on behalf of world Jewry, particularly by recruiting and training new generations of leaders among its academic youth. The English-language and higher educations they received in American universities played a welcome role in this mission. But without access to Yiddish and the YIVO tradition, he maintained, American Jewish youth would remain cut off from their heritage and consequently intellectually and psychologically fragmented. Only the legacy of a now-closed European "Yiddish era" in Jewish history, he was convinced, could provide it with the psychological wherewithal to withstand the challenges of the external world and empower it to lay the foundations for the next era in Jewish life, in which America would play a dominant role.[17] More than YIVO needed American Jewry, he was convinced, American Jewry needed YIVO.

Despite moments of despair, Weinreich was optimistic about the future of YIVO and American Jewry, if only by sheer force of will. Some of his YIVO colleagues, in contrast, rejected the idea that American-born Jewry could perpetuate the cultural traditions of eastern European Jewry, and they discouraged YIVO from investing its energies in what they considered futile goals. A few such as Raphael Mahler (in 1950), Jacob Lestschinsky (in 1959), Sol Liptzin (after retirement from City College in 1962), and Yudel Mark (in 1969) eventually relocated to Israel—some out of Zionist convictions, others for academic opportunities and/or out of the belief that Jewish culture, including Yiddish, possessed a brighter future in Israel than in America.[18] Despite long-standing opposition to Yiddish in official circles and in broader society, Israel was a state founded on the understanding they shared: that Jews constituted a nation. It devoted a significant share of its resources to furthering Jewish culture, including teaching Jewish history and literature at all levels of education. It also received an influx of Soviet Jews, many of them Yiddish speakers, in the 1970s.

While he never moved to Israel, Jacob Shatzky bequeathed a large part of his personal library and archives, including rare volumes and copies of materials he had collected in European archives, not to YIVO but to the Hebrew University and Israeli Historical Society, with whose archivists he had cordial relations. According to the contemporary Hebrew press, he did so because he believed that the future of scholarship about eastern European Jewry lay in Israel. YIVO did, however, also receive a substantial part of his collection.[19] Whatever Shatzky's motivations, the division of his collection between Jerusalem and New York suggests the perspective that in the post-Holocaust era, the Jewish people possessed two major world centers—both of which were, in large measure, the legacy of eastern European Jewry.

Weinreich too had high hopes for Jewish scholarship in Israel, but he possessed faith in the creative energies resident in American Jewry and its eventual "return" to Yiddish and its eastern European origins out of enlightened self-interest, even if he would not live to see this. Eventual frustration and disappointment with the shallowness of English-language American Jewish culture, he maintained, would lead a portion of its youth to plumb the depth and richness of its Yiddish past. As he expressed himself in his final year to his student, Israeli literature scholar Dan Miron,

> If American Jews still dream as a group, Yiddish is the language they speak in their dream. It is still the idiom of their collective unconscious. For their personality to become whole they—at least some of them—will have to go back to Yiddish one day. Otherwise, their enormous creative force will be blocked by an inner, psychic fragmentation. They will come back to look for their hidden parts of their national personality. Once they realize that their Jewishness, lived on an abstract level, is moribund, and the mere presence of the Jewish state cannot by itself revive it, they will have to come back. And there we shall be, waiting for them down in the Yiddish cellar with a strong torchlight in our hand. Somebody will have to spell out for them the contents of their dream, to elucidate the vision they saw with bleary eyes, and we, because we made Yiddish *visnshaft* the thing we live and die for, will be able to throw light and heal.[20]

Weinreich's death ushered in a new era in YIVO's history. This era, beginning in the 1970s, was characterized by the influx of members of a younger generation who had not known prewar Poland firsthand. While some had been educated in Yiddish schools or schools that taught Yiddish in the postwar United States, Canada, or Poland, increasing numbers had not grown up immersed in Yiddish language and culture.[21] For them, *College Yiddish* was often the first step toward uncovering the "lost continent" of Jewish eastern Europe and recuperating their collective inheritance. Their innovative efforts, which were instrumental in launching the contemporary wave of academic, artistic, political, and popular interest in eastern European Jewish culture and creating a space for the field in universities, would not have been possible, of course, without the infrastructure of scholarship and resources made available by the generation that built the Amopteyl into the American YIVO.

We may wonder how YIVO would have developed if its headquarters had transferred to Montreal, home of Canada's largest Jewish population into the 1970s, and not New York. The city was described in the 1940s and '50s by wistful Yiddishists, disappointed by the fate of Yiddish in the United States, as a "fortress of Yiddishism" thanks to its intense Yiddish cultural life that included day schools offering a significant part of their instruction in the language in those decades. Indeed, the city, where Jews were effectively seen as a distinct community alongside francophone Catholics and anglophone Protestants, was explicitly compared to Vilna.[22] Similarly, we may wonder what would have been the consequences of YIVO's existing Argentine branch assuming the mantle of the organization's postwar leadership. The relative weight of secular Yiddish cultural institutions, including schools, in communal life in Buenos Aires exceeded that in New York and possibly Montreal. Unfortunately, a comparative study of the trajectories and accomplishments of YIVO in New York and of IWO in Buenos Aires, whose history also awaits comprehensive scholarly treatment, is beyond the scope of this book.[23]

In both hypothetical cases, however, it is reasonable to assume that had YIVO established its postwar center outside the United States, it would likely have maintained a different relationship to the Yiddish diaspora. Rather than seeing itself as an American institution tasked with global Jewish leadership, it would likely have relied more on the financial support of and cooperation with other YIVO branches, strengthening a sense of belonging to a global Yiddish-speaking nation. Moreover, its presence in a smaller Jewish community and in a country where Jewish national cohesiveness was more pronounced and Jews' integration into general society less advanced would likely have contributed to greater appreciation for YIVO among rank-and-file Jews.

Be that as it may, such was not YIVO's fate. Moreover, Yiddishism eventually succumbed to the same forces of acculturation and language shift even in those diasporic communities that offered models of Jewish communal life closer to the eastern European ideal of cultural autonomy. Thus, in Montreal and Buenos Aires too, the dominant languages of non-Jewish society—English (prior to efforts to promote French associated with the Quiet Revolution) and Spanish, respectively—eventually supplanted Yiddish among Ashkenazic Jews, even if familiarity with, and often fluency in, Yiddish endured longer there than in the United States outside of *haredi* communities.

Ultimately, much of Max Weinreich's ambition for YIVO in America and the continuation of the YIVO tradition of the Jewish social sciences has been realized, if not entirely according to his vision or exclusively within YIVO. Weinreich and his generation of YIVO scholars would no doubt have been bitterly disappointed by the displacement of Yiddish as the institute's operating language, the effective cessation of its publication of original research by in-house serials (in English or Yiddish), and the disappearance of its graduate training division by the twenty-first century—precisely those features that made YIVO much more than an archive and library specializing in the heritage of eastern European Jewry. As he emphasized even during the uncertain period of early World War II, when Vilnius was under Lithuanian control and the city was flooded with Jewish refugees, scholarship and training, not popularization, were always YIVO's foremost mission—even if he encouraged exhibitions of YIVO collections and academic forums open to the broad public. Moreover, for many (if not most) in his generation, a YIVO without Yiddish as its dominant language of daily operations, scholarship, and public programming was no longer YIVO.

On the other hand, YIVO's flexibility with regard to language—as evidenced by compromises with English and its eagerness to translate *College Yiddish* and Weinreich's *Geshikhte fun der yidisher shprakh* into English and Hebrew—set a precedent that enabled it to avoid the obsolescence faced by many Yiddish cultural organizations that relied on competence in the language.[24] Moreover, the goal of using English to draw youth *to* Yiddish yielded a measure of success, as reflected in the longevity of the *zumer-program* and the generations of scholars, artists, and communal and cultural activists using the language (some in their everyday lives) who figure among its graduates. Conversely, YIVO's inflexibility with regard to politics—its aspirations to be above party politics and its rejection of scholarship in the service of predetermined conclusions—enabled it to attract forces from across much of the Jewish political-ideological spectrum, even if this brought often vague accusations (beyond the use of "YIVO Yiddish") of aloofness or estrangement from the working-class Jewish masses that emanated from some of the cultural and political organizations that it outlived. While unable to maintain its status as an organization with branches around the world, YIVO was careful to cultivate relations with academic institutions whose mandates overlapped with its own, especially in Israel—where an ever-growing part of the world Jewish population, especially eastern European Jews and their progeny, was to be found and an academic infrastructure was constructed for the study of Yiddish literature and eastern European Jewish history.

The notable exception was eastern Europe itself, which YIVO scholarship largely treated as a closed chapter in the Jewish experience after the Holocaust and the installation of communist regimes. After the 1940s, YIVO scholars seldom communicated directly with the few Jewish studies scholars, writers, and cultural figures who remained publicly active there. Occasional visitors from communist lands—such as Hersh Smolar, the editor of the Polish Yiddish newspaper *Folks-sztyme* in 1966—were received with a mixture of curiosity, Cold War suspicion, and the fear of endangering them in their home countries by greeting them too warmly in what was seen there as a bourgeois Jewish nationalist institution in the capitalist West. YIVO's attitudes toward the staff and scholarship of the Jewish Historical Institute in Warsaw (which was invited to participate in YIVO's December 1967 colloquium on "Imposed Jewish Governing Bodies Under Nazi Rule," but per Weinreich's subtle allusion to events of that year, "their representative could not come") and toward writings published in *Sovetish heymland* (which conveyed much anti-Western, pro-Soviet propaganda as well as occasional barbs directed at YIVO scholarship), for example, remain subjects in need of researchers' attention.[25] Once the opportunity presented itself, however, YIVO was quick to establish relations with students, scholars, and institutions throughout eastern Europe beginning in the late 1980s.[26] Significantly, *The YIVO Encyclopedia of Jews in Eastern Europe* covers not only the Holocaust but also postwar Europe, with many contributions by scholars who grew up there during the Soviet era.

In the period under study, YIVO's engagement with politics—Jewish or otherwise—was chiefly academic and confined to the past, at least as represented in its publications and public statements (individual associates were, of course, welcome to their own views). In the post–World War II era, it treated all manifestations of Jewish political life and culture that sought to sustain a future for Jews *qua* Jews rather than to promote the dissolution of a distinct Jewish consciousness—from Orthodoxy to socialism to secular nationalism—as manifestations of a Jewish national will for survival and products of a singular Jewish culture forged in Hebrew and Yiddish across the centuries in eastern Europe no matter how bitterly various factions had opposed each other.

Admittedly, YIVO's secularist, Diaspora Nationalist orientation contributed to a tendency, which existed in Vilna as well, to overlook Orthodox organizations and exclude communism. This was reflected, for example, in a conference Weinreich organized in 1964 on "Movements for Social Progress among East European Jewry"—by which he meant primarily the American Jewish labor movement and socialist and left-leaning forms of Jewish nationalism—and numerous talks and symposia YIVO hosted about the diversity of Jewish political life in eastern Europe and its role in forging the State of Israel.[27] Beyond a short-lived project to collect Hasidic folklore in the 1940s and some contributions about Yiddish in pre- and postwar Hasidic communities to YIVO publications, the American YIVO showed little interest in *haredi* communities—possibly the one segment of American Jewry that valued the eastern European Jewish tradition as much (although differently) as did Yiddishist circles and certainly the only one to succeed in fostering an ideology that perpetuated Yiddish as a language of multigenerational communal life on a large scale.

Weinreich's cohort laid the foundations for YIVO in America, but the institute naturally had to undergo its own unforeseeable organic processes to complete the transformation from immigrant institution to an American institute with eastern European roots. True, its ambitions in the early 1950s to become the *premier* archives and institute for the sociological and historical study of American Jewry went unrealized. Once rival institutions such as the American Jewish Historical Society, with which it now shares facilities in the Center for Jewish History, and the American Jewish Archives, founded in Cincinnati in 1947, instead came to fulfill this role. Further, the number of Jewish archives, research institutes, and think tanks in America has multiplied considerably since 1940. Nonetheless, YIVO has become home to the collections of several major American Jewish organizations, making its archives an essential locus for the writing of American Jewish history. Through its own publications, conferences, and teaching, it has also contributed significantly to the maturation of the field of American Jewish history, particularly to the study of immigrant and labor history as well as the Jewish history of New York City. And of course, scholars trained by YIVO have played a crucial role in the development of Jewish studies and Holocaust studies in American and other universities, where much of the social science and other research YIVO championed is carried out today.

Perhaps most indicative of the long-term success of YIVO's implantation in the "stony shores" of America despite the many challenges, controversies, transformations, and disappointments it has experienced over the decades (and will surely continue to face, like any other evolving institution) is neither its contemporary ability to draw unprecedented (albeit from the standpoint of the institution still inadequate) financial contributions from corporate, individual, and government sponsors using American fundraising techniques. Nor is YIVO's success to be measured chiefly by its twenty-first-century address alongside other prominent Jewish scholarly and cultural institutions at the well-appointed Center for Jewish History. Prestige and financial stability were never goals in and of themselves for YIVO but necessary means for pursuing its founding mission of creating scholarship "from the folk, for the folk, with the folk." Moreover, the gathering of research institutions under one roof has brought its share of advantages and disadvantages, with some arguing that YIVO has compromised too much of its autonomy and distinct character as a consequence.[28]

Rather, the strongest evidence for YIVO's long-term success is to be found in the enduring—and arguably, with the passage of time, increasing—relevance it possesses for contemporary generations eager to learn about eastern European Jewry and its impact on the larger world.

YIVO is today visited annually by thousands of researchers and students, many of them supported by its generous research grants, as well as by members of the lay public.[29] They make use of its collections, study in the *zumer-program*, or attend (both in person and via Zoom) its lecture series in Yiddish and English, exhibits and cultural events such as concerts, and adult education courses on a variety of subjects pertaining especially to eastern European Jewry and the American Jewish experience. Thanks largely to its efforts and inspiration, the study of Yiddish and all aspects of eastern European Jewish civilization, including its destruction, has not only continued beyond Weinreich's generation. It has become a flourishing part of academic life in the United States and Israel as well as in other countries—particularly in former cradles of Ashkenazic life such as Poland and Germany.

The folk YIVO serves today—the chiefly non-*haredi* descendants of Yiddish-speaking Jewry—is, however, quite different geographically, linguistically, politically, economically, and otherwise from the one it knew prior to World War II and in the early postwar decades. It took time for YIVO to calibrate its relationship to American Jewry and for American Jewry to recognize the value of YIVO as a resource and interpreter of the eastern European era in Jewish life. Indeed, through much of the period surveyed in this study, YIVO struggled to maintain its existence. And the project of "reclaiming" Jews' eastern European cultural heritage, in which YIVO played a dominant but not exclusive role, would not have been possible without the passing of generations and larger trends in American Jewish society and American and global politics—among them the Cold War (and its end), postwar prosperity, access to higher education, and the "search for roots" of the 1960s and '70s and beyond—that paved the way for a more positive evaluation of Yiddish language and culture as a supplement rather than a replacement to general American culture. But most importantly, this process would not have been possible without YIVO preserving, curating, and interpreting this heritage, holding the figurative torchlight of which Weinreich spoke.

While no longer functionally a Yiddishist or even a primarily Yiddish-speaking institution, YIVO has for many come to symbolize Yiddishism itself, including its association with the Jewish Diaspora. This includes those who ground their contemporary cultural and political commitments in the Diaspora-affirming tradition of the prewar Jewish labor movement, particularly the anti-Zionist Bund, that embraced Yiddishism and contributed extensively to the development of secular Yiddish culture. At least since the closing decades of the twentieth century, a part of the Jewish Left has come to see YIVO as the expression of an alternative to what they see as the dominant currents—socially and politically conservative, heteronormative, Hebrew- and Israel-centric—in post-Holocaust American Jewish life. Such an association has been reinforced in popular conception by the presence of politically progressive Jews among YIVO's staff; their participation in its activities, above all the *zumer-program*; and their involvement in YIVO-adjacent organizations, such as Yugntruf, and the broader Yiddish folk and cultural revival movement of the late twentieth century that was spearheaded by individuals with close ties to YIVO.[30]

As in past generations, the tension between YIVO's commitment to academic nonpartisanship and to meeting the needs and desires of its constituency has repeatedly erupted into conflict and controversy. Most recently, scarcely a year before the institute's centennial anniversary, YIVO found itself embroiled in a controversy related to the Israel–Hamas war that began with Hamas's invasion of Israel in October 2023. YIVO's announcement in 2024 of a three-part lecture series about the relationship between Nazi antisemitism and Islamicism in Hamas's ideology attracted some five thousand registrants, making the Zoom talks some of its best attended in recent memory.[31] It also drew outraged reactions from self-identified left-wing and progressive Jews close to YIVO. They accused it not only of deviating from YIVO's mandate to explore and promote Yiddish culture but also of seeking to advance a propagandistic, pro-Israel narrative of the war and the larger Israeli–Palestinian conflict that excluded Arab and Palestinian voices. In response, the event's organizers rejected such accusations as an implicit distortion of the Jewish Left's historic attitudes to a variety of subjects, including Zionism and Israel. They also saw it as a denial of YIVO's own history as a nonpartisan academic institution committed to free inquiry and engaged with topics of profound concern to the Jewish people as a whole—including antisemitism (as reflected, for example, in Weinreich's *Hitler's Professors*)—even if removed from Yiddish or eastern Europe.[32]

The dispute in the Yiddishist community, a reflection of the larger divide among American Jews over attitudes toward Israel, not only aroused bitter feelings and threatened to alienate a part of YIVO's audience, particularly young people who identify as anti-Zionist;[33] it also revived the question of what defines the YIVO tradition and to whom the institute "belongs" in the present day and in the future. Needless to say, the eastern European–born generation that founded YIVO and relocated its center to America during World War II functioned in a very different political and social context than twenty-first-century American Jewry. But such criticisms would be familiar to it in nature if not actual content. In its early decades in America, YIVO drew at times bitter criticism from those supporters who believed that it had strayed from the institute's founding mission and betrayed the values of its "true" constituency in attempting to court mainstream American Jewry or, as in the case of accepting German reparations, had engaged in Faustian compacts to achieve its aims.

As this book has hopefully demonstrated, Weinreich's generation viewed YIVO and Yiddish not as an alternative to the dominant currents in American Jewish intellectual and cultural life, despite the institute's own marginality from the perspective of much of American Jewry. On the contrary, it saw scholarship in the YIVO tradition and Yiddish, the basis of nearly a millennium of Jewish culture, as central to Jewish life and its future in America and beyond. Weinreich and his colleagues sought to make YIVO a part of the American Jewish mainstream in order to shape American Jewish life as much as possible. Then as now, both praise and condemnation testify to YIVO's enduring relevance. It remains a vital institution for that part of American Jewry that, no matter how politically and ideologically divided it finds itself, is committed to seeking meaning for contemporary life in the legacy of eastern European Jewish experience.

NOTES

Introduction

1 Y[udel] M[ark], "Funem folk, farn folk, mitn folk," *Der veg tsu der yidisher visnshaft*, 15 January 1926, YIVO Institute for Jewish Research, New York (hereafter: YIVO) RG 82 Tcherikower Archive YIVO Administration Records, folder 2396, cited in Cecile Esther Kuznitz, *YIVO and the Making of Modern Jewish Culture* (Cambridge University Press, 2014), 71.

2 Lucy S. Dawidowicz, *The War Against the Jews, 1933–1945* (Holt, Rinehart and Winston, 1975).

3 Estonia, with a tiny Jewish population of some 4,500 at the end of World War I, was the only state in the region to offer Jews full national cultural autonomy in the interwar period. On Jewish campaigns for cultural autonomy, see Ezra Mendelsohn's classic work, *The Jews of East Central Europe Between the World Wars* (Indiana University Press, 1983).

4 On the unsuccessful pursuit of Jewish national politics in the United States, see James Loeffler, "Nationalism Without a Nation?: On the Invisibility of American Jewish Politics," *Jewish Quarterly Review* 105, no. 3 (Summer 2025): 367–98.

5 On attitudes toward Yiddish in Israel in this period, see Rachel Rojanski, *Yiddish in Israel: A History* (Indiana University Press, 2020).

6 Max Weinreich, letter to Avrom Sutzkever, 9 January 1947 in Avrom (Avraham) Novershtern "Briv fun maks vaynraykh tsu avrom sutskever," *Di goldene keyt* 95/96 (1978): 173.

7 For an overview of mainly English-language historiography about Jews in eastern Europe until 2000, see Michael Stanislawski,

"Eastern European Jewry in the Modern Period, 1750–1939," in *The Oxford Handbook of Jewish Studies*, Martin Goodman, ed. (Oxford University Press, 2002), 396–411. The field has expanded tremendously in the last few decades as reflected in the various annotated bibliographies of sources on topics related to eastern European Jewry in the Oxford online bibliography series ("Jewish Studies," Oxford Bibliographies, accessed 14 December 2025, www.oxfordbibliographies.com/page/164).

8 Recent scholarship about institutions and scholars prior to World War II informing this study include Dan Rabinowitz, *The Lost Library: The Legacy of Vilna's Strashun Library in the Aftermath of the Holocaust* (Brandeis University Press, 2019); Natalia Aleksiun, *Conscious History: Polish Jewish Historians Before the Holocaust* (Littman Library of Jewish Civilization, 2021); Joshua Karlip, *The Tragedy of a Generation: The Rise and Fall of Jewish Nationalism in Eastern Europe* (Harvard University Press, 2013). Above all, Max Weinreich has fascinated scholars. Recent monographs treating him include Kenneth Moss's *An Unchosen People: Jewish Political Reckoning in Interwar Poland* (Harvard University Press, 2021); and Naomi Seidman's *Translating the Jewish Freud: Psychoanalysis in Hebrew and Yiddish* (Stanford University Press, 2024).

9 Among recent studies are David E. Fishman, *The Book Smugglers: Partisans, Poets, and the Race to Save Jewish Treasures from the Nazis* (ForeEdge, 2017); Elisabeth Gallas, *A Mortuary of Books: The Rescue of Jewish Culture After the Holocaust* (New York University Press, 2019); Nancy Sinkoff, *From Left to Right: Lucy S. Dawidowicz, the New York Intellectuals, and the Politics of Jewish History* (Wayne State University Press, 2020); Bilha Shilo, *Hashava ve-haḥmatsa. Tom ha-tekufa ha-eropit shel yivo* (Magnes Press, 2021); and Jason Lustig, *A Time to Gather: Archives and the Control of Jewish Culture* (Oxford University Press, 2022). Lustig's work stands out among these for its interest in questions about the contemporary YIVO.

10 Examples of scholarship about the history of Jews in America that discuss YIVO briefly include Edward S. Schapiro, *A Time for Healing: American Jewry Since World War II* (Johns Hopkins University Press, 1992); Eli Lederhendler, *New York Jews and the Decline of Urban Ethnicity, 1950–1970* (Syracuse University Press, 2001); and Daniel Soyer, ed., *The Jewish Metropolis: New York City from the 17th to the 21st Century*

(Academic Studies Press, 2021); see also Eli Lederhendler, "The Eastern European Jewish Past and Its Historians: Cultural Interventions in Postwar America," in *Reconstructing the Old Country: American Jewry in the Post-Holocaust Decades*, ed. Eliyana R. Adler and Sheila E. Jelen (Wayne State University Press, 2017), 23–43.

11 Cecile Kuznitz's 2002 overview of the field, no longer up to date but still invaluable, does not focus on the history of YIVO but discusses the impact of the prewar institute in shaping Yiddish studies. It also makes mention of several postwar YIVO contributions as well as of scholarship using YIVO collections. Many of the scholars cited worked under the institute's aegis or with its financial support (Cecile Kuznitz, "Yiddish Studies," in *The Oxford Handbook of Jewish Studies*, 341–71).

12 Jan Schwarz, *Survivors and Exiles: Yiddish Culture After the Holocaust* (Wayne State University Press, 2015); Rojanski, *Yiddish in Israel*; Anita Norich, *Discovering Exile: Yiddish and Jewish American Culture During the Holocaust* (Stanford University Press, 2007).

13 For a bibliography of scholarship about Max Weinreich, see Kalman Weiser, "Max Weinreich," *Oxford Bibliographies Online: Jewish Studies*, ed. Naomi Seidman, 2017. Within the last two decades, Jennifer Young, Daniel Soyer, and Jocelyn Cohen have written articles about Moses (Moyshe) Kligsberg and the autobiographical contests conducted by the American YIVO in the 1940s; Nancy Sinkoff's *From Left to Right* is an intellectual biography of Lucy Dawidowicz; Mark L. Smith's, *The Yiddish Historians and the Struggle for a Yiddish History of the Holocaust* (Wayne State University Press, 2019) gives significant attention to YIVO historians Isaiah Trunk and Philip Friedman; Alec Eliezer (Leyzer) Burko has contributed a dissertation about the YIVO Linguistics Circle: "Saving Yiddish: Yiddish Studies and the Language Sciences in America, 1940–1970" (PhD diss., Jewish Theological Seminary, 2019). Isaac Bleaman and Rakhmiel Peltz have written articles about Uriel Weinreich, and Zachary Baker has contributed several pieces about YIVO's library, including about its founder Mendel Elkin. The introduction to the *Guide to the YIVO Archives* (M. E. Sharpe, 1998), compiled and edited by Fruma Mohrer and Marek Web, is also an invaluable source about the history of YIVO's collections in America.

14 See, for example, Yudel Mark's "Di ershte yorn fun yivo," *Tsukunft* 81, no. 4 (April 1976): 130–36. Mark's personal memoirs that were recorded in Jerusalem in 1972 and are printed serially in the *Forverts* (New York) 2012–13 have far more to say about YIVO's pre–World War II than its postwar period. Similarly, Max Weinreich made frequent reference to the Vilna years in his speeches at YIVO conferences and gave a talk about the early history of the institute to staff members on the occasion of YIVO's fortieth anniversary in 1965. Excerpts of the speech were later broadcast on WEVD: Max Weinreich, "Dr. Max Weinreich Reminisces about the Early Days of YIVO (1965)" and "Historic YIVO Radio Program on WEVD," YIVO Institute for Jewish Research, accessed 14 December 2025, yivo.org/dr-max-weinreich-reminisces-about-the-early-days-of-yivo-1965.

15 The major article in the volume evaluating the American period is Joshua Fishman's brief contribution, "Der yivo in amerike," *Yivo bleter* 49 (1980): 98–101.

16 Zachary Baker, "Yiddish Publishing After 1945," in *Yiddish After the Holocaust*, ed. Joseph Sherman (Boulevard, 2004), 63.

17 Jan Schwarz, *Survivors and Exiles*.

18 Smith, *The Yiddish Historians*.

19 On the construction of Jewish usable past, see David G. Roskies, *The Jewish Search for a Usable Past* (Indiana University Press, 1999); and Steven J. Zipperstein, *Imagining Russian Jewry: Memory, History, Identity* (University of Washington Press, 1999).

20 Markus Krah, *American Jewry and the Re-Invention of the East European Jewish Past* (De Gruyter, 2018).

21 Jeffrey Shandler, *Homes of the Past: A Lost Jewish Museum* (Indiana University Press, 2024), 119–20.

22 To name but a few: Kalman Weiser, *Jewish People, Yiddish Nation: Noah Prylucki and the Folkists in Poland* (University of Toronto Press, 2011); Joshua Shanes, *Diaspora Nationalism and Jewish Identity in Habsburg Galicia* (Cambridge University Press, 2012); Jess Olson, *Nathan Birnbaum and Jewish Modernity* (Stanford University Press, 2013); Simon Rabinovitch, *Jewish Rights, National Rites: Nationalism and Autonomism in Late Imperial and Revolutionary Russia* (Stanford University Press, 2014); and Laura Almagor, *Beyond Zion: The Jewish Territorialist*

Movement (Littman Library of Jewish Civilization in association with Liverpool University Press, 2022).

23 On the Soviet case, see Gennadi Estraikh, *Soviet Yiddish: Language Planning and Linguistic Developments* (Clarendon, 1999); David Schneer, *Yiddish and the Creation of Soviet Yiddish Culture* (Cambridge University Press, 2004); Anna Shternshis, *Soviet and Kosher: Jewish Popular Culture in the Soviet Union, 1923–1929* (Indiana University Press, 2006); Elissa Bemporad, *Becoming Soviet Jews: The Bolshevik Experiment in Minsk* (Indiana University Press, 2013).

24 On *Sovetish heymland*, see Gennadi Estraikh, *Yiddish in the Cold War* (Legenda, 2008); and Eleanora Bergman, "Yiddish in Poland After 1945," in *Yiddish and the Left*, ed. Gennady Estraikh and Mikhail Krutikov (Legenda, 2001), 167–76.

25 On the flourishing Yiddish literary culture in America—above all New York—in the first half of the twentieth century and writers' pessimism about its declining readership, see Avraham Novershtern's monumental history of American Yiddish literature, *Kan gar ha'am ha-yehudi* (Magnes Press, 2015). For a broader, social scientific depiction of the state of Yiddish culture in the 1960s, see Joshua A. Fishman, *Yiddish in America: Sociolinguistic Description and Analysis* (Indiana University and Mouton, 1965).

26 On the postwar Bund, see Jack Jacobs, ed., *Jewish Politics in Eastern Europe: The Bund at 100* (Palgrave, 2001); Yosef Gorny, *Converging Alternatives: The Bund and the Zionist Labor Movement, 1897–1985* (SUNY Press, 2006); David Slucki, *The International Jewish Labor Bund After 1945: Toward a Global History* (Rutgers University Press, 2012); and "The Bund Archives Comes to YIVO," *Yedies fun yivo / Yivo News* (hereafter: *Yedies*) 178 (Fall 1992): 1*, 8*. Asterisks refer to English-language pages of *Yedies*.

27 Almagor, *Beyond Zion*.

28 Fradle Pomerantz Freidenreich, *Passionate Pioneers: The Story of Yiddish Secular Education in North America, 1910–1960* (Holmes & Meier Publishers, 2010); Naomi Prawer Kadar, *Raising Secular Jews: Yiddish Schools and Their Periodicals for American Children, 1917–1950* (Brandeis University Press, 2016); Sandy Fox, *The Jews of Summer: Summer Camp and Jewish Culture in Postwar America* (Stanford University Press, 2023).

29 Fox, *The Jews of Summer*, 141–47.

30 Sandy L. Fox, "'Laboratories of Yiddishkayt': Postwar American Jewish Summer Camps and the Transformation of Yiddishism," *American Jewish History* 103, no. 3 (July 2019): 279–301. On postvernacular Yiddish, see Kuznitz, "Yiddish Studies"; Jeffrey Shandler, *Adventures in Yiddishland: Post-Vernacular Language & Culture* (University of California Press, 2006); and Rebecca Margolis, *Yiddish Lives On! Strategies of Language Transmission* (McGill-Queen's University Press, 2023).

31 Christhard Hoffmann, ed., *Preserving the Legacy of German Jewry: A History of the Leo Baeck Institute, 1955–2005* (Mohr Siebeck, 2024).

32 Kuznitz, *YIVO and the Making*, 47–52.

33 Shlomo Noble, "The Yivo," *Contemporary Jewish Record* 7, no. 4 (1 August 1944): 387.

34 Kalman Weiser, "Where Is the Capital of Yiddishland?," in *Warsaw. The Jewish Metropolis: Essays in Honor of the 75th Birthday of Professor Antony Polonsky*, ed. Glenn Dynner and François Guesnet (Brill, 2015), 298–322; Efrat Gal-Ed, "Yiddishland: A Promise of Belonging," *Journal of Modern Jewish Studies* 20, no. 2 (2021): 141–69.

35 Marek Web, "The YIVO Archives—Where It All Began," typescript of speech delivered on the occasion of YIVO's sixtieth anniversary, 16 October 1988, p. 2, YIVO RG 100, YIVO, New York—General, box 74-9, folder 60th Anniversary Conference.

36 Kuznitz, *YIVO and the Making*, 10. For a valuable discussion of faith in objectivity and its relationship to politics in the pursuit of Jewish social science by Zionist scholars at the turn of the century, see Mitchell B. Hart, *Social Science and the Politics of Modern Jewish Identity* (Stanford University Press, 2000), ch. 1, esp. 49–55.

37 Kuznitz, *YIVO and the Making*, 175; Weiser, *Jewish People, Yiddish Nation*, 215–16.

38 Zachary Baker, "Die amerikanisierung der jiddischen Wissenschaft," *Judaica* 51, no. 4 (1995): 224.

39 The literature about the Czernowitz conference is substantial. For an overview and references, see Kalman Weiser, "Die jiddische Sprachkonferenz," in *Handbuch der Literaturen aus Czernowitz und der Bukowina*, ed. Andrei Corbea-Hoişie et al. (Metzler, 2023), 137–41. On the Hebrew University, see David N. Myers, *Re-Inventing the Jewish Past: European Jewish Intellectuals and the Zionist Return to History* (Oxford University Press, 1995).

40 On the work of YIVO's Terminological Commission, see Leybl Kahn, "Der terminologisher oyftu fun yivo," *Yivo bleter* 46 (1980): 229–41.

41 Kuznitz, *YIVO and the Making*, 113, 121–25; Weiser, *Jewish People, Yiddish Nation*, 186–87.

42 On the history of YIVO before World War II, see Kuznitz, *YIVO and the Making*, as well as her overview of the institute in *The YIVO Encyclopedia* 2:2090–96; Jacob Shatzky, "Finf un tsvantsik yor yivo," in *Shatski-bukh*, ed. E. Lifschutz. (YIVO, 1958), 303–17; and Lucy Dawidowicz, *From That Place and Time* (Bantam Books, 1989). The figures for YIVO's staff and students for the academic year 1938–39 are taken from Dawidowicz, *From That Place and Time*, 78, 89.

43 Leo Herskowitz et al., "New York City," in *Encyclopaedia Judaica*, 2nd ed. (Macmillan Reference, 2007), 15:212; Antony Polonsky, "Warsaw," in *The YIVO Encyclopedia of Jews in Eastern Europe*, ed. Gershon David Hundert (Yale University Press, 2008), 2:2001.

44 H. S. Linfield, "The Jewish Population of the United States," in *American Jewish Year Book, 1940–1941*, ed. American Jewish Committee (Jewish Publication Society, 1942), 219. For an overview of Yiddish culture in New York City, especially in the pre–World War II period, see Ayelet Brim, Eddy Portnoy, and Daniel Soyer, "Yiddish New York," in *The Jewish Metropolis: New York City from the 17th to the 21st Century*, ed. Daniel Soyer (Academic Studies Press, 2021), 91–114.

45 On the question of how to refer to Samuel Charney, see Eli Bromberg, "We Need to Talk About Shmuel Charney," *In geveb*, 2 October 2019, ingeveb.org/articles/we-need-to-talk-about-shmuel-charney (accessed 6 June 2023); and Gil Ribak, "My Mom Drank Ink: The 'Little Negro' and the Performance of Race in *Yente Telebende*'s Stage Productions," *In geveb*, 21 April 2023, ingeveb.org/articles/race-in-yente-telebende (accessed 1 March 2024).

46 Cecile Kuznitz, "YIVO Institute for Jewish Research in the United States," in *Encyclopedia of American Jewish History*, ed. Stephen H. Norwood and Eunice G. Pollack (ABC-CLIO, 2008), 768–69.

47 Kuznitz, *YIVO and the Making*, 270n271.

48 Natalia Aleksiun, 2010, "Lestschinsky, Jakob," *The YIVO Encyclopedia of Jews in Eastern Europe*, yivoencyclopedia.org/article.aspx/Lestschinsky_Jakob (accessed 13 August 2023); Kuznitz, *YIVO and the Making*, 182.

49 See Nina Warnke, "Of Plays and Politics: Sholem Aleichem's First Visit to America," *YIVO Annual* 20 (1991): 239–76; Chone Shmeruke, "Sholem Aleichem and America," *YIVO Annual* 20 (1991): 211–38; and Michael Brown, *The Israeli-American Connection* (Wayne State University Press, 1996).
50 Kuznitz, *YIVO and the Making*, 69.
51 Dawidowicz, *From That Place and Time*, 212–13.
52 *Tsvey yor arbet far dem yidishn visnshaftlekhn institut* (Vilna: YIVO, 1927), 47–48.
53 Jacob Shatzky, letter to Tcherikower, 5 October 1932, cited in Robert Moses Shapiro, "Jacob Shatzky, Historian of Warsaw Jewry," *Polin: Studies in Polish Jewry* 3 (2004): 205–6.
54 Lederhendler, "The Eastern European Jewish Past," 28–29.
55 *Barikht fun der konferents fun dem yidishn visnshaftlekhn institut (amerikaner opteyl)* (New York: YIVO, 1935), 4.
56 N. P. [Noah Pryłucki], "Yidishe folkslider oys kanade," *Yidishe filologye* 1 (1924): 235–36; M. Weinreich, "English un di imigrantn-shprakhn in amerike," *Yivo bleter* 3 (January–May 1932): 79–85.
57 Max Weinreich, "Fuftsik yor nokh tshernevits: a dermonung un a monung," *Di tsukunft* 63, no. 5–6 (May–June 1958): 222.
58 Uriel Weinreich, *Modern English-Yiddish Yiddish-English Dictionary* (New York: YIVO, 1990), xx–xi, xxiv–xxv.

Chapter 1

1 "Erklerung fun yidishn-visnshaftlekhn institut vegn ir vayterdiker tetikeyt," *Forverts*, 2 October 1939. Unless otherwise noted, all translations are mine. This chapter builds on my article, "Coming to America? Max Weinreich and the Emergence of YIVO's American Center," in *Choosing Yiddish: New Frontiers of Language and Culture*, ed. Lara Rabinovitch et al. (Wayne State University Press, 2012), 233–52.
2 Dov Levin, *The Lesser of Two Evils* (Jewish Publication Society, 1995), 198–217.
3 Minutes of the meeting of YIVO's temporary administration (YTA minutes), Vilna, 9–10 December 1939, YIVO RG 1.1 YIVO—Vilna Administration Records, box 3.1, folder 631.

4 Opening the 9–10 December meeting of the YTA, Zelig Kalmanovitch lamented, "I consider it my duty to honor the memory of all those who have died in the current *khurbn* of Polish Jewry" (YTA minutes, Vilna, 9–10 December 1939), p. 1.

5 For descriptions of the Szabad family, see Lucy Dawidowicz, *From That Place and Time* (Bantam Books, 1989), 139–42; and Gabriel Weinreich, *Confessions of a Jewish Priest* (Pilgrim Press, 2005), esp. 44–46, 54–56.

6 Dawidowicz, *From That Place and Time*, 139–42, 200; Weinreich, *Confessions of a Jewish Priest*, 36.

7 Max Weinreich, letter to Nathan Feinerman, 24 August 1939, YIVO RG 584 Max Weinreich Papers, folder 293b; Weinreich, *Confessions of a Jewish Priest*, 35; Bent Blüdnikov, "Max Weinreich in Copenhagen," 24 August 2014, www.yivo.org/max-weinreich-in-copenhagen (accessed 1 March 2024).

8 On Dawidowicz's experiences studying in Vilna, see Dawidowicz, *From That Place and Time*; and Nancy Sinkoff, *From Left to Right: Lucy S. Dawidowicz, the New York Intellectuals, and the Politics of Jewish History* (Wayne State University Press, 2020), 61–62.

9 Dov Levin, "The Jews of Vilna Under Soviet Rule, 19 September–28 October 1939," *Polin* 9 (1996): 107–36, 117; Yisroel Lempert, "Der goyrl fun yivo in historishn iberbrokh (1939–1941)," *Yivo bleter*, n.s., 3 (1997): 9–42.

10 Marek Web, "The YIVO Archives—Where It All Began," typescript of speech delivered on the occasion of YIVO's sixtieth anniversary, 16 October 1988, pp. 6–7, YIVO RG 100, box 74-9, folder 60th Anniversary Conference. I have used Web's translation here and added some items in brackets for the sake of clarity.

11 Max Weinreich, letter to Nathan Feinerman, 14 October 1939, YIVO RG 584, folder 293b.

12 Gershon Bacon, "National Revival, Ongoing Acculturation—Jewish Education in Interwar Poland," *Simon Dubnow Institut Jahrbuch* 1 (2002): 71–92.

13 Max Weinreich, letter to Nathan Feinerman, 14 October 1939, YIVO RG 584, folder 293b.

14 Nathan Feinerman, letter to Elias Tcherikower, 6 December 1939, YIVO RG 100A, YIVO, New York—Project Records, box 24, folder tet.

15 Meeting of Amopteyl Executive Office, 28 December 1939, YIVO RG 1.1 YIVO—Vilna Administration Records, box 33, folder 690.

16 Elias Tcherikower, letter to Nathan Feinerman, 15 November 1939, YIVO RG 100A, box 24, folder tet. On YIVO's activity in Paris until 1940, see Nick Underwood, *Yiddish Paris: Staging Nation and Community in Interwar France* (Indiana University Press, 2022), esp. ch. 2.

17 Nathan Feinerman, letter to Max Weinreich, 23 January 1940, YIVO RG 100A, box 28, folder M. Weinreich. See also the letter from the Rockefeller Foundation to Feinerman, 20 November 1939, YIVO RG 584, box 81, folder 696.

18 "Dr. maks vaynraykh fort op tsurik keyn yurop; hot durkhgefirt erfolgraykhe arbet farn vilner yidishn institut," *Forverts*, 6 July 1929. "Far dem yidishn vishnshaftlekhn institut. Barikht fun maks vaynraykhs kampanye in amerike," *Vilner tog* (Vilna), 6 September 1929; Cecile Esther Kuznitz, *YIVO and the Making of Modern Jewish Culture* (Cambridge University Press, 2014), 120.

19 On Sapir's career and his relationship to his Jewishness, see Edward Siskin, "The Life and Times of Edward Sapir," *Jewish Social Studies* 48, no. 3/4 (Summer–Autumn 1986): 283–92; and David Koffman, *The Jews' Indian: Colonialism, Pluralism and Belonging in America* (Rutgers University Press, 2019), 184–87.

20 "D'r maks vaynraykh kumt dinstik keyn amerike," *Der tog*, 17 March 1940. For details on Weinreich's year at Yale, see Barbara Kirshenblatt-Gimblett, "Coming of Age in the Thirties: Max Weinreich, Edward Sapir, and Jewish Social Science," *YIVO Annual* 23 (1996): 1–103; Jennifer Young, "Race, Culture, and the Creation of Yiddish Social Science: Max Weinreich's Trip to Tuskegee, 1932," in Rabinovitch, *Choosing Yiddish*, 217–32; and Leila Zenderland, "Social Science as a 'Weapon of the Weak': Max Weinreich, the Yiddish Scientific Institute, and the Study of Culture, Personality, and Prejudice," *Isis* 104, no. 4 (2013): 742–72.

21 Max Weinreich, letter to Leibush Lehrer, 25 January 1940, YIVO RG 507 Leibush Lehrer Papers, folder 30.

22 Max Weinreich, letter to Feinerman, 22 December 1939, YIVO RG 100A, box 28, folder M. Weinreich; Nathan Feinerman, letter to Elias Tcherikower, 5 December 1939, YIVO RG 100A, box 24, folder tet; Max Weinreich, letter to Nathan Feinerman, 15 December 1939, YIVO RG 584, folder 293b.

23 Max Weinreich, letter to YIVO Vilna, 5 January 1940. The letter is printed in its Yiddish original under the title "Di tsvey vovn: maks vaynraykh un di misye fun yivo," *Yedies* 183 (Fall 1996): 21–22.
24 Nathan Feinerman, letter to YIVO Vilna, 19 January 1940, YIVO RG 1.1, box 31, folder 664. Weinreich approved of issuing *Yivo bleter* with a title indicating its origins, such as "American *Yivo bleter*" (Weinreich, letter to Feinerman, n.d., YIVO RG 584, folder 293b).
25 Kuznitz, *YIVO and the Making*, 167.
26 Minutes of the Amopteyl Executive Office, 9 September 1939, p. 5, YIVO RG 1.1, box 33, folder 690.
27 Nathan Feinerman, letter to Elias Tcherikower, 5 December 1939.
28 Nathan Feinerman, letter to Max Weinreich, 21 November 1939, YIVO RG 584, folder 293b.
29 Catherine Collomp, "The Jewish Labor Committee, American Labor, and the Rescue of European Socialists, 1934–1941," *International Labor and Working Class History* 68 (2005): 112–33.
30 Kuznitz, *YIVO and the Making*, 119.
31 "Yidishe interesn," *Forverts*, 3 March 1940.
32 Minutes of the Amopteyl Executive Office, 21 September 1939, p. 3, YIVO RG 1.1, box 33, folder 690.
33 Meeting of Amopteyl, 21 September 1939, YIVO RG 1.1, box 33, folder 690.
34 Max Weinreich, letter to Nathan Feinerman, 25 September 1939, YIVO RG 584, folder 293b.
35 Max Weinreich, letter to Nathan Feinerman, 30 October 1939, YIVO RG 584, folder 293b.
36 Max Weinreich, letter to Nathan Feinerman, 25 September 1939. The folder also contains the five-page plan for Weinreich's proposed dictionary.
37 "Yivo-konferents in nyu-york," RG 1.1, box 32, folder VIII/672; "Yidishe interesn," *Forverts*, 16 January 1940.
38 "Yidishe interesn," *Forverts*, 9 January 1940.
39 *Buletin* (Central Jewish Library and Press Archives) 1 (January 1939): 4; "Fifteen Years of the YIVO Library and Archives," *Yedies* 50 (September 1953), 1*–2*; "Mendel Elkin (1873–1962)," *Yedies* 83 (July 1962), 1*, 5*; Zachary M. Baker, "The Yiddish Collections of the YIVO Library. Their History, Scope, and Significance," *YIVO Annual* 22 (1995):

257–59; Zachary Baker, "The Legacy of Mendl Elkin, the New York YIVO's First Librarian," speech delivered at the Center for Jewish History in New York City, 11 December 2012; Dina Abramowicz, "Mendel Elkin and the Beginning of the YIVO Library," unpublished speech, 1988. I thank Zachary Baker for sharing his and Dina Abramowicz's unpublished speeches from his personal collection.
40 "Fun der redaktsye," *Yivo bleter* 15 (1940): 1–2.
41 YTA minutes, Vilna, 27 January 1940, pp. 23–24, YIVO RG 1.1, box 3.1, folder 361.
42 Dov Levin, "Lithuania," *YIVO Encyclopedia of Jews in Eastern Europe*, 2011, yivoencyclopedia.org/article.aspx/Lithuania (accessed 2 March 2024).
43 See, for example, Moyshe Mandelman, "In freyd un leyd tsvishn litvishe yidn (fun 1938 biz 1940)," in *Lite*, ed. Mendel Sudarsky et al. (Jewish-Lithuanian Cultural Society, 1951), 1333–58.
44 Kalman Weiser, "The Jewel in the Yiddish Crown: Who Will Occupy the Chair in Yiddish at the University of Vilnius?," *Polin* 24 (2012): 232–44.
45 On this period, see Levin, "Jews of Vilna."
46 Joshua Karlip, "At the Crossroads Between War and Genocide: A Reassessment of Jewish Ideology in 1940," *Jewish Social Studies* 11, no. 2 (2005): 170–201.
47 Session of YTA, 10 March 1940, p. 15, YIVO RG 1.1, box 3.1, folder 631.
48 YTA minutes, 27 January 1940, pp. 14–15, YIVO RG 1.1, box 3.1, folder 361.
49 Amopteyl, letter to YIVO Vilna, 21 February 1940, YIVO RG 1.1, box 31, folder 664.
50 Amopteyl (Nathan Feinerman), letter to YIVO Vilna, 12 March 1940, YIVO RG 1.1, box 31, folder 663.
51 Zelig Kalmanovitch, letter to Max Weinreich, 17 May 1940, YIVO RG 584, box 30, folder 293b.
52 N. S. "A shtikl balans fun der arbet fun 'yivo,'" *Yidishe shtime* (Vilna), 6 June 1940; V., "Avire d'yivo," *Vilner togblat* (Vilna), 7 June 1940; "Profesorn fun vilner universitet oyf der perets-oysshtelung yivo" (YIVO RG 584, box 30, folder 293); Mandelman, "In freyd un leyd," 1349.
53 On the chair, see Weiser, "Jewel in the Yiddish Crown."

54 Dr. M. Weinreich, "Forverts-korespondent d'r maks vaynraykh dertseylt vi azoy er un andere zaynen farvundet gevorn in vilner pogrom," *Forverts*, 14 December 1931; "D'r maks vaynraykh arestirt far dem strayk gegn getos. Spetsiel keybl fun ben-nokhem" *Morgn-zhurnal* (New York), 22 October 1937.

55 Kalman Weiser, "The Chair for Yiddish in Weimar Germany That Wasn't," in *A Jew in the Street: New Perspectives on European Jewish History*, ed. Nancy Sinkoff et al. (Wayne State University Press, 2024), 241–66.

56 Sh. Niger, "Yidishe visnshaft antdekt amerike," 1940, YIVO RG 1.1, box 32, folder VIII/672.

57 Dawidowicz, *From That Place and Time*, 214; "Fifteen Years of the YIVO Library and Archives," *Yedies* 50 (September 1953), 1*–2*.

58 Zelig Kalmanovitch, letter to Max Weinreich, 17 June 1940, YIVO RG 584, box 30, folder 293b.

59 Zelig Kalmanovitch, letter to Max Weinreich, 1 July 1940, YIVO RG 584, box 30, folder 293b.

60 Society of Friends of the Yiddish Scientific Institute (Nathan Feinerman), letter to Zelig Kalmanovitch, 29 July 1940, YIVO RG 1.1, box 31, folder 664.

61 Shmerke Kaczerginski, *Tsvishn hamer un serp. Tsu der geshikhte fun der likvidatsye fun der yidisher kultur in sovetn-rusland* (Der emes, 1950), 28.

62 "Oykh der 'yivo' vert endlekh aroysgetsoygn fun zumf," *Tageblat* (Vilna), 16 August 1940; Leyzer Ran, *Ash fun yerushalayim de'lite* (Vilner Farlag, 1959), 176–79.

63 Kalman Weiser, *Jewish People, Yiddish Nation* (University of Toronto Press, 2011), 248–59; Lara Lempertienė, "The End of the Glorious Years: YIVO Under the Soviet Regime, 1940–1941," *Jahrbuch des Simon Dubnow-Instituts* 19 (2021/2022): 115–29.

64 Weinreich's dissertation (*Studien zur Geschichte und dialektischen Gliederung der jiddischen Sprache*) was reprinted, with an introduction including a biographical overview, by Jerold Frakes as *Geschichte der jiddischen Sprachforschung*, ed. Jerold Frakes (Scholars' Press, 1993).

65 "Nokh vegn inyen yivo (tsvey briv)," *Fraye arbeter shtime* (New York), 9 March 1956.

66 Y. Fogel, "Yidisher visnshaftlekher institut bashlist ibertsutrogn tetikeyt keyn amerike," *Forverts*, 1 October 1940.

67 Fogel, "Yidisher visnshaftlekher institut bashlist."
68 Fogel, "Yidisher visnshaftlekher institut bashlist"; Dawidowicz, *From That Place and Time*, 213–14; Max Weinreich, "S'iz itst 15 yor zint der grindung fun yidishn visnshaftlekhn institut," *Forverts*, 3 January 1941.
69 Max Weinreich, "Di yidishe visnshaft in der hayntiker tsayt," *Yivo bleter* 17 (1941): 3. For Weinreich's perspective in the mid-1930s, see his remarks in YIVO, *Der alveltlekher tsuzamenfor fun yidishn visnshaftlekhn institut. Tsum 10-yorikn yoyvl fun yivo. Opgehaltn in vilne fun 14tn bizn 19tn oygust 1935* (Vilna: YIVO, 1936).
70 On YIVO's and especially Weinreich's use of martial metaphors, see Kuznitz, *YIVO and the Making*, 172–73.
71 Kuznitz, *YIVO and the Making*, 12–13.
72 Kuznitz, *YIVO and the Making*, 5–6.
73 Weinreich, "S'iz itst 15 yor zint der grindung fun yidishn visnshaftlekhn institut."
74 P. Berman, "Di gantse yidishe inteligents in eyrope vert oygekoylet," *Forverts*, 2 June 1943.
75 For similar views, see Markus Krah, *American Jewry and the Re-Invention of the East European Jewish Past* (De Gruyter, 2018), ch. 2.
76 Max Weinreich, "A yidishe natsionale program oyf nokh der milkhome," in *Yidisher arbeter-komitet, Yidn nokh der milkhome. Barikht fun der ershter konferents fun forshungs-komitet baym yidishn arbeter-komitet* (Jewish Labor Committee, 1942), 51–80.
77 P. Berman [Max Weinreich], "Vos hot di yidishe literatur tsu gebn dem yungn yidishn dor?," *Forverts*, 16 February 1947.
78 Young, "Race, Culture, and the Creation," 220–22.
79 Max Weinreich, "Der yivo in yidishn lebn," *Yivo bleter* 23, no. 1 (January–February 1944): 10.
80 Max Weinreich, *Der veg tsu undzer yugnt. Yesoydes, metodn, problemen fun yidisher yugnt-forshung* (Vilna: YIVO, 1934), 169–71.
81 Eric L. Goldstein, *The Price of Whiteness: Jews, Race, and American Identity* (Princeton University Press, 2006), 204; "The Classification of Jewish Immigrants," *Yedies* 5 (November 1944): 3*.
82 Goldstein, *Price of Whiteness*, 206–8; James Loeffler, "Nationalism Without a Nation?: On the Invisibility of American Jewish Politics," *Jewish Quarterly Review* 105, no. 3 (Summer 2025): 373–74.

83 P. Berman [Max Weinreich], "Ken men ertsien dem yungn yidishn dor in amerike mit yidishkeyt fun der alter velt?," *Forverts*, 2 April 1944.

84 Max Weinreich, "Der yivo in a yor fun umkum," talk held at YIVO conference, 8 January 1943, YIVO RG 584, folder 4.

85 P. Berman [Max Weinreich], "Vos hot di yidishe literatur tsu gebn dem yungn yidishn dor?"; Max Weinreich, "Jews in a Gentile World," 1942 (?), typed manuscript, YIVO RG 584, box 4, folder 540a. This is a shortened, English-language version of Weinreich's "Yidn in a nit-yidisher velt," *Yivo bleter* 19 (1942): 250–60. It is a review of Isacque Graeber et al., *Jews in a Gentile World: The Problem of Antisemitism* (Macmillan, 1942).

86 Weinreich, "Der yivo in a yor fun umkum."

87 Weinreich, "Di yidishe visnshaft in der hayntiker tsayt," 11.

88 Weinreich, "Jews in a Gentile World," 259.

89 P. Berman [Max Weinreich], "Di gantse yidishe inteligents in eyrope vert oygekoylet"; M. Weinreich, "Di yidishe visnshaft in der hayntiker tsayt," 9.

90 Max Weinreich, "Der yivo un di problemen fun undzer tsayt," *Yivo bleter* 25 (1945): 3–18.

91 Hasia R. Diner, "American Jewish History," in *The Oxford Handbook of Jewish Studies*, ed. Martin Goodman (Oxford University Press, 2002), 472–75.

92 Diner, "American Jewish History," 472; Jason Lustig, "Building a Home for the Past: Archives and the Geography of American Jewish History," *American Jewish History* 102, no. 3 (July 2018): 375–99. Marcus is cited here on page 378.

93 Weinreich, "Di yidishe visnshaft in der hayntiker tsayt," 1–13. The quote appears on page 3.

94 On the ambivalent attitudes of immigrant Jews in America toward their home communities in eastern Europe, see Rebecca Kobrin, "The Shtetl by the Highway: The East European City in New York's 'Landsmanshaft' Press, 1921–39," *Proof Texts* 26, no. 1–2 (2006): 107–37; and Daniel Soyer, "Transnationalism and Americanization in East European Jewish Immigrant Public Life," in *Imagining the American Jewish community*, ed. Jack Wertheimer (Brandeis University Press, 2007), 47–66.

95 Paul Ritterband and Harold S. Wechsler, *Jewish Learning in American Universities: The First Century* (Indiana University Press, 1994), 202–7.

96 Hasia R. Diner, *The Jews of the United States, 1654–2000* (University of California Press, 2004), 207–15; Tony Michels, "Is America 'Different'? A Critique of American Jewish Exceptionalism," *American Jewish History* 96, no. 3 (2010): 201–24. The quote is from page 217.

97 Jeffrey S. Gurock, "While *Publications* Slept," *American Jewish History* 81, no. 2 (Winter 1993/1994): 214–15. On the assimilationist underpinnings of Wirth's study, see Daniel Schwartz, *Ghetto: The History of a Word* (Harvard University Press, 2019), ch. 3.

98 Both Kallen and Wirth were supportive of YIVO's work in the 1930s and the former would eventually serve on its Board of Directors. "Prof. Horace M. Kallen Honored," *Yedies* 126 (Summer 1973): 4*; Kirshenblatt-Gimblett, "Coming of Age in the Thirties," 80.

99 For a picture of the contents of the *American Jewish Year Book*, published by the American Jewish Committee, in this period, see Jonathan Sarna, "The Twentieth Century Through American Jewish Eyes: A History of the American Jewish Year Book, 1899–1999," *American Jewish Year Book* 100 (2000): 25–49.

100 On Dubnow's ideas about national cultural autonomy, see Simon Rabinovitch, *Jewish Rights, National Rites: Nationalism and Autonomism in Late Imperial and Revolutionary Russia* (Stanford University Press, 2014).

101 Max Weinreich, "Roshe-prokim fun a yidisher program oyf nokh der milkhome," *Tsukunft* (March 1942): 145–46. On Jews and nationality minority rights in the interwar period, see Carol Fink, *Defending the Rights of Others: The Great Powers, the Jews, and International Minority Protection, 1878–1938* (Cambridge University Press, 2004); and James Loeffler, *Rooted Cosmopolitans: Jews and Human Rights in the Twentieth Century* (Yale University Press, 2018).

102 On disillusionment with Diaspora Nationalism, see, for example, Joshua Karlip, *The Tragedy of a Generation: The Rise and Fall of Jewish Nationalism in Eastern Europe* (Harvard University Press, 2013); Weiser, *Jewish People, Yiddish Nation*; and Kenneth Moss, *An Unchosen People: Jewish Political Reckoning in Interwar Poland* (Harvard University Press, 2021).

103 Gil S. Rubin, "The Future of the Jews: Planning for the Postwar Jewish World, 1939–1946" (PhD diss., Columbia University, 2017), 66–67; Gennady Estraikh, "Jacob Lestschinsky: A Yiddishist Dreamer

and Social Scientist," *Science in Context* 20, no. 2 (2007): 215–37; Gur Alroey, "Demographers in the Service of the Nation: Liebmann Hersch, Jacob Lestschinsky, and the Early Study of Jewish Migration," *Jewish History* 20 (2006): 265–82.

104 "Toyznt mentshn bay erefenung fun konferents fun yidishn visnshaftlekhn institut," *Forverts*, 11 January 1942.

105 Jacob Lestschinksy, "Ershte ayndrukn fun amerikaner yidntum," *Der yidisher kemfer* 16 (June 1939): 8–9.

106 Weinreich, *Confessions of a Jewish Priest*, 38, 89–93.

Chapter 2

1 Mordkhe Schaechter, "Dem yivos yidish-oyftu: obzervatsyes un sakhaklen," *Yivo bleter* 46 (1980): 222.

2 "The Yivo," *Yedies* 1 (September 1943): 1*.

3 Shloyme Bikl, "Di tsvontsiktse 'yivo' konferents. Faktn un bamerkungen," *Der yidisher kemfer* (New York), 1 February 1946, 13.

4 Max Weinreich, "English un di imigrantn-shprakhn in amerike," *Yivo bleter* 3 (1932): 79–85; Yudel Mark, "Yidishe anglitsizmen. A por bamerkungen," *Yorbukh fun amopteyl* 1 (1938): 296–321.

5 See, for example, Sore Brener [Max Weinreich], "Yidishe olraytniks fun amerike un england oyf di trens nokh pariz un varshe," *Forverts*, 11 November 1922; Sore Brener, "'Genose baranov, antlayt mir ayer revolver,'" *Forverts*, 14 October 1923; and Kalman Weiser, "Where Is the Capital of Yiddishland?," in *Warsaw. The Jewish Metropolis: Essays in Honor of the 75th Birthday of Professor Antony Polonsky*, ed. Glenn Dynner and François Guesnet (Brill, 2015).

6 Max Weinreich, "Der yivo un di problemen fun undzer tsayt," *Yivo bleter* 25, no. 1 (January–February 1945): 11.

7 Cecile Esther Kuznitz, *YIVO and the Making of Modern Jewish Culture* (Cambridge University Press, 2014), 154.

8 Sol Liptzin, "Maks vaynraykh in amerike," *Di pen* 19 (February 1996): 26; "The Academic Council of Yivo," *Yedies* 6 (December 1944): 6*.

9 On pogroms, see Jeffrey Veidlinger, *In the Midst of Civilized Europe: The Pogroms of 1918–1921 and the Onset of the Holocaust* (Metropolitan Books, Henry Holt and Company, 2021).

10 Dr. Mark Wischnitzer, "Fun der bikher velt. Geshikhte fun der yidisher arbeter-bavegung in di fareynikte shtatn," *Di tsukunft* 49, no. 5 (May

1944): 316–19; Solomon F. Bloom, "The Sage of America's 'Russian' Jews," *Commentary* (New York), no. 1 (December 1945): 1–7. Only two volumes were ultimately published. A condensed, one-volume English translation by Aaron Antonovsky, *The Early Jewish Labor Movement in the United States*, was published by YIVO in 1961.

11 "Fifteen Years of the YIVO Library and Archives," *Yedies* 50 (September 1953): 1*–2*. For brief descriptions of Mark, Mahler, and Elias and Rebecca Lestschinsky, see Lucy Dawidowicz, *From That Place and Time* (Bantam Books, 1989), 212–14.

12 "Eliyohu tsherikover plutsem geshtorbn," *Yedies* 1 (September 1943): 2. On Tcherikower's life and career, see Joshua Karlip, *The Tragedy of a Generation: The Rise and Fall of Jewish Nationalism in Eastern Europe* (Harvard University Press, 2013).

13 "N. Faynerman, o"h," *Yedies* 3 (July 1944): 2.

14 On the trope of collecting to guard against cultural loss, see Itzik Gottesman, *Defining the Yiddish Nation: The Jewish Folklorists of Poland* (Wayne State University Press, 2003); Laura Jokusch, *Collect and Record!: Jewish Holocaust Documentation in Early Postwar Europe* (Oxford University Press, 2012); Kuznitz, *YIVO and the Making*, 9.

15 Dawidowicz, *From That Place and Time*, 250.

16 On the role of *zamlers* prior to World War II, see Kuznitz, *YIVO and the Making*, esp. 7, 73–74.

17 Cecile E. Kuznitz, "La Recherche yiddish dans le sillage de la destruction: 'le yivo affronte le monde de l'après-guerre', 1940–1953," in *Premiers savoirs de la Shoah*, ed. Judith Lindenberg (CNRS Éditions, 2017), 200–202; Jeffrey Shandler, *Homes of the Past: A Lost Jewish Museum* (Indiana University Press, 2024).

18 Daniel Soyer and Jocelyn Cohen, *My Future Is in America: Autobiographies of East European Jewish Immigrants* (New York University Press, 2006), 5.

19 Max Weinreich, "Di yidishe visnshaft in der hayntiker tsayt," *Yivo bleter* 17 (1941): 11.

20 In recent years, there has appeared a large body of scholarly literature about YIVO's autobiography contest in prewar Poland. Works include Jeffrey Shandler, ed. *Awakening Lives: Autobiographies of Jewish Youth in Poland Before the Holocaust* (Yale University Press, 2002); Kamil Kijek, "Max Weinreich, Assimilation and the Social Politics of Jewish

Nation-Building," *East European Jewish Affairs* 41, no. 1–2 (2011): 25–55; Barbara Kirshenblatt-Gimblett, "Coming of Age in the Thirties: Max Weinreich, Edward Sapir, and Jewish Social Science," *YIVO Annual* 23 (1996): 1–103; Leila Zenderland, "Social Science as a 'Weapon of the Weak': Max Weinreich, the Yiddish Scientific Institute, and the Study of Culture, Personality, and Prejudice," *Isis* 104, no. 4 (2013): 742–72; Jennifer Young, "Race, Culture, and the Creation of Yiddish Social Science: Max Weinreich's Trip to Tuskegee, 1932," in *Choosing Yiddish: New Frontiers of Language and Culture*, ed. Lara Rabinovitch et al. (Wayne State University Press, 2012), 217–32; and Ido Bassok, "Le-she'elat erkan ha-histori shel otobiografiot bene no'ar mi-osef yivo," *Mada'e ha-yahadut* 44 (2007): 137–64.

21 Max Weinreich, letter to Alexander M. Dushkin, Jewish Education Committee of New York, 11 June 1940, YIVO RG 584, folder 570a; "Budget for 1944," p. 3, YIVO RG 584, folder 314.

22 Moses Kligsberg, "Sotsial-psikhologishe problemen arum dem yivo konkurs oyf oytobiografies," *Yivo bleter* 21 (1943): 262–75; it appeared in English as Moses Kligsberg, "Socio-Psychological Problems Reflected in the YIVO Autobiography Contest," *YIVO Annual of Jewish Social Science* 1 (1946): 241–49; Moses Kligsberg, "Jewish Immigrants in Business: A Sociological Study," *American Jewish Historical Quarterly* 56, no. 3 (March 1967): 283–318; Soyer and Cohen, *My Future Is in America*, 5–9; Daniel Soyer, "Yiddish Scholars Meet the Yiddish-Speaking Masses: Language, the Americanization of YIVO, and the Autobiography Contest of 1942," in *Yiddish in America: Essays on Yiddish Culture in the Golden Land*, ed. Edward S. Shapiro (University of Scranton Press), 55–79; Moses Kligsberg, "Di yidishe yugnt-bavegung in poyln tsvishn beyde velt-milkhomes," in *Shtudyes vegn yidn in poyln, 1919–1939*, ed. Joshua A. Fishman (New York: YIVO, 1974), 137–228. For an evaluation of Kligsberg's approach to the study of youth and its differences from Weinreich's approach, see Jennifer Young, "Generationwechsel. Moyshe Kligsberg und di *yungt-forshung*," in *Impulse für Europa. Tradition und Moderne der Juden Osteuropas*, ed. Manfred Sapper (BWV Berliner-Wissenschaft, 2008), 313–19.

23 "Biographical Note," *Guide to the Papers of Moses Kligsberg*, pp. 4–6, YIVO RG 719 Moses Kligsberg Papers; "Moyshe Kligsberg, 1902–1975," *Yedies* 134 (July 1975): 1*, 1–2

24 Sandy Feiner, interview with author, Toronto, 23 February 2023.
25 Moses Kligsberg, "The Study of Man: The Golden Land," *Commentary* 5, no. 5 (May 1948), www.commentary.org/articles/moses-kligsberg/the-study-of-man-the-golden-land/.
26 Kligsberg, "The Study of Man." Leibush Lehrer critiques aspects of Kligsberg methodology in a letter to the editor under the title "The Immigrant Type" in the June 1948 issue of the same journal.
27 Moses Kligsberg, "American Jewish Soldiers on Jews and Judaism," *YIVO Annual of Jewish Social Science* 5 (1950): 256–65; the original appears in Yiddish in *Yivo bleter* 31–32 (1948): 233–43; Kuznitz, "La Recherche yiddish," 198–99.
28 Max Weinreich, letter to Uriel Weinreich, 14 April 1946, Weinreich Family Papers, University of Michigan, box 9. For a negative evaluation of Elkin's skills as a librarian, see Ezekiel Lifschutz, Diary, 24 April and 28 May 1962, Ezekiel Lifschutz Private Collection, P130/202, Central Archives for the History of the Jewish People, Jerusalem (hereafter Lifschutz, Diary).
29 Zachary M. Baker, "The Card Catalogs of the YIVO Library: A Memoir," 13–14 (Zachary Baker, personal collection).
30 Dina Abramowicz, untitled eulogy for Mendel Elkin, 1962 (Zachary Baker, personal collection). See also Yudel Mark's speech on the anniversary of the tenth anniversary (*yortsayt*) of Elkin's death, "Mendl elkin tsu zayn 10tn yortsayt," *Yivo bleter* 44 (1973): 292–95. On Elkin's character and activities, see also Jacob Glatstein, *Prost un poshet. Literarishe eseyen* (Fanny Gladstone, 1978), 312–15.
31 On Lansky's work to save Yiddish books from destruction, see his *Outwitting History: The Amazing Adventures of a Man Who Rescued a Million Yiddish Books* (Algonquin Books of Chapel Hill, 2004).
32 "Mendel Elkin (1873–1962)," *Yedies* 83 (July 1962): 5*.
33 "Our New Building," *Yedies* 1 (September 1943): 2*; "Di heym fun visnshaftlekhn institut," *Yedies* 1 (September 1943): 2; Milton R. Konvitz, "Yivo Comes to Morningside," *Commentary* 4 (1 January 1947): 48–54.
34 Zosa Szajkowski, "Der yivo un zayne grinders. Katalog fun der oysshtelung tsum 50-yorikn yoyvl fun yidishn visnshaftlekhn institut," *Yivo bleter* 46 (1980): 64.
35 M. Weinreich, "Der yidisher visnshaftlekher institut in yidishn gaystikn lebn fun amerike," *Forverts*, 20 January 1946.

36 Affidavit of Markus Uveeler, 1 February 1947, p. 1, in "YIVO OAD 18," National Archives and Record Administration (NARA), College Park, MD, RG 260 Records of US Occupation Headquarters, World War II; Berl Kuczer, *Geven a mol varshe: zikhroynes* (Kultur-opteylung baym dzshoynt in frankraykh, 1955), 282. Uveeler's name is also sometimes spelled Yuviler and Youviller.

37 "Eighteenth Annual Conference of the Yivo," *Yedies* 2 (February 1944): 2*.

38 "Di yidishe geto in varshe," *Yivo bleter* 16, no. 2 (November–December 1940): 200–201; Kuznitz, "La Recherche yiddish," 192.

39 "Shloyme mendelson (1896–1948)," *Yedies* 25 (February 1948): 2; S. Mendelsohn, *Vi azoy lebn poylishe yidn in di getos / The Polish Jews Behind the Nazi Ghetto Walls* (New York: YIVO, 1942); V. Shulman, "Zayn lebn un veg," in *Shloyme mendelson. zayn lebn un shafn* (Unzer tsayt, 1949), 16–18, 28; Mortkhe Velvl Bernshteyn, "Mendelsohn, Shloyme. March 30, 1896—February 9, 1948," in *Leksikon fun der nayer yidisher literatur*, trans. and ed. Joshua Fogel, congressforjewishculture.org/people/2795/Mendelson-Shloyme-March-30-1896-February-9-1948; Weinreich, "Der yivo un di problemen fun undzer tsayt," 15; Kuznitz, "La Recherche yiddish," 202–3.

40 "Petition of the American Jews to the President Concerning Nazi Persecutions of the Jews," *Yedies* 1 (September 1943): 3*.

41 Max Weinreich, "Der yivo in yidishn lebn," *Yivo bleter* 23, no. 1 (January–February 1944): 8–9.

42 "The Battle of the Warsaw Ghetto," *Yedies* 3 (July 1944): 1. The talk was published in *Yivo bleter* 23, no. 1 (January–February 1944) and also circulated as a brochure in English translation to various Jewish organizations, government offices, scholars, and interested individuals.

43 "Di 18te yerlekhe konferents fun yivo iz adurkh mit groys erfolg," *Yedies* 2 (February 1944): 3.

44 Sh. Mendelsohn, *The Battle of the Warsaw Ghetto* (New York: YIVO, 1944); Salomón Mendelson, *La resistencia desesperada en el ghetto de Varsovia* (IWO, 1944); "The Battle of the Warsaw Ghetto," *Yedies* 3 (July 1944): 3; Kuznitz, "La Recherche yiddish," 202–3.

45 "Jewish Cultural Work in Poland," *Yedies* 5 (November 1944): 6*. On Ringelblum and the *Oyneg shabes* project, see Samuel D. Kassow, *Who Will Write Our History? Emanuel Ringelblum, the Warsaw Ghetto, and the Oyneg Shabes Archive* (Indiana University Press, 2007).

46 "Memorial Meeting for Three Jewish Historians," *Yedies* 5 (November 1944): 1*. On Bałaban and Schipper, see Natalia Aleksiun, *Conscious History: Polish Jewish Historians Before the Holocaust* (Littman Library of Jewish Civilization, 2021).
47 "Yizker," *Yivo bleter* 26, no. 1 (September–October 1945): 3–19.
48 Weinreich, "Der yivo un di problemen fun undzer tsayt," 16.
49 Weinreich, "Der yivo un di problemen fun undzer tsayt," 3–18.
50 Weinreich, "Der yivo in yidishn lebn."
51 Max Weinreich, "Der yivo in a yor fun umkum," talk held at YIVO conference, 8 January 1943, YIVO RG 584, folder 4.
52 Weinreich, "Der yivo in yidishn lebn."
53 "Basic Facts About Yiddish," *Yedies* 17 (November 1946): 4*. The pamphlet was slightly updated and reissued online in 2014: YIVO, "Basic Facts About Yiddish," YIVO Institute for Jewish Research, accessed 14 December 2025, www.yivo.org/cimages/basic_facts_about_yiddish_2014.pdf.
54 Sol Liptzin, trans. and ed., *Peretz* (New York: YIVO, 1947).
55 Shlomo Noble did much of YIVO's translation work from the time he started working in YIVO in 1944 until the 1970s. He recalls that he, like others, was pessimistic that English translations of Yiddish scholarship would find an audience. (Rakhmiel Peltz, "Intervyu mit d'r nobl [opgehaltn dem oygust, 1985 in piksvil, n'y]," p. 2, YIVO RG 747 Shlomo Noble Papers, box 4.)
56 P. Berman [Max Weinreich], "Vos hot di yidishe literatur tsu gebn dem yungn yidishn dor?"; Berman, "Ken men ertsien dem yungn yidishn dor in amerike mit yidishkeyt fun der alter velt?"
57 Berman, "Ken men ertsien dem yungn yidishn dor in amerike mit yidishkeyt fun der alter velt?"
58 Berman, "Vos hot di yidishe literatur tsu gebn dem yungn yidishn dor?"
59 Max Weinreich, letter to Samuel Charney, 10 May 1945; Max Weinreich, letter to Samuel Charney, 20 June 1945, YIVO RG 360 Papers of Shmuel Niger, folder 723.
60 Dawidowicz, *From That Place and Time*, 217; "Di yivo-aspirantur in amerike," YIVO RG 100A, box 110; "Registration for New Candidates to the Dr. C. Szabad Research Training Division (Aspirantur)," YIVO RG 100, box 78, folder 6.

61 "1946 Budgeting Bulletin for Membership Agencies," p. 3, YIVO RG 584, folder 314.

62 For details on the *aspirantur*'s first year, see YIVO, *Kurtser barikht far di ershte akht khadoshim 1941* (Yiddish Scientific Institute, 1941), 2–3. On the Vilna aspirantur, see Kuznitz, *YIVO and the Making*, 154–57.

63 Arnold Gurin, chair, Seminar Committee, letter, 16 November 1945, YIVO RG 100, box 78, folder 8.

64 Lucy Shildkret, letter to Elias Picheny, 8 March 1946, YIVO RG 100, box 78, folder 9.

65 "Di yivo-aspirantur in amerike," YIVO RG 100A, box 110; Alec Eliezer Burko, "Saving Yiddish: Yiddish Studies and the Language Sciences in America, 1940–1970" (PhD diss., Jewish Theological Seminary, 2019), 116.

66 Max Weinreich, letter to Avrom Sutzkever, 30 January 1947 in Avrom (Avraham) Novershtern, "Briv fun maks vaynraykh tsu avrom sutskever," *Di goldene keyt* 95/96 (1978): 176.

67 Dawidowicz, *From That Place and Time*, 217; "In der aspirantur," *Yedies* 1 (September 1943): 5; "Open Courses in the Research Training Division—Aspirantur 1945/6," *Yedies* 9 (June 1945): section 2.

68 "A Neglected Movement," *Reconstructionist*, 21 January 1944, cited in "The Reconstructionist About the Yivo," *Yedies* 2 (February 1944): 4*.

69 Of more than 7,000 contributors worldwide, YIVO counted 4,119 individuals and 558 organizations paying membership dues in 1947. "The Yivo Serves," *Yedies* 25 (February 1948): 3*; "Report of the Administration," *Yedies* 25 (February 1948): 3*, 5*.

70 "Yivo Conference Outlines Broad Program," *Yedies* 7 (February 1945): 3*; "Organization and Budget of the YIVO in 1953," *Yedies* 52 (March 1954): 3*; "Organization and Budget of YIVO in 1954," *Yedies* 56 (March 1955): 3*.

71 Jeffrey Shandler, "Homes of the Past: The Story of a Lost Museum," lecture, Center for Jewish History and the YIVO Institute for Jewish Research, New York, 19 May 2022, posted on 23 May 2022 by Center for Jewish History, www.youtube.com/watch?v=F_K630-2T1Y.

72 "YIVO's Budget," *Yedies* 44 (March 1952): 4*.

73 Max Weinreich, "Der yivo in zayn finf un tsvontsiksn yor," p. 8, speech read at opening of 24th conference of YIVO, Saturday, 18 February 1950, YIVO RG 552 Papers of Uriel Weinreich, box 40, folder 421.

74 Weinreich, "Der yivo in zayn finf un tsvontsiksn yor," 3–5.
75 Weinreich, "Der yivo in zayn finf un tsvontsiksn yor," 10.
76 Henry L. Lurie and Max Weinreich, eds., "Jewish Social Research in America: Status and Prospects; A Symposium," *YIVO Annual of Jewish Social Science* 4 (1949): 168, cited in Jason Lustig, "Building a Home," 385.
77 Weinreich, "Der yivo in zayn finf un tsvontsiksn yor," p. 9.
78 Cited in Jason Lustig, "Building a Home for the Past: Archives and the Geography of American Jewish History," *American Jewish History* 102, no. 3 (July 2018): 386.
79 Mark Uveeler in Lurie and Weinreich, eds., "Jewish Social Research," 297–98. See Lustig, "Building a Home," esp. 378–87, for a fuller treatment of these discussions.
80 "YIVO to Establish Central Archives on Jews in America," *Yedies* 38 (September 1950): 1*–2*.
81 Ascher Penn, *Yidishkeyt in amerike. A vegvazyer tsu dem gaystikn yidishn lebn in der tsveyter helft fun 20tn yorhundert* (Bibliotek "Yidishkeyt in amerike," 1958), 557–69.
82 "Dina Abramowicz" and "Hirsh Abramovitsh (Hirsz Abramowicz)" in Fogel, *Leksikon fun der nayer yidisher literatur*, yleksikon.blogspot.com/search?q=abramowicz; Joseph Berger, "Dina Abramowicz, 90, Librarian and Yiddish Expert, Dies," *New York Times*, 9 April 2000; Zachary Baker, "Dina Abramowicz," accessed 14 December 2025, jwa.org/encyclopedia/article/abramowicz-dina. "Dina Abramowicz, 1909–2000," *Yedies* 190 (Summer 2000): 6; "YIVO Appoints New Staff Members," *Yedies* 27 (June 1948): 4*; "Library News," *Yedies* 172 (Autumn 1987): 12; Jeff Sharlet, "Keeper of a Civilization," *Der Pakntreger / The Book Peddler* 21 (1996): 9–21.
83 Kuznitz, *YIVO and the Making*, 104–5; Nachman Meisel, "Iz der yivo umparteyish?," *Yidishe kultur* (New York), no. 2 (February 1944): 61; "Shete va'adot shel anshe lashon veḥeker," *Davar* (Tel Aviv), 12 February 1953; Morris U. Schappes, "Knowledge Limited and Timid," *Morgn frayhayt* (New York), 2 February 1946; Morris U. Schappes, "Facts for Lestschinsky," *Morgn frayhayt*, 15 February 1947. The quote is taken from Schappes's article "Right Wing Scholarship," *Morgn frayhayt*, 7 February 1948.

84 Dr. H. Frank, "Vos felt fort dem yivo in amerike?," *Fraye arbeter shtime*, 10 and 17 January 1947.

85 Dr. H. Frank, "Vos felt fort dem yivo in amerike?," *Fraye arbeter shtime*, 17 January 1947.

86 For a similar exposition of his views, see Yudel Mark, "Tsu der yoyvl konferents fun yivo," *Der yidisher kemfer*, 12 January 1951, 4–5.

87 Yudel Mark, letter to Shloyme Bikl, 5 February 1946, YIVO RG 100, box 82. For Bikl's criticism of Mark's views, see Bikl, "Di tsvontsiktse 'yivo' konferents," 13–14.

88 Max Weinreich, letter to Uriel Weinreich, 27 January 1946, Weinreich Family Papers, box 9.

89 Shlomo Noble, "Di 20ste yivo konferents," *Der yidisher kemfer* (1 February 1946): 14.

90 On the institute, see Boaz Cohen, "Dr. Jacob Robinson, the Institute of Jewish Affairs and the Elusive Jewish Voice in Nuremberg," in *Holocaust and Justice: Representation and Historiography of the Holocaust in Post-War Trials*, ed. Dan Michman and David Bankier (Yad Vashem, Berghahn Books, 2010), 81–100.

91 Gennady Estraikh, "Jacob Lestschinsky: A Yiddishist Dreamer and Social Scientist," *Science in Context* 20, no. 2 (2007): 231–32.

92 "Twenty-Fifth Anniversary of the Yiddish Scientific Institute," *Jewish Labor Bund Bulletin* (New York) 4, nos. 1–2 (1951): 3. See also "Nokh der konferents fun yivo," *Unzer tsayt*, 1 January 1954, 24–25.

93 Joshua D. Zimmerman, "TSYSHO," *YIVO Encyclopedia of Jews in Eastern Europe*, 12 February 2010, encyclopedia.yivo.org/article/147 (accessed 27 July 2025); Kalman Weiser, *Jewish People, Yiddish Nation* (University of Toronto Press, 2011), 215–18.

94 Burko, "Saving Yiddish," 33, 41–42; Hannah Kliger and Rakhmiel Peltz, "The Secular Yiddish School in the United States in Sociohistorical Perspective. Language or Cultural School?," *Linguistics and Education* 2 (1990): 4–5.

95 Eli Lederhendler, *New York Jews and the Decline of Urban Ethnicity, 1950–1970* (Syracuse University Press, 2001), 28.

96 Kliger and Peltz, "Secular Yiddish School," 3; Burko, "Saving Yiddish," ch. 1.

97 B. Weinryb, "Yivo Annual of Jewish Social Science. Vol. IV," *Jewish Quarterly Review* 42, no. 3 (January 1952): 328.

98 B. Weinryb, "Yivo Annual," 326–28. The quote is from page 328.

99 "Zitsung fun der visnshaftlekher kolegye," 14 February 1952, YIVO RG 100, box 138, folder visnshaftlekhe kolegye 1951–52.

100 "Tsu der zitsung fun der shats-komisye, yuni 5, 1951," YIVO RG 584, folder 569a.

101 "Board of Directors Meets," *Yedies* 42 (September 1951): 1*.

102 "YIVO's Scope World-Wide," *Yedies* 45 (June 1952): 4*.

103 Mark, "Tsu der yoyvl konferents fun yivo," 4–5.

104 On Yiddish culture in Argentina, see Mariusz Kałczewiak, *Polacos in Argentina: Polish Jews, Interwar Migration, and the Emergence of Transatlantic Jewish Culture* (University of Alabama Press, 2020); and Jan Schwarz, *Survivors and Exiles: Yiddish Culture After the Holocaust* (Wayne State University Press, 2015). William Pimlott, "YIVO's Foreign Sections: Building Transnational Immigrant History in the Wake of the Holocaust," manuscript draft, 7–8. I thank the author for providing me with a copy of his unpublished work. He has subsequently given a talk at YIVO on this subject: William Pimlott, "Taking Yiddish Science Global: YIVO's Foreign Branches, 1925–1994," YIVO Institute for Jewish Research, 17 September 2025, www.youtube.com/watch?v=haaLOM8004M.

105 "A History of Ladino in Manuscript in YIVO," *Yedies* 69 (December 1958): 6*.

106 Max Weinreich, letter to Uriel Weinreich, 23 June 1946, Weinreich Family Papers, box 9; P. Berman [Max Weinreich], "Yidisher forsher brengt grus fun shvartse yidn in etiopye," *Forverts*, 5 June 1951; P. Berman, "Undzere brider in tsofn-afrike," *Forverts*, 18 January 1953; P. Berman, "Yisroel tsvishn mizrekh un mayrev," *Forverts*, 21 June 1953.

107 "On the Threshold of the State of Israel," *Yedies* 27 (June 1948): 6, 7*; "Problems of Integration of the American Jewish Community," *Yedies* 31 (February 1949): 2*; "The Jews in the Muslim Countries," *Yedies* 33 (June 1949): 7*.

108 "Public Lectures at YIVO," *Yedies* 45 (June 1952): 3*.

109 "From the Declaration Read at the Opening of the Conference," *Yedies* 25 (February 1948): 2*.

110 Max Weinreich, letter to Leibush Lehrer, 15 July 1948, YIVO RG 507 Leibush Lehrer Papers, folder 30.

111 Weinreich to Lehrer, 15 July 1948, YIVO RG 507 Leibush Lehrer Papers, folder 30.

112 On Yiddish in post–World War II Israel, see Rachel Rojanski, *Yiddish in Israel: A History* (Indiana University Press, 2020). On the case of the Yiddish chair at the Hebrew University, see also Abraham Novershtern, "Between Town and Gown: The Institutionalization of Yiddish at the Israel Universities," in *Yiddish in the Contemporary World*, ed. Gennadi Estraikh and Mikhail Krutikov (Legenda and University of Oxford Press, 1999), 1–19.

113 On the attempt to create a Yiddish chair at the Hebrew University in 1927, see Arieh Leyb Pilowsky, *Tsvishn yo un neyn: yidish un yidish-literatur in erets-yisroel, 1907–1948* (Veltrat far yidish un yidishe kultur, 1986), 141–91.

114 Benzion Dinaburg, letter to Max Weinreich, 7 November 1949, YIVO RG 584, box alef 6, folder 22.

115 Max Weinreich, letter to Uriel and Beatrice Weinreich, 7 February 1950, Weinreich Family Papers, box 12, folder 8.

116 On Sadan's contributions to Yiddish scholarship, see Novershtern, "Between Town and Gown," 10–15.

117 Max Weinreich, letters to Uriel Weinreich, 5 March 1950 and 25 June 1950, Weinreich Family Papers, box 12, folder 8.

118 "Protokoln fun yivo farvaltung zitsung, dem 24tn April, 1948," YIVO RG 100, box 48-7, folder protokoln fun der farvaltung fun yivo 1948; "Protokoln fun yivo farvaltung, dem 21tn februar, 1948," YIVO RG 100, box 48-7, folder protokoln fun der farvaltung fun yivo 1948.

119 A. Menes, "Vos darf zayn der veg fun yivo—der 'vilner' oder der 'nyu-yorker'?," *Forverts*, 10 February 1952; M. Mratshni, "Tsayt-komentarn," *Fraye arbeter shtime*, 15 February 1952; A. Menes, "Nokh amol vegn di meynungs-farsheydnheytn in yivo," *Forverts*, 9 March 1952; "Yivo oyfn sheydveg," *Frayer yidisher klub buletin* (New York) 26 [1956?].

120 "Yivo oyfn sheydveg."

121 Joshua Fishman, interview with author, Bronx, New York, 26 August 2010; Ezekiel Lifschutz, "D'r maks vaynraykh," in his unpaginated notebook titled "Notitsn vegn shraybers vos ikh hob gekont," Ezekiel Lifschutz Private Collection, P130-201, Central Archives for the History of the Jewish People, Jerusalem.

122 Chana Mlotek, interview with author, New York, 2 July 2009.

123 Max Weinreich, letter to Abraham Golomb, 30 October 1952, YIVO RG 584, folder 545A.

124 For debates about reconstituting YIVO's sections, see YIVO RG 100, box 138, folder 2 Visnshaftlekhe kolegye 1952–53, esp. 20 October 1952, 3 November 1952, and 11 February 1953.

125 "The Cahan Folklore Club at Yivo," *Yedies* 29 (November 1948): 4*; "Y.l. kahan yugntklub far folklor baym yivo," *Yedies* 29 (November 1948): 4; "Fun an intervyu mit bine silverman-vaynraykh," *Yedies* 173 (Autumn 1988): 9; "Yidishe folkor- un etnografye-forshung," *Forverts*, 26 May 1974.

126 "Dr. Mark Wischnitzer, Jewish Historian, Dies; Was 75," *JTA*, 15 October 1955, www.jta.org/archive/dr-mark-wischnitzer-jewish-historian-dies-was-73; "Dr. Wischnitzer, Jewish Historian," *New York Times*, 18 October 1955.

127 Mark L. Smith, *The Yiddish Historians and the Struggle for a Yiddish History of the Holocaust* (Wayne State University Press, 2019), 112–13.

128 Kuznitz, *YIVO and the Making*, 96–99.

129 "Formation of a Social Science Circle," *Yedies* 61 (June 1956): 3*; "Geshafn baym yivo a krayz far sotsiale visnshaftn," *Yedies* 61 (June 1956): 5; David C. Engerman, "Social Science in the Cold War," *Isis* 101 (2010): 393–400.

130 "Linguistic Circle Organized at YIVO," *Yedies* 45 (June 1952): 4*; "Geshafn gevorn a lingvistisher krayz baym yivo," *Yedies* 45 (June 1952): 8.

131 Ezekiel Lifschutz, "Leybush lehrer," in Lifschutz, Diary, 19 September 1967.

132 "Judah A. Joffe," YIVO RG 552, box 40, folder 422.

133 Max Weinreich, letter to Uriel and Beatrice Weinreich, 11 December 1949, Weinreich Family Papers, box 11, folder 3.

134 M. Weinreich, "Vegn baytn dem englishn nomen fun yivo," 31 December 1949, YIVO RG 552, box 40, folder 422; Weinreich, "Der yivo in a yor fun umkum"; "YIVO Board of Directors Meets," *Yedies* 57 (June 1955): 3*.

135 Weinreich, "Der yivo in a yor fun umkum"; Max Weinreich, "Vegn di tsiln fun yivo baym onheyb fun zayn tsveytn fertl yorhundert," 30 May 1951. The comments are contained in "Tsu der zitsung fun der shats-komisye, yuni 5, 1951," YIVO RG 584, folder 569a.

136 The title "Jewish Scientific Institute" appeared for a period on its letterhead, but this change was not reported in *Yedies*. See debates about the character of YIVO's work and changing its name in the minutes

of the Committee on Research for 5 January 1955 (YIVO RG 100, box 138); A. Golomb, "Vu iz der yidisher visnshaftlekher institut?" *Di fraye arbeter shtime*, 30 December 1955.

137 Joseph Gar, *Viderklangen. Oytobiografishe fartseykhenungen*, vol. 2 (Farlag "Hamenora," 1971), 140–42.

138 Chaim Gininger, letter to Solomon Birnbaum, 13 November 1951, Nathan and Solomon Birnbaum Family Archives, Gininger folder.

139 Shikl (Joshua) Fishman, "Zikhroynes vegn maks vaynraykh," *Yivo bleter* n.s., no. 3 (1997): 353.

140 Joshua Fishman, interview with author; Ezekiel Lifschutz, "D'r maks vaynraykh," in his "Notitsn vegn shraybers."

141 Mordkhe Schaechter, "Dem yivos yidish-oyftu," 192–228.

Chapter 3

1 "3-Year Slum Plan Relocates 5,935," *New York Times*, 21 October 1957; Alice Kessler-Harris, "1048 Fifth Avenue," in *American Places: Encounters with History; A Celebration of Sheldon Meyers*, ed. William E. Leuchtenberg (Oxford University Press, 2000), 233–39; "YIVO Installed in Its New Home," *Yedies* 59 (December 1955): 4; Ascher Penn, *Yidishkeyt in amerike. A vegvazyer tsu dem gaystikn yidishn lebn in der tsveyter helft fun 20tn yorhundert* (Bibliotek "Yidishkeyt in amerike," 1958), 557–69.

2 Sh. Esterman, "Forshteyer fun der yidisher prese kumen oyf a bazukh in der nayer gebayde fun 'yivo,'" *Forverts*, 4 January 1956.

3 "YIVO's New Home Being Prepared for Occupancy," *Yedies* 57 (June 1955): 4*; "YIVO Installed in Its New Home," 4*.

4 Ezekiel Lifschutz, "R' khayim liberman" in his "Notitsn vegn shraybers vos ikh hob gekont," Ezekiel Lifschutz Private Collection, P130-201, Central Archives for the History of the Jewish People, Jerusalem.

5 On the ERR's activities in Vilna and specifically in YIVO, see David E. Fishman, *The Book Smugglers: Partisans, Poets, and the Race to Save Jewish Treasures from the Nazis* (ForeEdge, 2017); and Maria Kuhn-Ludewig, *Johannes Pohl (1904–1960): Judaist und Bibliothekar im Dienste Rosenbergs. Eine biographische Dokumentation* (Laurentius, 2000).

6 For introductions to *Judenforschung*, see Alan E. Steinweis, *Studying the Jew: Scholarly Antisemitism in Nazi Germany* (Harvard University

Press, 2006); and Dirk Rupnow, *Judenforschung im Dritten Reich. Wissenschaft zwischen Politik, Propaganda und Ideologie* (Nomos, 2011). On the fate of Jewish cultural treasures during the war, see David Fishman, *Embers Plucked from the Fire: The Rescue of Jewish Cultural Treasures in Vilna / Shaytelekh aroysgerisn fun fayer: dos oprateven kultur-oytsres in vilne*, 2nd ed. (New York: YIVO, 2009); and Fishman, *The Book Smugglers*.

7 On the Strashun Collection, see Dan Rabinowitz, *The Lost Library: The Legacy of Vilna's Strashun Library in the Aftermath of the Holocaust* (Brandeis University Press, 2019).

8 Kalman Weiser, *Jewish People, Yiddish Nation* (University of Toronto Press, 2011), 269–71; Fishman, *The Book Smugglers*, chs. 3, 14.

9 Herman Kruk, *The Last Days of the Jerusalem of Lithuania: Chronicles from the Vilna Ghetto and the Camps, 1939–1944*, ed. Benjamin Harshav, trans. Barbara Harshav (New York: YIVO and Yale University Press, 2002), 296.

10 Cited in Barry Trachtenberg, *The Holocaust and the Exile of Yiddish: A History of the Algemeyne Entsiklopedye* (Rutgers University Press, 2022), 154; Fishman, *Embers Plucked from the Fire*, 4–5.

11 On Šimaite, see Julija Šukys, *Epistolophilia: Writing the Life of Ona Šimaitė* (University of Nebraska Press, 2012). For a fuller, riveting account of the activities of the Paper Brigade and the recovery of Vilna materials after the war, see Fishman, *The Book Smugglers*.

12 Fishman, *The Book Smugglers*, 67–68; Lucy Dawidowicz, *From That Place and Time* (Bantam Books, 1989), 263; Bilha Shilo, *Ein Drama in Akten. Die Restitution der Sammlungen des Wilnaer YIVO* (Vandenhoeck & Ruprecht, 2022), 27–32.

13 Fishman, *The Book Smugglers*, 166–67.

14 Elisabeth Gallas, "Preserving East European Jewish Culture—Lucy Dawidowicz and the Salvage of Books After the Holocaust," *Simon Dubnow Institute Yearbook* 11 (2012): 76–83. The most important sources about the restitution of YIVO materials consulted for this study are Fishman, *The Book Smugglers*; Mark Glickman, *Stolen Words: The Nazi Plunder of Jewish Books* (Jewish Publication Society, 2016); Dana Herman, "*Hashavat Avedah*: A History of Jewish Cultural Reconstruction, Inc." (PhD diss., Department of History, McGill University, 2008); Elisabeth Gallas, *A Mortuary of Books: The Rescue of*

Jewish Culture After the Holocaust (New York University Press, 2019); Rabinowitz, *The Lost Library*; Nancy Sinkoff, *From Left to Right: Lucy S. Dawidowicz, the New York Intellectuals, and the Politics of Jewish History* (Wayne State University Press, 2020); and Shilo, *Ein Drama in Akten*. An abbreviated version of Shilo's work appears in English as "When YIVO Was Defined by Territory: Two Perspectives on the Restitution of YIVO's Collections," in *Contested Heritage: Jewish Cultural Property After 1945*, ed. Elisabeth Gallas, Anna Holzer-Kawalko, Caroline Jessen, and Yfaat Weiss (Vandenhoeck & Ruprecht, 2020), 79–89. For this author's review of Shilo's book: Kalman Weiser, review of Bilha Shilo, *Ein Drama in Akten. Die Restitution der Sammlungen des Wilnaer YIVO* (Vandenhoeck & Ruprecht, 2022), in *Central European History* 56, no. 4 (December 2023): 652–54.

15 Nancy Sinkoff, "Lucy S. Dawidowicz and the Restitution of Jewish Cultural Property," *American Jewish History* 100, no. 1 (January 2016): 124; Shilo, *Ein Drama in Akten*, 39–42.

16 Bilha Shilo, "'Funem folk, farn folk, mitn folk': The Restitution of the YIVO Collection from Offenbach to New York," *Moreshet* 14 (2017): 370, 386; Sinkoff, "Dawidowicz and the Restitution," 126.

17 Shlomo Noble, "The Yivo," *Contemporary Jewish Record* 7, no. 4 (1 August 1944): 391. On Noble's life and career, see Jonathan Boyarin, *A Storyteller's Words: The Education of Shlomo Noble in Europe and America* (Holmes & Meier, 1994). The transcript and recordings of an interview conducted by Rakhmiel Peltz with Noble are found in YIVO RG 747.

18 "Jews in Palestine Seek Methods to Retrieve at Peace Table Own Assets Stolen by Nazis," *New York Times*, 7 April 1944.

19 See Justin D. Cammy and Avraham Novershtern, "Afterward: Written in Moscow, Summer 1944," in Abraham Sutzkever, *From the Vilna Ghetto to Nuremberg: Memoir and Testimony*, ed. and trans. Justin Daniel Cammy (McGill-Queen's University Press, 2021), 319–73; Ralph Parker, "Poet Partisan from Vilna Ghetto Says Nazis Slew 77,000 of 80,000," *New York Times*, 15 April 1944; and Joshua Rubinstein, "Jewish Anti-Fascist Committee," *YIVO Encyclopedia of Jews in Eastern Europe*, 2011, yivoencyclopedia.org/article.aspx/Jewish_Anti-Fascist_Committee (accessed 10 April 2023).

20 "What Is Left of the YIVO in Vilna?," *Yedies* 4 (September 1944): 7*.

21 Uriel Weinreich, "Nekome far der boben," 1945, Weinreich Family Papers, University of Michigan, Ann Arbor, Special Collections Library, box 9; Fishman, *The Book Smugglers*, ch. 19; Avrom Sutzkever, "A vort tsum zekhtsikstn yoyvl fun yivo," *Goldene keyt* 116–17 (1986): 234–40.

22 Fishman, *The Book Smugglers*, 168.

23 Jason Lustig, *A Time to Gather: Archives and the Control of Jewish Culture* (Oxford University Press, 2022), 61.

24 Shilo, *Ein Drama in Akten*, 43–44; Shilo, "'Funem folk, farn folk, mitn folk,'" 371.

25 Sinkoff, *From Left to Right*, 81–82.

26 Fishman, *The Book Smugglers*, chs. 16–17.

27 Fishman, *The Book Smugglers*, ch. 18.

28 Mark Tolts, 2010, "Population and Migration: Migration Since World War I," *The YIVO Encyclopedia of Jews in Eastern Europe*, yivoencyclopedia.org/article.aspx/Population_and_Migration/Migration_since_World_War_I (accessed 30 August 2023); Avinoam Patt and Michael Berkowitz, ed., *"We Are Here": New Approaches to Jewish Displaced Persons in Postwar Germany* (Wayne State University Press, 2010).

29 Fishman, *The Book Smugglers*, ch. 20; Shilo, *Ein Drama in Akten*, 34–36.

30 Fishman, *The Book Smugglers*, chs. 20–22.

31 Fishman, *The Book Smugglers*, chs. 2, 20–21, 28; Shilo, *Ein Drama in Akten*, 36–37; Laura Lempertienė, "Looted? Abandoned? Saved? The Provenance and Status of Jewish Documents in the State Document Repositories of Lithuania," in *Treuhändische Übernahme und Verwahrung. International und interdiziplinär betrachtet*, ed. Olivia Kaiser et al. (V & R Unipress, 2018), 317; Joshua Rubenstein, "Jewish Anti-Fascist Committee," *The YIVO Encyclopedia of Jews in Eastern Europe*, 2011, yivoencyclopedia.org/article.aspx/Jewish_Anti-Fascist_Committee (accessed 10 April 2023).

32 "Three Outstanding Diaries in YIVO's Archives," *Yedies* 22 (September 1947): 1*, 2*, 8*; "The Work of the YIVO in 1947," *Yedies* 24 (December 1947): 1*–2*; "Unique Manuscript in the Possession of YIVO," *Yedies* 26 (April 1948): 4*.

33 Kalmanovitch's Hebrew-language diary (published in Israel as *Yoman be-geto vilna u-khetavim min ha-'izavon she-nimtse'u*

ba-harisot [Tel Aviv, 1977]) was translated into Yiddish by Yudel Mark and appeared in *Yivo bleter* in 1951 (Zelig Kalmanovitch, "A togbukh in vilner geto," *Yivo bleter* 35 [1951]: 18–92). An English translation was subsequently published in *YIVO Annual* (Zelig Kalmanovitch, "A Diary of the Nazi Ghetto in Vilna," *YIVO Annual of Jewish Social Science* 8 [1953]: 9–81). For a new English translation uniting fragments of the diary from YIVO's collection in New York and the Gaon Museum's collection in Vilnius: Zelig Kalmanovich, *Hope Is Stronger Than Life: Vilna Ghetto Diary*, trans. Olga Lempert (Vilna Gaon Museum of Jewish History, 2021). Herman Kruk's diary appeared as *Togbukh fun vilner geto*, ed. Mordechai W. Bernstein (New York: YIVO, 1961). Decades after Kruk's death, a full reconstruction and translation of the diary with additional pages subsequently found in Israel and Lithuania was produced by Benjamin and Barbara Harshav (Kruk, *Last Days of the Jerusalem of Lithuania*).

34 "Fun di vilner arkhiv oytsres," *Yedies* 27 (June 1948): 5.

35 On Szajkowski, see Lisa Leff, *The Archive Thief: The Man Who Salvaged French Jewish History in the Wake of the Holocaust* (Oxford University Press, 2015).

36 "Oystsugn fun z. shaykovskis briv, fun berlin, dem 11tn sept. 1945," YIVO RG 100, box 46-8, folder Shaykovski, Z.

37 M. Weinreich, letter to Z. Szajkowski, 28 September 1945, YIVO RG 100, box 46-8, folder Shaykovski, Z.

38 Dawidowicz, *From That Place and Time*, 268–70; Shilo, *Ein Drama in Akten*, 48–49.

39 Max Weinreich, letter to Uriel Weinreich, 17 March 1946, Weinreich Family Papers, box 9; Fishman, *The Book Smugglers*, ch. 23.

40 On the activities of the JCR from its founding until its dissolution in 1977, see Dana Herman, *Hashavat Avedah* and Gallas, *A Mortuary of Books*, esp. ch. 2.

41 Research Staff of the Commission on European Jewish Cultural Reconstruction, "Tentative List of Jewish Cultural Treasures in Axis-Occupied Countries," *Jewish Social Studies* 8 (1946), H. 1, supplement, entries 248–49. Dan Rabinowitz disputes the number of books (Rabinowitz, *The Lost Library*, 105).

42 Grace Cohen Grossman, "Scholar as Political Activist: Salo W. Baron and the Founding of the Jewish Cultural Reconstruction," in *For*

Everything a Season: Proceedings of the Symposium on Jewish Ritual Art, ed. Joseph Guttmann (Cleveland State University Press, 2000), 149–51; Wacław Wierzbieniec, "Kielce," *The YIVO Encyclopedia of Jews in Eastern Europe*, 18 August 2010, yivoencyclopedia.org/article.aspx/Kielce (accessed 25 March 2024).

43 Fishman, *The Book Smugglers*, ch. 27.

44 Fishman, *The Book Smugglers*, ch. 27.

45 Shilo, *Ein Drama in Akten*, 77.

46 Fishman, *The Book Smugglers*, ch. 27. The quotation is cited on page 224.

47 Fishman, *The Book Smugglers*, ch. 27; Shilo, *Ein Drama in Akten*, 54–56.

48 See Weinreich's statement, certified by a notary, and stamped (with the Nazi eagle) by the German consulate in New York from 18 April 1941, Weinreich Family Papers, box 12.

49 Shilo, *Ein Drama in Akten*, 5; Fishman, *The Book Smugglers*, 225.

50 Max Weinreich, letter to Leibush Lehrer, 20 July 1946, YIVO RG 507, folder 30; Sinkoff, *From Left to Right*, 71–73, 375n34. Chana Mlotek recalled the breakdown in their relationship being primarily due to Weinreich's failure to defend Shildkret from criticisms for the perceived shortcomings of a YIVO conference she agreed to organize alone in 1946 in order to permit Weinreich time to write *Hitler's Professors* (Chana Mlotek, interview with author).

51 Dawidowicz, *From That Place and Time*, 278.

52 Max Weinreich, letter to Uriel Weinreich, 9 December 1945, Weinreich Family Papers, box 9; Sinkoff, *From Left to Right*, 85; Leff, *The Archive Thief*, 125–26.

53 Max Weinreich, letter to Uriel Weinreich, 17 March 1946, Weinreich Family Papers, box 9; Fishman, *The Book Smugglers*, ch. 23.

54 Dawidowicz, *From That Place and Time*, 312–14; Sinkoff, *From Left to Right*, 83–84.

55 Dawidowicz, *From That Place and Time*, 316.

56 Dawidowicz, *From That Place and Time*, 318.

57 Dawidowicz, *From That Place and Time*, 324; Shilo, *Ein Drama in Akten*, 70.

58 Max Weinreich, letter to Uriel Weinreich, 8 August 1946, Weinreich Family Papers, box 9.

59 Sinkoff, *From Left to Right*, 89.

60 Fishman, *The Book Smugglers*, ch. 27; Dawidowicz, *From That Place and Time*, 324–26; Shilo, *Ein Drama in Akten*, 57–60; Rabinowitz, *The Lost Library*, 412.

61 Col. S. J. Pomrenze, "The Restitution of Jewish Cultural Treasures After the Holocaust: The Offenbach Archival Depot's Role in the Fulfillment of U.S. International and Moral Obligations (A First Hand Account)," *Proceedings of the 37th Annual Convention of the Association of Jewish Libraries, Denver, CO, June 23–26, 2002*, 1–9; "YIVO Library Is Back Home," *Yedies* 40 (March 1951): 2*.

62 Fishman, *The Book Smugglers*, ch. 27; Sinkoff, "Dawidowicz and the Restitution," 117–47; Shilo, "'Funem folk, farn folk, mitn folk,'" 362–412.

63 Rabinowitz, *The Lost Library*, 112–13. Weinreich's affidavits are found in "YIVO OAD 18," National Archives and Record Administration (NARA), College Park, MD, RG 260 Records of US Occupation Headquarters, World War II. Weinreich offered this explanation to Lucy Shildkret: "The [Strashun Library] is connected to the Historic-Ethnographic Society to which we were closely tied in a variety of other, smaller collections. Last year in Vilna, a central Jewish library was in the process of being created and it was clear to everyone that YIVO was the natural center. The Strashun Library's books were already in the YIVO building, on 18 Wiwulski Street, when the Germans began to remove them." Max Weinreich, letter to Libe Shildkret, 26 February 1947, cited in Sinkoff, "Dawidowicz and the Restitution," 129.

64 "YIVO's Associated Libraries" in "YIVO OAD 18," NARA RG 260. YIVO and the Jewish Ethnographic Society reached an agreement in 1928 for YIVO to house library and archival collections belonging to the Ethnographic Society. That same year, as YIVO was embarking on a campaign to construct a building with modern storage facilities, the idea of housing the Jewish Ethnographic Society, the Strashun Library, and YIVO all under one roof was discussed by Vilna intellectuals active in these institutions. As Moyshe Shalit of the Jewish Ethnographic Society then explained, placing them under YIVO's roof "would create the possibility of concentrating in one place in Vilna a great scholarly and artistic treasure with conditions for further growth." Cecile Kuznitz, "An-sky's Legacy: The Vilna Historic Ethnographic Society and the Shaping of Modern Jewish Culture," in *The Worlds of S. An-sky: A Russian Jewish Intellectual at the Turn of the*

Century, ed. Gabriella Safran and Steve Zipperstein (Stanford: Stanford University Press, 2022), 333.

65 Rabinowitz, *The Lost Library*, 108; Marc J. Yuveeler, letter to Seymour Pomrenze, 5 June 1947; "YIVO's Associated Libraries," affidavit by Zofia Sofie Ehrlich née Dubnow, 2 July 1946 in "YIVO OAD 18," NARA RG 260.

66 Max Weinreich, letter to Seymour Pomrenze, 14 February 1947, American Jewish Historical Society, New York, Lucy S. Dawidowicz Papers, box 52, folder 1, cited in Rabinowitz, *The Lost Library*, 113. On Rubinstein, see Hirsz Abramowicz, *Farshvundene geshtaltn*, (Tsentrale farband fun poylishe yidn in Argentine, 1958), 163–70.

67 "Barikht fun dem yidishn visnshaftlekhn institut tsum 31stn detsember. Di arbet fun yivo in yor 1938/39, bizn oysbrokh fun der milkhome," YIVO RG 1.1, box 37, folder 632, Minutes and Reports of the Central Board, 1939–40.

68 In her memoirs, Dawidowicz tells that Weinreich communicated to her not long after arriving in New York that, shortly after the outbreak of the war, "the trustees of the Strashun Library, also fearing for the safety of their library, asked the Vilna YIVO to ship their library, too, and to be responsible for its security." On these grounds, she urged Joseph A. Horne, the OAD director who succeeded Bencowitz, to treat the Strashun books as YIVO property (Dawidowicz, *From That Place and Time*, 318–19).

69 For an interpretation that disputes the veracity of YIVO's claims to the Strashun collection, see Rabinowitz, *The Lost Library*, ch. 6; and Dan Rabinowitz, "The Vanishing of the Strashun Library," *Tablet*, 15 February 2022, www.tabletmag.com/sections/history/articles/vanishing-strashun-library. Fishman is less critical but maintains that "Weinreich may have fibbed to obtain more books" (Fishman, *The Book Smugglers*, 196).

70 Sinkoff, *From Left to Right*, 93.

71 "YIVO Library Is Back Home," 1*–2*; Shilo, *Ein Drama in Akten*, 70–72.

72 Rabinowitz, *The Lost Library*, 143–52; Shilo, *Ein Drama in Akten*, 71–72. According to Frida Shor, the Strashun books were sold in the early twenty-first century by Heichal Shlomo to a yeshiva, where they remained uncatalogued at the time of her investigation (Frida Shor, *Mi-"lekute shoshanim" ve'ad "brigadat ha-ne'yar." Sipuro shel bet 'eked ha-sefarim 'al shem strashun be-vilna* [Deyonun, 2012], 205–6).

73 Ezekiel Lifschutz, "R. khayim liberman," in his "Notitsn vegn shraybers"; Khayim Leyb Fuks, "Liberman, khayim," in Fogel, ed., *Leksikon fun der nayer yidisher literatur*, yleksikon.blogspot.com/search?q=liberman.
74 Shor, *Mi-"lekute shoshanim,"* 143–45, 206–7.
75 Ezekiel Lifschutz, "R. khayim liberman"; Zachary Baker, personal communication, 21 April 2025.
76 I thank Cecile Kuznitz for sharing this insight.
77 Shilo, *Ein Drama in Akten*, 79-80; Kateřina Čapková, "Between Expulsion and Rescue: The Transports for German-Speaking Jews of Czechoslovakia in 1946," *Holocaust and Genocide Studies* 32, no. 1 (Spring 2018): 66–92.
78 Shilo, *Ein Drama in Akten*, 87–90.
79 Gallas, *A Mortuary of Books*, 177–80.
80 Shilo, *Ein Drama in Akten*, 108–9.
81 Shilo, *Ein Drama in Akten*, 108–9.
82 Shilo, *Ein Drama in Akten*, 100–113.
83 "Vilna Collection Augmented. Library Acquires Rare Jewish Periodicals," *Yedies* 41 (June 1951): 3*.
84 Max Weinreich, *Hitler's Professors: The Part of Scholarship in Germany's Crimes Against the Jewish People* (Yiddish Scientific Institute, 1946); 2nd revised ed. (Yale University Press, 1999), 77.
85 It appeared in Yiddish as "Hitlers profesorn. Der kheylek fun der daytsher visnshaft in daytshlands farbrekhns kegn yidishn folk," *Yivo bleter* 27, nos. 1–2 (1946): 1–160, 209–312; it was published in book form in 1947.
86 The materials constitute YIVO's "Berlin Collection" (RG 215); Leff, *The Archive Thief*, 129–36.
87 Daniel Jonah Goldhagen, *Hitler's Willing Executioners: Ordinary Germans and the Holocaust* (Alfred A. Knopf, 1996).
88 Leo Spitzer, letter to Max Weinreich, 28 April 1946, YIVO RG 584, folder 164a.
89 Max Weinreich, letter to Leo Spitzer, 7 June 1946, YIVO RG 584, folder 164a.
90 See, for example, "War Department Acknowledges Yivo's Assistance," *Yedies* 22 (September 1947): 6*.
91 Sinkoff, "Dawidowicz and the Restitution," 125; "Yivo-materialn genutst in protses fun prof' shtark," *Yedies* 21 (June 1947): 5; Rupnow, *Judenforschung im Dritten Reich*, 292.

92 Max Weinreich, letter to Uriel Weinreich, 22 November 1945, Weinreich Family Papers, box 9. On Dawidowicz's relationship with Weinreich, see Sinkoff, *From Left to Right*; and Dawidowicz, *From That Place and Time*.

93 Max Weinreich, letter to Uriel Weinreich, 13 January 1946, Weinreich Family Papers, box 9.

94 Weinreich, *Hitler's Professors*, 6.

95 Weinreich, *Hitler's Professors*, 7.

96 Samuel Kassow, "Avant-propos," in *Hitler et les Professeurs. Le rôle des universitaires allemands dans les crimes contre le peuple juif*, trans. Izabelle Rozenbaumas (Belles Lettres, 2013), xii–xiii; Nicolas Patin, "Max Weinreich, Hitler et les professeurs. Le rôle des universitaires allemands dans les crimes commis contre le peuple juif, Paris, Belles Lettres, 2013, 393 p., ISBN 978-2-251-44469-7," *Revue d'histoire moderne & contemporaine* 63–64 (2017): 241–43.

97 On this subject, see Bernard M. Levinson and Robert P. Eriksen, ed., *The Betrayal of the Humanities: The University During the Third Reich* (Indiana University Press, 2022).

98 On the case of Beranek, see Weiser, "One of Hitler's Professors: Max Weinreich and Solomon Birnbaum Confront Franz Beranek," *Jewish Quarterly Review* 108, no. 1 (February 2018): 106–24.

99 Kalman Weiser, "The Chair for Yiddish in Weimar Germany That Wasn't," in *A Jew in the Street: New Perspectives on European Jewish History*, ed. Nancy Sinkoff et al. (Wayne State University Press, 2024), 241–66; H. Kloss, "Das Jiddische Wissenschaftliche Institut in Wilna," *Nation und Staat. Deutsche Zeitschrift für das europäische Minoritätsproblem* 3 (November 1929): 139–41.

100 Heinz Kloss and Edith Pütter, ed., *Statistik, Presse und Organisationen des Judentums in den Vereinigten Staaten und Kanada* (Selbstverlag der Publikationsstelle, 1944).

101 Weiser, "One of Hitler's Professors."

102 Thus, Uriel Weinreich announced that Beranek's monograph was published "with support of the Reichsintitut für die Geschichte des neuen Deutschlands while the author was a member of the Nazi party." Uriel Weinreich, "Western Traits in Transcarpathian Yiddish," in *For Max Weinreich on His Seventieth Birthday: Studies in Jewish Languages, Literature, and Society*, ed. Lucy S. Dawidowicz et al. (The Hague: Mouton, 1964), 248.

103 Dovid Eliyohu (David) Fishman, "Bamerkungen vegn vaynraykhs role in der antviklung fun der yidisher visnshaft," *Yivo bleter* 3, n.s. (1997): 298–307.

104 Weinreich refused to have his dissertation published by a German publisher after World War II. It was posthumously published by Jerold C. Frakes under the title *Geschichte der jiddischen Sprachforschung* (Scholars Press, 1993).

105 "Zitsung fun der visnshaftlekher kolegye. Montik dem 12tn may 1952." YIVO RG 100, box 138, folder 1.

106 Cited in "Arkhiv fun yidn unter der natsisher memshole," *Yedies* 8 (April 1945): 3. See also "Archives of Jewish Life Under the Nazis," p. 5* in the same issue.

107 Fruma Mohrer and Marek Web, eds., *Guide to the YIVO Archives* (New York: YIVO, 1998), xviii; Hasia R. Diner, *We Remember with Reverence and Love: American Jews and the Myth of Silence After the Holocaust, 1945–1962* (New York University Press, 2009), 94–95.

108 Diner, *We Remember with Reverence*, 93; Moyshe Kligsberg, "YIVO, New York" in *D'Auschwitz à Israël*, ed. Isaac Schneersohn (Centre de documentation juive contemporaine, 1968), 445. On *yizker-bikher*, see Jack Kugelmass and Jonathan Boyarin, ed., *From a Ruined Garden: The Memorial Books of Polish Jewry*, 2nd expanded ed. (Indiana University Press, 1998).

109 "Close Cooperation with the Polish Historical Commission," *Yedies* 16 (September 1946): 7*; Samuel Kassow, *Who Will Write Our History? Rediscovering a Hidden Archive from the Warsaw Ghetto* (Indiana University Press, 2007), 218. See Kassow's book for a full treatment of the *Oyneg shabes* project.

110 Nakhmen Mayzel, "Mehuma u-mevukha ba-mosadot ha-yehudi'im be-amerika," *La-merḥav*, 24 December 1954.

111 "Public Lectures at YIVO," *Yedies* 45 (June 1952): 3*.

112 Louis H. Sobel, letter to the "Conference on Jewish Materials Claims Against Germany, Inc., New York City," 27 March 1953, p. 1, YIVO RG 584, file 74.

113 Mayzel, "Mehuma u-mevukha." On the Freeland League, see Laura Almagor, *Beyond Zion* and Adam Rovner, *In the Shadow of Zion: Promised Lands Before Israel* (New York University Press, 2014). For further discussion and Steinberg's protest letter, see Mendel Elkin, "Y. N. Shteynberg,

der yivo-tuer," in *Yitshok Nakhmen Shteynberg (gedenk-bukh). Der mentsh, zayn vort, zayn oyftu* (I. N. Steinberg Book Committee, 1961), 444–46.

114 Sobel, 1.

115 "YIVO Embarks on a Series of Major New Projects," *Yedies* 53 (June 1954): 1*–2*.

116 "Yad Vashem and Yivo Conclude Agreement," *Yedies* 52 (March 1954): 1*; Max Weinreich, letter to Uriel and Beatrice Weinreich, 12 November 1949, the Weinreich Family Papers, box 11, folder 3.

117 "Yad Vashem and Yivo Conclude Agreement," 7*.

118 Natalia Aleksiun, "The Central Jewish Historical Commission in Poland, 1944–1947," *Polin* 20 (2008): 74–97; Mark L. Smith, *The Yiddish Historians and the Struggle for a Yiddish History of the Holocaust* (Wayne State University Press, 2019), ch. 4; Ada Schein, "'Everyone Can Hold a Pen: The Documentation Project in the DP Camps in Germany,'" in *Holocaust Historiography in Context: Emergence, Challenges, Polemics and Achievements*, ed. David Bankier and Dan Michman (Yad Vashem, 2008), 103–23.

119 Smith, *The Yiddish Historians*, 102. For a personal account of work on the project, see Joseph Gar, *Viderklangen. Oytobiografishe fartseykhenungen*, vol. 2 (Farlag "Hamenora," 1971).

120 Smith, *Yiddish Historians*, 112.

121 Smith, *Yiddish Historians*, 112–13.

122 Philip Friedman and Jacob Robinson, *Guide to Jewish History Under Nazi Impact* (New York: YIVO, 1960); Phillip Friedman, *Bibliografiya shel ha-sefarim ha-'ivri'im 'al ha-sho'a ve-'al ha-gevura* (Yad Vashem, 1960); and Phillip Friedman and Joseph Gar, *Bibliografye fun yidishe bikher vegn khurbn un gvure* (New York: YIVO, 1962).

123 Biographical note, YIVO RG 483 Papers of Isaiah Trunk; Smith, *Yiddish Historians*, 26–27, 84.

124 Isaiah Trunk, *Lodzher geto* (New York: YIVO and Yad Vashem, 1962). It was later published in English by Trunk's student, historian Robert Moses Schapiro as *Łódź Ghetto: A History*, trans. and ed. Robert Moses Shapiro (Bloomington: Indiana University Press, 2006); "Archives of the Lodz Judenrat at YIVO," *Yedies* 27 (June 1948): *1–*2.

125 Isaiah Trunk, *Judenrat: The Jewish Councils in Eastern Europe Under Nazi Occupation* (New York: Macmillan, 1972).

126 "Colloquium on the German-Imposed Jewish 'Representations,'" *Yedies* 104 (December 1967): 1*.

127 Shatzky is quoted in Jan Schwarz, *Survivors and Exiles: Yiddish Culture After the Holocaust* (Wayne State University Press, 2015), 104.

128 Raul Hilberg, "The Development of Holocaust Research—A Personal Overview," in Bankier and Michman, 25–36.

129 On the contributions of the group of survivor scholars who wrote primarily in Yiddish, see Smith, *The Yiddish Historians*. On Friedman specifically, see Roni Stauber, "Philip Friedman and the Beginning of Holocaust Studies," in Bankier and Michman, 83–102. On Trunk, see Véronique Mickisch, "Jewish Historiography Between Socialism and Nationalism: A Portrait of Historian Isaiah Trunk," *Jewish Social Studies* 21, no. 1 (Winter 2022): 150–84.

130 "The YIVO and the Eichmann Affair," *Yedies* 76 (October 1960): 4*; "Der yivo un der aykhman-inyen," *Yedies* 76 (October 1960): 4.

131 Diner, *We Remember with Reverence*, 93; I take the term "myth of silence" from the subtitle of Diner's book. Kuznitz, "Yiddish Studies," 556–57.

132 "Warsaw Ghetto Exhibition Touring the Country," *Yedies* 90 (June 1964): 2*.

133 YIVO RG 100, box 138, folder 4 Visnshaftlekhe-kolegye 1954, minutes of meeting 1 December 1954.

Chapter 4

1 Rebecca Margolis, *Yiddish Lives On! Strategies of Language Transmission* (McGill-Queen's University Press, 2023), x; Alec Eliezer Burko, "Saving Yiddish: Yiddish Studies and the Language Sciences in America, 1940–1970" (PhD diss., Jewish Theological Seminary, 2019), 17.

2 Boris Smolyar, "Hundert yor yidishe imigratsye keyn amerike," *Forverts*, 5 June 1966.

3 Uriel Weinreich, "Yiddish Studies at Columbia University," *Freeland* (New York) January–February 1953: 14; "Dr. A. A. Roback, Noted Psychologist and Strong Supporter of Yiddish, Dead," *JTA* 8 June 1965, www.jta.org/archive/dr-a-a-roback-noted-psychologist-and-strong-supporter-of-yiddish-dead. Roback's book received largely negative reviews from Yiddish and English critics. He defended his work in his

Psychology Through Yiddish Literature: Apologia Pro Vita Yiddicia (Sci-Art Publishers, 1942).

4 "Yiddish in the Curriculum of American Colleges," *Yedies* 23 (November 1947): 3; Anonymous, "Some Facts About Yiddish Instruction in NY Since 1947," 3 July 1952, YIVO RG 584, folder 27d; Jeffrey S. Gurock, *Jews in Gotham: New York Jews in a Changing City, 1920–2010* (New York University Press, 2012), 48.

5 P. Berman [Max Weinreich], "Yidishe literatur far der amerikaner yugnt," *Forverts*, 1 June 1947.

6 Moshe David, "Ha-lashon ha-yidit meta, hi shayekhet la-teḥum ha-akademi, savur prof' liptsin," 23 February 1973. Joshua Fishman recalled that Liptzin's Yiddish was full of Anglicisms and Germanisms but that he easily made himself understood (Joshua Fishman, interview with author, Bronx, New York, 26 August 2010).

7 Stuart Dow, "The Man Who Made Yiddish Respectable," *Jerusalem Post*, 6 May 1989.

8 Sol Liptzin, letter to Max Weinreich, 28 July 1947, YIVO RG 584, folder 263.

9 Liptzin to Weinreich, 28 July 1947, YIVO RG 584, folder 263; Kalman Weiser, "Saving Yiddish, Saving American Jewry: Max Weinreich in 1940s New York City," in *Languages of Modern Jewish Culture: Comparative Perspectives*, ed. Anita Norich and Joshua Miller (University of Michigan Press, 2016), 215.

10 Max Weinreich, letter to Sol Liptzin, 25 July 1947, YIVO RG 584, folder 263.

11 Mordkhe Asnim, "Di studentn," *Yugntruf* 9, no. 1 (September–October 1948): 6–7; "Weinreich, Internationally Famous Philologist, Author, Teaches Yiddish," *UCLA Bruin* (Los Angeles), 27 July 1948; "Yivo Grants 12 Scholarship for Study of Yiddish Language and Literature," *Yedies* 27 (June 1948): 5*; "Courses in Yiddish and Yiddish Folklore at the University of California," *Yedies* 28 (September 1948): 3*.

12 Max Weinreich, "Der yivo in yidishn lebn," *Yivo bleter* 23, no. 1 (January–February 1944): 8–9; Joshua Fishman, interview with author.

13 "Yivo Grants 12 Scholarships," 5*. For information about Weinreich's time at UCLA and developments in the lives of course participants, see Mark L. Smith's 2014 article, "UCLA's First Yiddish Moment: Max

Weinreich at UCLA in 1948," *UCLA: The UCLA Alan D. Leve Center for Jewish Studies*, escholarship.org/uc/item/4bz3jowz.

14 Zaynvl Diamant, "Mlotek, Yoysef [Joseph] (July 25, 1918–July 2, 2000)," in Fogel, *Leksikon fun der nayer yidisher literatur*, congressforjewishculture.org/people/2829/Mlotek-Yoysef. On the collection of testimonies, see Miriam Schulz, *Der Beginn des Untergangs. Die Zerstörung der jüdischen Gemeinden in Polen und das Vermächtnis des Wilnaer Komitees* (Metropol, 2016).

15 Max Weinreich, "Problemen fun yidishn kiem in amerike," *Di tsukunft* (May 1951): 203–7.

16 P. Berman [Max Weinreich], "Vu mir haltn mit lernen yidish in di amerikaner universitetn," *Forverts*, 4 September 1952.

17 For student evaluation from Max Weinreich's courses at CCNY, see YIVO RG 584, folder 214. Wolf Younin published a series of articles about Yiddish in universities August-September 1953 in the *Tog morgen-zhurnal*.

18 Uriel Weinreich, *Yidish la-universita. Mavo la-lashon yidish ve-tarbuta* (Magness Press, 1977).

19 Jeffrey Shandler, "*College Yiddish*: An Appreciation," in Uriel Weinreich, *College Yiddish: An Introduction to the Yiddish Language and to Jewish Life and Culture* 6th rev. ed. (New York: YIVO, 1999), 3; Isaac Bleaman, "Uriel Weinreich: Contact Linguist, Historical Linguist, and Yiddishist Par Excellence," *Journal of Jewish Languages* 5 (2017): 131–33; "Uriel Weinreich (1926–1967)," *Yedies* 102 (June 1967): 1–2, 1*–2*.

20 Max Weinreich, letter to Uriel Weinreich, 15 July 1946, Weinreich Family Papers, box 9.

21 Rakhmiel Peltz, "Uriel vaynraykh: di brik tsvishn mizrekh-eyrope un amerike," *Afn shvel* 378–79 (Winter/Spring 2018): 45.

22 Shandler, "*College Yiddish*: An Appreciation," 1–7; Jeffrey Shandler, *Adventures in Yiddishland: Post-Vernacular Language & Culture* (University of California Press, 2006), 86.

23 Weinreich, *College Yiddish*, 30.

24 Weinreich, *College Yiddish*, 82.

25 Weinreich, *College Yiddish*, 58.

26 Weinreich, *College Yiddish*, 144.

27 Weinreich, *College Yiddish*, 34.

28 Weinreich, *College Yiddish*, 35.

29 On the lack of religious education and traditional Jewish observance in his upbringing, see Gabriel Weinreich's memoir, *Confessions of a Jewish Priest* and Lucy Dawidowicz, *From That Place and Time* (Bantam Books, 1989), 116.

30 Weinreich's appreciation for the role of Judaism as a religious culture in shaping Yiddish and Ashkenazic life is evident in, for example, his essay "Yidishkayt and Yiddish. On the Impact of Religion on Language in Ashkenazic Jewry," in *Mordecai M. Kaplan Jubilee Volume*, ed. Moshe Davis (Jewish Theological Seminary, 1953), 481–514.

31 On YIVO's relationship to *Commentary*, see Markus Krah, *American Jewry and the Re-Invention of the East European Jewish Past* (De Gruyter, 2018), ch. 2.

32 Ralph Weiman, "*College Yiddish* by Uriel Weinreich. Yiddish Scientific Institute—YIVO. 397 pp. $4.50," *Commentary* 10 (1 January 1950): 98–99.

33 Allan F. Hubbell, "A Yiddish Grammar," *American Speech* 25, no. 3 (October 1950): 210.

34 S. Lomanitz, "Books Abroad," *American Speech* 24, no. 2 (Spring 1950): 202.

35 Max Weinreich, letter to Uriel and Beatrice Weinreich, 1 May 1950, Weinreich Family Papers, box 12.

36 On Atran and the creation of the Yiddish chair at Columbia, see Andrew Sunshine, "The Making of a Chair: Uriel Weinreich and the Yiddish Chair at Columbia University," in *EYDES (Evidence of Yiddish Documented in European Societies): The Language and Culture Atlas of Ashkenazic Jewry*, ed. Marvin Herzog et al., vol. 5 (Max Niemayer Verlag, 2008), 305–26.

37 Max Weinreich, letter to Regina Weinreich, 29 November 1951, Weinreich Family Papers, box 12.

38 Sunshine, "The Making of a Chair," 323, note 38.

39 Andrew Sunshine, "Weinreich, Uriel (1926–1967)," in *Encyclopedia of Language & Linguistics*, ed. Keith Brown, 2nd ed., vol. 13 (Elsevier, 2006), 543–44; Sunshine, "The Making of a Chair," 306–26; Bleaman, "Uriel Weinreich," 135.

40 Uriel Weinreich, ed., *Field of Yiddish: Studies in Language, Folklore, and Literature* (Linguistic Circle of New York, 1954); Uriel Weinreich, ed., *Field of Yiddish: Studies in Language, Folklore, and Literature*, Second

Collection (Mouton, 1965); Marvin I. Herzog et al., eds., *Field of Yiddish: Studies in Language, Folklore, and Literature*, Third Collection (Mouton, 1969).

41 Rakhmiel Peltz, "Recovering Uriel Weinreich's Research on Yiddish Culture in Eastern Europe," lecture, YIVO Institute for Jewish Research, 12 March 2013, www.youtube.com/watch?v=uE25FIF-0EA; Peltz, "Uriel vaynraykh," 49–50.

42 William Labov and Gillian Sankoff, *Conversations with Strangers* (Cambridge University Press, 2023), 13. On Uriel Weinreich's scholarly contributions, particularly as a general linguist, see Bleaman, "Uriel Weinreich," and also William Labov, "Uriel Weinreich: Builder on Empirical Foundations," *Journal of Jewish Languages* 5 (2017): 253–66.

43 Ruth Wisse, "The Poet from Vilna," *Jewish Review of Books* (online edition, Summer 2010).

44 On Baron's career at Columbia, which is widely seen as marking the beginning of Jewish studies in America, see Rebecca Kobrin, ed., *Salo Baron: The Past and Future of Jewish Studies in America* (Columbia University Press, 2022) and Robert Liberles, *Salo Wittmayer Baron: Architect of Jewish history* (New York University Press, 1995).

45 On Columbia's attitudes toward Jews in the first half of the twentieth century, see Stephen H. Norwood, "Complicity and Conflict: Columbia University's Response to Fascism, 1933–1937," *Modern Judaism* 27, no. 3 (October 2007): 253–83. Also, "Columbia and Its Forgotten Jewish Campus," the first episode of the podcast *Gate Crashers*, www.tabletmag.com/sections/community/articles/gatecrashers-podcast-jews-ivy-league#e1ed7f29b180.

46 Uriel Weinreich, "Yiddish Studies at Columbia University," *Freeland* January–February 1953, 14; S. Regensburg, "Di katedre far yidish in brandayz-univerzitet," *Forverts*, 27 October 1960; Edward S. Schapiro, *A Time for Healing: American Jewry Since World War II* (Johns Hopkins University Press, 1992), 76–92.

47 Shandler, *Adventures in Yiddishland*, 16; Deborah Dash Moore, *At Home in America: Second Generation New York Jews* (Columbia University Press, 1981).

48 On American Jewish attitudes toward the eastern European past, see Steven J. Zipperstein, *Imagining Russian Jewry: Memory, History, Identity* (University of Washington Press, 1999). On *Life Is*

with People, see Krah, *American Jewry*, esp. ch. 7; and Barbara Kirshenblatt-Gimblett, introduction to *Life Is with People: The Culture of the Shtetl*, Mark Zborowski and Elizabeth Herzog (Schocken, 1995), ix–xlviii. On American Jewish ambivalence, Rachel Kranson, *Ambivalent Embrace: Jewish Upward Mobility in Postwar America* (University of North Carolina Press, 2017); Hasia R. Diner, *The Jews of the United States, 1654–2000* (University of California Press, 2004), 283–91; and Daniel Soyer, *Jewish Immigrant Associations and American Identity in New York, 1800–1939* (Wayne State University Press, 2001), ch. 8.

49 Diner, *Jews of the United States*, ch. 8; Schapiro, *A Time for Healing*, 201–3. On the postwar development of Jewish studies in the context of cultural changes among American Jewry, see Schapiro, *A Time for Healing*, 70–93; Paul Ritterband and Harold S. Wechsler, *Jewish Learning in American Universities: The First Century* (Indiana University Press, 1994), ch. 8; and Leon A. Jick et al., "Jewish Studies," *Encyclopaedia Judaica*, ed. Michael Berenbaum and Fred Skolnik, 2nd ed., vol. 11 (Macmillan Reference USA, 2007), 316–27. On interest in Yiddish specifically, see Joshua Fishman, "Di sotsiologye fun yidish in amerike: 1960–1970 un vayter," *Di goldene keyt* 75 (1972): 110–27; Joshua A. Fishman, *Yiddish in America: Sociolinguistic Description and Analysis* (Indiana University; the Hague: Mouton & Co., 1965); and Leonard Prager, "Yiddish in the University," *Jewish Quarterly* 22, nos. 1–2 (1974): 31–40.

50 Kalman Weiser, "The 'Orthodox' Orthography of Solomon Birnbaum." *Studies in Contemporary Jewry* 20 (2004): 284–86; Dovid Katz, "The Religious Prestige of the Gaon and the Secular Prestige of Lithuanian Yiddish," in *The Gaon of Vilna and the Annals of Jewish Culture*, ed. Izraelis Lempertas (Vilnius: 1998), 187–99; Dovid Katz, "Naye gilgulim fun alte makhloykesn: di litvishe norme un di sikhsukhim vos arum ir," *Yivo bleter*, n.s., no. 2 (1994): 205–57.

51 Max Weinreich, "Vegn englishe elementn in undzer kultursphrakh," *Yidishe shprakh* 1, no. 2 (1941): 34.

52 Max Weinreich, "Amerikaner yidish," in *Algemeyne entsiklopedye*, vol. 3 (Dubnov-fond, 1936), 320–22.

53 Gabriel Weinreich recalls, for example, that speaking Yiddish well in his family in postwar America meant speaking "consistently"

(*oysgehaltn*)—that is, without mixing dialectal pronunciations (Gabriel Weinreich, interview with author, Ann Arbor, MI, 18 July 2009).

54 Teresa L. McCarty, "Questions for Gella Schweid Fishman," *Language Policy* (2010) 9:360. On Yiddish schools, see Fradle Pomerantz Freidenreich, *Passionate Pioneers: The Story of Yiddish Secular Education in North America, 1910–1960* (Holmes & Meier, 2010); Naomi Prawer Kadar, *Raising Secular Jews: Yiddish Schools and Their Periodicals for American Children, 1917–1950* (Brandeis University Press, 2016); and Burko, "Saving Yiddish," ch. 1.

55 Uriel Weinreich, "Tsu der frage vegn a normirter oysshprakh," *Yidishe shprakh* 11 (1951): 27.

56 Max Weinreich, "A merkverdiker tsuzamenfor fun frume yidishe shrayber in poyln," *Forverts*, 13 August 1939.

57 Rakhmiel Peltz, "The Politics of Research on Spoken Yiddish," in *Politics of Yiddish: Studies in Language, Literature, and Society*, ed. Dov Ber Kerler (AltaMira Press, 1998), 64–67.

58 Solomon Poll, "The Role of Yiddish in American Ultra-Orthodox and Hassidic Communities," *YIVO Annual* 13 (1965): 125–52, reprinted in Joshua A. Fishman, *Never Say Die! A Thousand Tears of Yiddish in Jewish Life and Letters* (Mouton Publishers, 1981), 197–218; Yosseph Shilhav and Lewis Glinert, "Holy Land, Holy Language," *Language and Society* 20 (1991): 59–86.

59 Kalman Weiser, "The Fallenness of *Haredi* Folk," *Journal of Jewish Identities* (forthcoming, 2026).

60 "Session of the Social Science Circle," *Yedies* 82 (April 1962): 2*. For more extensive discussion of efforts to promote Yiddish in postwar "Hungarian" Hasidic communities in Brooklyn, see Chaya Rachel Nove, "Phonetic Contrast in New York Hasidic Yiddish Vowels: Language Contact, Variation, and Change" (PhD diss., City University of New York, 2021), esp. 14–32.

61 Burko, "Saving Yiddish," 86; Alec Eliezer Burko, "Did the YIVO Linguists Disregard Hasidic Yiddish?," YIVO Institute for Jewish Research, 29 June 2022, www.youtube.com/watch?v=S9AgbDD8440&t=2308s.

62 On *klal* Yiddish: *Gramatik fun der yidisher klal-shprakh* (Alveltlekher kultur-kongres, 1978).

63 Holocaust survivor Gininger, who felt indebted to Weinreich for his assistance in coming to America and finding employment, faced poor health and financial hardships. Unable to establish a satisfying career, he chiefly blamed Uriel Weinreich for not employing him to teach language courses at Columbia and accused his student Mordkhe Schaechter of "stealing" his ideas. On Birnbaum's attitudes toward YIVO and its standardization of Yiddish, see Kalman Weiser, "*Yiddish: A Survey and a Grammar* in Its Historical and Cultural Context," in K. Weiser et al., eds., 2nd revised ed. of Solomon Birnbaum, *Yiddish: A Survey and a Grammar* (University of Toronto Press, 2016), xxiv–lvii; and on Gininger's attitudes, see Chaim Gininger, "A bukh tsu lernen yidish," *Yivo bleter* 33 (1949): 210. On Gininger's relationship to the Weinreichs and YIVO, see his correspondence with Birnbaum in the Gininger folder in the Nathan and Solomon Birnbaum and Family Archives, Toronto, ON, and Gininger's collection in YIVO (RG 1384 Papers of Chaim Gininger).

64 Kalman Weiser, "Where Is the Capital of Yiddishland?," in *Warsaw. The Jewish Metropolis: Essays in Honor of the 75th Birthday of Professor Antony Polonsky*, ed. Glenn Dynner and François Guesnet (Brill, 2015), 298–322; Cecile Esther Kuznitz, *YIVO and the Making of Modern Jewish Culture* (Cambridge University Press, 2014), 168–72; Weiser, "The 'Orthodox' Orthography."

65 Max Weinreich, "Di ershte yidishe tsaytungen in amerike un zeyer aynflus oyf der yidisher shprakh," *Forverts*, 22 August 1937; Tony Michels, *A Fire in the Their Hearts: Yiddish Socialists in New York* (Harvard University Press, 2005), ch. 2.

66 Burko, "Saving Yiddish," 127–28.

67 For more on debates about *daytshmerish*, see Hirshe-Dovid Kats (Dovid Katz), *Tikney-takones. Fragn fun yidisher stilistik* (Oksforder Yidish Press and Oxford Centre for Post-Graduate Hebrew Studies, 1993), esp. 166–85.

68 Kuznitz, *YIVO and the Making*, 84.

69 Yudel Mark, "Neologizmen bay maks vaynraykhn," in *Maks vaynraykhn tsu zayn zibetsikstn geboyrn-tog / For Max Weinreich on His Seventieth Birthday: Studies in Jewish Languages, Literature, and Society*, ed. Lucy S. Dawidowicz et al. (Mouton, 1964), 412–35. See also Burko, "Saving Yiddish," esp. ch. 2; Dan Miron, "Between Science and Faith: Sixty Years of the YIVO Institute," *YIVO Annual* 19 (1990): 13.

70 Yitskhok Varshavski [I. B. Singer], "Der yidish vos m'hot geredt in alter heym vert fargesn," *Forverts*, 13 March 1944.

71 M. K., "A diskusye vegn der shprakh in di oysgabes fun yivo," *Yidishe shprakh* 2 (1942): 49–50.

72 Beatrice Weinreich, "A bintl perzenlekhe zikhroynes," Max Weinreich memorial, YIVO, 4 December 1994, Weinreich Family Papers, box 1.

73 M. K., "A diskusye vegn der shprakh," 51. The translation is Leyzer Burko's (Burko, "Saving Yiddish," 100).

74 YIVO RG 100, box 49-9, folder algemeyns 1949. Weinreich described Shatzky's manuscript to his son Uriel as "carelessly written" (Max Weinreich, letter to Uriel Weinreich, 3 February 1946, Weinreich Family Papers, box 9). Shatzky completed only three of four volumes of his *Geshikhte fun yidn in varshe* prior to his death.

75 Mordkhe Schaechter, "Fun folkshprakh tsu kultursphrakh," in YIVO, *Der eynheytlekher yidisher oysleyg* (New York: YIVO and Yiddish Language Resource Center of the Yiddish League, 1999), 40.

76 "Fun folk tsu folk," *Forverts*, 24 November 1955.

77 "Fun folk tsu folk," *Forverts*, 20 December 1955.

78 Schaechter, "Fun folkshprakh tsu kultursphrakh," 40–41.

79 Such measures included the elimination of an apostrophe to offset elements of Hebrew-Aramaic origin from elements of other provenance in a specific word and the suppression of the "silent" (*shtume*) *ayin* before the *nun* in words such as "yedens, merstens, untervegens, trayben, krekhtsen, shtupen" (each one's, mainly, on the way, drive, moan, push) where he maintained that the *ayin* actually represented an audible vowel. He also objected to YIVO's use of a *daled* to represent the affricate in such words as *haldz* (instead of *halz*—neck—in the newspaper's system), the pluralization of words such as *arbeter* (worker) with a *samekh* (*arbeters* instead of *arbeter*), and the placement of a hyphen in compound words of more than three syllables (e.g., *arbeter-ring*, "Workmen's Circle") or between compound words containing nouns of both Semitic and non-Semitic origin, for example (*dire-gelt* for "rent"). Shimen Weber, "Darf men endern dem yidishn oysleyg?" *Forverts*, 31 December 1965.

80 Weber, "Darf men endern dem yidishn oysleyg?"

81 Shimen Weber, "A lektsye vi azoy tsu shraybn yidish," *Forverts*, 13 May 1961.

82 "The First World Conference of Yiddish Studies," *Yedies* 68 (July 1958): 1*–2*, 5*–8*; "A Significant YIVO Exhibition. The Yiddish Language: Its History and Study," *Yedies* 68 (July 1958): 3*–4*.

83 "Durkhfirung fun eynheytlekhn oysleyg," *Lebnsfragn*, 1 April 1959.

84 "Naye shtendike yivo-zamlers in eyrope," *Yedies* 39 (December 1950): 6; Mordkhe Schaechter, interview with author, New York City, 26 October 1994. On the Freeland League after World War II, see Laura Almagor, "A Territory, but Not a State—The Territorialists' Visions for a Jewish Future After the Shoah (1943–1960)," *S:I.M.O.N. (Shoah: Intervention. Methods. Documentation.)* 1 (2022): 93–108.

85 Max Weinreich, letter to Uriel and Beatrice Weinreich, 23 August 1951, Weinreich Family Papers, box 12.

86 See, for example, Shimen Weber, "A lektsye vi azoy tsu shraybn yidish," *Forverts*, 13 May 1961. Avrom Shulman praised Schaechter's devotion to Yiddish but objected to words such as "yert zikh" (grows a year older, has a birthday) and "parshoyndlekh" (persons) ("Dr. maks vaynraykh, 'yert zikh tsum 70stn mol' . . ." *Forverts*, 20 March 1965). Yankev Raykh scoffed, for example, at *nayert* (rather) as an antiquated word found in his mother's old-fashioned Bible translations. "Emeser mame-loshn oder gekintselter yidish," *Forverts*, 23 June 1968. Aaron Zeitlin (*Der tog morgn-zhurnal* [New York], 13 September 1969) cautioned Schaechter to remember that "a philologist is not a law-giver of a language but its caretaker and guardian" (cited in B. Raynus, "Shtrikhn," *Fraye arbeter shtime*, 1 October 1969).

87 "Guide to Standardized Orthography Published," *Yedies* 78 (April 1961): 5*; Schaechter, "Fun folkshprakh tsu kultursprakh," 76–83; Burko, "Saving Yiddish," 102, 197.

88 Max Weinreich, letter to Meylekh Ravitch, 17 February 1961, Meylekh Ravitch Collection, Archive, the Hebrew University, Jerusalem, ARC 4 1540.

89 YIVO, *Takones fun yidishn oysleyg* (Vilna: YIVO, 1937); "A Course in Standardized YIVO Orthography," *Yedies* 95 (September 1965): 1*; "Exhibit on Yiddish Orthography," *Yedies* 96 (December 1965): 3*; Rakhmiel Peltz, "Planning for the Jewish Future: Standards for Yiddish in the 20th and 21st Centuries," lecture, YIVO Institute for Jewish Research, New York, 17 February 2015, www.youtube.com/watch?v=TBfacK3roBA. Schaechter's course formed the basis of his

publication "Fun folkshprakh tsu kultursphrakh" in YIVO, *Der eyn-heytlekher yidisher oysleyg*.

90 Yitskhok Varshavski [I. B. Singer], "Der yidish vos m'hot geredt in alter heym vert fargesn"; Yitskhok Varshavski, "Tsvey oyfgabes farn yidishn visnshaftlekhnn institut," *Forverts*, 25 December 1948.

91 Burko, "Saving Yiddish," 154.

92 Burko, "Saving Yiddish," 155–57. An example of a positive review is Dr. H. Frank, "A naye shatskamer fun undzer shprakh-oytser," *Fraye arbeter shtime*, 29 September 1950. For excerpts of positive reviews, see "YIVO Publication Accorded Enthusiastic Reception," *Yedies* 38 (September 1950): *6; and "Oprufn vegn yivo-oysgabes," *Yedies* 38 (September 1950): 6.

93 Burko, "Saving Yiddish," 156–57.

94 Burko, "Saving Yiddish," 158–60.

95 Ezekiel Lifschutz, Diary, 14 December 1968, Ezekiel Lifschutz Private Collection, P130/202, Central Archives for the History of the Jewish People, Jerusalem.

96 Burko, "Saving Yiddish," 150.

97 Kuznitz, *YIVO and the Making*, 53; Mark, "Zikhroynes fun yudl mark," *Forverts*, 28 September 2012.

98 Yudel Mark, letter to Dov Sadan, 21 May 1965, YIVO RG 540, folder 219, cited in Burko, "Saving Yiddish," 5; Lifschutz, "Dr. Max Weinreich." Miriam Hoffman attributes to Mark and Weinreich a rivalry that was also rooted in what she sees as Weinreich's jealousy of the physical attractiveness and popularity of the tall and handsome Mark, who was considered an excellent orator despite possessing a high-pitched voice (Miriam Hoffman, interview with author, New York City, 14 May 2013).

99 Burko, "Saving Yiddish," 165.

100 Cited in Burko, "Saving Yiddish," 167.

101 Mordecai Kosover, *Arabic Elements in Palestinian Yiddish: The Old Ashkenazic Jewish Community in Palestine, Its History and Its Language* (Ruben Mass, 1966); Isaac Rivkind, *Der kamf kegn azartshpiln bay yidn, a shtudye in finf hundert yor yidishe poezye un kultur-geshikhte* (New York: YIVO, 1946). His best-known lexicographic study is *Yidishe gelt in lebnsshteyger, kultur-geshikhte un folklor. A leksikologishe shtudye* (Ha-akademya ha-amerikanit le-mada'e ha-yahadut, 1959).

102 M. Mratshni, “Tsayt-komentarn,” *Fraye arbeter shtime*, 28 January 1955.
103 Burko, “Saving Yiddish,” 103, 170–72.
104 Burko, “Saving Yiddish,” 165–68. Lifschutz deplored what he considered the carelessness with which the *Leksikon* was edited, noting that is “It is dry and full of errors since the deaths of Shatzky and Niger” (Lifschutz, Diary, 18 February 1962). On the *Algemeyne entsiklopedye*, see Barry Trachtenberg, *The Holocaust and the Exile of Yiddish: A History of the Algemeyne Entsiklopedye* (Rutgers University Press, 2022).
105 The Yiddish *Forverts*, for example, introduced in 2013 a rubric titled “Idish mit an alef” for writings by authors originating in *haredi* circles, where the silent alef remains in use: blogs.yiddish.forward.com/yiddish-with-an-aleph/index.html. The dictionary (and its orthographic controversy) is likely the only one to be the subject of an opera: composer Alex Weiser and librettist Ben Kaplan’s 2024 *The Great Dictionary of the Yiddish Language* (www.alexweiser.com/works/the-great-dictionary-of-the-yiddish-language).
106 Burko, “Saving Yiddish,” 176–78.
107 Burko, “Saving Yiddish,” 32.
108 Yudel Mark, “The Great Dictionary of the Yiddish Language,” *Jewish Cultural News* 6 (6 October 1973): 2–4; Burko, “Saving Yiddish,” 177.
109 Yudel Mark, “Dr. maks vaynraykh,” *Forverts*, 9 February 1969.
110 Shikl (Joshua) Fishman, “Zikhroynes vegn maks vaynraykh,” *Yivo bleter* n.s., no. 3 (1997): 352–53.
111 “Oyfklerung fun yivo,” in *Groyser verterbukh fun der yidisher shprakh*, ed. Judah A. Joffe and Yudel Mark (Komitet farn groysn verterbukh fun der yidisher shprakh, 1961), 7.
112 Joffe and Mark, *Groyser verterbukh*, 22–23.
113 A. Shin, “Di debate arum verterbukh,” *Fraye arbeter shtime*, 1 September 1960.
114 S. Dingol, “Di vokh in yidishn lebn,” *Der tog* (New York), 2 July 1960; A. Shin, “Di debate arum groysn verterbukh,” *Fraye arbeter shtime*, 15 September 1960.
115 Leyzer [Alex Eliezer] Burko, “Nokh tsvey bend funem nisht-farendiktn ‘groysn verterbukh’ zaynen itst tsutritlekh onlayn,” *Forverts*, 13 May 2024, forward.com/yiddish/612736/two-volumes-of-the-uncompleted-great-yiddish-dictionary-are-now-online/. The scans of the

additional two volumes and more information about the project can be found here: yiddish5-6.com/.

116 Uriel Weinreich, "Multilingual Dialectology and the New Yiddish Atlas," *Anthropological Linguistics* 4, no. 1 (1962): 6–22; Robert King, "On the Uses of Yiddish Language Geography," *Shofar* 17 (1998): 81–98.

117 Janina Wurbs, "A Treasure Trove in a Hotel Lobby—Songs of the Ben Stonehill Collection at the YIVO Sound Archives," *European Journal of Jewish Studies* 8 (2014): 127–36. Miriam Isaacs has produced a website with digitized songs from this collection: stonehilljewishsongs .wordpress.com/.

118 The book, which yielded a highly romanticized image of the shtetl, itself proved tremendously influential as one of the primary texts—alongside Sholem Aleichem's stories of Tevye—for the Broadway musical *Fiddler on the Roof.* While favorably reviewed by Weinreich and in the Yiddish press, Yudel Mark considered the study a methodologically flawed distortion of shtetl life that was also full of basic errors about Jewish culture (Yudel Mark, "The Shtetl in Retrospect: Pseudo Science," *The Jewish Frontier* [June 1952]: 25–27.) Steven J. Zipperstein, "Underground Man: The Curious Case of Mark Zborowski and the Writing of a Modern Jewish Classic," *Jewish Review of Books* Summer 2010.

119 Asher Penn, "Yidishe froy krigt a doktor-titl far ir arbet vegn yidish," *Der tog morgn-zhurnal*, 22 June 1953.

120 King, "Yiddish Language Geography," 81–98; Andrew Sunshine, "Computers and the *Language and Culture Atlas of Ashkenazic Jewry*: The 1960s," *Jewish Folklore and Ethnology Review* 16, no. 1 (1994): 13–14; Miriam Hoffman, *A Breed Apart: Reflections of a Young Refugee* (Yiddishkayt Press), 147–56.

121 Burko, "Saving Yiddish," ch. 5.

122 A. Varshever, "Vos yivo hot dergraykht in zayne 40 yor," *Der tog*, 10 May 1966. I thank Gennady Estraikh for helping me to identify A. Varshever.

123 Varshever, "Vos yivo hot dergraykht."

124 Boris Smolyar, "Poblik skul lerer oyf yidishe kursn," *Forverts*, 24 July 1966.

125 "Yivo vet aroysgebn vaynraykhs geshikhte fun yidisher shprakh," *Der tog*, 2 May 1966.

126 Max Weinreich, “Der yivo in finftn tsendling. Referat fun maks vaynraykh bay der efenung fun der fertsikster yoyvl-konferents fun yivo dem 30stn April 1966,” 5, YIVO RG 584, folder 716b.
127 Lifschutz, Diary, 21 January 1965.
128 “Jewish Participation in Social Progress Movements,” *Yedies* 91 (September 1964): 1*.
129 See, for example, Meylekh Ravitsh’s mixed comments about Joshua Fishman and Moses Rischin (Meylekh Ravitsh, “24ste konferents fun yivo,” *The Australian Jewish News*, 6 April 1950) and Ezekiel Lifschutz praise for Zvi Gitelman’s “good Yiddish diction (without strong signs of English)” (Lifschutz, Diary, 21 January 1965).
130 “YIVO vet aroysgebn vaynraykhs geshikhte fun yidisher shprakh.”
131 “Shmuel Lapin Appointed General Secretary of YIVO,” *Yedies* 99 (September 1966): 4*; “Shmuel Lapin, 43, Expert on Yiddish,” *New York Times*, 6 February 1973.
132 “Dorem-amerikaner yidn gefinen zikh in klem tsvishn kemfndike koykhes, hert yivo-konferents,” 24 December 1964; “Isidore David Passow Appointed Executive Secretary of the YIVO,” *Yedies* 84 (October 1962): 4*.
133 Irena Klepfisz, “Remembering the Warsaw Ghetto Uprising Today,” *Tablet*, 24 April 2017, www.tabletmag.com/sections/news/articles/remembering-warsaw-ghetto-uprising. Lapin’s wife, Chava, a Montreal-born and raised chemist educated in that city’s Yiddish secular schools, would too come to play an important role in the institute, particularly following her husband’s untimely death in 1973.
134 “Committee on Research Planning,” *Yedies* 84 (October 1962): 4*.
135 Weinerich, “Der yivo in finftn tsendling,” 8–9.
136 Weinreich, “Der yivo in finftn tsendling,” 11.
137 Burko, “Saving Yiddish,” 81–82.
138 On this subject, see Kalman Weiser, “‘Barg-aroyf’ or ‘Uphill’? Max Weinreich and the Changing Meaning of the First Yiddish Language Conference in Czernowitz, 1908–1958,” in *Zukunft der Sprache, Zukunft der Nation. Debatten um jüdische Sprache und Literatur im Kontext von Mehrsprachigkeit und Nationbuilding*, ed. Carmen Reichert et al. (De Gruyter, 2022), 17–36.
139 Burko, “Saving Yiddish,” 85.

140 The most prominent scholarly opponents of YIVO Yiddish-language norms in the late twentieth century were Solomon Birnbaum and the much younger Yiddish scholar Dovid Katz. Both offer their own spelling conventions. Birnbaum's *Yiddish: A Survey and a Grammar* represents a neotraditionalist school of Yiddish linguistics and language standardization that abjures YIVO's secularism but shares a staunch anti-*daytshmerish* stance. Katz's *Tikney-takones*, in contrast, argues for recognition of borrowings from modern German as a genuine element of the language that adds semantic and stylistic nuance when wielded by capable writers.

141 Mordkhe Schaechter maintained that this was evidence of the influence of non-*haredi* publications (personal communication, 9 March 1996) but a thorough investigation of this phenomenon and the reasons behind it remains a desideratum. See also Shikl (Joshua) Fishman, "Vos kenen mir zikh oplernen fun english?," *Forverts*, 8 March 2002.

Chapter 5

1 "Groyser oylem bay efenung fun yivo konferents; baern ondenk fun gelerntn uriel vaynraykh," *Forverts*, 9 April 1967; William Labov, interview with author via Zoom, 12 June 2023; Alec Eliezer Burko, "Saving Yiddish: Yiddish Studies and the Language Sciences in America, 1940–1970" (PhD diss., Jewish Theological Seminary, 2019), 370.

2 An excerpt from Heschel's eulogy appears in Rakhmiel Peltz, "Uriel vaynraykh: di brik tsvishn mizrekh-eyrope un amerike," *Afn shvel* 378–79 (Winter/Spring 2018): 73–74.

3 Chana Mlotek, interview with author.

4 "Groyser oylem bay efenung fun yivo konferents" and "41st Conference Demonstrates YIVO's Growth," *Yedies* 102 (June 1967): 1*, 7*.

5 "Tsvey khosheve gest referentn bay efenung fun 'yivo' konferents," *Forverts*, 10 March 1967; "Di yivo konferents hert referatn vegn alter un nayer literatur," *Forverts*, 11 April 1967; Khone Shmeruk, *Peretses yiesh-vizye. Interpretatsye fun y.l. peretses bay nakht oyfn altn mark* (New York: YIVO, 1971).

6 Lifschutz, Diary, 10 April 1967.

7 "Jewish Research Institute Plans New Center Here," *New York Times*, 10 April 1967.

8 "Yivo proklamirt forshung oyfboy fund lekoved 80 yorikn yoyvl fun yudl borenshteyn," *Forverts*, 10 April 1967; "Dr. yehude shapiro vet onfirn mit nay-geshafenem tsenter far hekhere yidishe shtudyes baym 'yivo,'" *Forverts*, 26 September 1967; "Dr. Judah J. Shapiro Heads Advanced Studies Program," *Yedies* 103 (September 1967): 1*–2*; "Dr. yehude y. shapiro firt on mit program far hekhere yidishe shtudyes," *Yedies* 103 (September 1967): 1, 5.

9 "Charter for Yivo Center for Advanced Jewish Studies Obtained," *Yedies* 108 (December 1968): 4*.

10 Israel Steinbaum, *Di geshikhte fun yidishn lerer seminar un folksuniversitet in nyu-york, 1918–1968* (Jerusalem: published by committee, 1979); Burko, "Saving Yiddish," 64–66; Yudel Mark, "Vegn a fareynikung vos iz noytvendik," *Kultur un dertsiung* (New York) 7 (December 1959): 1–3; Gershon Winer, *A Memoir: Victory in Defeat* (Jerusalem: n.p., 2009), 31–34; Max Weinreich, letters to Uriel Weinreich, 10 and 13 December 1959, Weinreich Family Papers, box 10.

11 Judah Shapiro, letter to Max Weinreich, 31 January 1968, YIVO RG 658 Julius Borenstein Papers, folder 1968.

12 See, for example, Boris Smolyar, "Di rol fun 'yivo' in amerikaner yidishn lebn," *Forverts*, 9 November 1969; "'yivo'-tsenter far hekhere shtudyes fayerlekh geefnt," *Forverts*, 10 November 1969; "YIVO Center for Advanced Jewish Studies Begins Activities," *Yedies* 110 (Summer 1969): 1*.

13 Max Weinreich, letter to YIVO Administration, 28 September 1967, YIVO RG 584, box 429.

14 Judah J. Shapiro, "High School Yiddish Program," memorandum, 12 September 1967, pp. 1–2, YIVO RG 658, box 1966.

15 Shapiro, "High School Yiddish Program," p. 2.

16 Lifschutz, Diary, 27 September 1967.

17 "The Uriel Weinreich Yiddish Language Program," *Yedies* 107 (September 1968): 3*, 8*.

18 Judah Shapiro, letter to Max Atran, 25 October 1968, YIVO RG 658, folder 1968.

19 Dr. Mordecai Kossover, "Kolombiya-universitet nokh di umruen," *Forverts*, 17 November 1968.

20 "The Research Planning Committee of YIVO," *Yedies* 106 (June 1968): 8*. The other, European-born members of the committee were

Mordkhe Schaechter, the Yiddish literature scholar and ancient Near East specialist Michael Astour, and Columbia University economist Alexander Erlich.

21 James Matisoff, interview with author via Zoom, 7 February 2024.

22 Y. Shmulevitsh, "A vikhtiker kurs fun yidish in kolombiya universitet," *Forverts*, 19 August 1968; "The Uriel Weinreich Yiddish Language Program at Columbia University," *Yedies* 105 (March 1968): 1*–2*; "Akademisher limed fun yidish oysgebreytert," *Yedies* 105 (March 1968): 1–2; "The Uriel Weinreich Yiddish Language Program. A New Approach to the Teaching of Yiddish," *Yedies* 107 (September 1968): 3*, 8*.

23 "Di yidish-program fun kolumbiye un yivo,"*Yedies* 107 (September 1968): 6. See also Zachary Baker, "Getting in on the Ground: Confessions of a Yiddish Impersonator," Rosaline and Mayer Feinstein Lecture Series, Association of Jewish Libraries, 2006, p. 6, jewishlibraries.org/wp-content/uploads/2021/05/Zachary-Baker-.pdf.

24 "The Uriel Weinreich Yiddish Language Program," *Yedies* 107 (September 1968): 3*, 8*.

25 Lifschutz suggests that this was Max Weinreich's idea (Lifschutz, Diary, 27 September 1967).

26 Judah Shapiro, letter to Max Atran, 25 October 1968, YIVO RG 658 folder 1968.

27 "'Yivo' halt-op konferents fun gezelshaftlekhe tuer vegn yidish in amerike," *Forverts*, 3 October 1968.

28 Uriel Weinreich, "Memorandum" about Yiddish-English school dictionary, 1952, Weinreich Family Papers, box 1; Z. Zilberberg-Kholeva, "Uriel vaynraykh—tsu zayn 1tn yortsayt," *Forverts*, 7 April 1968; "Yiddish-English and English-Yiddish Concise Dictionary Prepared for Press," *Yedies* 93 (February 1965): *1, *4; Burko, "Saving Yiddish," 313–14.

29 Uriel Weinreich, *Modern English-Yiddish Yiddish-English Dictionary* (New York: YIVO, 1990). The citation is from Eisig Silberschlag, "Modern English-Yiddish Yiddish-English Dictionary by Uriel Weinreich," *Books Abroad* 44, no. 1 (Winter 1970): 141–42. An overview of reviews can be found in Burko, "Saving Yiddish," 331–38.

30 Boris Smolyar, "Yidish in kolombya universitet," *Forverts*, 24 March 1968.

31 Weinreich, *Confessions of a Jewish Priest* (Pilgrim Press, 2005), 97.

32 Shmuel Lapin, letter to Max Weinreich, 3 July 1968, YIVO RG 658, folder 1968.

33 Lifschutz, Diary, Monday 21 February 1966.

34 Max Weinreich, *Geshikhte fun der yidisher shprakh* (New York: YIVO, 1973); Max Weinreich, "The Reality of Yiddish Versus the Ghetto Myth: The Sociolinguistic Roots of Yiddish," in *To Honor Roman Jakobson: Essays on the Occasion of His Seventieth Birthday* (1967), 2199–2211. For a broader discussion of Weinreich's writing of his *Geshikhte*, see Burko, "Saving Yiddish," ch. 4.

35 Weinreich, letter to Pinkhos Schwartz, 30 May 1957, YIVO RG 584, folder 327.

36 Ruth Wisse, "The Poet from Vilna," *Jewish Review of Books* (online edition, Summer 2010).

37 The full translation, including notes, appeared in 2008: Max Weinreich, *History of the Yiddish Language*, ed. Paul Glasser, trans. Shlomo Noble, with the assistance of Joshua A. Fishman, 2 vols (Yale University Press, 2008).

38 The literature critiquing Weinreich's theories about the origins and development of Yiddish is sizable. For an overview, see Alexander Beider, *Origins of Yiddish Dialects* (Oxford University Press, 2016).

39 Of the group of YIVO's founders and builders, four remained alive: Abraham Golomb (Mexico City), Yudel Mark (Jerusalem), Aaron Steinberg (London), and Khayim-Shloyme Kazdan (New York).

40 "Bay levaye fun dr. m. vaynraykh," *Forverts*, 1 February 1969.

41 "Memorial Meeting for Dr. Max Weinreich," *Yedies* 109 (Spring 1969): 3*.

42 "Declaration of YIVO at the Memorial Meeting for Dr. Max Weinreich," *Yedies* 109 (Spring 1969): 3*.

43 For descriptions of Weinreich, see the sources listed in Weiser, "Max Weinreich." Jacob Glatstein, "Maks vaynraykhs binyen," *Der tog*, 6 February 1970.

44 "Shmuel Lapin (1930–1973)," *Yedies* 125 (Spring 1973): 5*; "Joseph Berg Executive Director of YIVO," *Yedies* 131–32 (Fall–Winter 1974–75): 3*; "Morris Laub Elected Chairman of YIVO," *Yedies* 137 (June 1976): 1*; "In Memory . . ." *Yedies* 178 (Fall 1992): 3.

45 "Hannah Fryshdorf (1920–1989)," *Yedies* 174 (Spring 1989): 15; Bolek Ellenbogen, "Bolek elnbogens bamerkungen bay der hazkore in

ondenk frun khane frishdorf, vos iz forgekumen in yivo-binyen dem 15tn yanuar, 1989," *Yedies* 174 (Spring 1989): 16; David Fishman, "YIVO Centennial Celebration," YIVO Institute for Jewish Research, 11 November 2025, www.youtube.com/watch?v=kxBEhxUMT7Y&t=4078s.

46 Volf Yunin, "Shprakhvinkl," *Forverts*, 12 August 1974; "Students Organize *Krayzn* at Max Weinreich Center," *Yedies* 137 (June 1976): 3*; "Folklore *Krayz* Hears Guest Speakers," *Yedies* 140 (March 1977): 3*.

47 "Working Papers in Yiddish and East European Jewish Studies," *Yedies* 131–32 (Fall–Winter 1974–75): 6*.

48 Joshua A. Fishman, "YIVO in America," *Yedies* 134 (July 1975): 8*.

49 Isaiah Trunk, "Yerlekhn yivo ovnt '50 yor yivo,'" Jewish Public Library Montreal, 13 September 1975, www.yiddishbookcenter.org/collections/archival-recordings/frances-brandt/fbr-471_4470/annual-yivo-evening-50-years-yivo-yehiel-yeshaya-trunk.

50 Trunk, "Yerlekhn yivo ovnt '50 yor yivo'"; "The Fall Semester at the Max Weinreich Center," *Yedies* 135 (December 1975): 6*.

51 Trunk, "Yerlekhn yivo ovnt '50 yor yivo.'"

52 Trunk, "Yerlekhn yivo ovnt '50 yor yivo.'"

53 Cecile Esther Kuznitz, *YIVO and the Making of Modern Jewish Culture* (Cambridge University Press, 2014), 99, 159–60, 195–98.

54 David Margolick, "Workmen's Circle: 85 Years of Aid to Jews," *New York Times*, 10 November 1985. On the comparative resilience of Yiddish in Canada, see Rebecca Margolis, *Yiddish Lives On! Strategies of Language Transmission* (McGill-Queen's University Press, 2023); and David G. Roskies, "Yiddish in Montreal: A Utopian Experiment," in *An Everyday Miracle: Yiddish Culture in Montreal*, ed. Ira Robinson et al. (Véhicule Press, 1990), 22–38. On Montreal in comparison with Vilna, see Kalman Weiser, "Vilna on the Saint Lawrence: Montreal as the Would-Be Haven for Yiddish Culture," in *No Better Home?: Canada, Its Jews, and the Question of Home*, ed. David Koffman (University of Toronto Press, 2021), 56–69.

55 Diner, *Jews of the United States*, ch. 8.

56 Steven M. Lowenstein, letter to Mr. Joseph Berg, Executive Director, 26 September 1975, YIVO RG 100, box 75-1, folder 161; David Myers, "Remembering Steven M. Lowenstein, Prominent Jewish Historian," *Forverts*, 2 June 2020.

57 Barbara Kirshenblatt-Gimblett, interview with author, Toronto, 9 November 2013.

58 Yudel Mark, "Vegn dem matsev fun yidishn visnshaftlekhn institut," *Kultur un dertsiung* 1 (January 1957): 2.

59 William Pimlott, "'My First Year in England': The Lost YIVO Autobiography Competition and Yiddish Science in Britain, 1937–1971," unpublished essay. I thank Dr. Pimlott for sharing his work with me. An expanded version of the essay has since appeared: William Pimlott. "Global British Jewish History: YIVO in Britain, 1937–71," *Jewish Social Studies* 29, no. 3 (Fall 2024): 119–55.

60 Jan Schwarz, *Survivors and Exiles: Yiddish Culture After the Holocaust* (Wayne State University Press, 2015), ch. 4; "40 yor yivo in Argentine," *The Australian Jewish News*, 16 August 1968. The Argentine YIVO suffered a devastating blow when a terrorist drove an explosives-laden van into the building of the Asociación Mutual Israelita Argentina (AMIA), resulting in eighty-five fatalities and injuring over three hundred. The crime has been widely attributed to Hezbollah with the backing of Iran. YIVO New York's head librarian Zachary Baker traveled to Buenos Aires to help ascertain the extent of damage to library and archival collections ("YIVO Librarian to Buenos Aires After Bombing," *Yedies* 180 [Spring 1995]: 8, www.iwo.org.ar/). YIVO in New York naturally provided whatever assistance it could to help IWO in Buenos Aires restore its collections and resume its normal operations.

61 See, for example, "'YIVO' forum vert geefnt in miami bitsh dem 11tn yanuar," *Forverts*, 3 January 1964; "Nayes fun groys miami," *Forverts*, 30 November 1969; "Friends of YIVO," *Yedies* 172 (Autumn 1987): 8.

62 For example, Israel Shenker, "What's Nu? Bagel-and-Bus Tours of Jewish New York," *New York Times*, 5 May 1976. Reporter David Margolick described it as "an academic research and resource center on Eastern European Jewry and Jewish culture" ("Institute Seeking to Recreate the 'Face' of Russian Jewry," *New York Times*, 13 November 1983).

63 See, for example, Israel Schenker, "Yiddish Institute Preserves the Past," *New York Times*, 13 October 1970. For a retrospective description, see, for example, Henry Sapoznik, *Klezmer! Jewish Music from Old World to Our World* (Schirmer Books, 1999), 180–81.

64 Estelle Gilson, "YIVO Institute for Jewish Research. History and Mission on Fifth Avenue Where Jewish Scholarship Lives," *Forverts*, 17 June

1979. The report itself appeared in English in the *Forverts*, a concession to linguistic realities. Baker, "Getting in on the Ground," 6.

65 "First Phase Completed of Yiddish Catalogue Project," *Yedies* 139 (December 1976): 1*–2*; "YIVO Archives Receives NEH Grant," *Yedies* 146 (September 1978): 3*.

66 "Major Federal Grant for Max Weinreich Center," *Yedies* 131–32 (Fall–Winter 1974–75): 1*; "YIVO Library News," *Yedies* 170 (Winter 1986–87): 11.

67 Baker, "Getting in on the Ground," 4.

68 Norich estimates that NEH grants made up to 40 percent of the institute's budget in the late 1970s (Samuel Norich, interview with author, 28 November 2022).

69 Gilson, "YIVO Institute for Jewish Research"; Baker, "Getting in on the Ground," 7.

70 Baker, "Getting in on the Ground," 5.

71 Ezekiel Lifschutz, "Vi azoy tsu prezervirn dos gedrukte yidishe vort," *Tsukunft* 69, no. 3 (April 1963): 105–8; Dina Abramowicz, "Der goyrl fun yidish bukh," *Tsukunft* 83, nos. 7–8 (July–August 1977): 233–36.

72 Fruma Mohrer and Marek Web, eds., *Guide to the YIVO Archives* (New York: YIVO, 1998), xix; "YIVO's Landsmanshaftn Project Underway," *Yedies* 144 (March 1978): 1*–2*.

73 Baker, "Getting in on the Ground," 4.

74 Barbara Kirshenblatt-Gimblett, interview with author. Anita Norich, interview with author, Toronto, 15 February 2023.

75 Lifschutz, "Zoza Shaykovski (Shayke Fridman)," in his "Notitsn vegn shraybers vos ikh hob gekont," Ezekiel Lifschutz Private Collection, P130-201, Central Archives for the History of the Jewish People, Jerusalem. See also comments about Szajkowski scattered throughout his diary.

76 Lisa Leff, "Rescue or Theft? Zosa Szajkowski and the Salvaging of French Jewish History After World War II," *Jewish Social Studies* 18, no. 2 (Winter 2012): 3.

77 Lisa Leff writes of Szajkowski that after a rupture with YIVO colleagues in the early 1950s, "A few friendships were rebuilt—with Riva Tcherikower, Moshe Kligsberg, and Max Weinreich—but he remained largely alienated from his coworkers who found him strange and difficult" (Leff, *The Archive Thief*, 147, 199–200). Lifschutz, "Zoza Shaykovski (Shayke Fridman)," in his "Notitsn vegn shraybers."

78 Zachary Baker, personal communication, 21 October 2024.

79 Hass Weinberg recalls that *Yivo-menies* ("YIVO Obstacles," a play on the title of its newsletter *Yedies fun yivo*), the English-language parodic journal made by the staff each Purim, quipped that "Der yivo-binyen falt ayn baym araynhakn a mezuze" (The YIVO building collapses with the affixing of a mezuzah). Bella Hass Weinberg, interview with author via Zoom, 12 November 2023. Shaindel Fogelman, a secretary, and Faige Lederman, who operated the switchboard, were other Orthodox employees.

80 Cecile E. Kuznitz, "The Future of the YIVO Library," 29 January 2020, katz.sas.upenn.edu/resources/blog/future-yivo-library.

81 Henry Sapoznik, interview with Christa Whitney, Madison, WI, 20 March 2012, www.yiddishbookcenter.org/collections/oral-histories/interviews/woh-fi-0000275/henry-sapoznik-2012.

82 Zachary Baker, interview with author via Zoom, 17 January 2023.

83 Mordkhe Schaechter, "Tsu ale mitglider fun der farvaltung fun yivo, fun der forsh- un oysshul-komisye un fun personel fun yivo," 11 December 1975, YIVO RG 100, box 75-1, folder 161.

84 Chava Lapin, interview with author, Queens, NY, 19 November 2022; "Yiddish Was the Fourth Language at YIVO," Christa Whitney, interview with Paul Glasser, Association for Jewish Studies Conference, Washington, DC, 19 December 2011, www.yiddishbookcenter.org/collections/oral-histories/excerpts/woh-ex-0002510/yiddish-was-fourth-language-yivo.

85 Chava Lapin recalls, for example, Bolek Ellenbogen and Hannah Fryshdorf typically speaking Polish among themselves just as North American-born Yiddish speakers of her generation were accustomed to speaking English among themselves (Chava Lapin, interview). David Engel, "Poland Since 1939," YIVO Encyclopedia of Jews in Eastern Europe, 2010, encyclopedia.yivo.org/article/18 (accessed 19 July 2025). On March 1968, see Anat Plocker, *The Expulsion of Jews from Communist Poland: Memory Wars and Homeland Anxieties* (Indiana University Press, 2022).

86 Mohrer and Web, *Guide to the YIVO Archives*; Leyzer [Alec Eliezer] Burko, "Ongezeener poylish-yidisher yivo-arkhivist marek veb iz avek," *Forverts*, 20 May 2021; "YIVO Center for Advanced Jewish Studies," *Yedies* 115 (Fall 1970): 2*. On Web's experiences in Poland

prior to 1968, see Marek Web, "Marek Web—Journalist, Warsaw," "We Are Here": Jewish Narratives of Poland's March 1968 Events as Told to Teresa Toranska, accessed 15 December 2025, wearehere68.com/the-journalist-marek-web/.

87 Lucjan Dobroszycki, *Reptile Journalism: The Official Polish Language Press Under the Nazis 1939–45*, trans. Barbara Harshav (Yale University Press, 1994); Lucjan Dobroszycki, ed., *Chronicle of the Lodz Ghetto, 1991–1994*, trans. Richard Lourie et al. (Yale University Press, 1984).

88 I model this use of "polysystem" on Chone Shmeruk's application of the concept to Jewish society's use of multiple languages in interwar Poland ("Hebrew-Yiddish-Polish: A Trilingual Jewish Culture," in *The Jews of Poland Between Two World Wars*, ed. Yisrael Gutman et al. [University Press of New England, 1989], 295–311).

89 Program, "YIVO Center for Advanced Jewish Studies, 1970–1971," 1–4, YIVO RG 100, box 43, folder 322; "YIVO Center for Advanced Jewish Studies Begins Activities," *Yedies* 110 (Summer 1969): 2*.

90 *Yedies* 135 (December 1975); *Yedies* 173 (Autumn 1988); interview with Jack Kugelmass, interviewed by Christina Whitney, Association for Jewish Studies Conference, Boston, MA, 21 December 2010, www.yiddishbookcenter.org/collections/oral-histories/excerpts/woh-ex-0000489/yivo-institute.

91 Samuel Norich, interview with author.

92 Its instructors and consultants in the years 1970–1972 alone included such today well-known scholars as Benjamin Hrushovski (Harshav), Haim Blanc, Isaiah Trunk, Irving Howe, Raphael Mahler, Marvin Herzog, Edward Stankiewicz, Ruth Wisse, Oscar Janowsky, Alexander Erlich, Jacob Robinson, Marshall Sklare, Solomon Birnbaum, Dan Miron, Zosa Szajkowski, Rachel Erlich, Shlomo Noble, Barbara Kirshenblatt-Gimblett, Chana Mlotek, Beatrice Weinreich, Zvi Gitelman, Moses Rischin, Dina Abramowicz, Ezekiel Lifschutz, Mordkhe Schaechter, and Lucy Dawidowicz (Program, "YIVO Center for Advanced Jewish Studies, 1970–1971," 4–10; Program, "Max Weinreich Center for Advanced Jewish Studies," 9, 14–17, YIVO RG 100, box 43, folder 322). Their students went on to become leading figures active today. To mention but one year, for example, *Yedies* in 1979 profiled eleven current Max Weinreich Center students and graduates who were already on paths to careers in Jewish education, museum work,

and above all, academia: Batya Braun, Shifra Epstein, Mark Friedman, Eric Goldman, Janet Hadda, Neil Jacobs, Jack Kugelmass, Jean Lowenstamm, Hana Wirth-Nesher, Anita Norich, and Susan Slotnick ("Some of Our Graduates—What Are They Doing Now?," *Yedies* 149 [June 1979]: 3*).

93 Cecile E. Kuznitz, "Yiddish Studies," in *The Oxford Handbook of Jewish Studies*, ed. Martin Goodman (Oxford University Press, 2002), 341–71.

94 Mordkhe Schaechter, memorandum to N. Reich, 9 June 1974, YIVO RG 100, box 74-1, folder 152; "New Editor of YIVO Annual," *Yedies* 138 (September 1976): 5*; "YIVO Appoints Research Director," *Yedies* 173 (Autumn 1988): 12; David G. Roskies, personal communication, 3 November 2024. *Yidishe shprakh* was revived after a hiatus of almost twenty years with the publication of an issue edited by Paul Glasser and Yankl Salant combining material gathered for a planned 1990 issue with material written years later.

95 Kuznitz, "Yiddish Studies," 341–571.

96 Nancy Sinkoff, *From Left to Right: Lucy S. Dawidowicz, the New York Intellectuals, and the Politics of Jewish History* (Wayne State University Press, 2020), 70; Jeffrey Shandler, "'The Time of Vishniac': Photographs of Pre-War East European Jewry in Post-War Contexts," *Polin* 16 (2003): 313–33.

97 "YIVO Exhibit Featured at Jewish Museum," *Yedies* 136 (March 1976): 1*, 4*; "YIVO's Image Before My Eyes Published by Schocken Press," *Yedies* 143 (December 1977): 1*–2*; "YIVO's Documentary Film Wins Coveted Award," *Yedies* 155 (Winter 1980): 7*; "Photography View," *New York Times*, 2 May 1976; Lucy S. Dawidowicz, "A Vanished World," *New York Times*, 9 April 1978; Janet Maslin, "'Image Before My Eyes,' Jewish Life in Prewar Poland," *New York Times*, 19 March 1981.

98 These include Michael Alpert, Adrienne Cooper, Henry Sapoznik, Alicia Svigals, Loren Sklamberg, and Jennie Romaine.

99 "Derklerung fun yidishn pen-tsenter vegn yidish-visnshaftlekhn institut (yivo)," *Forverts*, 2 June 1976.

100 Sh. L. Shnayderman, "Geyt di yivo oyf naye vegn," *Forverts*, 17 May 1977.

101 For example, "Report on the 36th Annual YIVO Conference," *Yedies* 82 (April 1962): 1*–2*; "The Fight Against Religion in Soviet Russia," *Yedies* 93 (February 1965): 2*.

102 "YIVO Exhibitions: A Century of Ambivalence," *Yedies* 173 (Autumn 1988): 4.
103 "Project Judaica: From Dream to Reality," *Yedies* 177 (Spring 1992): 1.
104 "YIVO Benefit: A Tribute to Neil Simon," *Yedies* 171 (Summer 1987): 16; "YIVO Benefit: Enter Joseph Papp," *Yedies* 175 (Spring 1996): 6; Samuel Norich, interview with author.
105 Jeffrey Edelstein, "Pigs and Christmas; Yitshak, Yitskhok, Isaak, Isac, Ayzik, Eizik and Itshe: Creating a 'Modern' Jewish Encyclopedia," *Journal of Modern Jewish Studies* 5, no. 3 (2006): 349–354; Laura Engelstein, "The YIVO Encyclopedia," *The Jewish Quarterly Review* 100, no. 4 (Fall 2010): 731–43.
106 Gershon David Hundert, "Preface to the Print Edition," *The YIVO Encyclopedia of Jews in Eastern Europe*, 2010, encyclopedia.yivo.org/about/preface (accessed 19 July 2025).
107 Edelstein, "Pigs and Christmas," 351.

Conclusion

1 Emanuel Zingeris, "Bikher un mentshn: vegn dem goyrl fun yidishe un hebreishe bikher-fondn in lite," *Sovetish heymland* 7 (July 1988): 70–73; David E. Fishman, *The Book Smugglers: Partisans, Poets, and the Race to Save Jewish Treasures from the Nazis* (ForeEdge, 2017), 249–50; Menachem Kaiser, "Paper Brigade: The Incredible Story of the Vilnius Archives," *Jewish Quarterly* 247 (February 2022): 7–9.
2 Stefanie Halpern, "A History of YIVO's Prewar Archival Collections from 1925 to 2001," *Judaica Librarianship* 22 (2022): 25–27; Fishman, *The Book Smugglers*, 249–50.
3 To cite but one example, Lifschutz notes hearing in 1960 from a visiting scholar from Poland that the scholar had seen piles of unsorted books belonging to the Vilna YIVO in the University of Vilnius (Lifschutz, Diary, 5 August 1964).
4 Aleksander Srebrakowski, "The Nationality Panorama of Vilnius," *Studia z Dziejów Rosji i Europy Środkowo-Wschodniej* 55, no. 3 (2020): 48; Dov Levin, "Lithuania," *YIVO Encyclopedia of Jews in Eastern Europe*, 2011, yivoencyclopedia.org/article.aspx/Lithuania (accessed 2 March 2024). Today, after the emigration of much of the city's

Jewish community since the end of the communist era, Vilnius's Jewish population numbers fewer than three thousand.

5 Pamela Bruzzese, "Distributing the Past: Jewish Cultural Property in Lithuania," *New York University Journal of International Law and Politics* 31, no. 1 (Fall 1998): 152–55.

6 "A Jewish Heritage Endangered," *New York Times*, 29 November 1996.

7 Cited in Halpern, "History of YIVO's Prewar," 36. The version that appeared in *The New York Times* is slightly condensed and more restrained in tone, making no reference to the nature of the collections and omitting the phrase "After more than a half century of abysmal neglect of the Judaic treasures that remained hidden in Europe"; Alan Nadler, "Lithuania Has No Right to Keep Jewish Archive," *New York Times*, 5 December 1996.

8 Michael Specter, "Piles of Storied Jewish Books Are Languishing in Lithuania," *New York Times*, 24 November 1996.

9 Halpern, "History of YIVO's Prewar," 27–36; Jason Lustig, *A Time to Gather: Archives and the Control of Jewish Culture* (Oxford University Press, 2022), 158–65.

10 Jonathan Brent, "The Last Books," *Jewish Ideas Daily*, 1 May 2013, www.jewishideasdaily.com/6413/features/the-last-books/; Kaiser, "Paper Brigade," 16; Halpern, "History of YIVO's Prewar," 20, 29; Joseph Berger, "A Trove of Yiddish Artifacts Rescued from the Nazis, and Oblivion," *New York Times*, 18 October 2017; "YIVO Makes Archives of Yiddish Life Available Online," *New York Times*, 5 January 2022; "The Edward Blank YIVO Vilna Online Collections," vilnacollections.yivo.org/Scope-of-Project; Andrew Silow Carroll, "From Reverent to Raunchy, YIVO's Vast Archives of Yiddish Life Are Reunited Online," *The Times of Israel* (Jerusalem), 13 January 2022, www.timesofisrael.com/from-reverent-to-raunchy-yivos-vast-archives-of-yiddish-life-are-reunited-online/.

11 Kaiser, "Paper Brigade," 16–17; Jelena Subotić, "Correspondence," *Jewish Quarterly* 248 (2022): 96–97.

12 Olga Zabludoff, "YIVO, Lithuania, and Lies About the Holocaust," *The Algemeiner*, 13 November 2014, www.algemeiner.com/2014/02/13/yivo-lithuania-and-lies-about-the-holocaust/. See the extensive objections to YIVO's cooperation with the Lithuanian government on Yiddish scholar Dovid Katz's website: defendinghistory.com/.

13 Subotić, "Correspondence," 97. On the concept of double genocide in Lithuania and elsewhere in eastern Europe, see Michael Shafir, "Ideology, Memory and Religion in Post-Communist East Central Europe: A Comparative Study Focused on Post-Holocaust," *Journal for the Study of Religions and Ideologies* 15, no. 44 (Summer 2016): 52–110. On Judeo-Bolshevism, see Paul Hanebrink, *A Specter Haunting Europe: The Myth of Judeo-Bolshevism* (Belknap Press of Harvard University Press, 2018).

14 Cecile E. Kuznitz, "Correspondence," *Jewish Quarterly* 248 (2022): 100. Historian Jason Lustig (Lustig, *A Time to Gather*, 164–65) suggests that YIVO's press releases about the digital joining of materials in the YIVO Vilna's possession prior to September 1939 with materials that were not creates the misleading impression of restoring a unitary collection that had not previously existed as such. The provenance of files is, however, clearly indicated online: vilnacollections.yivo.org/Browse.

15 Yudel Mark, "Tsu der yoyvl konferents fun yivo," *Der yidisher kemfer*, 12 January 1951.

16 Max Weinreich, "Der yivo in a yor fun umkum," talk held at YIVO conference, 8 January 1943, YIVO RG 584, folder 4.

17 I borrow the concept of a "Yiddish era" from Max Weinreich, "Ashkenaz: di yidish-tkufe," *Yivo bleter* 35 (1951): 7–17. See also Naomi Seidman, *Translating the Jewish Freud: Psychoanalysis in Hebrew and Yiddish* (Stanford University Press, 2024), ch. 7.

18 Mahler lectured on Jewish economic history at the Tel Aviv School of Law and Economics before joining the faculty of Tel Aviv University in 1959. Liptzin was a founder of Bar-Ilan University and the American College in Jerusalem and taught at both for many years. Mark continued his work on the *Groyser verterbukh* in cooperation with the Hebrew University. (Robert Moses Schapiro, "Raphael Mahler," *The YIVO Encyclopedia of Jews in Eastern Europe*, 12 February 2010, encyclopedia.yivo.org/article/562 [accessed 17 October 2024].) "Leshtshinski, Yankev," in Fogel, *Leksikon*, congressforjewishculture.org/people/3163/Leshtshinski-Yankev; Wolfgang Saxon, "Solomon Liptzin, 94, Educator and Advocate of Yiddish Study," *New York Times*, 18 November 1995; Alec Eliezer Burko, "Saving Yiddish: Yiddish Studies and the Language Sciences in America, 1940–1970" (PhD diss., Jewish Theological Seminary, 2019), 220–23.

19 "Dr. Jacob Shatzky, Noted Jewish Historian, Dies in New York; Was 62," *JTA*, 14 June 1956, www.jta.org/archive/dr-jacob-shatzky-noted-jewish-historian-dies-in-new-york-was-62; "'Izvono shel d'r shatski—la-universita ha-'ivrit," *La-merḥav* (Tel Aviv), 16 May 1957. Much of YIVO archivist Ezekiel Lifschutz's personal writings, including his diary from the 1960s and observations about YIVO colleagues, is found in Jerusalem's Central Archives for the History of the Jewish People. As reflected in his diary, Lifschutz was doubtful about the future of Jewish scholarship in America. But it is also likely that he wished for his private reflections to be deposited away from the milieu and individuals it described for fear of offending them (Yochai Ben-Ghedalia, personal communication, 6 November 2024).

20 Dan Miron, "Between Science and Faith: Sixty Years of the YIVO Institute," *YIVO Annual* 19 (1990): 14–15.

21 On Yiddish schools in Canada, see Rebecca Margolis, *Yiddish Lives On! Strategies of Language Transmission* (McGill-Queen's University Press, 2023). On Poland, see Eleanor Bergman, "Yiddish in Poland After 1945," in *Yiddish and the Left*, ed. Gennadi Estraikh and Mikhail Krutikov (Taylor and Francis, 2001), 167–75.

22 Kalman Weiser, "Vilna on the Saint Lawrence: Montreal as the Would-Be Haven for Yiddish Culture," in *No Better Home?: Canada, Its Jews, and the Question of Home*, ed. David Koffman (University of Toronto Press, 2021), 56–69.

23 I thank William Pimlott for sharing his essay comparing YIVO's activity in Britain and Argentina, "YIVO's Foreign Sections: Building Transnational Immigrant History in the Wake of the Holocaust." Literature scholar Alan Astro offers a preliminary comparison of the situation of Yiddish (including YIVO) in Canada, the United States, and Argentina: "Persistencia del ídish en Argentina: reflexiones comparativas con Estados Unidos y Canadá," work in progress, 8 July 2014, www.ides.org.ar/sites/default/files/attach/Persistencia_Idish.pdf.

24 In 1971, an agreement was concluded between YIVO and Mosad Bialik in Jerusalem to publish Weinreich's *Geshikhte fun der yidisher shprakh* in Hebrew (YIVO RG 100, box 43, folder 304). The translation was to be undertaken by Dov Sadan. What became of the project is unknown to me.

25 Max Weinreich, "Aims and Scope of the Colloquium," in *Imposed Jewish Governing Bodies Under Nazi Rule*, (YIVO, 1972), 10.

26 On Smolar's visit to YIVO, see Lifschutz's diary, 7 April 1966.

27 "Jewish Participation in Social Movements," *Yedies* 91 (September 1964): 1–2*, 8*.

28 Nathaniel Popper, "Board Fight, Staff Cuts at Yiddish Center," *Forverts*, 18 February 2009, forward.com/news/103173/board-fight-staff-cuts-at-yiddish-center/.

29 "Fellowships & Awards," YIVO Institute for Jewish Research, accessed 15 December 2025, yivo.org/Fellowships.

30 On the Yiddish language and cultural revival movement, including *Yugntruf*, see Jeffrey Shandler, *Adventures in Yiddishland: Post-Vernacular Language & Culture* (University of California Press, 2006); and Rebecca Margolis, *Yiddish Lives On! Strategies of Language Transmission* (McGill-Queen's University Press, 2023).

31 Alex Weiser, personal communication, 25 September 2025. The lectures have as of October 2025 drawn collectively more than twenty thousand viewers: Jeffrey Herf and Matthias Künzel, "Hamas and the Origins of Islamic Antisemitism," Part I, YIVO Institute for Jewish Research, 26 February 2024, www.youtube.com/watch?v=kMUwrhjheHA; Jeffrey Herf and Benny Morris, "Colonialism, Racism, and the Arab Israeli War of 1948," YIVO Institute for Jewish Research, 25 March 2024, www.youtube.com/live/RT16_J6-Qdk; Jeffrey Herf et al., "Responses to October 7th," YIVO Institute for Jewish Research, 16 April 2024, www.youtube.com/live/4lLhayifkec.

32 P. J. Grisar, "A Yiddish Institution Will Discuss Hamas—Many in the Yiddish World Say They're Promoting Propaganda," *Forverts*, 13 February 2024, forward.com/culture/581709/yivo-hamas-yiddish-webinars-controversy-zionism/; Irena Klepfisz, "YIVO Is My Intellectual Home. Its Webinars on Hamas Are Misguided," *Forverts*, 15 February 2024, forward.com/opinion/583263/yivo-hamas-webinars-controversy/.

33 On the divide in contemporary Yiddishist circles, see Rukhl Schaechter, "A Painful Split in the Yiddishist Community Since Oct. 7," *Forverts*, 26 September 2024, forward.com/yiddish-world/656976/split-yiddish-yiddishist-oct-7-warsaw-ghetto-uprising-klezkanada/. See also Rokhl Kafrissen's response ("My Great Grandfather Wasn't a Bundist," 4 December 2018, medium.com/@rokhlk/my-great-grandfather-wasnt-a-bundist-4fba2f186ab9) to Molly Crabapple's "My Great Grandfather the Bundist," *New York Review of Books*, 6 October 2018.

ADDITIONAL SOURCES CONSULTED

Interviews

Kolya Borodulin, interviewed by author via Zoom, 16 December 2022.

Itzik Gottesman, interviewed by author via Zoom, 9 January 2023.

Benjamin Harshav, interviewed by author, North Haven, CT, 27 August 2010.

Irena Klepfisz, interviewed by Christina Whitney, Brooklyn, NY, 25 September 2017. www.yiddishbookcenter.org/collections/oral-histories/interviews/woh-fi-0000981/irena-klepfisz-2017

Dan Miron, interviewed by author, New York City, NY, n.d., 2001.

Rakhmiel Peltz, interviewed by author, Philadelphia, PA, 10 October 2023.

Jeffrey Shandler, interviewed by author via Zoom, 12 January 2023.

Lorin Sklamberg, interviewed by author, Toronto, ON, 2 September 2024.

Gabriel Weinreich, interviewed by Mark H. David, Ann Arbor, MI, 5 April 2012.

Ruth Wisse, interviewed by author via telephone, 18 December 2013.

Renate Zeitlin, interviewed by author, Englewood, NJ, 8 July 2012.

Archival Materials

YIVO Institute for Jewish Research, New York

- RG 356 Jacob Shatzky Papers
- RG 453 Mendel Elkin Papers
- RG 455 Papers of Abraham Golomb
- RG 546 Judah A. Joffe Papers
- RG 540 Papers of Yudel Mark
- RG 682 Papers of Mordkhe Schaechter

RG 1243 Papers of Hannah Fryshdorf
RG 1300 Rachel (Shoshke) Erlich Papers
RG 1542 Papers of Marvin Mikhl Herzog

Daily Press

Kol Ha'am (Tel Aviv)

Uncited Secondary Sources

Fishman, Joshua A., ed. *Studies on Polish Jewry, 1919–1939: The Interplay of Social, Economic and Political Factors in the Struggle of a Minority for Its Existence*. YIVO Institute for Jewish Research, 1974.

Goldberg, Sol, Scott Ury, and Kalman Weiser, eds. *Key Concepts in the Study of Antisemitism*. Palgrave Macmillan, 2021.

Moss, Binyomin (Kenneth). "Tsienizm in dem goles-natsionalistishn gedank. Maks vaynraykh in palestine." *Afn shvel* 356–57 (2012): 21–27.

Noble, Shlomo. "Dos yor in yivo." *Der yidisher kemfer* (17 January 1947): 7, 15.

Norich, Anita. "Yiddish Literary Studies." *Modern Judaism* 10, no. 3 (1990): 297–309.

Rogov, David. "Di oytsres fun yivo." *Di tsukunft* 99, no. 2 (November–December 1995): 3–9, 40.

Rogov, David. "60 yor yivo: 1925–1985." *Di goldene keyt* 116–17 (1985): 232–33.

Roskies, David. "Hoyptshtromen fun der hayntiker yidisher literatur-forshung." *Di goldene keyt* 94 (1977): 145–60.

Shandler, Jeffrey. *Yiddish: A Biography*. Oxford University Press, 2020.

Silverman Weinreich, Beatrice. *Yiddish Folktales*. Pantheon Books, 1988.

Trunk, Isaiah. "Yivo un di yidishe historishe visnshaft." *Yivo bleter* 46 (1980): 242–54.

Yudkoff, Sunny S. "The Joy of Joys: A Reception History of Leo Rosten's Yiddish Lexicon." *AJS Review* 46, no. 2 (2022): 374–97.

INDEX

Page numbers in *italics* refer to figures.

Aaroni, Rabbi Abraham, 122
Abramowicz, Dina, 74, 93, 196, 227, 242, *243*
Abramowicz, Hirsz, 93
Academy of Sciences of the Soviet Socialist Republic of Lithuania, 48
Albright, William F., 68
Algemeyne entsiklopedye, 239
Allied Control Council, 131
American Jewish Archives, 91–92, 256
American Jewish Committee, 52, 59
American Jewish Historical Society, 91–92, 256
American Jewish youth: Weinreich's analysis of, 8; YIVO's focus on, 82–84, 250
American Jewry and the Re-Invention of the East European Jewish Past (Krah), 7–8
Amopteyl (*Amerikaner opteyl*), 20–25; absorbs Central Jewish Library and Press Archives, 39–41; expansion of, 39; 1940 conference, 38–39, 194; and recovery of YIVO materials, 137; versus YIVO in Vilna, 248–50; as YIVO's world center, 1, 2. *See also* YIVO Institute for Jewish Research; YIVO Institute for Jewish Research, headquarters transferred to NYC
antisemitism, 53, 55–56, 58. *See also* Holocaust
Arendt, Hannah, 129
Argentine YIVO (Fundación IWO–Instituto Científico Judío en Argentina), 101, 252–53, 320n60
Ashkenazic Jewish people, 191–93, 210
Asociación Mutual Israelita Argentina (AMIA), 320n60
aspirantur, 19, 33, 84–87, 127, 158, 203
Associated Libraries, 135–39
Astour, Michael, 316n20
Atran, Frank (Efroym Zalmen), 169, 171
Atran Chair for Yiddish at Columbia University, 169–71, 206
Atran Foundation, 169, 205, 208
Austerlitz, Robert, 205
autobiographical essay contests, 70–73

Baker, Zachary, 7, 223, 227, 320n60
Bałaban, Majer, 81
Baron, Salo, 56–57, 68, 129, 140–41, 152, 171
"Basic Facts About Yiddish" booklet, 83

"Battle of the Warsaw Ghetto, The" (Mendelsohn), 80
Bencowitz, Isaac, 133, 135
Beranek, Franz, 145–47, 298n102
Bereze, David, *21*
Berg, Joseph, 213
Bergmann, Arthur, 141, 142
Bergmann, Hugo, 140, 141, 142
Birnbaum, Solomon, 46, 176, 315n140
Biržiška, Mykolas, 45
Bogorod, Solomon, 208
Borenstein, Julius (Yudel), 111, 202
Bratkowsky, Joan, 214
Brent, Jonathan, 246
Bund, the, 10, 258
Burko, Leyzer, 188, 198
Butler, Nicholas, 171

Cahan, Yehuda Leib (Y.L.), 21, 39, 44, 135. *See also* Y. L. Cahan Folklore Club
Callen, Horace, 59
Center for Jewish History, 1, 237, 256
Central American Jewish Archive, 92
Central Jewish Committee of Poland, 149
Central Jewish Historical Commission of Poland, 149, 152
Central Jewish Library and Press Archives, 39–41
Century of Ambivalence exhibit, 236
Charney, Samuel (Shmuel Niger), 21, 39, 43, 46, 49–50, 100, 108–9, 195
City College in New York City (CCNY), 159, 160
Claims Commission / Claims Conference, 150, 153, 186–87
climate control, 224–25
Cohen, Gerson D., 206
College Yiddish (U. Weinreich), 158, 160, 163–68, 173, 176, 194, 195, 252
College Yiddish Association, 147
Columbia University: Atran Chair for Yiddish at, 169–71, 206; Uriel Weinreich Yiddish Summer Program, 204–8, 212, 216, 241
Commentary, 168
Commission for the Implementation of Standard Yiddish Orthography, 182, 183
Commission on European Jewish Cultural Reconstruction, 129–30, 140–41
Commission to Collect and Process Documents of Jewish Culture, 123–24, 125
Committee for Saving Treasures of the Diaspora, 141–42
Committee on Research, 104–5, 110, 185
Committee on Research Planning, 170, 196, 206, 316n20
conservation, 224–25
Council of Jewish Federations and Welfare Funds, 88
Czechoslovakia, reclamation of cultural treasures in, 140–42

Dawidowicz, Lucy (Lucy Shildkret), *18*, 31–32, 132, 133–34, 138, 141, 219, 294n50, 296n68
Dawidowicz, Szymon, 179
daytshmerish, 177, 178
dialectology, 191–93
Diner, Hasia R., 15
Dingol, Solomon, 190
Dinur, Ben-Zion, 151
Dobroszycki, Lucjan, 230, 234
Dollard, John, 34, 68
double consciousness, 53
Dubnow, Simon, 45, 51, 119–20, 137
Du Bois, W. E. B., 53

Edward Blank YIVO Vilna Online Collections Project, 246–47, 248

Eichmann, Adolf, 15
Einsatzstab Reichsleiter Rosenberg (Reichsleiter Rosenberg Taskforce; ERR), 113, 116
Einstein, Albert, 68, 143
Eisenberg, Leah M. (Manya), 111
Eisner, Gustav, *21*
Elboym, Moyshe, 194
Elkin, Mendel, 41, 73–74, *75*
Ellenbogen, Bolek, 228, 322n85
English language, 67–68, 228–29, 253–54, 282n55
Erlich, Alexander, 316n20
Erlich, Henryk, 196
Erlich, Shoshke (Rachel), 196, 209, 214
Erlich, Sofia Dubnow, 137
essay contests, 70–73

Faks, Sh., *21*
Feinerman, Nathan (Naftole), 33–34, 36, 39, 43, 69
Fiddler on the Roof, 195, 313n118
Field of Yiddish, The (U. Weinreich), 170
Fishman, David, 213–14
Fishman, Joshua (Shikl): career of, 162, 219; and Committee on Research Planning, 196; on conflict between Weinreich and Uveeler, 105; and *Geshikhte fun der yidisher shprakh*, 211; on Liptzin's Yiddish, 302n6; and Project Judaica, 237; speaks at YIVO's fiftieth annual conference, 214–15; and summer program, 206; on Weinreich's composure, 189–90; on Weinreich's recruiting of Yiddish-speaking youth, 161; as Weinreich's student, 162; and Yiddish maintenance, 198; and *Yivo bleter*, 233; and YIVO Center for Advanced Jewish Studies, 203
Fogelman, Shaindel, 322n79
Folk Arts Program ("KlezKamp"), 234–35
folk arts revival, 234–35
Folks-sztyme (Voice of the People), 9
Ford, Henry, 58
Forverts, 146–47, 180–81
Fox, Sandy, 11
Freeland League, 10, 183
Freidenreich, Fradle Pomerantz, 11
Friedman, Philip, 107, 152, 153
Friends of YIVO Societies, 13, 15, 100, 220
Frydman, Szajke (Zosa Szajkowski), *77*, 122, 127–28, 143, 182, 183–84, 210, 225–26, 321n77
Fryshdorf, Hannah, 196, 213–14, 322n85
fundraising, 77–78

German culture, Weinreich as betrayed by, 147–48
German language: *daytshmerish*, 177, 178; relationship to Yiddish, 166
Geshikhte fun der yidisher arbeter-bavegung in di fareynikte shtatn (History of the Jewish Labor Movement in the United States), 68–69, 89
Geshikhte fun der yidisher shprakh (*History of the Yiddish Language*) (M. Weinreich), 201, 209–12, 328n24
Ghetto, The (Wirth), 58–59
Gininger, Chaim, 38, 110, 176, 308n63
Gitelman, Zvi, 236
Glasser, Paul (Hershl), 211
Glatstein, Jacob, 177–78, 190
Glazer, Nathan, 108, 172
Glueck, Nelson, 91
Goldhagen, Daniel, 143
Goldshmidt, Eliyohu Yankev, 115
Golomb, Abraham, 106
Gordon, Jacob, 41
Gotthardt, Herbert, 113
Grade, Chaim, 133
Greenberg, Eliezer, 172

groyser verterbukh fun der yidisher shprakh, Der (The Great Dictionary of the Yiddish Language), 184–91
Guide to Standardized Yiddish Orthography, The (Schaechter), 183

Hamas, 258–59
Hand, Wayland D., 161
Handlin, Oscar, 56–57, 91
haredi, and Standard Yiddish, 175–76
Harkavy, Alexander, 208, 209
Harkavy, Tzvi, 138
Harman, Avraham, 151–52
Hasidic movement, 167
Hass Weinberg, Bella, 227–28, 322n79
Hebrew University, 16, 103–4, 122, 141–42
Heichal Shlomo, 296n72
Herzl, Theodor, 126, 167
Herzliah Hebrew Teachers' Institute, 203, 206
Herzog, Elizabeth, 192
Herzog, Marvin (Mikhl), 171, 191, 193, 202, 206, 231
Heschel, Abraham Joshua, 81, 200, 212
Hirschbein, Peretz, 75
Historians' Circle, 107
Historic-Ethnographic Society, 295n63
Hitler's Professors (M. Weinreich), 142–48
Hoffman, Ben-Zion (Tsivyen), 169, 178, 179
Hoffman, Mendel, 193
Hoffman, Miriam, 193, 311n98
Holocaust: birth of Holocaust studies, 148–54; in *College Yiddish*, 165; emotional damage of, 64; and plunder of YIVO, 113–17; and recovery of YIVO materials, 112–13, 117–26, 155–56; reparations for, 149–50, 186–88; and Weinreich's *Hitler's Professors*, 142–48; YIVO's education on, 78–82
Homes of the Past: A Lost Jewish Museum (Shandler), 8
Horne, Joseph A., 296n68
Howe, Irving, 172
Hundert, Gershon D., 238–39

Image Before My Eyes exhibition, 234
immigrant essay contests, 70–73
Institute for German Work in the East (Institut für deutsche Ostarbeit), 117
Institute for Jewish Culture, 48
Institute for Research on the Jewish Question (Institut zur Erforschung der Judenfrage), 114, 116, 117
International Workers Order (IWO), 94
Israel: and challenges facing YIVO, 3; in *College Yiddish*, 167; Jewish scholarship in, 250–51; language shift of European Jews in, 2. *See also* Zionism
Israel–Hamas war, 258–59
Isserles, Rabbi Moses, 49

Jakobson, Roman, 85, 164, 169
Jewish Anti-Fascist Committee, 125
Jewish Cultural Association (*Yidisher kultur-farband*, IKUF), 94
Jewish Cultural Reconstruction Inc. (JCR), 129–30
Jewish Cultural Society (Lithuania), 242
Jewish Ethnographic Society, 136, 137, 295n64, 296n68
Jewish Historical Institute (Żydowski Instytut Historyczny), 9, 149, 254
Jewish Labor Committee, 36, 37, 52, 56, 59, 79, 169

Jewish Museum (Vilna). *See* Museum of Jewish Art and Culture (Jewish Museum)
"Jewish Scientific Institute," 288n136
Jewish Social Science research symposium, 91
Jewish Teachers Seminary, 203
Jofen, Jean, 108, 192
Joffe, Judah A., 22, 38, 39, 69, 109, 158, 186, 187, 188
Joint Distribution Committee (Joint or JDC), 36–37

Kaczerginski, Shmerke, 115, 123–25, 133
Kadar, Naomi Prawer, 11
Kahan, Borukh Virgili, 84
Kahn, Leonard (Leybl), 162
Kalmanovitch, Zelig: death of, 81; diary of, 126, 292n33; and German looting of YIVO, 116; on honoring Holocaust victims, 269n4; and Soviet occupation, 32, 47, 48; on YIVO in Vilna, 35, 42–43, 44; and YIVO's transferring of headquarters to NYC, 35, 38
Kapel, Aleksander (Alexander Mukdoyni), 23–24
Kaplan, Mordechai, 87–88
Katz, Dovid, 315n140
Kirshenblatt-Gimblett, Barbara, 231, 234
klezmer and Jewish folk arts revival, 234–35
Kligsberg, Moses (Moyshe), 71–73, 185
Kloss, Heinz, 145, 146, 147
Knox, Israel, 201–2
Kosover, Mordecai, 39, 187
Kovner, Abba, 123, 124
Krah, Markus, 7–8
Kruk, Herman, 115, 126
Kuznitz, Cecile, 5, 22, 37, 263n11

Labov, William, 170
Language and Culture Atlas of Ashkenazic Jewry, The (LCAAJ), 191–93
languages, spoken in YIVO, 228–30, 253–54, 322n85. *See also* English language; Polish language; Yiddish language
Lansky, Aaron, 74
Lapin, Chava, 314n133, 322n85
Lapin, Shmuel, 196, 209, 213
Laub, Morris, 213
League for Yiddish, 10, 183
Lederman, Faige, 322n79
Leff, Lisa, 226
Lehrer, Leibush, 20, 21, 22, 43, 108, 111, *121*, 195, 198
Lehrer, Lipe, 39
Leivick, H., 37–38, 76, 177–78
Leksikon fun der nayer yidisher literatur, 149–50, 312n104
Lerer, Moyshe, 48
Lestschinsky, Jacob, 20, 22, 43, 54, 60–61, 95–96, 195, 250
Liberman, Chaim, 139
"Life, Struggle, and Uprising in the Warsaw Ghetto" exhibition, 156
Life Is with People (Zborowski and Herzog), 192, 313n118
Lifschutz, Ezekiel, 182, 185, 195, 224, 312n104, 328n19
Linguists Circle, 108
Liptzin, Sol, *159*, 160–61, 201, 250, 302n6, 327n18
literary Yiddish, 173–74
Lowenstein, Steven, 219
Lunski, Khaykl, 114, 115, 139
Lurie, Harry, 91
Lustig, Jason, 327n14

Mahler, Raphael, 20, 250, 327n18
Marcus, Jacob Rader, 56–57
Margolick, David, 320n62

Maritain, Jacques, 68
Mark, Yudel, *189*; and *Der groyser verterbukh fun der yidisher shprakh* (The Great Dictionary of the Yiddish Language), 186–89; on *Life Is with People*, 313n118; as New York resident, 22; relocates to Israel, 250, 327n18; and reorganization of YIVO, 107; on reparations, 150; and standardization of Yiddish, 198; Weinreich's relationship with, 95, 186, 188, 189, 311n98; and *Yidishe shprakh*, 233; and YIVO Center for Advanced Jewish Studies, 203; on YIVO in Vilna, 248–49; on YIVO's mission, 2, 95
Martinet, André, 164, 169
Matisoff, James, 206
Max Weinreich Center, 211, 214, 215–16, 223, 231–33, 235, 241
Mayer, Leo A., 118
Mendelsohn, Shloyme, 79, 80
Michels, Tony, 58
Mielnik, Deborah Rosenblum, 206
Milwitzky, William, 101
Minkoff, N. B., 158
Miron, Dan, 171, 219
Mlotek, Chana (Eleanor) Gordon, *77*, 106, 162, 219, 294n50
Mlotek, Joseph (Yosl), 162, 180
Modern English-Yiddish Yiddish-English Dictionary (U. Weinreich), 193, 201, 208–9
Mohrer, Fruma, 228
Molotov-Ribbentrop Pact, 29
Montreal, 252–53
Moore, Deborah Dash, 231, 233
Mosad Bialik, 328n24
Moscovitch, Wolf, 191
"Movements for Social Progress among East European Jewry" (M. Weinreich), 255
Mratshni, M., 187
Mukdoyni, Alexander (Aleksander Kapel), 23–24
Museum of Jewish Art and Culture (Jewish Museum), 123–24, 125, 131
Museum of Jewish Homes of the Past, 70, 89

Nadich, Rabbi Judah, 128
Nadler, Alan, 245
National Conference of Jewish Communal Service, 91–92
National Endowment for the Humanities (NEH), 223
New York City. *See* Amopteyl; YIVO Institute for Jewish Research, headquarters transferred to NYC
New York Times, The, 118–19, 222, 234, 245
Niger, Shmuel (Samuel Charney), 21, 39, 43, 46, 49–50, 100, 108–9, 195
Noble, Shlomo, 95, 118, 139, 194–95, 210, 211, 233, 282n55
Norich, Samuel, 224, 242, 244, 321n68

Odoner, Morris (Moyshe), *21*
Offenbach Archival Depot (OAD), 128, 133, 134
Office of Military Government of the United States (OMGUS), 128, 132
Opatoshu, Joseph, 36, 177–78
Oyneg shabes project, 149
Oytser fun der yidisher shprakh (Thesaurus of the Yiddish Language) (Stutchkoff), 184–85

Paper Brigade, 115–16, 119, 123, 124, 242
Papp, Joseph, 237
Passow, Isidore David, 196
People's University, 203
Peretz, Y. L., 45, 83–84, 167
Pinkas ha-kehilot (Encyclopedia of Communities) project, 153
Pinson, Koppel S., 132–33

Pludermakher, Gershon, 41
Pohl, Johannes, 113, 114
Poland: Central Jewish Committee of Poland, 149; Central Jewish Historical Commission of Poland, 149, 152; and promotion of Yiddish culture, 9; Warsaw Ghetto, 78–79, 80–81; *Yidn in poyln* (Jews in Poland), 38; YIVO lacks support in, 17–18
Polish language, 229–30
politics, YIVO's engagement with, 255
Poll, Solomon, 175
Pomrenze, Israel Chaim, 133, 135
Pomrenze, Seymour, 133, 134, 135, 141
"postvernacular" culture, 11–12
postwar era, Jewish life in, 59–62
proaspirantur, 19, 33, 84
Project Judaica, 236–37
Pryłucki, Noah, 17, 20, 24, 48, 81, 114, 115

racial classification of Jews, 54–55
rare works, 224
Raykh, Yankev, 310n86
Reconstructionist, The, 87–88
refugees, 42
Reichel, Rabbi Leo, 80
Reichssicherheitshauptamt (RSHA, Reich Security Main Office), 114, 116–17
reparations, 149–50, 186–88
Research Training Program, 84, 86–87
Reyzen, Zalmen, 13, *18*, 32, 81
Ringelblum, Emanuel, 20, 80–81, 95, 149
Rivkind, Isaac, 187
Roback, Abraham Aaron, 158–59, 301n3
Rollansky, Samuel, 182, 221
Rosenberg, Alfred, 113
Rosenfarb, Chava, 180
Roskies, David, 227, 233
Rubinstein, L., 180
Rubinstein, Rabbi Isaac, 137
Sadan, Dov, 104, 203
salvage ethnography, 70
Sapir, Edward, 34
Sapoznik, Henry, 228
Schaechter, Mordkhe: Baker studies with, 227; and campaign for YIVO orthography and spelling, 180, 182–83, 310n86, 315n141; and Committee on Research Planning, 316n20; on emotional impact of Holocaust, 64; on English spoken in YIVO, 228–29; Gininger's accusations against, 308n63; and *The Language and Culture Atlas of Ashkenazic Jewry*, 193; and summer program, 206; on Weinreich, 111; and *Yidishe shprakh*, 233
Scheck, Ze'ev, 142
Schiff, Jacob, 76
Schipper, Ignacy (Yitshok), 81
Schneiderman, Sh. L., 235
Schwartz, Pinchos (Shmuel Kruk), 126, 196
Schwarz, Jan, 7
self-study commissions, 100–102
Seraphim, Heinz Peter, 142–43
Shalit, Moyshe, 295n64
Shandler, Jeffrey, 8
Shapiro, Judah, 202, 205–6, 207
Shatzky, Jacob, 15, 21–22, 23, 37, 39, 69, *164*, 179, 195, 250–51
Shildkret Dawidowicz, Lucy, *18*, 31–32, 132, 133–34, 138, 141, 219, 294n50, 296n68
Shilo, Bilha, 117, 142
Shmeruk, Khone, 202, *204*
Shor, Frida, 296n72
Shtif, Nokhem, 12–13, 17
Shulman, Avrom, 310n86
"Silver Age" of Yiddish publishing, 6–7
Šimaite, Ona, 116
Singer, Isaac Bashevis, 149, 178, 184, *204*
Sklare, Marshall, 108

Slobin, Mark, 228
Smith, Mark L., 7
Smits, M., 180
Smolar, Hersh, 254
Smolyar, Boris, 157
Sobel, Louis H., 150
Social Science Circle, 108
Sovetish heymland (Soviet Homeland), 9, 254
Soviet Union: occupation of Vilna, 29, 32, 42, 47–48; and promotion of Yiddish culture, 9; and reclamation of cultural treasures in Czechoslovakia, 141; YIVO under, 47–48
Spitzer, Leo, 143
Standard Yiddish (*klal-yidish*), 173–77
Standard Yiddish Orthography, 179, 182, 183
Stanislawski, Michael, 245
Stark, Johannes, 143
Stefan Batory University, 45–46
Steinberg, Isaac N., 10, 150
Strashun Library, 114–15, 136, 137, 138–39, 295nn63–64, 296n68, 296n72
Stutchkoff, Nahum, 184–86, 187
Subotić, Jelena, 247
suburbs, Jews' movement into, 171–72
summer programs, 204–8, 212, 216, 241
Survivors and Exiles: Yiddish Culture After the Holocaust (Schwarz), 7
Sutzkever, Avrom, 85–86, 115, 119–20, 123–25, 133, 182, 211
Szabad, Stefania, 31, 120
Szabad, Tsemach, 84
Szajkowski, Zosa (Szajke Frydman), *77*, 122, 127–28, 143, 182, 183–84, 210, 225–26, 321n77

Takones fun yidishn oysleyg (Rules of Yiddish Spelling), 180, 183, 184, 188
Tcherikower, Elias (Elye), 20, 33–34, 43, 47, 68–69, 195
Tcherikower, Rebecca (Rive), 69
"Tentative List of Cultural Treasures in Axis-Occupied Countries," 129
Trunk, Isaiah, 153, 154, 215–17
Tsanin, Mordkhe, 182
Tsivyen (Ben-Zion Hoffmann), 169, 178, 179
TSYSHO (*Tsentrale yidishe shul organizatsye*) schools, 97, 218
Tyshchenko, Dmytro, 191

Ulpis, Antanas, 242
University of Vilnius, chair for Yiddish language and literature at, 45–46, 47–48
Uriel Weinreich Yiddish Summer Program (*zumer-program*), 204–8, 212, 216, 241
Uveeler, Mark, 78, 91, 95, 100, 105–6, 111, 151

Vanderbilt mansion, 112, 222–23, 225, *232*
Varshavski, Yitskhok. *See* Singer, Isaac Bashevis
Varshever, A., 194
vidervuks (regrowth), 201
Vilna / Vilnius: German looting of YIVO in, 113–17; Jewish population of, 244, 325n4; Jewish refugees in, 42; rediscovery of archives and library from, 239–40; Soviet occupation of, 29, 32, 42, 47–48; YIVO in, 12–20, 22–23, 42–47, *120*, 248–49; YIVO materials from, 117–26, 242–48. *See also* YIVO Institute for Jewish Research, headquarters transferred to NYC

Warsaw Ghetto, 78–79, 80–81, 156
Web, Marek, 228, 230, 242, 244

Weber, Shimen, 181, 309n79
Weiner, Sh., *21*
Weinreich, Beatrice (Bina) Silverman, 162, *164*, 192, 219
Weinreich, Gabriel, 31, 34, 163–64, 212, 306n53
Weinreich, Max: on abuse of Stefan Batory University students, 45–46; and American Jewish youth, 8, 82; on American Jewry, 51–59; on American support for YIVO, 38; with Amopteyl founders, *21*; applies for US citizenship, 131; arrives in New York, 43–44, 62–63; and *aspirantur*, 85; and Atran Chair for Yiddish at Columbia University, 169; background of, 49; as chair for Yiddish language and literature, 46; on cooperation with Strashun Library and Jewish Ethnographic Society, 295n63, 296n68; death of, 212–13, 240, 251–52; and death of Uriel, 200–201; declines Hebrew University chair position, 103–4; on disintegration of Yiddish, 174; education of, 17; on Elkin, 74; and establishment of YIVO, 13; experience with American academia, 34–35; on financial support for YIVO, 89–91; on future of Jewish scholarship, 251; on German culture, 147–48; and German looting of YIVO, 114, 115; *Geshikhte fun der yidisher shprakh* (*History of the Yiddish Language*), 201, 209–12, 328n24; *Hitler's Professors*, 142–48; on Holocaust, 79, 82; and immigrant essay contest, 71; impact on YIVO, 49–51, 110–11, 209, 249–50; influence on *College Yiddish*, 167; Kalmanovitch's correspondence with, 47; on language, 68; Mark's relationship with, 95, 186, 188, 189, 311n98; Mlotek's relationship with, 294n50; "Movements for Social Progress among East European Jewry," 255; opposes YIVO name change, 108–9; and outbreak of war, 31–32; personality of, 213; on postwar Jewish life, 59–62; and reclamation of cultural treasures in Czechoslovakia, 140–41; and recovery of YIVO materials, 112–13, 117–18, 119–20, 122, 126–28, 130, 134–35, 138; and reorganization of YIVO, 102–6; and restoration of YIVO's library, 126–28, 130; Shildkret as assistant to, 132; and standardization of Yiddish, 178–80, 182, 183, 185, 188, 189–90; with students at City College, *159*; Szajkowski's relationship with, 225–26; vision for YIVO, 4–5, 249–50, 253; writings on Yiddish language in US and Canada, 24; on Yiddish and YIVO, 157; and Yiddish in American academia, 159–60, 161–62; on Yiddish transmission, 33, 198; and *Yivo bleter*, 43; and YIVO Center for Advanced Jewish Studies, 202, 203; with YIVO instructors, *18*; and YIVO's Associated Libraries, 136; on YIVO's financial support, 15; and YIVO's fortieth annual conference, 195, 196–97, 264n14; on YIVO's new office in NYC, 76; and YIVO's self-study commission, 100, 101–2; and YIVO's transferring of headquarters to NYC, 30, 31–35. *See also* Max Weinreich Center
Weinreich, Regina, 31, 34

Weinreich, Uriel: as *aspirantur*, 87; and Atran Chair for Yiddish at Columbia University, 169–71; and Beranek, 147, 298n102; and campaign for YIVO orthography and spelling, 180, 182; *College Yiddish*, 158, 160, 163–68, 173, 176, 194, 195, 252; and Committee on Research Planning, 196; death of, 200–201; education of, 163–64; Gininger's accusations against, 308n63; and *The Language and Culture Atlas of Ashkenazic Jewry*, 191–93; *Modern English-Yiddish Yiddish-English Dictionary*, 193, 201, 208–9; recognized at YIVO annual conference, 201–2; relocates to United States, 34, 43; on Standard Yiddish, 174–76; travels to western Europe with parents, 31; Uriel Weinreich Yiddish Summer Program, 204–8, 212, 216, 241; as US Army soldier in Germany, 120; and Yiddish in American academia, 198–99; in YIVO seminar, *164*; and YIVO Yiddish, 158, 160, 162

Weinryb, Bernard Dov, 98

Weizmann, Chaim, 189

Winchevsky, Morris, 39

Winter, Ella, 119

Wirth, Louis, 58–59

Wischnitzer, Mark, 107

Wisse, Ruth, 171, 202, 211, 219

Wissenschaft school, 56

Wolf, Meyer, 191

Yad Vashem, 151–53

Yalta Conference (1945), 122

Yedies fun yivo, 65–67, 81, 87–89, 101–2, 126, 150, 207, 233

Yeshiva University, 91–92

Yiddish culture: decline of, 12; growing interest in, 172–73; in Lithuania, 33; promotion of, 9–10; scholarship and sources on, 10–12

Yiddish Historians and the Struggle for a Yiddish History of the Holocaust, The (Smith), 7

Yiddishism: Kalmanovitch's confidence in, 42–43; as tool for building American Jewish identity, 11–12; Weinreich's devotion to, 53–54; YIVO as symbolizing, 257–58

Yiddish language, 157–58; in American academia, 158–63, 198–99; and Atran Chair for Yiddish at Columbia University, 169–71; "Basic Facts About Yiddish" booklet, 83; campaign for YIVO orthography and spelling, 179–84, 309n79, 310n86, 315n140; and *College Yiddish*, 163–68; decline of, in America, 67–68; evolution of, 210; *Geshikhte fun der yidisher shprakh* (*History of the Yiddish Language*), 201, 209–12, 328n24; growing interest in, 172–73; *Der groyser verterbukh fun der yidisher shprakh* (The Great Dictionary of the Yiddish Language), 184–91; *The Language and Culture Atlas of Ashkenazic Jewry*, 191–93; literary Yiddish, 173–74; relationship to German, 166; spoken by Liptzin, 302n6; spoken by Weinreich family, 306n53; spoken in YIVO, 228–29; Standard Yiddish (*klal-yidish*), 173–77; transmission of, 198; YIVO's relationship to, 16–17; YIVO Yiddish, 177–79

Yiddish literature, 83

Yiddish PEN (Poets, Essayists, Novelists) Club, 235
Yiddish schools and camps, 10–11, 33, 97–98, 198, 218, 226
Yiddish-speaking communities, 2–3, 6
yidishe gezelshaftlekhkeyt, 86, 94
Yidishe shprakh, 76–77, 187, 232, 233
Yidn in poyln (Jews in Poland), 38
YIVO and the Making of Modern Jewish Culture (Kuznitz), 5
YIVO Annual, 233
Yivo bleter (*YIVO Pages*), 7, 23, 36, 38, 41, 43, 78–79, 81, 105, 152–53, 232–33
YIVO Center for Advanced Jewish Studies, 201–8
YIVO Encyclopedia of Jews in Eastern Europe, The, 238–39, 255
YIVO Institute for Jewish Research: American audience drawn to, 234–36; American division of, 20–25; archives of, 216, 224–25, 239–40; Argentine YIVO, 101, 252–53, 320n60; Associated Libraries, 135–39; challenges facing, 3–4; changed attitudes toward Yiddish, Yiddishism, and Diaspora Nationalism, 9; commemorative writing on, 6–7; conflicts and controversy in, 258–59; cooperation with Strashun Library and Jewish Ethnographic Society, 295nn63–64, 296n68; creative rejuvenation of, 240–41; criticisms of, 93–100; education on Holocaust, 78–82; engagement with politics, 255; establishment of, 12–13; evolution of, 236–40, 255–56; expands publications, 76–77; fiftieth annual conference of, 214–50; finances of, 13, 14–15, 18–19, 77–78, 87–92, 100–101, 223–24, 237–38, 283n69; focus on American Jewish youth, 82–84, 250; Folk Arts Program ("KlezKamp"), 234–35; fortieth annual conference of, 194–97, 264n14; fundraising for, 77–78; German looting of, 113–17; growth of, 12; and *Der groyser verterbukh fun der yidisher shprakh* (The Great Dictionary of the Yiddish Language), 184–91; history and impact of, 1; and Holocaust studies, 148–54; housed in Vanderbilt mansion, 112, 222–23, 225, *232*; hypothetical choices and outcomes of, 252–53; impact of Weinreichs' deaths on, 200–201; impact on Jewish scholarship and public life in America, 6; instructors of, *18*; languages spoken in, 228–30, 253–54, 322n85; library of, 73–74, 112, 126–32, 216; mission of, 2–3, 12, 17, 65, 69, 96; name change of, 288n136; new generations in, 226–30; 1940 conference, 38–39, 194; as nonpartisan, 19–20; as Old World institution, 222–26; postwar indirection of, 65; proposed name change for, 108–9, 110; and publication of *Geshikhte fun der yidisher shprakh*, 211; and reclamation of cultural treasures in Czechoslovakia, 140–42; recovery of materials of, 112–13, 117–26, 132–35, 242–48; relationship to Yiddish, 16–17; relationship with eastern European institutions, 254–55; relevance of, 256–57; relocates in New York City, 74–76, 112; reorganization of, 102–8;

YIVO Institute for Jewish Research (*continued*): Research Training Program, 84, 86–87; scholarship on, 5–9; self-study commission, 100–102; under Soviet rule, 47–48; success of, 256–57; supporters of, 13, 14–15; as symbolizing Yiddishism, 257–58; transitional period of, 4–5; in Vilna, 12–20, 22–23, 42–48, 64–65, *120*, 248–49; in Vilna versus United States, 216–19; Weinreich's ambition for, in America, 253; following Weinreich's death, 212–14, 240–41, 251–52; Weinreich's impact on, 49–51, 110–11, 209, 249–50; Weinreich's vision for, 4–5, 249–50; as world institution, 220–22; following WWII, 1–2; Yiddish literary figures distance themselves from, 177–78. *See also* Amopteyl; YIVO Institute for Jewish Research, headquarters transferred to NYC

YIVO Institute for Jewish Research, headquarters transferred to NYC, 1, 3, 62–63; American support for, 35–42; events leading to, 29–30; and forging path in America, 65–78; Weinreich's dilemma concerning, 31–35. *See also* Amopteyl

Yivo-menies, 322n79

YIVO Yiddish, 177–79

Y. L. Cahan Folklore Club, 107, 170

youth: Weinreich's analysis of, 8; YIVO's focus on, 82–84, 250

zamlers, 14, 70, 148, 155

Zborowski, Mark, 192

Zeitlin, Aaron, 149

Zhitlovski, Khayim, 39

Zingeris, Emanuelis, 242, 246

Zionism, 2, 37; anti-Zionism of Bund, 10, 258

zumer-program (Uriel Weinreich Yiddish Summer Program), 204–8, 212, 216, 241